Classic Motorcycle Restoration and Maintenance

Classic Motorcycle Restoration and Maintenance

Nigel Clark

The Crowood Press

First published in 2015 by
The Crowood Press Ltd
Ramsbury, Marlborough
Wiltshire SN8 2HR

www.crowood.com

British Library Cataloguing-in-Publication Data
A catalogue record for this book is available from the British Library.

ISBN 978 1 84797 881 3

Disclaimer
Safety is of the utmost importance in every aspect of an automotive workshop. The practical
procedures and the tools and equipment used in automotive workshops are potentially
dangerous. Tools should be used in strict accordance with the manufacturer's recommended
procedures and current health and safety regulations. The author and publisher cannot accept
responsibility for any accident or injury caused by following the advice given in this book.

Typeset and designed by D & N Publishing, Baydon, Wiltshire.

Printed and bound in Singapore by Craft Print International Ltd.

contents

acknowledgements

This list is relatively short as most of the information in this book is based on experience gained over several years of restoring old British motorcycles of varying shapes and sizes. Of course, there is a great deal of technical detail of which I neither know nor deem necessary to know particularly deeply, as there are others who specialize in these fields and it is to them I turned for their advice and for that I express much gratitude. They have given freely of their immense skills and knowledge, and without their help I could not have completed the task of compilation and I thank them all.

Accreditation must go to the following for allowing use of their copyrighted documents:

Joachim Seifert of Norton Motors Group, for permission to use extracts and diagrams from various Norton documents; Colin McSeveny of Smiths Group, for permission to use extracts and diagrams from various Smiths Industries documents; Dave Bennett of BSA Company Ltd, for permission to use extracts and diagrams from various BSA documents; the University of Birmingham, for the archive images of the BSA factory; Lucas Electrical, for permission to use extracts and diagrams from various Lucas documents; and Triumph Motorcycles, for permission to use images from various brochures.

Special mention must go to Dave Flintoft, BSA Gold Star specialist, engineer par excellence and all round good egg, who spent far too many unprofitable hours demonstrating and advising me on various engineering tasks; the ever-pleasant Bob Wylde, for his time and patience with wheel building; Ferret, the electrical magician; Adrian Hill, of Morris Lubricants, for his advice on oils; Boyer Bransden, for their electronic ignitions; Jan de Jong at ABSAF; Kate Emery at Norvil Motorcycles; and Ben Coombes and the ace team at Amal and Burlen Fuel Systems. There are others too – my late pal Bob Byatt, for his saintly patience and ever willingness to help me out, sorely missed, and to Katapultgrafik for the artwork.

Thanks also must go to – in alphabetical order – Pete Adams, Paul Andrews, Neil Beadling, Steve Clark, Mike Powell and Tony Pearson.

introduction

Classic > *adjective* **1** Judged over a period of time to be the highest quality. **2** Remarkably typical. Synonyms – *adjective* **1** Definitive, enduring, exemplary, masterly, outstanding, archetypal, paradigmatic, quintessential. *Noun* **1** Masterpiece, a work of art of established value.

The origin of the word, like much of our rich language, comes from the Latin *classicus*, meaning 'belonging to a class or division' and later 'of the highest class'.

In the years since the Second World War the term has been used more loosely, initially to represent designs of outstanding merit, and latterly, more generally, to represent items which, to put it bluntly, are simply old.

It's a term that is now widely open to interpretation. Taking aircraft as an example, it is surely fair to adorn the likes of the Supermarine Spitfire, Avro Lancaster and Vulcan, English Electric Lightning and others of similar ilk with the description. Likewise Sir

Nigel Gresley's fabulous, art deco Pacific Streamliner locomotives, or those wonderful coachbuilt beauties from Messrs Rolls Royce and Bentley, or George Brough's hand-built specials, or Phil Vincent's super-fast V-twins, or the all-conquering racing Nortons from Birmingham…

The list is probably endless and each has its own argument for and against. What about Honda's little 50cc step-thru moped? 'What about it?', you may ask. It's a throwaway utility vehicle of no particular value apart from a basic means of getting from place to place, particularly in less developed countries, where it is often used as family transport. Images are regularly seen of the poor little thing overloaded with husband, wife, several children, animals, bales of straw, boxes of fruit, you name it. So how then can it be a classic? Well, it's been in production in various specifications and sizes for over half a century and has sold tens of millions of units and continues to do so to this day. In that case, the dic-

tionary definition of 'definitive' and 'enduring' certainly applies, though to be fair the 'Nifty Fifty' is at the opposite end of the scale to the likes of the Velocette Venom Thruxton when it comes to desirability – and market value. Having said that, would a peasant farmer from the developing world swap his Honda for a Thruxton? Certainly not in the practicality stakes, as a Thruxton would be no use to him whatsoever; but then, in his situation there is no classic status, his bike is simply everyday transport – and that of course is what most of our so-called classics once were.

Nowadays, anything with any age to it is deemed classic. As the classic car market has seen the prices of exotica climb to extraordinary heights, so has that vacuum formed below it sucked up the prices of lesser, more run-of-the-mill vehicles. As said market shows no sign of diminishing and the banks' interest rates continue to stagnate, the investors have realized that a good return can be had from

Once upon a time a Coventry Eagle V-twin such as this was just an old motorcycle; now it's a very expensive and very sought-after commodity.

the classic motorcycle. This has had two effects on the market. The first is that prices for machines with a genuine history and provenance have rocketed, which in turn has flushed out onto the market many machines that have been tucked away for years, as owners finally cash in.

Not many years ago, anyone who had an old motorcycle, or car come to that, was seen as being, shall we say, at worst not particularly well off, or at best some form of eccentric. However, many such people eventually had the last laugh, as the old rubbish they stored away in their sheds and hen huts steadily became valuable and sought-after machines. Those hoarders now have an extremely healthy pension pot!

A BRIEF HISTORY LESSON

The story of the fairly rapid implosion of the British motorcycle industry, followed not long afterwards by that of the car industry too, is well documented in many other books, and while today such industries are looked back upon through those familiar rose-tinted spectacles, hindsight now shows that the demise was without doubt inevitable – though it need not have been so.

As the men (and women of course) returned from the war and factories geared up for massive export production to try to pay off the crippling debts incurred, the attitude of the country's workforce had changed. Having endured five years of conflict, followed by

at least another five years of rationing and hardship, people wanted a better life, certainly better than that of the immediate pre-war years, and they were prepared to make a stand for it.

As far as the factory management was concerned, the easiest and most sensible way in which to get production into full swing was to give the pre-war designs a bit of a facelift and make as many as possible. Bear in mind of course that many factories, particularly the smaller ones, had ceased

motorcycle production altogether to concentrate on the necessities of the war effort, making anything from aircraft parts to generators and ball bearings. So with the outbreak of peace, they had no new designs and even those lucky enough to have any tooling survive at all were left behind as the likes of Triumph had a head start. Many never reappeared at all.

The government had requisitioned all Triumph production to be for the military, but the original Coventry factory was bombed out in the devastating blitzkrieg raid of November 1940. As is (or at least was) the British way, with backs to the wall, a temporary factory was established in Warwick, tooling repaired and made good and production restarted in double quick time. Meanwhile, a new factory was built at Meriden, a village between Coventry and Birmingham, and one Edward Turner set about designing a twin-cylinder machine, which, once the war was over, would be ready to set new standards and leave the opposition floundering in Triumph's wake. The other factories had to follow suit, though many soldiered on for a few more years with outdated designs, eventually shrinking away to nothing.

After the Second World War, people wanted some fun and the motorcycle was a perfect way to find it.

The Bracebridge Street Norton factory in Aston, Birmingham, immediately post-war.

Norton left their original home in the early 1960s but the facade has changed very little.

The actual Norton factory building was around the back on Aston Brooke Street. Sadly this iconic old building has gone, replaced by a sprawling mail sorting office.

The Meriden Triumph factory in its prime.

The pre-war Triumph Tiger 100, a breathtaking sports machine, within the financial reach of most and a standard by which all others would be judged. Its production was delayed by six years due to the onset of war in 1939.

As the austere 1950s turned into the swinging 1960s, industrial relations in general were deteriorating across industry as a whole. In the motorcycle industry problems were legion. As the Italians showed that their multi-cylinder machines were the future on the racetrack, outpacing the previously all-conquering British singles, the small, almost elite, band of designers, in particular Bert Hopwood and Doug Hele and their associated henchmen, were busy designing and building prototype machines, which could have easily taken on and beaten the world's best and led to a range of road-going motorcycles of an advanced design and specification, the likes of which had never been seen before. However, that would have meant retooling for manufacture and development, which spelled expense to the company accountants and a loss of dividend to the shareholders, so inevitably, and no doubt immensely frustratingly for said designers, practically all such designs were vetoed in favour of simple updates to the existing machines – many of which, such as the Matchless G3 range, could be readily traced back to the despatch riders' favourite machine of the Second World War.

Carefree summer days, fun and pretty girls at the seaside – or so the marketeers would have you believe.

To say most management in the motorcycle industry was complacent is an understatement. They had a strange belief that their machines' shortcomings, oil leaks being a prime example, were quite acceptable to the customer, who liked nothing better on a Sunday but to repair, maintain and clean his machine in order that it would get him to work for the following six days. However, there was much more.

The factory buildings – Triumph excepted – were at best Victorian, the machine tools were equally as old and worn and the management was weak in the face of an increasingly militant workforce and powerful left-wing trade unions.

It's an obvious scenario now. Post war, the Japanese and the Germans had to start from scratch, with a clean sheet of paper and a piece of land. As such, their factories were state of the art, as were their designs. Already

With roots harking back to the DR's favourite mount, the AJS and Matchless trials bikes of the 1950s and 1960s were first-class machines for the job.

several years old at the start of the war, and having run flat out during it, there was little hope of the weary old British factories being able to compete without the all too lacking enormous investment. While the defeated countries began with nothing to lose and everything to gain, our home industries struggled on to pay off the war debts mentioned previously – export or die, was the call.

There is a story that when Norton production was transferred from the hallowed ground of Bracebridge Street, Birmingham to AMC parent company headquarters, in Plumstead, London, in 1962, the machine operators there ruined a colossal amount of Dominator crankcases because the bearing holes didn't line up. Eventually the old, retired, ex-Bracebridge Street machinist was contacted for his advice, to which he asked 'Didn't you take the plank?', the folklore reckoning being that the boring machine was so worn that a piece of wood was wedged into place to keep it running true. Whether there's any truth in the tale or not is really irrelevant – without doubt the Norton factory tooling was well past its sell-by date, and indicative of the industry as a whole.

Ignorance is bliss, and even as warnings were being voiced about the potential threat of the oriental machines, it was naively believed that they were only interested in small machines and the world would continue to buy big British bikes. As we all know now, by the time our factories woke up to the fact that the Japanese could build big, reliable bikes of a much higher specification and, most importantly, at a fairly competitive price, the writing was already on the wall. For sure, when the remains of the industry was lumped together into one company, they put up a fairly good rearguard action but the dogma of varying political factions ruined what chance that ever had.

CLASSIC ROOTS

Even as the factories returned to peace time output, there was a faction of motorcycle enthusiasts who felt it necessary to try and preserve the two-wheeled heritage of the early years. In April 1946 a meeting was held at the Lounge Cafe, Hog's

The view down Armoury Road in the 1960s – houses along one side, the mighty BSA factory on the other.

The front of the BSA factory did not go overboard with its advertising of Ariel.

BSA main gates. The concrete-framed building on the left (Truscon) and the single-storey section of traditional building beyond it are the only remnants of the once sprawling factory. The Truscon building is privately owned and in poor condition and subject to an ongoing effort to have it listed and restored. The other buildings still house the successful BSA guns company. All the other magnificent old buildings have long since gone to make way for faceless industrial units.

Back, near Guildford in Surrey, where thirty-eight enthusiasts gathered to discuss the forming of a club for owners of machines manufactured prior to December 1930. The Vintage Motor Cycle Club was born.

Over the years the club has seen myriad changes, but while keeping abreast of times and attitudes, it has remained more or less true to its roots, with a rolling twenty-five year eligibility date, which of course now entitles

The racing section of the Vintage Motor Cycle Club threw a lifeline to those who still wanted to race on their old motorcycles.

Because the VMCC cut-off date for the racing section was, initially at least, 1958, owners of later race machines formed their own race club – the Classic Racing Motorcycle Club.

many Japanese machines to take part. This is a bone of contention with many, for as the once great names of the home industry all went to the wall in the face of the unrelenting onslaught from the land of the rising sun, those who lamented this loss circled their wagons and stood by their old bikes.

As the swinging sixties turned into the strife-torn seventies, it must be borne in mind that the cessation of world hostilities was still only a couple of decades past and for many, the atrocities of the Japanese during that conflict were still quite raw in the mindset of a generation. Understandably, there was much resentment. However, there was a new generation reaching motorcycling age who had been fortunate enough to be raised in an environment without world war or many of its repercussions, and most carried no such emotional baggage. The new Japanese machines were brightly coloured, stylish, reliable, fast and affordable and

the youngsters hocked themselves up with years of monthly payments – and so it went on. The British motorcycle industry was dead and buried.

For over a decade the Japanese big four – Honda, Yamaha, Suzuki and Kawasaki – held sway but for those who took notice, it was plain to see that at grass roots level something was afoot.

For example, in those heady days of the 1960s, an ordinary national road race meeting – in which the country's top privateers, on their Nortons, Matchless and AJS singles, and the sidecar crews with their BSA and Triumph outfits – would make up the programme, would often attract a crowd of perhaps 30,000 fans, while an international meeting, where the big prize money attracted the world champions, could see crowds of twice that. As the Japanese two-strokes steadily crept up the capacity classes – the 351cc over-bored Yamaha twin killed off the 500cc British singles, having already done away

with them in the 350cc classes (even though it was invariably the same bike, capacity was rarely checked) – and the world champions stayed away, the crowds lost interest and attendances dropped hugely.

What had become of all those bikes, which were no longer competitive? Some were no doubt sold on for next to nothing while others were unceremoniously dumped into the back of the shed. Then someone had a bright idea. Why not start a club, a bit like the VMCC, but purely for race bikes, where these old bangers could compete again, against similar machines? Enter the Classic Racing Motorcycle Club.

This gave the bikes a new lease of life, encouraged more to join, attracted excellent crowds of like-minded enthusiasts and generally went from strength to strength.

As the modern motorcycle horsepower race grew out of hand during the 1980s and bikes became physically bigger, the enthusiasts of the earlier machines faced a problem: spares, or rather the lack of them. As former agencies of the British marques turned over to the Japanese, many cashed in on the scrap value of the parts held in stock in favour of the faster-selling contemporary machine parts, while others just boxed them away out of sight and out of mind, selling too few to warrant more attention. It became difficult for anyone running or restoring a post-war British bike to find good-quality spares, and practically impossible for owners of pre-war machines. To make matters worse, imported pattern parts began to flood the market and many were, to say the least, of dubious quality. They were ill fitting, incorrectly threaded, manufactured of the wrong material or not hardened so they wore out at an alarming rate, or worse, broke up and caused damage to other previously serviceable parts.

Something had to be done about it, and slowly but surely it was. If a part was needed and it was no longer available, or at least not to a satisfactory standard, the old adage 'what man has made, man can make again' came into play. Marque enthusiasts within owners clubs often found themselves not alone in needing a part or parts and invariably there would be a retired engineer within their ranks, or even a working or self-employed engineer who could undertake machining operations within his own time. He would be asked, or take it upon himself, to make a certain part and this inevitably led to others requesting his services. Then perhaps the owners club would put out the word that they had a batch of said parts available for sale to members, they would sell out and more would be ordered, along with further requests for different parts. From this, improvements were made, replica items in stainless steel instead of the original mild steel and so on, and as technology and materials improved, so did the quality of the replica parts.

Many has been the time that an engineer enthusiast found himself redundant and with nothing to lose, started up in business making specialist parts for certain machines. His business would increase as word spread and a wider range of parts became available, and from this perhaps the engineer would then digress into other marques. Another common story is that of the engineer who began producing parts for his own machines, followed by the same for his friends and colleagues and then the general public, until such time as his sideline was so big that he had to quit the day job to concentrate on his new business.

This new cottage industry blossomed and reputable businesses established themselves as manufacturers of top-quality replica parts, engine and gearbox parts, clutch parts, wheel rims, brake shoes and so on. The list grew in both number and complexity, with pressed steel cycle parts, cylinder barrels and heads, carburettors, electrical systems, crank and gearbox cases being added, until eventually it became possible to build a complete machine entirely from newly manufactured spare parts. Who would have ever imagined in the early 1980s, when enthusiasts were struggling to extend the life of their weary and obsolete old Amal carburettor by boring out the body and sleeving the throttle slide, that twenty years hence it would be possible to buy any of Amal's excellent range of motorcycle carburettors off the shelf; or that brand new Manx Nortons could be had from no fewer than two manufacturers in England, one in Australia and engines from at least one other; or that BSA's Gold Star or Matchless's G85 engines could be bought new, likewise Weslake's four-valve twin, or a complete new Norton Commando, Dominator or Vincent Black Shadow – or, to put the icing on the cake, a Brough Superior…

ABOVE LEFT: Brand new and readily available, Matchless G85 engines …

ABOVE MIDDLE: …and Gold Star BSA too.

ABOVE RIGHT: Complete Norton Dominators can be built from new parts by Norvil Motorcycles.

RIGHT: … likewise Commandos in any style or era.

A brand-new Vincent Black Shadow, sir? No problem, that'll be £a lot, please.

There were also a canny few who, when various former dealers were retiring, selling up, or simply changing allegiance, moved quickly to snap up any remaining genuine period stock – and what a terrific amount there was still out there. Add to this a whole host of specialist refurbishment services and it's fair to say that the older motorcycle has never had it so good!

The demand for tricky-to-manufacture cycle parts, such as petrol tanks, oil tanks and toolboxes, has been met by a legion of pretty skilled tin bashers across India. A few years ago it was accepted that such items, particularly replica mudguards, would probably need varying amounts of work to make them fit correctly. This is not so much the case any more as the craftsmanship has increased dramatically, with many parts being as good, if not better, than original, and by virtue of the labour situation in their place of origin, prices can be very competitive.

THE RIGHT TIME

Sadly, long gone is the time when a basket case, middleweight BSA, for example, would set you back ten or fifteen pounds: you would need to add a couple of zeros onto those figures now. As mentioned previously, as the top-end machines such as the Broughs, Coventry Eagles, McEvoys, Vincents and so on have climbed to unbeliev-

able values in the market, they have brought up in their wake, more everyday machines – which will form the basis of this publication – and there seems to be no end in sight. That's no slight on more humble machinery; quite the contrary – there can be as much fun and enjoyment in restoring and riding an everyday classic as an exotic, and spares are easier to come by too.

Small-capacity machines, originally designed as commuters, or basic machines with which the factory could woo youngsters in an effort to steer their product loyalty toward bigger machines once they had passed their test, have found favour in the offroad competition sphere. BSA's 250cc C15 and its bigger brother, the 350cc B40 – both essentially derived from the smaller sibling, Triumph's Tiger Cub – can be converted into highly competitive trials bikes, along with Royal Enfield, Ariel, AJS and Matchless heavyweights, not to mention the plethora of regular lightweight names powered by the proprietary Villiers engine. Once considered unsuitable, now even the BSA Bantam is becoming a pre-65 trials force to be reckoned with.

This diversification has spawned a spares and service industry all of its own, with several trials specialists offering all manner of parts from a spark plug to a complete rolling chassis.

Akin to the days when 'racing improved the breed', all these developments can be successfully transposed onto everyday classics to improve starting, stopping and overall reliability. This in turn brings more older motorcycles back onto the road, and the more they are used the more parts they need so the whole process just gathers momentum.

SO WHY A CLASSIC?

There are so many reasons why a classic motorcycle is a good idea. First and foremost is the F word – Fun. Now, it may be exhilarating to travel at twice the legal limit in a straight line or experience acceleration that will slick tyres and ruin chains within hundreds rather than thousands of miles, but the former is strictly illegal on the Queen's highways and the latter is extremely expensive. What's more, once the initial buzz has worn off, it all becomes a little boring.

Modern motorcycles, without doubt, are sensational. High-tech and practically faultless in all that they do, they have reached a stage nowadays where they are indeed so good that their clinical excellence can become simply dull. That is something that can never be said of a classic. As realization of this dawns on more and more former riders of modern machinery, they now turn to a more sedate but equally fulfilling classic.

Character is a difficult thing to pigeon-hole. Is it the sound of a classic? Is it the timeless styling? Note how modern manufacturers have lately begun to introduce traditionally styled machines into their range again as the vast majority of buyers turn away from the race replica, so long beloved in the UK. Is it the fact that in comparison to the modern machine, the average classic neither goes, stops or handles as well? Is it because they vibrate more? Is it because they were essentially made and hand built by human beings instead of computerized machines and robots? It's impossible to say, except that it's probably a combination of all these things and more, because two seemingly identical machines will have distinctly different characters and idiosyncrasies. Like the proverbial Friday afternoon car, some classics will be better than others, yet they will be made up of the same parts and assembled in the same manner. One thing is guaranteed, however: they'll both form a relationship with the owner. There will be times of overwhelming joy, grin-inducing fun, hammer-wielding frustration and head-in-hands despair, but the beauty of it all is that whatever problem arises, it can generally be fixed in your own workshop. You can be back on the road in double quick time, the bad times forgotten.

Classic ownership can bring about some strange encounters. Park your old motorcycle on the market square, in the car park, outside the supermarket, at the filling station, and on your return you will find someone standing by it who will want to talk to you about it – anyone from the glassy-eyed old chap who used to run one just like it when he was younger, to the BMX-mounted kid who loves bikes but has never heard of the make that the badge on your fuel tank so proudly boasts. They'll want to see you start it – a fingers-crossed time for a first kick effort, the audience-induced poor start can be most embarrassing – and listen to it as you ride away, all the while ignoring the gleaming superbike next to it. Such simple things can be enormously satisfying and you know that they'll be telling their friends about that lovely old Norton, or BSA, or Triumph or whatever they saw.

The unusual sound of a passing classic, compared to the commonplace howl of the modern 4-cylinder machine, will stop people in their tracks, have them stare and stick up a thumb or simply grin inanely.

Another positive incentive for choosing and old motorbike is economics, for most classics are tax exempt. Based on the age of the vehicle – four-wheelers are included too – and the presumption of limited mileage, a rolling twenty-five-year exemption, applicable to any vehicle, was introduced by the Conservative government but in 1997; when the Labour party took over, they put the brakes on the rolling system and applied a cut-off date of 1 January 1973. Understandably this proved unpopular: for example, if your machine was built on 31 December 1972 and your mate's was built two days later, he'd pay full tax while you wouldn't pay any. In 2104 the rolling

You'll always find nice bikes and interesting people to talk to at any classic or vintage gathering.

There's no better way to blow away the winter cobwebs than a ride out on your favourite classic.

With a middleweight classic and some nice weather, there's nothing finer than exploring the country lanes at a steady pace.

Park up your classic and watch people ignore the modern bikes to come and look at yours.

system was reinstated, but now only for vehicles forty years old or more.

What's more, in a rare moment of inspired thinking, the Conservative/ Lib-Dem coalition government of 2012 decided that, seeing as the vast majority of classic owners cosseted and maintained their vehicles to a high standard, it was unnecessary for them to have to try to get their classics to conform to the ever-increasing standards of the modern day MoT test. Since November 2012, all vehicles built or registered prior to 1 January 1960 no longer have to undergo a mandatory MoT test, though it remains optional should the owner feel so minded.

So, now you've no MoT to pay for, as well as no tax – but what about insurance? Well, that's another bonus, because many insurance brokers realize that classic owners not only look after their machines extremely well, but they also respect their bikes' age and ride them accordingly, thus not being the high-speed risk of the modern superbike. Generally speaking, classics don't come out during the bad weather months, so the only real risk to consider is that of theft. As such, there are several specialist insurers who have excellent packages available to the classic owner, with agreed value, limited mileage and a variety of other inducements, which can make comprehensive insurance very reasonable indeed. What's more, multi-bike cover can be cheap, because, after all, it's only possible to ride one bike at once.

Another thing to bear in mind is component life. For drive chains and tyres this can be measured in years rather than miles, fuel consumption is invariably excellent and the simplicity of home maintenance keeps running costs to a bare minimum. There's never been a better time to own a classic, so what are you waiting for?

Triumph was the last of the British mainstream motorcycles to fall.

2

which classic?

How long is a piece of string? Your choice of classic depends on any number of things – your engineering and mechanical skills, self-confidence, available space, security, tools and of course the size of your wallet.

Common sense must prevail: while the initial enthusiasm to set about your project will be all-consuming, if it's, say, in a lock-up garage half a mile or more from your eighth-floor flat, a cold, wet and windy evening after a day's work will soon temper that enthusiasm and before long your classic will be advertised on ebay as an unfinished project and without doubt you will finish up out of pocket.

Also think about your future plan for the classic. Once you've restored it and it's running well, are you going to keep it for years or do you fancy selling it and getting another different project? Bear in mind that it costs almost as much to restore a small bike as it does a big one but the

returns are much less, as per Ford's old adage 'big car, big profit, small car, small profit.'

If it's your first restoration, then avoid the temptation to buy a basket case, that is, a bike that has been completely dismantled, because no matter how much the owner insists that all parts are present and correct, you can bet your life, there will be something missing. It might be, indeed it probably will be, only a small component part, but sod's law dictates that the part gone awol will be critical to the assembly of a whole load of others. Likewise, unless you are an experienced restorer or you are intending to build up a classic without particular reference to its original specification, avoid the loosely assembled machine with obvious parts missing, as this will prove to be an expensive exercise in parts gathering – unless of course, it's such a bargain price that it would be foolish to ignore it.

Having said that though, endless hours trawling through boxes at various autojumbles – if you can justify the extortionate and ever-increasing gate prices of the major shows and events – can be both great fun and incredibly frustrating at the same time, but enormously satisfying if the sought-after part eventually turns up. Even after all these years, parts do still keep turning up but you'll stand just as good a chance of finding what you need on ebay. Often you can spot a part for your machine and discover that the seller has many other parts for sale too; in such a case it's always worth contacting him to see if he has the very part you need.

If you can, find a complete machine. Don't worry too much if it's rusty, oily, or even that it doesn't run, just make sure that it's pretty much in one piece. It may be that it's simply been stored up for years in less than ideal conditions and the damp has affected the electrical system or the ignition, or of course

ABOVE: An incomplete project such as this BSA B33 is not too bad a start because most of the missing parts are available as pattern replicas – the important parts are all present.

LEFT: The seller will say it's all there but you can bet your life it won't be.

it may be that it's worn out or broken somewhere inside, but providing the kick start will turn over the engine it's a good enough place to start. If it doesn't, then at least there is an element of leverage with regard to the bartering process, especially if the seller also doesn't know quite why it's seized. The overall acceptable standard of decay is relative to each individual so making the final decision on whether or not the project is too far gone, too much like hard work, too expensive for what it is or simply too daunting is down to you.

Naturally, the best buy is one that is a runner but probably needs work to make it either reliable or more aesthetically pleasing. Surface rust on wheel rims and bright works is not detrimen-

tal to anything other than the look of the bike; likewise oil leaks are not a problem except again to the appearance of the bike, the state of your riding gear and the place where you park the bike. All these aspects can be greatly improved if not entirely cured.

So where do you start? Well, with all the previous preliminaries taken care of, it's a case of practicalities. Choose a mainstream marque for which parts are interchangeable across a variety of ranges. Take BSA, for example, the Small Heath, Birmingham concern was once the biggest motorcycle manufacturer in the world, with one in four machines being a BSA, so there were many made and many still around. During a set period, say between 1958 and 1961

as a snapshot, the twin-cylinder range shared cycle parts, suspension, brakes, electrics, even the gearbox with the single-cylinder range, and the frames were practically the same too, so a mudguard or an oil tank from a single will fit a twin as it is the same part. The only difference is the colour scheme.

This greatly eases the search for parts. Leaving only the engine as the individual aspect, even then most parts are interchangeable between the 350cc and the 500cc singles, and the 500cc and 650cc twins. What's more, the great number of these machines still being used on the road has resulted in most parts becoming available again as newly manufactured and on the shelf. This applies equally, of course,

Amazingly enough this Thunderbird was a pretty good runner, though later investigation showed a blocked sludge trap and a plethora of rotten metal.

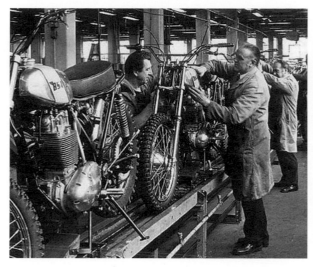

ABOVE: *At one time, one in four motorcycles throughout the world was a BSA.*

RIGHT: *Velocette owners are a passionate bunch: once a Velo man, always a Velo man.*

to the likes of Triumph, Norton, Royal Enfield and most other major marques.

Velocette were renowned for their quality engineering and the marque has a very loyal and passionate following, but they do have one or two unusual design features, the clutch and primary drive arrangement being the most obvious. The clutch itself, and hence the primary drive system, is positioned in between the crankcases and the outboard drive sprocket. Whilst this makes changing the gearing with the sprocket an easy operation, to actually reach the clutch is more difficult. What's more, because of its position within the limited space, it is a very narrow clutch with a unique scissor-type operating mechanism, which can be tricky to set up correctly. Indeed the factory service book states 'Before attempting any adjustment of the clutch it is important that the operation of the clutch is fully understood ...'

A situation where you have to remove a pressed steel cover to reveal the gearbox sprocket and then secure a steel peg through one of three holes in its centre, then locate it into one of the castellations in the shock absorber spring behind it and then rock the rear wheel backwards or forwards, depending on whether the clutch is slipping or dragging, calls for a bit of considered thought and no little concentration. If that does not do the trick, there are three pages of optional treatments in the manual ... The Velocette clutch is not a strong assembly and will not stand a lot of abuse, but when set up perfectly and used correctly it is a very light and sweet unit. Superb machines the Velocettes undoubtedly are, but perhaps not the ideal choice for the first-time restorer.

Consider a few other more obvious aspects of classic ownership too, some of which will have a bearing on the restoration and maintenance costs. A twin cylinder engine, for example, obviously has, in some areas, twice the component parts of a single. Two exhaust pipes and two silencers instead of one, two con rods and two pistons instead of one, four valves, rocker arms and cam followers instead of just two, often two carburettors and so on.

Unit or pre-unit? In other words does the engine have the gearbox in with it, or does it have a separate gearbox? Does the idea of having to dismantle the gearbox together with the engine fill you with dread, because of course the gearbox can be treated as a completely separate entity in a pre-unit system. With a pre-unit system, the engine can be restored and put to one side before tackling the gearbox, or the other way round; and if the frame or rolling chassis is already prepared then the gearbox can be fitted into the frame to await its engine. The main advantage of the unit engine is that the primary

Triumph's Bonneville, the epitome of the British twin.

BSA's much-loved A7/A10 range with the separate gearbox was superseded by the not so popular unit-construction A50/A65.

The A50 and A65 engine was dubbed the 'Power Egg' for obvious reasons.

drive chain runs between constant fixed centres, any slack or wear being taken up by means of a chain tensioner, and it's generally easier to keep clean, whereas the separate gearbox has to be physically moved back and forth to adjust primary chain tension and it's sometimes quite awkward to keep the area between the back of the engine and the front of the gearbox clean. In the latter case, there is also the issue of maintaining an oil-tight seal between the gearbox shaft and the inner primary drive case, because the case has to be slotted to allow adjustment movement of the gearbox, whereas this does not apply in the unit engine.

Then there is the frame – rigid, plunger or swinging arm. Of the three, arguably the first and last are the best bets. The rigid is straightforward with no suspension parts to have to consid-er other than a well-sprung saddle; and the swinging arm, which is removable from the mainframe, is supported on simple tubular bushes with a couple of sprung dampers. It's relatively easy to remove and refit, along with readily available new bushes and so on, but there is the potential cost of new dampers, whereas with a rigid frame all that needs to be considered is the paint finish. The plunger system was an attempt to introduce an element of suspension by allowing wheel movement within an adapted rigid frame. It's a system accommodated within a limited, closed ends space, and is accordingly not the easiest arrangement to work on; even when in good condition, it leaves much to be desired when compared to the systems that came before and after. Triumph's sprung hub works on the same principle but in an even more complicated manner, as the plunger arrangement is built into a huge rear-wheel hub, rather than the frame itself – thus giving the rigid frame an extended lease of life.

KNOW THY BEAST

Before you take the plunge on the bike you fancy, read up about it as much as you can, buy or borrow books on the marque and model and learn the basic differences between the year ranges. A classic example is the BSA heavyweight range of 1956 and 1957, which used Ariel full-width all-alloy hubs in their wheels. This was essentially because BSA, as Ariel's parent company, wanted to use up most of Ariel's four-stroke range component parts, as the direction they were sending their subsidiary was down the two-stroke road with the Leader and Arrow. A year before the change, BSA used single-sided hubs and in 1958 went onto full-width steel hubs.

Take a trip to a classic gathering such as Founder's Day, the VMCC's annual premier one-day gathering, invariably at Stanford Hall, near Lutterworth in Leicestershire, take photographs of similar machines and see what other owners have done to theirs. Better still, talk to the owner if you can find him, take his number and don't be afraid to call him and ask his advice if you get stuck – most classic owners are only too pleased to help others, even if it's only by advice from personal experience.

Join the owners club. Not only do you get a monthly magazine full of information, technical advice, anecdotes

All you need to know is available out there.

BSA used their subsidiary Ariel's elegant full-width alloy hubs in 1956 and 1957.

BSA called time on the Ariel four-stroke and used up the available wheel hub stock on their own machines.

If there's one thing you feel you'd like to know, just ask – most owners will be only too happy to talk to you about their bike.

and dates of gatherings, you may also find there is a local branch where you can go along and meet other owners and enthusiasts who will welcome you into their fold and help you with your rebuild. The owners clubs invariably have a spares scheme too, from where you can obtain good-quality remanu-factured parts, or even new old stock components. Naturally there is also a for sale and wanted section, where club members advertise their surplus wares, and you will find that the spe-cialist retailers are advertised within

the pages of the journal too. Another facility offered by the owners club is a dating service. If your purchase has no documents with it – logbook, tax disc and so on – the frame number can be cross-referenced with the factory records to prove the date of manufac-ture. A dating certificate from the club will satisfy the DVLA and you will be able to gain an age-related number plate for your bike. These are registra-tion numbers that were allocated en masse to areas where the take-up of newly registered vehicles was small,

for example the remote corners of Scotland. As such there are still many registrations from the correct period that have never been issued and are still available, and they look far more in keeping with a classic than a rather obvious 'Q' plate. This applies also for 1960s and 1970s vehicles with a suffix letter.

The VMCC is an extremely useful club of which to be part. They too have branches – or as they're called, 'sec-tions' – country-wide and are behind many top-class classic events. Within

Membership of the VMCC is practically obligatory with an old motorcycle.

their Burton upon Trent HQ they have a breathtaking library, full of books, documents, factory records, trophies, brochures, photographs and much more. As a member you are eligible to spend time in the library to research whatever you feel like researching and there's a full-time staff always willing to help you. The VMCC also has an excellent monthly journal and there is a team of marque specialists, whose sole objective is to answer queries and put people right on various aspects of that particular company's wares. Indeed, for the larger marques there are also subsection specialists, such as for twins, singles, lightweights, two-strokes and so on. Whilst the club has to be run at a profit, like any other business, its main agenda is to keep old motorcycles on the road and their profile high, so it will not rip you off for their services, unlike other well-known commercial archives.

The club also has an excellent and very comprehensive transfer service, from where the transfers can be purchased for your motorcycle's correct year of manufacture.

Once you have built up a little knowledge about your subject, you'll feel far more confident when you assess a machine with a view to buying and can spot obvious items that are incorrect, or purport to be something they are not. If you are still not too sure, then take someone with you who is more experienced in classic matters. Whilst the vast majority of classic owners and enthusiasts are perfectly honest, there are inevitably those who are, shall we say, economical with the truth and the last thing you want to be doing is paying well over the odds for what is essentially a wreck.

PRELIMINARY CHECKS

Assume you've made your choice and you've found a bike that, for all intents and purposes, is complete but not running. Ascertain the length of time it has been out of service, for if it has been standing still for several years, do not under any circumstances try to get it to start. There may be countless problems inside that have arisen simply due to its inactivity, which could result in further damage to what might otherwise be a fairly light rescue mission. Corrosion may have rusted the bore, the piston rings may be stuck in their grooves, or worse, stuck to the bore, in which case forced movement may break them and ruin a perfectly serviceable cylinder barrel. Likewise corrosion may have affected the bearings, the big ends, camshaft faces and other parts. What's more, despite the sump perhaps being full of old, black oil, the residue from the combustion process within it may have wreaked havoc on every metal surface immersed therein.

In the case of twin-cylinder engine, there's a good chance that the sludge trap will be full too. The sludge trap is a tube that runs through the centre of the crank where the heavyweight deposits – such as combustion by-products, carbon and so on – carried within the oil are collected. Eventually, this tube fills and becomes blocked, thus restricting oil flow to the big ends and resulting in expensive engine failure.

Of course, if it's only been stood for a relatively short time and it turns over on depression of the kick start, then after a few preliminary checks it may be all right to see if it will fire up.

Putting it simply, if there's fuel and oil present and a spark occurring at the right stage of the combustion process, then there's no real reason for it not to fire. However, if the fuel has been in the tank for a long time, it may have 'died'. Leaded fuel used to take on a distinct smell when it was past its best, not to mention a pretty murky colour. Modern unleaded fuel has a very short shelf life – if not in a sealed container, then it may be a matter of just months. It may look fine and smell fine, but will probably be useless when trying to fire up an engine. Furthermore, it may have left a residue in the carburettor on evaporation, restricting or, worse, bunging the jets up completely.

Let's assume at this point that the bike has not been standing too long. Firstly, take the fuel pipes off the taps under the tank and drain off the old petrol and dispose of it in a responsible manner. Underneath the crankcases you will see a plate or a hexagon headed screw into the sump. Undo this and allow the old oil to drain off into a suitable receptacle and then temporarily tip it through a filter back into the tank – a fine, domestic, tea strainer-like sieve will be adequate. Do not run on this old oil for many minutes, only for long enough to see if the engine will run.

Remove the spark plug and clean it with a wire brush, check the contact on the end has a small gap between it and the central core point, fit it back into its holder on the end of the lead and lay it against the cases, cylinder head, barrel and so on.

Remove the ignition points cover and slowly turn over the engine and see if the contact breaker points open and close. While they're at their open point, gently insert a sliver of fine emery paper and clean the mating faces of the points.

At this point, a swift swing on the kick start should induce the click of a spark at the plug. If so, replace the plug in the head, fit the lead and add some fuel to the tank. Let it fill the carburettor, flood the carburettor by means of the tickler button on the

The sludge trap from a 1955 Triumph – sludge indeed.

Old petrol, particularly unleaded, can leave behind a residue capable of blocking the system.

Undo the sump plug.

Let all the oil that has gathered in the sump run out into your collecting vessel.

No matter how quick you are, the oil will be quicker and run over your fingers.

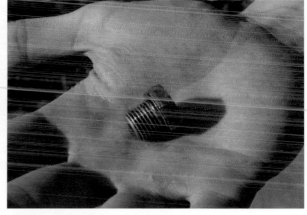

The sump plug may be covered in metallic particles, which will give a good indication of the engine oil condition. Clean the threads before replacing.

float chamber and with a bit of luck, after one or two kicks, the engine should start. Don't rev the engine too hard but keep it running and have a look inside the oil tank, where you should eventually see a regular squirt from the return pipe just under the filler neck. That tells you that the oil pump is working. Don't be alarmed if it takes a minute or two, it has to

circulate right through the engine before it returns to the tank.

If the twin-cylinder engine has never been rebuilt, despite it appearing to be in good condition, can you afford to take the risk of running it as is, especially regarding the sludge trap? If you've a single, then you will not have this problem, as invariably the big end bearing arrangement is different.

Remember the old adage 'better safe than sorry'.

Now, without wishing to sound patronizing or condescending, all this assumes that the new owner is mechanically savvy enough to know what the above terms mean and where said items – points, plug lead, big ends and so on – are found. These items will be covered in more detail in later chapters.

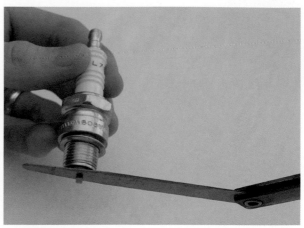

Sometimes, like in the case of this Norton, the area around the sump plug is tight and needs a special spanner. In this case, simply grinding the edges off the hexagon of a box spanner is all that's required.

Use your feeler gauges to get the correct spark plug gap.

Amal 276 carburettor. The tickler button can be seen on top of the float chamber.

It will take a minute or so for the oil to travel throughout the engine before returning to the tank.

Shelves are just so useful, but the more you have, the more you'll find to fill them.

3

getting started

Setting out your workshop space is critical, but as mentioned earlier, this all depends on personal circumstances. Some may have a spacious workshop, others a domestic garage, and other still just a garden shed, so some of the following may not be applicable to everyone purely on the grounds of elbow room.

Obviously, the main thing to start with is a bench. Anything will do as long as it's sturdy enough to take the weight of the engine and is at a comfortable working height. A purpose-built wooden bench permanently fixed to the wall is ideal, though angle iron or another such support system is perfectly fine. The top can be boarded with heavy duty ply, blockboard, softwood planks, MDF or similar – all are adequate, especially if topped with a sheet of white-faced hardboard. The latter not only gives a jointless surface, it also helps with light distribution and makes spotting wayward nuts and bolts easier. It's

also fairly oil-resistant and easy to clean down. Avoid chipboard, even the fine-density flooring grade, unless you're intending to finish it with hard board, because not only is it a difficult and not very secure material to screw into, by its very nature it is absorbent, and if left wet, will swell and break up.

There again, it's not difficult to pick up a length of unwanted kitchen worktop, which is invariably chipboard based but will have an impervious surface finish and may have a posh rounded nose to it and a jazzy surface finish. It may seem an obvious thing to say, but ensure it's level, front to back as well along its length, as there's little more annoying than having things rolling about on the bench. Also, make sure it's of a good working height that does not have you bending or stretching. If your kitchen worktop height suits you, base the height on that.

It's always useful to have a shelf above your bench, so you can have

important items readily to hand at all times without cluttering up bench space – for example, a battery charger, the leads of which can be lowered to a battery on the bench when required but rolled up out of the way when not. Likewise, you could have a mini radio system with its push buttons instantly accessible and cables running up the wall and across to wherever you position the speakers. It's a good place also to store everyday items such as scissors, pencils, marker pens, tape measure and that all-important workshop manual. The shelf doesn't have to be anything industrial, just a couple of domestic brackets and a length of suitable board.

The same applies elsewhere in the workshop: the more shelf space you have, the more you'll find to fill it. Oils, greases and various lubricants, paints, cleaners, fuel additives, polishes, distilled water, boxes of nuts, bolts, screws, washers, bulbs, fuses – you name it, it will find its way onto the shelves.

A white-topped surface helps you spot things when they go missing and also helps with the light distribution.

A small shelf over the bench is ideal for the battery charger and radio.

The more light you have on the bench the better.

Once that's set up to your satisfaction, make sure you have a light source directly over the bench, be it a fluorescent tube, an angle-poise type arrangement, a rack of spotlights or just an odd bulb or two. Make sure that when you're standing over an item of work, the light does not cast the shadow of your head and shoulders onto it. There is nothing more frustrating than having to move to one side in order to be able to see what you need to see.

Also, make sure your bench is supplied by an adequate number of sockets. You may need to have, say, a battery charger, a drill and the grinder all available to you at one time, not to mention perhaps the radio or the fan heater. Extension leads are all well and good, but they do get in the way and are a tripping hazard.

It may seem obvious, but a clock is fairly important too, especially if you don't wear a watch. Not only does it give you an indication of how long you've been in the workshop, but it also allows you to time tasks, for example in the course of preparation of a rust removal immersion or painting.

Next you'll need a substantial vice. Once your bench is where you want it, think about where you will primarily stand when working – usually directly in front of a window – and do not place your vice there. Fix it to one end, but not too close to the wall in case you have to hold something long or tubular, in which case you may not have left adequate room between the vice jaws and the wall for your item's length. You want it to be just far enough away not be in your way when working, but close enough to be used in all circumstances. Size-wise, it will need to have at least 6in jaws and a fairly wide opening capability, to accommodate, for example, the crankcases or gearbox shell.

Take your time …

Get a strong vice. One like this has seen some serious service over the years but will still last for generations.

Have a look around the autojumbles or the car boot sales – vices often turn up beneath the counters for reasonable prices, and most vendors will accept an offer as they'll not want to cart the thing home with them if they can help it. Alternatively, there are the internet auction sites, but obviously if a good, cheap vice isn't local, it'll cost a bomb to transport; be patient and one within acceptable travelling distance should turn up before too long. Likewise the high street tool and hardware stores will have new ones in stock, though you may have to pay a little more for them. In the case of the latter, the vice may come complete with soft jaws, or at least such things may be available from the same place. Soft jaws are usually lengths of strong nylon or plastic right angles, which simply drop over the serrated faces of the vice's steel jaws and prevent the serrations marking the object to be held while still maintaining good grip. An alternative is to make a pair. It's easy

and cheap enough to buy a length of aluminium angle and cut it to suit the vice jaws – the remainder will inevitably come in for something else useful later.

A double-ended bench grinder is a most useful tool that can save hours of laborious filing. Get one as big and as powerful as you can accommodate and afford, within reason of course. Six-inch diameter wheels are the most common and are generally adequate, but if you can go for the 8in do so, as the motor is a little more powerful and the wheels, by virtue of their size, will last longer.

Like the vice, consider carefully where you position the grinder on the bench with regards to space either side and below. The grinder will have a coarse wheel on one end and a fine wheel on the other. If you have the luxury of space, a real treat is to have the grinder mounted on an independent stand, which gives completely unhindered space below the wheels. This can

also double up as a polishing machine, with the grinding wheels swapped for buffing mops, where it is necessary to have space below to enable the mops to access the nooks and crannies of the item being polished. However, if this is indeed a luxury too far, there are other ways round it. For example, a simple electric motor, or of course a second grinder, bolted down on the free end of a bench or worktop, is more than adequate to utilize as a polisher, provided the motor is powerful enough. Anything above ¾hp will be sufficient for home workshop polishing. Less than this and the pressure of the item to be polished on the mop will stop it.

The beauty of the double-ended grinder is that there are several variations on the theme. For example, an excellent addition to the grinder kit is a linishing wheel. This is a strong but flexible rubber wheel, which fits onto the grinder shaft in place of the grinding wheel, and around which is

Soft jaws are a temporary means of holding something firmly in the vice without the serrations of the vice jaws marking it.

A bench grinder with a reasonably powerful motor and coarse and fine stone wheels can save a terrific amount of time.

A free-standing electric motor of reasonable output can be converted to use as a basic buffing machine.

slipped a hoop of abrasive sheet. The rubber wheel is slotted so that when it begins to revolve, the inertia expands the wheel – akin to a dragster's rear tyres – and grips the hoop. The hoops are available in any number of grades of abrasive and are ideal for gradually smoothing out the coarse markings of the grinding wheels prior to polishing.

A pillar drill, bench mounted, is regularly a better bet than the hand-held equivalent during a restoration, purely on the grounds that the drill is fixed and the item to be drilled is also fixed, therefore ensuring totally accuracy and eliminating the chance of the drill bit slipping to one side, or being applied out of plumb.

Again, the high street tool stores have an excellent selection and likewise many can be found on the auction sites. The pillar drill and its adjustable position bed can also be used at times in a similar manner to a milling machine, that is as a cutter rather than a drill, simply by fitting a cutting tool in place of the bit.

Any classic motorcycle restoration inevitably means oil, grease and muck. So treat yourself to a parts washer. It might seem extravagant, but if nothing else, it keeps all the muck and oily residues in one place and saves splashing it all over the workbench and floor, or if it's a warm summer's day, all over the grass – which it will of course kill, leaving a less than impressive brown patch on your lawn.

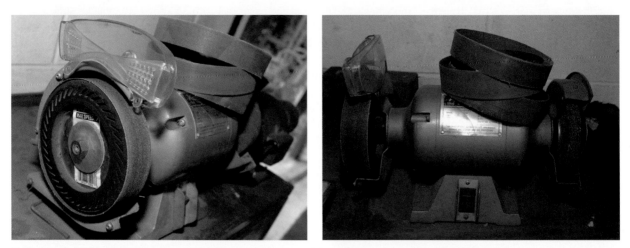

The bench grinder can also be utilized as a linisher if fitted with the appropriate expanding rubber wheel and sanding belt.

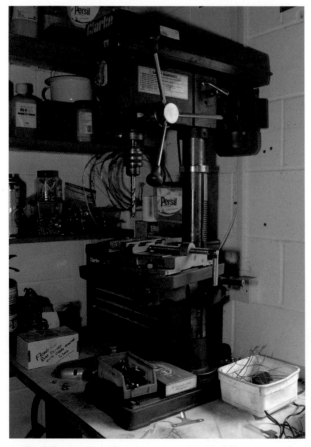

A pillar drill maintains perfect alignment and avoids drilling at an angle or to one side.

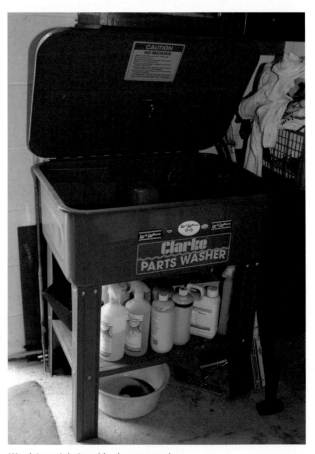

Worth its weight in gold – the parts washer.

There are some superb parts washers available, in varying sizes and capacities, some bench mounted, some free standing, some with filtered, recirculating systems, others just mere containers. What they all have, though, is a removable, internal perforated shelf on which the item to be cleaned can sit, which allows the fluid back into the sump. That this shelf is removable gives the choice of being able to soak the item in the fluid, as well as being manually brushed. Any old penknife or screwdriver and paint brush will help proceedings and when the sump has a build-up of sludge, it can be emptied by means of a removable plug in the bottom of the tank, allowing easy cleaning before replenishment.

As far as degreasing fluid goes, paraffin was always a favourite at one time because it was an inexpensive commodity; but like everything else these days that's not the case any more and there are better fluids available, which act in an emulsifying fashion – that is, they will degrease and then disperse in water, usually in a milky fluid, taking the grease with them. The parts washer will hold a fair amount of degreasing fluid but it lasts for a very long time and can be reused many times as the solids settle to the bottom of the sump, leaving the fairly clean fluid above it. It's worthwhile contacting the lubricants companies directly here because they will probably be able to supply a 5-gallon, or 25-litre, drum of their own branded degreaser at a much better rate than buying smaller quantities on the high street. Better still, if you have a friendly garage owner, see if he will buy it through his business for you: that way you'll get it at trade price rather than retail price.

Of course, there are some parts of the machine that will not fit in a parts washer, the mainframe for example, and these will have to be degreased manually with a brush. As always in such matters, please consider the environment when and where such a task is undertaken and dispose of your mess responsibly.

If you have a power washer for your drive or for use on your car, this is an ideal tool to use when washing down your degreased engine: the high pressure jet of hot soapy water takes no prisoners when to comes to getting in between the cylinder fins and other similar places.

A compressor is a must, if it's only to save manual effort when it comes to inflating tyres, and with the influx of Asian imported goods over the last few years, there are some competitively priced, good-quality units on the market, though as always it pays to shop around and haggle a bit. Go for the biggest air tank capacity, highest pressure and most powerful motor you can afford, especially if you're going to indulge in paint spraying or blast cleaning. The latter exercise, in particular, uses up a lot of compressed air and it's unbelievably frustrating to have to keep waiting for the compressor to catch up with the job. With an adequately sized compressor, you then have the choice of either air-assisted or electrically powered hand tools, such as grinders, sanders, cutters and so on.

If such jobs are not on your itinerary, then a lesser machine will be more than adequate for tyre inflation, blow-gun cleaning of swarf and muck from parts and of course drying parts once they're out of the parts washer and cleaned.

Again, depending on the size of your workshop and your wallet, a blast cleaning cabinet is exceptionally useful. To have the facility to blast clean parts in your own workshop, as and when you need them, is a real boon to any restoration, as it saves not only a lot of money, but also a colossal amount of time. If you do get one, you'll wonder how you ever got by without one before.

RIGHT: A pressure washer can blast water into nooks and crannies where a brush can't reach.

BELOW LEFT AND RIGHT: A powerful compressor will run both your blasting cabinet and spray gun, as well as powering numerous air tools.

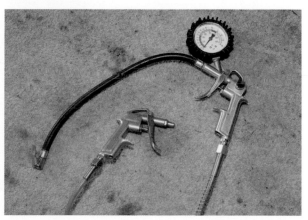

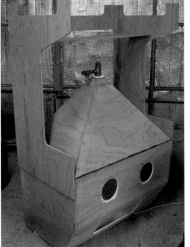

ASA blast cabinet in the process of construction.

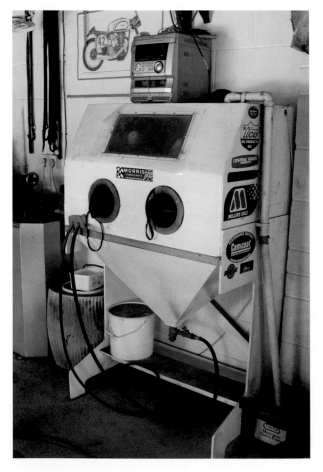

ASA blast cabinet that's been in solid service for a few years.

There are cabinets available in varying sizes and capacities but if you are, or know someone who is, fairly handy with a wood saw then there is a basic kit available from Anglo Scott Abrasives in Lancashire, which comprises a fully dimensioned working drawing, which enables you to construct your own with a couple of large sheets of ply or MDF, and very good it is too. As well as the plan, it comes complete with all fittings, blast guns and hoses, a large tub of iron oxide shot and another of glass beads, cabinet base mesh, internal light and a roll of clear film to protect the Perspex viewing window from the blast medium.

Another workshop boon is the hydraulic workbench. With variable heights, not only does it allow you to stand upright while you're working on the bike, thus saving cold and aches and pains from kneeling on the workshop floor, but it also enables you to see the lower reaches of the project without having to roll around on your back. Not many years ago there was only one main supplier in the UK and as such their products were ridiculously expensive, but now both UK-engineered and imported benches as available for very much less. Some are very basic and necessitate the use of an independent trolley jack, but for not a lot more, either scissor- or parallelogram-legged units are available with an integral jacking unit, which are more convenient. Most have a removable ramp at one end, which makes loading the bike onto the ramp simple, and also a removable panel, which facilitates the dropping out of wheels while the bike is on the ramp. At the front there is an adjustable guide, which clamps around the tyre and holds the bike straight and firm.

Some benches also have hooks beneath the table, so that the bike can also be strapped down if required. This is very useful if your bike has no centre stand. Under most circumstances, however, the bike will be quite secure on its centre stand without straps, though sometimes it may be necessary to have said centre stand up on a panel of wood in order to allow the rear wheel to turn without touching the bench table top.

A hydraulic workbench – you'll wonder how you ever got by without it.

HAND TOOLS

A form of heat is useful. Not so much to keep you warm on cold days – though that's always handy as you'll be more inclined to venture into the workshop if you know you can keep warm – but more as a means to heat up component parts. A plumber's gas-powered blow lamp is ideal, with the 2kg gas bottle, which makes for convenience and ease of carriage. These lamps do not have the ferocity or the pinpoint accuracy of the experienced welder's oxy-acetylene torch, but they can usually get steel to glow red, which is more often than not hot enough. Many is the time when such heat is the catalyst that breaks the bond and frees off rusted together parts.

Likewise, a steel stud in an alloy case. If it's stuck and will not undo with the tried and tested lock nut method, do not force it, as there's a better chance it will break the alloy in which it's stuck. Apply the heat locally, don't be afraid to give it plenty – it'll need far more heat than the lamp's capability to damage or melt the alloy – and then try to move the stud. As the alloy expands at a faster rate than steel when subjected to heat, 99 per cent of the time it will free off easily. It's the same principle when trying to release bearings or bushes from crankcases. The bearings are steel, bushes often bronze; neither expand at anything like the same rate as alloy, so again apply the heat as if your life depended on it, and with a firm tap they will simply fall out. The same applies in reverse, when replac-

ing or refitting bearings and bushes: simply heat up the cases, drop in the bearing and allow to cool. Some people prefer to apply the heat in a more general manner by putting the cases in the domestic oven. This is fine, but bear in mind that, by their very nature, the cases will give off quite strong fumes and trapped oil may find an escape, so, for the sake of domestic harmony, ensure you have the full blessing of your better half before you go down this route!

A heat gun is also an advisable piece of kit to have around the workshop. The basic domestic paint-remover type is perfect, for situations where heat is required but not a naked flame, for example on metal that's to be, or has been, painted.

In any workshop environment, an element of organization is necessary, if only to enable you can find a certain tool when you need it. As such, tools drawers and cabinets are ideal. If you ensure you've replaced the tool in the correct drawer when you've finished with it, you'll be able to go straight to it the next time you need it without having to turn the workshop upside down in the search for it. What's more, such a regime makes for a tidy bench, where items and parts can be readily spotted. Most high street tool stores have varying ranges and prices of such cabinets, but of course a small set of domestic drawers is equally adequate, space permitting.

Keep those plastic tubs that dishwasher tablets come in (or butter or

ABOVE: Getting your tools organized like this is simple enough, but keeping them this way takes a bit more effort.

LEFT: Two types of very useful point heat – a naked flame and a hot air gun.

ice cream), as they're really useful for putting the nuts, bolts and washers in while you're dismantling, or for newly refinished parts awaiting assembly. That way it keeps every related item together. They're also handy for draining oil into, catching petrol from the tank or carburettor and for holding the degreaser if you choose to do a bit of cleaning outside, away from your parts washer. They readily available and disposable as and when they break. You can also buy lightweight trays, which are magnetized, thus holding every metal component in place within them – useful in a situation where you may accidentally kneel on, step on or kick it flying.

Another useful item is a roll of light wire, off-cuts from domestic electrical wiring stripped down to a copper core, which is ideal for tying items together in the correct order, such as clutch parts or wheel bearings and spacers and so on. It's also ideal for hanging parts from a rack to be painted.

Treat yourself to a good-quality set of screwdrivers, a mix of large and small, long and short, Phillips head and standard, and resist the temptation to use them as chisels, though you can be forgiven for using them occasionally to prise something apart.

An impact driver can be pretty useful at times too. Again these come in varying qualities, but a good one should last you years. For the uninitiated, it's a ratcheted screwdriver, which, when impacted by a hammer blow, forces the ratchet to twist the head round by a small amount, usually enough to free off a stubborn screw – or in the worst case, rip the head off it!

Of course, no workshop should be without that most maligned of all tools, the hammer. For such use as described above, a mid-weight ball-pein hammer is adequate, though if you have access to a builder's traditional lump hammer or similar, that's more than enough. As well as the 'big hammer' it's worth investing in a rubber-headed mallet, for those times when you have to tap an alloy case or a shaft perhaps. The rubber head is tough enough to deliver a firm application but malleable enough not

LEFT AND BELOW LEFT: A dedicated drawer for each type of tool – screwdrivers, ring spanners, open-ended spanner, allen keys and so on – means you'll always know just where to find the tool you want when you want it.

Cheap and cheerful, but old ice cream tubs are just so useful.

Tying things together, tying things up for spraying, poking out holes – you'll always find a use for a length of sturdy but bendable wire.

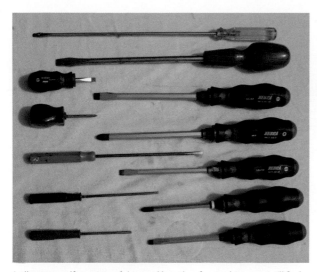

Collect yourself a variety of sizes and lengths of screwdrivers – you'll find that you will use them all at one time or another.

An impact driver will often free a seized screw but make sure the screw head is sound otherwise it may simply break off.

to mark the alloy or damage threads. Nylon-headed mallets are also available, though these are not quite so forgiving, and can be used alongside the traditional copper-headed mallet. Again, if applying against a shaft or something with a thread, the copper is soft enough to prevent damage.

A wire brush is one of those workshop hardy annuals that we take for granted yet is one of the most useful tools, for cleaning up nuts and bolts, gummed up with old grease and muck, paint or rust, cleaning the sooty spark plug and so on. Most tool stalls at autojumbles have them on sale usually at no more than 50p or £1.

Another £1 autojumble regular is the telescopic magnet. When collapsed, it's

about the size of a regular ballpoint pen, but extends like an old-fashioned car aerial to maybe a couple of feet. On the tip is a small, magnetized button, which can get into those little places where a dropped washer or nut inevitably falls and where your fingers can't reach.

A Dremel, or something along those lines, will save you a huge amount of time with the file. Also, as it has varying speeds, you can use it to clean out, for example, bolt holes in frames that have been painted, without the paint chipping as it would using say a penknife or even a round file. They have any number of different attachments, for grinding, sanding, cutting, de-burring and so on, and also have the

option of a flexible shaft for ease of access into tight corners where the main tool won't fit.

It's useful to have a selection of punches of differing thickness, as something often has to be knocked out of, or indeed into, a narrow space.

A peg spanner is handy when the need arises to turn an item, such as a crankshaft shock absorber nut, which is circular with castellations. It's also useful to have two so the other one can work on the splines of the shaft as shown here.

A measuring device is vital. Again autojumbles will turn up perfectly satisfactory 6 or 12in inch steel rulers, which also make for excellent straight edges. A vernier scale micrometer

ABOVE: The hammer is derided as a tool of brute force and ignorance but no workshop worth its salt can do without a good selection. From the top: engineer's ball pein, wooden mallet, copper head, rubber mallet.

RIGHT: Wire brushes of all shapes and sizes are available and fairly cheaply too, so treat yourself to a few and get things clean.

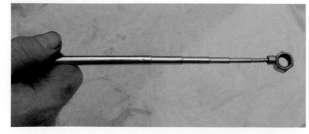

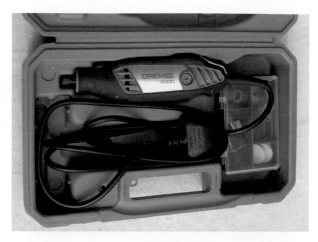

ABOVE: It might be cheap and it might be simple but when you can't reach that washer you've dropped into the deepest reaches of the engine, the telescopic magnet is a godsend.

RIGHT: With its variable speed and variety of heads, the Dremel can take care of some quite precise work.

Deliver a knockout with a series of punches.

Peg spanners are ideal for working on castellated items like splined crankshafts.

gives an exceptionally accurate measurement, though can be a little trying on the eyes; the digital LED caliper may not read to quite the same accuracy, but it's near enough and easier to see. What's more, with just the press of a button, it will read in either inches or millimetres and it also has two sets of jaws, one for external measurement and one for internal. The vernier calliper is a very accurate device, and there are many variations designed for specific purposes.

A pair of strong pliers and at least one pair of long-nosed pliers, and a pair of adjustable, locking grips are necessary for those awkward bits and pieces where the hexagon has been worn off the head. Sometimes you have to turn to the most agricultural equipment to succeed. For example, if an old fork leg is stuck fast in the yokes, only a big set of Stillsons will shift it: crude, but highly effective.

Of course, you'll need some spanners, and, generally speaking, if you're tackling an old British bike, most of them will need to be imperial. Unfortunately, with everyday socket sets being metric, the imperial spanner comes with a bit of a premium. They don't have to be brand new, though, and the autojumble and the internet

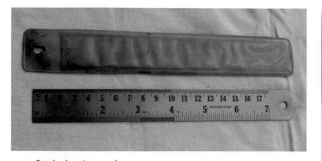

ABOVE: Steel rules give good accuracy.

RIGHT: If you need to change spectacles to read a micrometer, then an LED calliper is a big help.

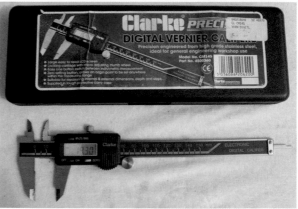

ABOVE LEFT: Most ordinary micrometers measure up to 1in – beyond that you have to buy individual larger micrometers – but this is a high-quality and expensive combination micrometer, which can measure up to 4in. The measuring anvils, to accommodate the appropriate length, are shown to the right and the central pieces are the exact length in inches to check the opening and reading when the anvil is selected and fitted.

ABOVE RIGHT: A micrometer that can read both imperial and metric. A little involved and not the most popular instrument.

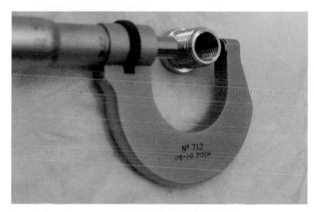
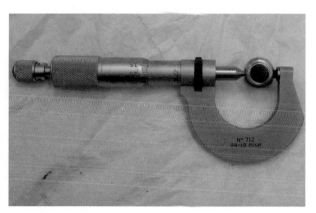

A specialist micrometer to measure the root of threads.

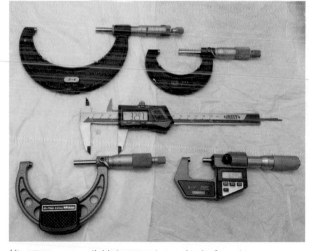
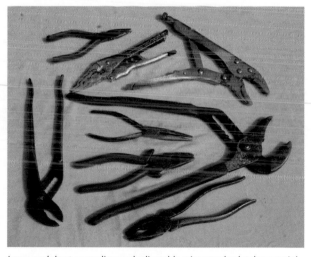

Micrometers are available in many sizes and styles for various applications.

Long- and short-nose pliers and adjustable grips are absolutely essential when needs must.

auction sites will turn up good-quality second-hand bargains, so go for open-ended and ring spanners, plus the obligatory socket set with long tommy bar and ratchet. It might seem rather expensive but bear in mind that most of those enviable collections of equipment you see in other peoples' workshops have been accumulated over many years, often handed down from father to son, and a good spanner will last a lifetime.

Keep a notebook of some kind on that shelf above the bench, along with a few pencils, a ballpoint or two and a marker pen. That way, you can make notes on what is what. For example, differentiate between the exhaust pushrod and the inlet pushrod by wrapping a piece of insulation tape around one and making a note in the

Classic spanners such as this often have a manufacturer's name embossed on them and are for a specific purpose, such as use on cylinder head nuts and spark plug.

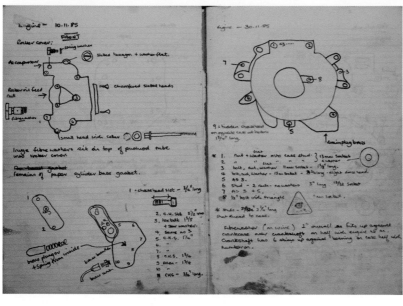

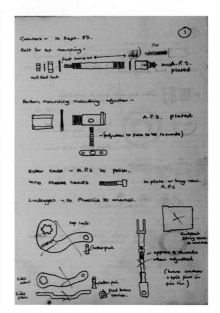

It might sound silly, but if you draw the shape of certain items and make notes on the lengths and sizes, then you will not be confused as to what goes where when parts return from the platers.

book of which it is. Also, if and when you send items off to the plating shop, it pays to trace nuts, bolts, washers and fittings into the book, dimension them and caption them accordingly; then, on their return all bright and shiny, you'll know exactly what goes where and what might have gone missing.

The head torch is a great invention, as it allows independent use of both hands, while maintaining a light source fixed on the job in hand. The little LED torches give off a very bright light and can be trained on those areas that are in the shade of the workshop lights.

There are countless other bits and pieces that you'll need, or that at least will be a big help, over the course of the restoration, many of which you can pick up here and there as and when you need them – items such as wire wool, sanding paper, flap wheels, timing disc, electrical wire stripper and crimping tool, multimeter, coarse and fine files, hand-held electric drill, buffing mops and polishes and so on.

A set of taps and die is always useful, as a means of forming, repairing or

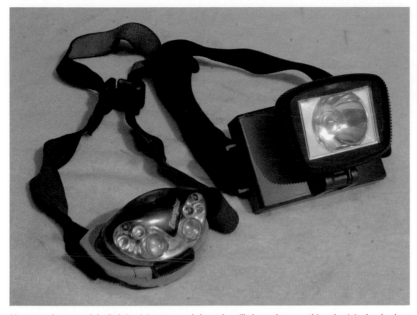

No matter how good the lighting is in your workshop, there'll always be something that's in the shade at some time. That's when the adjustable head torch comes into its own as it allows free use of both hands.

cleaning threaded holes and forming, repairing or cleaning the threads of a stud or bolt. The majority of high street tap and die sets will be metric, however, so not the best kit for an older machine whose nuts and bolts will be generally some form of imperial size.

One thing that might not immediately spring to mind is a digital camera. These days most people have an excellent camera built into their mobile phones, and this is perfectly adequate for recording just how things are before you start the dismantling process. It might seem obvious at the time, but six months down the road, you can bet your life you'll have forgotten what goes in what order and where. If you can refer back to a big colour picture on your pc screen, it makes life a whole lot easier come the reassembly.

Grind off rough welds or sharp edges with these little rotary burrs.

This image was taken at the dismantling stage of a restoration in order to provide a reference for where certain brackets and covers were placed and how. This is extremely useful when at the reassembly stage and it also makes for a good record of your efforts on completion.

Know your Thread

Excluding trained engineers, there exists within the realms of the home mechanic a general misconception that certain thread forms are the same. For example, a UNC stud will screw into a Whitworth hole and it will seem, on the face of it, perfectly adequate. However, the thread angle or profile is different, therefore working efficiency, yield strength and vibration resistance are compromised. It's a very involved little world, the world of threads, but it is worth at least a basic knowledge in order to assess what may be required with regard to damaged threads on your project.

There are several thread forms available, but only a few are regularly found on old motorcycles, which we'll examine a little closer in due course:

BSW – British Stand Whitworth
BSP – British Standard Pipe
BSF – British Standard Fine
BSB – British Standard Brass
BSC – British Standard Cycle
BA – British Association
CEI – Cycle Engineers' Institute
UNC – Unified National Coarse
UNF – Unified National Fine.

The last two are part of the standard American Unified Thread Standard.

It all began in the UK, when one Joseph Whitworth, a screw manufacturer, took a long look at all the various thread forms that were available on the market during the mid-1800s and proposed a basic standard to which all manufacturers should comply in order to simplify the system for both trade and customer alike. He recommended a thread angle of 55 degrees and a standard number of threads per inch depending on the diameter, which was eventually taken up as British Standard. BSW is a coarse thread, and while suitable for heavy industry applications, it does tend to loosen easily under vibration. The threads are cut deeply so have an increased thread engagement compared to a not-so-deep fine thread but are not as strong.

Just after the turn of the twentieth century, the Whitworth standard was modified to include a fine thread more suitable for use in the fledgling automotive industry – BSF. It used the same 55-degree thread angle but has better vibration resistance and torque strength.

Whitworth also proposed a hexagon head standard but it varied with the size of the bolt diameter and as such Whitworth

has a hexagon and spanner size that relates to the bolt's shank (thread) rather than across the hexagon flats. Further confusion is caused by the fact that BSF hex size can be one size smaller than its corresponding BSW equivalent. As such a $^7/_{16}$in BSF head is the same as a $^3/_8$in Whitworth – the spanner jaw being 0.71in wide for both heads across their flats. To reduce steel consumption during the Second World War, BSW and BSF were standardized to the latter's dimensions, which stayed in place thereafter. So post-war hexagon heads will be common to both BSF and BSW. Often spanners will be marked up, for example, as 1/4W-5/16BS – which means that the jaw is suitable for $^1/_4$in Whitworth or $^5/_{16}$in BSW/BSF.

BSP follows Whitworth in having a 55-degree thread angle and is used in situations where a metal to metal, male-female seal is required, as in plumbing fittings and in the case of motorcycles, petrol and oil pipe unions for example.

BSC, or as it's more commonly known, 'Cycle Thread', has a 60-degree thread angle, a fine thread and a shallow thread depth, which maximizes the core diameter and gives excellent strength. Regular sizes from $^1/_4$in to $^3/_4$in have 26 TPI, but other sizes often use just 20 TPI.

CEI also has a 60-degree thread angle but was largely superseded by BSC, which retained the profile but dropped all but the most common sizes. Typically, BSA continued to specify CEI into the 1960s, despite it being an obsolete thread from. It also used 26 TPI but some of the smaller fasteners, such as spoke threads, could use anything up to 62 TPI.

BSB was used on brass tube and has a constant 26 TPI irrespective of diameter. It has a 55-degree thread angle and is often confused with BSC. It's used mainly on classics for cable adjusters and other similar brass fittings.

BA is often confused with, but is not interchangeable with, metric. It has an odd thread angle of 47.5 degrees (metric 60 degrees) and is commonly used for instrument fasteners below $^1/_4$in.

True to form, the Americans went their own way. In 1865 William Sellers proposed a thread standard using a 60-degree thread angle but with differing TPI depending on the diameter. This was accepted and became American Standard (National) Coarse – NC – and (National) Fine – NF. Unlike Whitworth's typically British precision cutting of rounded crests (the prominent part of the thread, external or internal) and roots (the base of the thread groove), the American Standard used flat roots and crests, making them easier and cheaper to manufacture. These were still imperial and had pitch measured in TPI, but the spanner size was determined by the 'Across Flats' measurement of

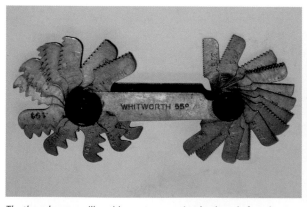

The thread gauge will enable you to recognize the thread of sundry bolts.

Every good workshop should have a box of assorted nuts and bolts.

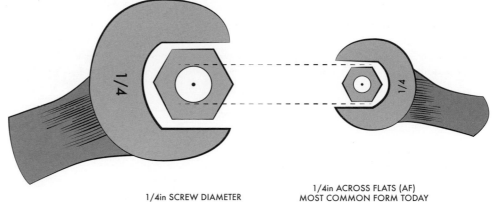

Often spanners will be marked up, for example, as 1/4W-5/16BS, which means that the jaw is suitable for ¹⁄₄in Whitworth or ⁵⁄₁₆in BSW/BSF.

1/4in SCREW DIAMETER

1/4in ACROSS FLATS (AF)
MOST COMMON FORM TODAY

CONFUSION CAN ARISE WITH 'CLASSIC' PRE-WAR SPANNERS OF THE
EARLY WHITWORTH ERA – (LEFT) – BOTH 1/4in BUT VERY DIFFERENT SIZES.

the hexagon bar from which the bolt was formed. Don't confuse the letters AF, meaning 'Across Flats' with AF used incorrectly to indicate 'American Fine' thread – there is no American Fine, it's National Fine and should be called NF or UNF. After the Second World War, it was generally recognized that all these threads and sizes, which allowed for a perfect size for every application, was getting ridiculously confusing, so Britain, Canada and the USA agreed to standardize. So it was that NF and NC became UNF (Unified National Fine) and UNC (coarse). Most vehicle and motorcycle manufacturers switched to these and they remain the most commonly used imperial thread form.

So that's the history and the mechanics, but in reality it is easy to get crossed up – pun intended. For example, take a ¹⁄₄in bolt with 26 TPI; it's probably British Cycle, but it could also be BSF or BSB – both also 26 TPI but with different thread profiles. Any nut from these forms will fit but if it's not exactly the right one then there will be an inherent lack of holding force, vibration resistance, fatigue and strength characteristics.

To correctly identify your bolt, firstly measure across the flats of the hexagon head, assuming they've not been chewed up by ham-fisted previous owners or been shaped up and/or polished – the latter will have involved removing metal thus the head will be fractionally smaller than originally. UNF and UNC are fractional, for example ¹⁄₄in, ⁵⁄₁₆in, ⁷⁄₁₆in, whereas BSF, BSW and BSC are not, for example 0.445in, 0.525in, 0.60in.

A thread gauge is necessary to ascertain the TPI and profile. As in the image, it's akin to a set of feeler gauges except these have teeth, which coincide with set thread forms. Further details on all threads can be found in the engineer's bible – the Zeus Precision Pocket Book, readily available at all tool stockists on via the internet.

Here's a table of details for quick reference:

Standard	Thread Angle	Thread Profile
BSW	55 degrees	Round crest/root
BSP	55 degree	Round crest/root
BSF	55 degrees	Round crest/root
BSB	55 degrees	Round crest/root
BSC	60 degrees	Round crest/root
BA	47.5 degrees	Round crest/root
CEI	60 degrees	Round crest/root
UNC/UNF	60 degrees	Flat crest/root

The Zeus book has all the information on threads you'll ever need to know.

Taps and Dies

Now you're familiar with the threads available, armed with your thread gauge you can now ascertain exactly what tap or die you need to make or make good a fitting on your classic project.

Most budget-priced tap and die sets found on the high street will be either metric or a combination of metric and NF, often followed by the letters AF in brackets. NF? Why the initials of this old terminology are still found on modern equipment is a mystery, when if nothing else it should be UNF. What's more, the inclusion of the letters AF is even more confusing as this applies to the nut size used on the bolt, which has just been threaded with the appropriate die and has nothing to do with the thread itself.

So, for example, in the set shown there are metric plus the NF imperial – the latter of which includes 1/8NF44, 5/32NF36, 1/4NF28, 5/16NF24 and 1/2NF20. These figures represent first the size – ¹⁄₈, ⁵⁄₃₂; then the thread form – NF (UNF); and finally the TPI – 44, 36.

It does not follow, however, that your project will necessarily have UNF nuts, bolts and studs and therefore you may find you need one or two regular-sized BSF taps and dies. Ebay is a great place to find good, used taps and dies, or you can root around on the tool stalls at your local autojumble.

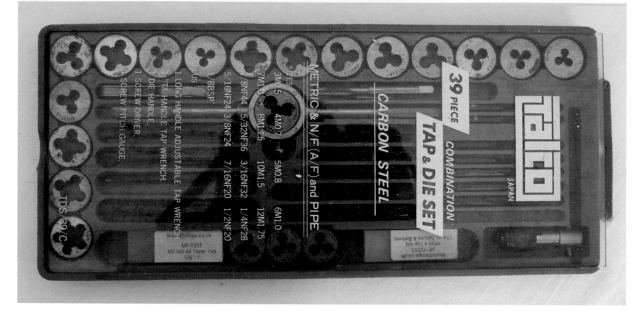

Taps and dies are more tools that will last a lifetime if looked after.

Taps

There are several types of tap available for various types of work and material but for the home restorer, it's unlikely that there will be any need go further than the common basic hand tap. These are straight flute tools, which are generally for manual operation but can also be for machine tapping under the correct situation. Hand taps can be purchased individually or in sets of three, which include a bottom, second and taper tap. The bottom tap has a chamfered lead-in of a couple of threads, the angle of the lead being around 18 degrees. These are used to produce threads as far down and as close to the bottom of a blind hole as possible, such as a crankcase mouth barrel stud, where the maximum strength is required in the hole to hold down the barrel.

Second taps have a lead of three to five threads at 8 degrees per side. These are the most common and popular and can be used for through holes, or blind holes where the thread does not need to reach right to the bottom. Taper taps have a lead of seven to ten threads at 5 degrees per side. This 'point', the taper lead, distributes the cutting force over a larger area, and the tapered shape helps guide the thread to start. As such, a taper tap can be used to start a thread prior to, or instead of, a second or bottom lead tap, or for through holes.

Take note: in the UK bottom taps are often referred to as 'plugs', while in the US it's the second taps that are called 'plugs'. This can add to an already confusing arena, so if and when you order a new tap from a distributor, it's wise to use the terms bottom, second and taper. Just to throw in a further aspect of potential confusion, second taps are sometimes called 'intermediates', and taper taps 'firsts'.

If you have an existing hole, the thread of which is damaged and let's say the stud from it is missing, then see if there are any more holes the same – again such as the crankcase mouth barrel mounting studs. If there are, and they're sound, use the lock-nut method (and the heat gun) to remove the stud and identify the size and thread by means of your thread gauge. You can then obtain the correct tap to screw into the damaged hole. If the damage

Taps have a distinctive shape and form plus they have their thread size and type marked on them.

is light, perhaps only in the mouth of the hole but preventing the replacement stud from screwing in, the tap will quickly fall into place within the undamaged remaining threads and clean them out as well as forming a new thread in the damaged mouth area.

If the internal threads are severely damaged or stripped, it may be necessary to drill the hole slightly oversize and cut a new thread with a slightly larger tap, but bear in mind that the bigger you go, the weaker the area around the stud. If there is insufficient metal to undertake this safely, then the hole must be tapped and helicoiled to standard size – see further details later.

In virgin metal the first thing is to ascertain the size of the hole to be drilled to accommodate your tap. Taking a ¼in BSF as an example, find yourself a set of screw-thread tables, from the internet, your distributor or from your local tame precision engineer and you will see that there will be lists of tapping and clearance drills. In this case the table states the drill bit should be 5.3mm or a No. 4 – the same thing. Now, this is where your pillar drill comes into its own. With the part to be drilled secure and central beneath the bit, drill it slowly and carefully to the required depth and then slightly countersink the mouth with a slightly larger bit. Next remove the drill bit and replace it with the first (taper) tap. If you have not moved either the part or the drill, then the tap should be centrally positioned over the drilled hole. Lower it to the hole and with copious amounts of cutting fluid around it, begin to turn the chuck manually to start the cut. The idea is to get a slack handful of well-cut threads into the hole, which will form a good guide for the remaining part of the operation and guarantee a straight entry. If you enter out of line at this stage the job is lost – you'll end up with a thread that is biased to one side of centre and you run the risk of breaking either the part or the tap.

Turn a little, then when resistance is felt, turn the tap back half a turn to break and clear the cutting swarf.

Once these initial threads are formed, the part can be removed from the drill and placed in the vice, and the tap fitted to its tommy bar-style wrench. Even the though the tap has a square head, do not be tempted to use a conventional spanner because it will apply off-centre leverage. However, if you don't have a proper wrench – though you should have if you're intending to use your taps properly – but you have a socket that fits securely, this can be used as a temporary measure with its T bar. Continue to turn the tap into the hole, lubricating regularly and reversing the tap accordingly. If it clogs, remove it fully and clean both the tap and the hole. Once the taper has gone as far as it can, repeat the operation with the second tap and lastly the plug tap, ensuring the base of hole is free from swarf and muck at all times. Finally, thoroughly clean out the hole, give it a good sharp blast of compressed air and, with the threads lubricated with light oil, proceed to screw in the stud.

Dies

Dies are a little more difficult to handle, as starting them squarely on the bar to be threaded needs concentration, a good eye and lots of care, not to mention fair effort. Insert the die into its holder, noting that the thread has a ground taper on one side to enable the bar to feed into the die and begin threading easily (note also that if the die is in the holder the right way round, that is with the taper outward, then the size of the die cannot be seen because it's on the opposite face, which faces into the holder – one of those strange, unexplainable things that has always been). Initially tighten the centre screw into the die slot until the die has spread to the holder's full diameter, then tighten the two adjacent screws to secure it firmly.

To ease alignment of the die onto the bar, a slight taper turned or filed onto the very top of the bar helps. Use plenty of lubricant and as with the tap, reverse regularly to free off the swarf. Another method is to use your lathe. Make the bar half an inch or so longer than the finished requirement and turn down said half inch a few thou' more than the core diameter of the thread, which you will have ascertained from your list of tables. This slightly smaller diameter will set you off in perfect alignment and you can progress then over the bar proper, cutting or parting off the smaller section when complete. If your lathe has a tailstock die holder, then you can hold the die squarely while you feed it the bar perfectly aligned into it – this will require turning the chuck manually.

Once the first cut has been made, try the appropriate nut for size, as with some materials the die can remove more metal per pass than others and it may be necessary to make several cuts, each time closing the die a little, by adjusting the screws in the holder. Other materials may need little more than a once-over with the fully open die, followed by a slightly tighter 'chase' cut to clean up the edges.

You'll soon realize if you've started the die on a slight angle as the finished screw thread will have an offset shoulder rather than being central. Like everything else, practice makes perfect.

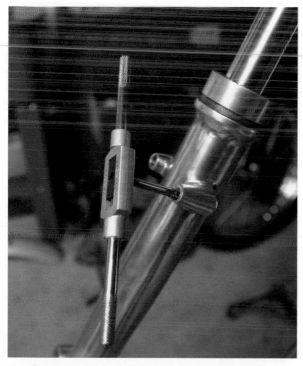

Extending the thread length internally on a fork leg lug with an appropriate tap.

Securing the die in the holder.

Know your Thread *continued*

Tapping drill sizes for metric coarse and fine threads

Thread size	Drill(mm)	Thread size	Drill(mm)	Thread size	Drill(mm)
M1 × 0.25	0.75	M9 × 0.75	8.3	M18 × 2	16
M1.2 × 0.25	0.95	M9 × 1	8	M18 × 2.5	15.5
M1.4 × 0.3	1.1	M9 × 1.25	7.8	M20 × 1	19
M1.6 × 0.35	1.25	M10 × 0.5	9.5	M20 × 1.5	18.5
M1.8 × 0.35	1.45	M10 × 0.75	9.3	M20 × 2	18
M2 × 0.4	1.6	M10 × 1	9	M20 × 2.5	17.5
M2.2 × 0.45	1.75	M10 × 1.25	8.8	M22 × 1	21
M2.5 × 0.45	2.05	M10 × 1.5	8.5	M22 × 1.5	20.5
M2.6 × 0.45	2.15	M11 × 1	10	M22 × 2	20
M3 × 0.35	2.65	M11 × 1.25	9.8	M22 × 2.5	19.5
M3 × 0.5	2.5	M11 × 1.5	9.5	M24 × 1	23
M3.5 × 0.35	3.15	M12 × 0.5	11.5	M24 × 1.5	22.5
M3.5 × 0.6	2.9	M12 × 0.75	11.3	M24 × 2	22
M4 × 0.5	3.5	M12 × 1	11	M24 × 3	21
M4 × 0.7	3.3	M12 × 1.25	10.3	M25 × 1.5	23.5
M4.5 × 0.5	4	M12 × 1.5	10.5	M25 × 2	23
M4.5 × 0.75	3.75	M12 × 1.75	10.3	M27 × 3	24
M5 × 0.5	4.5	M13 × 1	12	M30 × 3.5	26.5
M5 × 0.75	4.25	M14 × 1	13	M33 × 3.5	29.5
M5 × 0.8	4.2	M14 × 1.25	12.8	M36 × 4	32
M6 × 0.5	5.5	M14 × 1.5	12.5	M39 × 4	35
M6 × 0.75	5.25	M14 × 2	12	M42 × 4.5	37.5
M6 × 1	5	M15 × 1	14	M45 × 4.5	40.5
M7 × 0.5	6.5	M15 × 1.5	13.5	M48 × 5	43
M7 × 0.75	6.25	M16 × 1	15	M52 × 5	47
M7 × 1	6	M16 × 1.25	14.8	M56 × 5.5	50.5
M8 × 0.5	7.5	M16 × 1.5	14.5	M60 × 5.5	54.5
M8 × 0.75	7.25	M16 × 2	14	M64 × 6	58
M8 × 1	7	M18 × 1	17	M68 × 6	62
M8 × 1.25	6.8	M18 × 1.5	16.5	M72 × 6	66

To calculate tapping drill size for metric threads, subtract the pitch from the major diameter and select the next size up drill.

UNC and UNF threads

UNC	Drill (mm)	UNF	Drill (mm)
1/4.20	5.1		
5/16.18	6.6	1/4.28	5.5
3/8.16	8	5/16.24	6.9
7/16.14	9.4	3/8.24	8.5
1/2.13	10.8	7/16.20	9.9
9/16.12	12.2	1/2.20	11.5
5/8.11	13.6	9/16.18	12.9
3/4.10	16.5	5/8.18	14.5
7/8.9	19.5	3/4.16	17.5
1in. 8	22.2	7/8.14	20.5
1.1/8.7	25	1in. 12	23.2
1.1/4.7	28.2	1.1/8.12	26.5
1.3/8.6	30.8	1.1/4.12	29.5
1.1/2.6	34	1.3/8.12	32.8

BSW and BSF threads

BSW	Drill (mm)	BSF	Drill (mm)
1/8.40	2.54	3/16.32	3.97
3/16.24	3.7	1/4.26	5.37
1/4.20	5.08	5/16.22	6.8
5/16.18	6.5	3/8.20	8.3
3/8.16	7.9	7/16.18	9.7
7/16.14	9.3	1/2.16	11.1
1/2.12	10.6	9/16.16	12.7
9/16.12	12.2	5/8.14	14.1
5/8.11	13.6	11/16.14	15.6
3/4.10	16.5	3/4.12	16.9
13/16.10	18.1	13/16.12	18.5
7/8.9	19.4	7/8.11	19.9
15/16.9	21	1/10	22.9
1in.8	22.2	1.1/8.9	25.8
1.1/8.7	24.9	1.1/4.9	28.9
1.1/4.7	28.1	1.3/8.8	31.8
1.3/8.6	30.7	1.1/2.8	34.9
1.1/2.6	33.9	1.5/8.8	38.1
1.5/8.5	36.2	1.3/4.7	40.8
1.3/4.5	39.4	1.7/8.7	44

SAFETY

Basic workshop safety is really just common sense, and the lack of its application is the primary cause of most home workshop mishaps. The first thing to do when commencing any task is give yourself plenty of room to work and that goes for around your feet too. Clutter on the floor, electrical extension cables and so on, can easily be out of mind when concentrating on the job in hand on the bench and to step back without thinking could result in a fall and damage to both yourself and the work. The same applies on the bench – move away other items to give a reasonably clear working space.

It may be an obvious statement but do not use a liquid-fuelled portable heater, such as the traditional paraffin stove, simply for fear of knocking it over and spilling the fuel, which could catch fire. In an ideal situation, of course, such an appliance could be positioned permanently behind a fixed mesh guard, thus limiting the chance of spillage accidents. A bottled gas appliance is better, as it will not spill, though be aware it is still a naked flame and susceptible to vapours.

It's fair to say that eye protection is probably the most important aspect. You've only one pair of eyes, and while we do take them for granted, we are all well aware just how uncomfortable, nay, downright painful, an eye injury can be. You know whenever you peel a citrus fruit, it invariably squirts straight in your eye; it's the same in the workshop – if you're drilling, machining, sanding, grinding, cutting, in fact undertaking any task that results in flying sparks, shards or debris, the odds are that something will fly into your eye. So always wear a pair of safety glasses.

Likewise, if you're making a dust, wear a simple face mask to prevent inhalation, and if you're working with a noisy grinder, for example, over a long period of time, wear ear plugs too.

Thin but strong latex gloves are readily and cheaply available these days to protect the skin of your hands against potential adverse reactions to the chemicals within oils, greases and

Look after your eyes, ears and throat– they're the only ones you'll get.

Making a dust? Keep it out of your lungs with a simple disposable face mask.

other associated vehicle maintenance by-products. If you can't get on with working in gloves, no matter how thin they may be, then use a good-quality barrier cream before starting work, which will not only protect your skin but also make cleaning your hands much easier afterwards. There are many proprietary barrier creams along with emulsifying cleaners, which will also moisturize your skin after washing, not leaving them dry, itchy and prone to cracking. There's no shame in using your wife's hand cream afterwards either to aid the situation.

Pay attention to the tools you're using too; for example, if you're using an angle grinder, keep the guard in place if you can because the disc takes no prisoners and will, on contact with your finger, take it straight to the bone and the worse case scenario doesn't bear thinking about.

When you're grinding or cutting, bear in mind also which way the sparks are going to fly. Obviously you don't want them flying into your face, or even onto your clothes, but also ensure they're not heading toward that container where you keep the petrol for your lawnmower… Likewise, don't have them showering anything that's been painted, such as your car, because they will pock mark the finish and ruin

it. A carpet on the workshop floor helps maintain an element of comfort, but beware of those sparks if it's suffered from fuel or oil spills.

A fire extinguisher is hopefully something you'll never have to use in your workshop but should you ever need one, and you've got one to hand, it might mean the difference between a close thing and a catastrophe. In an ideal world, two extinguishers should be on hand, one containing water for general fires and the other a dry powder unit for electrical fires, though generally speaking, if the workshop wiring is up to standard then the latter is less likely as most electrical appliances, except for perhaps a battery charger, are switched off at night.

If you're working on a lathe or a grinder or indeed anything that turns, keep an eye on loose clothing, such as baggy sleeves or open shirts, for these machines can grab and take your hands into their works within a split second.

Ventilation is important too. With the advance of modern paints, it's now possible to spray in cold, damp weather because they contain a chemical hardener, whereas in the days of traditional cellulose it was necessary to have warm, dry air to effect the drying process. As such there may be a temptation to paint with the workshop doors closed to keep out the cold, in which case you would be well advised to invest in some form of filtered air flow mask, as breathing in the fumes is unadvisable. Another obvious point regarding ventilation – and we've all done it – is firing up the engine with the doors closed. Even in a short period of time the exhaust of carbon monoxide can be dangerous, so if you have to strike it up, either rig up some form of flexible pipe arrangement to get the gases out, or open the door. The latter is probably the best option, as without cooling air on the engine you'll soon find your exhaust pipe glowing red – so spare a thought for the exhaust valve in the cylinder head!

ABOVE: Barrier cream prevents skin damage from chemicals in oils and chemicals, plus it makes cleaning easier with degreaser and helps to prevent drying of the skin. Using moisturising cream for the hands is nothing to be ashamed of – your skin is as important as anything else.

LEFT: Watch the sparks from the angle grinder – and where's the guard?

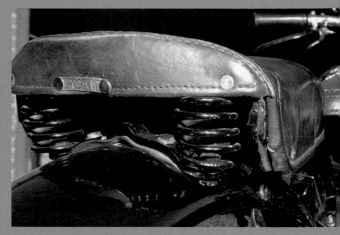

Single saddle fixings are pretty straightforward.

4

stripping down

CYCLE PARTS

Your workshop is all ready to accommodate the classic you've bought to restore, the tools are all laid out in their respective places, the bench is clean and clear and you're ready to rock and roll. Stop right there! With that initial surfeit of enthusiasm, it's all too easy to strip everything down in one fell swoop. Resist, because that enthusiasm will wane, inclination to head out to the workshop on a cold winter's night will disappear and frustration at an apparent lack of progress will seep in. Don't worry, though, most amateur restorers inevitably hit that 'mid-term' stasis, but after a short while away, the urge to crack on returns and your time in the workshop will be enjoyable once again.

So, formulate a plan and list the order in which you're going to do each job. Find yourself some boxes of varying

sizes; if you can find some tea chests even better, because big bits can go in one or even two and the containers of smaller component parts can go in the other, keeping all the parts you have in one place until you need them. Unbolt the fuel pipes and the petrol tank fixing bolts and remove the tank. With a single top-tubed frame, like Triumph, the fuel tanks sit on lugs projecting from that top tube, with thick rubber washers, often top hat-shaped, cushioning the tank base from the lugs. Without them, the metal to metal contact and the inherent vibration would, before too long, cause the tank to fracture. Norton was similar before the introduction of their famous twin tubed cradle Featherbed frame, where the tank sat on top of the two top tubes, again on rubber buffers, fixed by a central over-the-top strap. BSA had a similar arrangement to Triumph but also had a through bolt, on a rubber bush,

through the tank itself, which mated with a fixed nut on the frame tube.

Unscrew the fuel taps and drain out that smelly old fuel – disposing of it responsibly of course – then refit the taps and tip into the tank anything that will prevent corrosion attacking the inside while the tank is in storage. There are proprietary fluids designed and marketed especially for this purpose, but any light oil, diesel or paraffin will suffice for a good, long time, especially if, when you're passing by, you occasionally give the tank a slosh around. It can be cleaned out at a later date. This of course presumes that the tank will be in need of refinishing, and an extra scratch or two at this present time, while in the tea chest, will be of no consequence.

Remove the saddle next. With a single saddle, there will be a bolt through the front fixing to the frame and two individual springs, which fix the saddle to the frame. It may be a little awkward to get the spanner through the spring coils onto the fixing nuts, so a thin spanner helps. Also, if the nuts are rusted up, a good soaking in penetrating oil beforehand will do no harm. Undo the front bolt and lift up the saddle nose, then slip the bolt back through the saddle fixing and screw the nut back on – that way you'll know what it is and where it is. Likewise, unscrew the springs from the frame and leave them attached to the saddle for now.

A dual seat may well have the same sort of fitting up front, or maybe just a plain bracket with a slot in either

Keep what you're not working on at the moment out of the way in a big box.

ABOVE: The pillion saddle is sprung and fits on its own framework on the top of the back mudguard but it's not very forgiving.

RIGHT: Springs bolt up to the underside of the saddle.

side, which slides over a horizontal pin on the frame top tube. At the back, the seat base will have two internally threaded sockets, which coincide with appropriately positioned lugs on the frame, or a bracket bolted to the rear mudguard, through which extended hexagon-headed bolts are screwed to hold the seat in place. Put the seat and tank in the tea chest.

Now turn to the mudguards. The front has a pair of support stays front and back. Early machines had a one-piece U-shaped rear stay, with a horse-shoe lug on it, which was held in place by a fixed bolt on the lower portion of the guard. This doubled as a support stay and also as a stand to lift the wheel

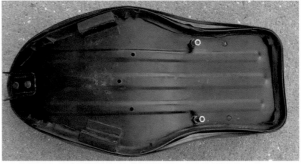

ABOVE: Rear-fitting bolts directly to frame lugs or mudguard brackets as the swinging arm frame does away with the need for a sprung saddle.

LEFT: The front of dual-seat fixing works on exactly the same principle as the sprung saddle.

BSA frame layout showing the dual-seat front fixing and bracket on the mudguard for rear fixing.

off the ground, to enable wheel removal in the case of a puncture. The fixing nuts would be loosened so that the stay fell downward, then tightened to keep it in place while the wheel was removed. For a rider stranded alone in the middle of nowhere, inevitably in the dark and rain, to undertake such a task must have been extremely difficult, if not practically impossible. Fortunately you will probably never have to tackle such an operation, due to comprehensive breakdown cover from the classic insurance experts – who will save you the damage you would do to the paintwork on your stay.

Later machines with improved ground clearance and improved centre stands had no need for this stay-cum-stand, simply holding the base of the mudguard in place with a couple of tubular stays. Likewise the front stays. Undo the nuts and bolts securing the stays and, for the time being at least, screw them back into the holes within the stays. Check, too, if the stays are the same at each end; if so, no problem, but if one end has a longer flat than the other, then write that down in your little book, for example, 'front mudguard rear stays, long flat to guard, short flat to forks' – that way you'll know how they fitted, because you will forget. Alternatively, use that digital camera and take a close-up of the stay, so you can refer to it further down the line. To be doubly sure, bolt the stays back to the guard in their rightful positions once it's off the bike and add it to the tank and seat box.

Some machines also have a Y-shaped fitting to hold the mudguard to the fork legs. The Y will have a curved middle to enable it to fit between the forks and the guard itself, so it can't really go back in the wrong place.

Turning to the rear mudguard, there is a little more involvement, namely the rear light.

If you're going to change the wiring loom – and if you're undertaking a restoration, it's obviously advisable – then for ease of removal, simply snip the wires under the rear mudguard. However, for potential assistance on the layout, unscrew the rear light lens, which will expose the two screws holding the lamp fitting to the number plate assembly. Unscrew them and the fitting will come away. The two wires to the lamp fitting will probably be integral, so trace the wires' path under the mudguard until you find a connection. Pull apart the connection, remove the lamp fitting by pulling the wires through the mudguard hole and then reassemble it all and add it to the storage box. The number plate fitting may have a separate number plate, which can be removed; if so, it may well be the embossed alloy type, which can be readily repainted at a later date.

It may, however, simply be painted numbers/letters or ones stuck directly

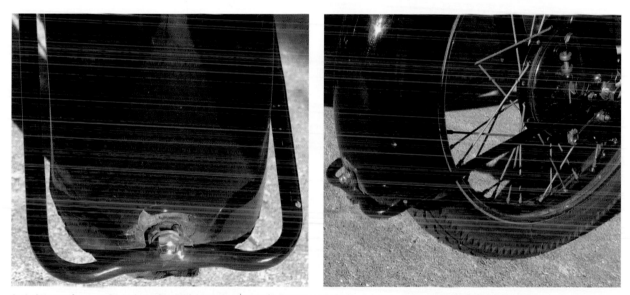

Period Norton front mudguard stay fixes with horseshoe lug central to the mudguard.

BSA front stay fitted to mudguard side valances with two lugs. This stay looks in poor condition but it is solid and will come up a treat after blasting, filling and painting.

Embossed alloy letters on a plate that bolts to the rear light console.

Front number plates are not a legal requirement today but serve as a decorative item if required.

onto the fitting, which then gives a later option of merely repainting or fitting an embossed alloy plate, which are readily available from the very same company who made them in the 1950s!

The number plate fitting can be unbolted from the guard and it might be a good idea to refit loosely the rear lamp fitting, thus keeping the assembly together.

The mudguard stays can simply be unbolted but there will be some form of bracket arrangement, which fastens the foot of the guard to some part of the mainframe. Take a photograph of this in place before you remove it; you'll be amazed how such a simple fixing can so easily be forgotten when it comes to reassembly. Remove it and refit to the guard before putting it all away in the box.

Now, remove the silencer and exhaust header pipe. The former will be simply a bracket to the frame and a bolt-up clip around the exhaust pipe,

Originally registration numbers would have been hand-painted, like here.

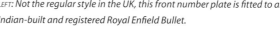

ABOVE: *Triumph, like their bikes in general during the Edward Turner era, gave their number plates a bit of style.*

LEFT: *Not the regular style in the UK, this front number plate is fitted to an Indian-built and registered Royal Enfield Bullet.*

Period-style number plates and rear lamps available today for Royal Enfield.

Jazzy-styled rear lamp on an early BSA A65.

or the hammer and drift. With the latter system, there is a big risk that if the flange is stuck fast, you will break off the fins, so give the threads as good a soaking with penetrating oil as you can. Alternately, use your blow lamp to heat up the flange and the port and use those grips. Work the flange back and forth, and once it's free, use the penetrating oil. Iron head machines used an iron flange, later models used alloy flanges, which are even more prone to breaking under the hammer. It's a difficult temptation to resist but you'll kick yourself if you succumb and break them.

With the exhaust system in the box, move to the front and remove the headlamp glass. With the most common Lucas headlamp, there will be a small screw on the very top of the headlamp body. This screws into a small L-shaped fitting, the tang of which hooks up beneath the lip of the chrome

though it will probably be a little bit stuck with carbon and burned-on oil and may need some penetrating oil and certainly some twisting back and forth before it slides off the pipe. The pipe itself may be merely a push fit into the exhaust port, in which case some gentle rocking should free it off. Norton, however, had a securing flange, which screwed into the port. These invariably are 'star'-shaped, with multiple fins, to allow the use of a suitable C spanner. Most of us do not possess such a tool and have to resort to either big grips

Use an appropriate C spanner on the exhaust rose if you can because a clout against one of the fins will eventually cause a breakage.

An unobtrusive little screw secures the clip that holds the headlamp rim in place.

plated headlamp rim to keep it tight against the shell. Once undone, prise off the rim. You'll note that elsewhere on the rim there is another tang, which connects into an appropriate slot in the rim to line everything up correctly. Disconnect the bulb holder from the rear of the lens. If there is a pilot light underslung beneath the main headlamp, then this lens is held in place by a simple spring clip. Release the clip and the whole assembly comes away.

Somewhere on the headlamp shell there will be one or more switches; they may be screwed into place, in which case the screws will be visible from the outside, or they may be held into place by spring clips on the underside. Either way they are simple to remove. If you are considering reusing the wiring loom, then take note of which colour wire is attached to which connection, make notes and take a photograph too if you can. Having said that, more often

than not you will find sundry bits of incorrectly coloured lengths of wire, odd, incorrect and regularly missing fittings, poor connections and joins wrapped up in various colours of insulation tape – in which case, rip it out and put it to one side for use when 'you just need a bit of wire'.

A good handbook or manual will have an appropriate wiring diagram in the back if you wish to make up a loom, and electrical specialists will have both

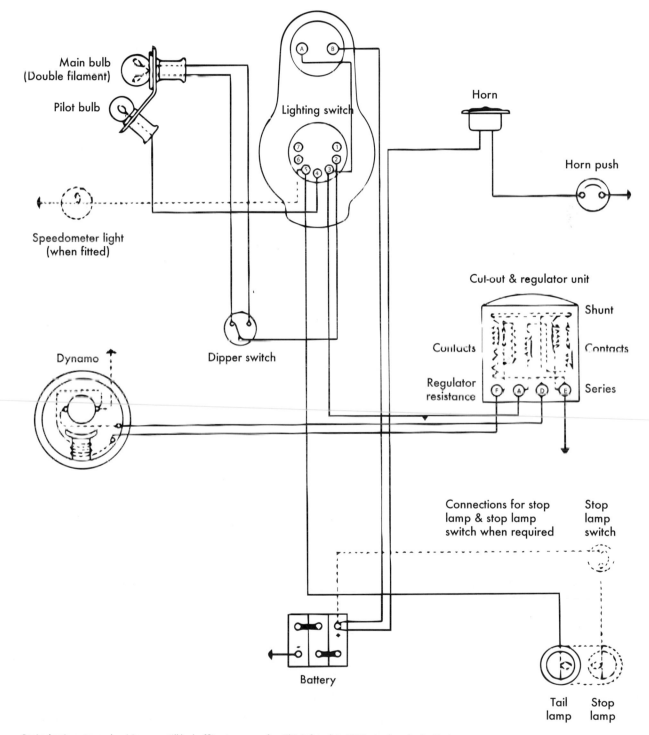

Basic classic motorcycle wiring can still be baffling to many of us. This is for a late 1940s single-cylinder Norton.

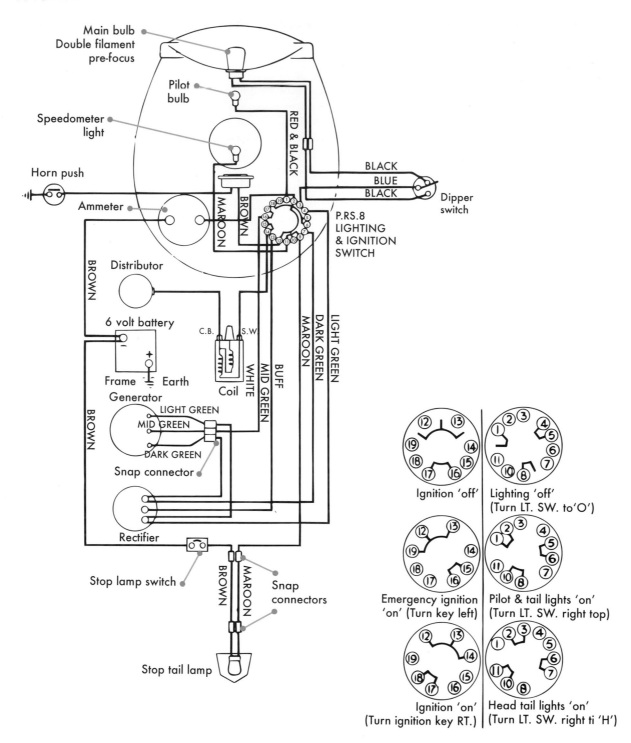

Triumph's twin diagram is a little more involved.

the requisite materials as well as ready-made looms and matching diagrams on their shelves.

The headlamp shell is removable by simply undoing a couple of bolts either side, which secure it to the brackets on the forks.

Certain marques have their own unique take on headlamp surrounds. Triumph have their 'nacelle'; likewise,

BSA Royal Enfield have what they term a 'casquette', and Velocette and Ariel all have their individual methods of removal and reassembly. The former two have part of the assembly within the fork arrangement, which means the forks have to be removed from the yokes to remove or refit the shrouds.

If you now take a look at the oil tank, you'll see that essentially like a domes-

tic heating system, there is a flow and return system. In general, British classic motorcycles are dry sump engines, that is they do not carry their oil in the sump but in a separate tank.

Royal Enfield have a slightly different system, in that while they too are dry sump engines, their oil is carried within a discrete compartment within the crankcases.

Triumph's nacelle is instantly recognizable.

BSA's take on the enclosed headlamp ran from 1958 through to the end of the pre-unit series in 1962 and into the early unit series.

Wet sump engines carry their oil within the sump, as in your car. The oil tank's main outlet fitting is usually at the front of the tank close to the bottom and has a basic gauze filter through which the oil flows, by gravity, down the pipe to a fitting, often marked F (flow), at the back of the crankcase. This connects directly to the oil pump within the cases. Having been pumped around the engine, the oil heads off back to the tank to cool a little but somewhere along the return line – if you have an ohv model, of course – there is a form of tee-off junction, which takes a flow of oil to the rocker shafts. (This doesn't apply to a side-valve engine.) This oil lubricates and cools the rocker assembly and then falls down the pushrod tubes, returning to the sump to be scavenged by the pump and returned to the tank via the pump and the R pipe – more on this later. The remaining returning oil, which has missed the tee-off exit, returns to the tank via a pipe, which connects into the top of the tank above the working level of the oil. There is also a breather pipe from the tank,

Despite having disappeared in the late 1960s on the heavyweight twins, Indian-built Bullets retained the casquette until quite recently.

Velocette only went so far with the enclosed headlamp fashion, essentially fitting a cover to mate with the upper edges of the headlamp-supporting ears of the fork shrouds.

Ariel always made very elegant castings.

Later Ariel went with fashion with their individually styled headlamp shroud.

Oil pipes flow to the pump, around the engine and then back to the tank.

A rigid-framed Norton oil tank.

which may or may not be routed along the back mudguard to vent behind the bike. There will be a drain-off plug somewhere at a low point or under the base of the oil tank, either a small hexagon or, in the case of BSA, a large chrome-plated hexagon nut low on the face.

Take care when draining the tank, as they all seem to have been de-signed to pour the oil over every-where on the bike, so have plenty of rags on hand to soak up the inevitable spills. It pays to spend a few minutes cobbling up some means of directing the flowing oil into a container – for example, a length of domestic waste pipe, maybe a couple of inches or so in diameter, with the ends cut into half to form a channel into which the oil can disperse. It's practical, cheap and always comes in handy for future oil changes, so keep it safe but not so safe you can't find it next time you need it!

With the pipes removed, unbolt the oil tank from the frame. It may well be on some form of rubber-mounted

An early swinging arm-framed Triumph oil tank.

Swinging arm-framed BSA Gold Star oil tank.

Sprung hub Triumph showing oil tank position.

bracket to prevent fracture through vibration, so take photographs, make notes and bolt everything back together once you've removed it, oil pipes *et al* – that way you'll not have to remember how they fitted together.

It might be worthwhile at this stage to wash out the oil tank a little because there will inevitably be a lot of sludge in the bottom and you can bet your life it'll seep out into your storage box. Don't be afraid to be a little crude here, a good stick or an old screwdriver poked into any available hole will be more than adequate to dislodge some of the thick stuff at the bottom. Give it a few swills with paraffin and then use your degreaser until the residue has disappeared and the tank is fairly clean. Once washed out, give it a good slosh of oil, diesel or paraffin to prevent it from rusting inside.

Opposite there'll be a toolbox; this can simply be unbolted, but as with the oil tank, take note of any bracketry, which may double up as mudguard supports and so on.

So now you've got the bare bones of the bike in front of you and you'll be able to see more clearly what condition

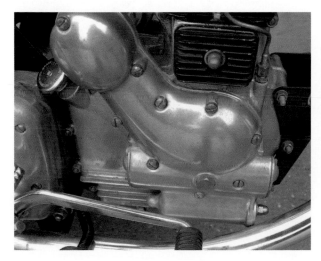

ABOVE: *Broken studs are best removed before any cosmetic work begins.*

LEFT: *Royal Enfield carry their oil in a compartment within the crankcases.*

it's in. At this stage, have a close look around the frame to see if you can see any obvious damage, such as missing or broken lugs, brackets, sheared-off bolts or studs, for these will need repairing while the frame is bare.

ENGINE ANCILLARIES

Magneto and Dynamo

If your machine has a single-cylinder engine and is fitted with a magneto, it will probably have a dynamo piggy-backing on it. The Lucas mag-dyno was a stock fitting to countless machines before the onset of the alternator. The magneto is the 'spark maker' and, in theory at least, the bigger the swing on the kick start, the bigger the spark the mag will produce. The magneto is connected to the engine via the timing gears, and the dynamo interlocks with it, so they all spin together, the magneto creating the sparks at the right time within the engine's cycle and the dynamo producing electricity to keep the battery charged.

The dynamo has two connections to it, the fittings held in place by a small fibre plate secured by a small screw. Undo this and pull out the connections. The dynamo is secured to the magneto by means of a wraparound strap, which bolts into the magneto body. The dynamo also has a long, thin stud, which projects through the face of the magneto and is held in place by nut. With this removed and the strap loosened, the dynamo will simply pull out of place.

The magneto is not so simple to remove as often it is bolted to a platform, with the bolts underneath screwing up into the body, with regard to

Lucas MagDyno fitted to a BSA Gold Star. Note the position of the pick up for the HT lead behind the unit.

Lucas MagDyno fitted to a rigid-framed Norton. Note the pick up at the front of the unit.

Short-bodied dynamo to Norton mag-dyno.

Long-bodied dynamo to BSA Gold Star mag-dyno.

dismantling, it is easier to remove it once the engine is on the bench. BSA, however, simply sit the magneto onto the platform with appropriate pegged feet in corresponding slots in the platform and secure it in place by means of a strap, which hoops over the dynamo and pulls everything down as one onto the platform. There will also be an advance and retard cable from the handlebars to the magneto, which manually adjusts the ignition timing. The magneto fitting has a nipple slot in it for the cable, so the cable can be removed without recourse to touching the mag at this stage.

If you've gone for a twin-cylinder machine, the magneto will have a triangular face that mates with a similar triangular face on the engine cases and bolts together with three studs and nuts. Once these are undone, the mag can be removed, and the rest is the same as on the single. However, the dynamo will be elsewhere, more than likely in its own little housing within the front engine plates. This will entail removing the timing cover to access the drive end of the dynamo; then it will pull out.

Later engines, from the mid 1950s, mostly gave up on the dynamo, swapping to the more efficient and more powerful alternator. This is fixed in the primary drive cover so does not need to be disturbed at this moment.

The carburettor is just a pair of nuts to undo against the inlet manifold on the cylinder head. Leave the throttle and air lever cables in place and simply remove both the twist grip and lever from the handlebars and add to your box as a complete unit.

The Big Bits

Simply to prevent double hernias and dislocated discs it's now time to remove a few bits from the engine itself, in order to make it lighter to lift out of the frame.

The top is the obvious place to start, so remove the rocker cover. Most machines have a rocker cover, which is a separate assembly to the cylinder head and it's invariably alloy, even if the head is cast iron. Norton, however, had an overly complicated one-piece casting for their twins. When they launched their first twin, the Model 7, this was all cast iron and a seriously weighty lump, but as the machine steadily developed into the Dominator range, the head and rocker box unit was cast in alloy. They missed a golden opportunity at that stage to simplify it by splitting it into two separate castings, but cost was always an issue and they obviously felt their system was good – which to a certain extent it was, indeed it still is, for if nothing else it obviates the need for gaskets, thus preventing potential leaks. What's more the head-cum-rocker box carried on right up to the demise of the Commando and is still available new today. Arguably, BSA's A50/65 range had the best idea, with a one-piece rocker cover, which was just that, a cover. Like a car engine, the cover can be removed to give unfettered access to the complete rocker assembly, which is actually on the cylinder head, rather than within the cover, thus making for easy adjustment.

Of course, if your chosen project is a side valve you can effectively ignore this part because there is no rocker gear for you to strip! Have a good look around the cover, or read up what your manual says about it first, because apart from the obvious bolts and studs, which screw down through the cover into the cylinder head, there is often a sneaky little screw or two hidden away beneath some tab or lug on the head, which screws upward into the cover, and unless you find it and remove it you'll be pulling out your hair over why the rocker cover won't budge.

When you think about a twin-cylinder engine, one of the valves should be under spring pressure most of the time so, in theory, once the fasteners are loosened the upward pressure of the spring on the valve should push up one corner of the rocker cover. On a single, of course, it's easier to have both valves closed and for sure the rocker cover will be stuck to the head with old gaskets, invariably gummed up with some form of sealing medium, so it may be necessary to bring out the rubber hammer to apply a little persuasion. Likewise, heat on the joint areas can help.

Once the cover is free, put the securing bolts back into their holes and secure them in their rightful places with a bit of insulation tape around each thread, or wire them all together, so

Norton single rocker cover.

Norton used their elaborate head-cum-rocker box casting for all their twin-cylinder models.

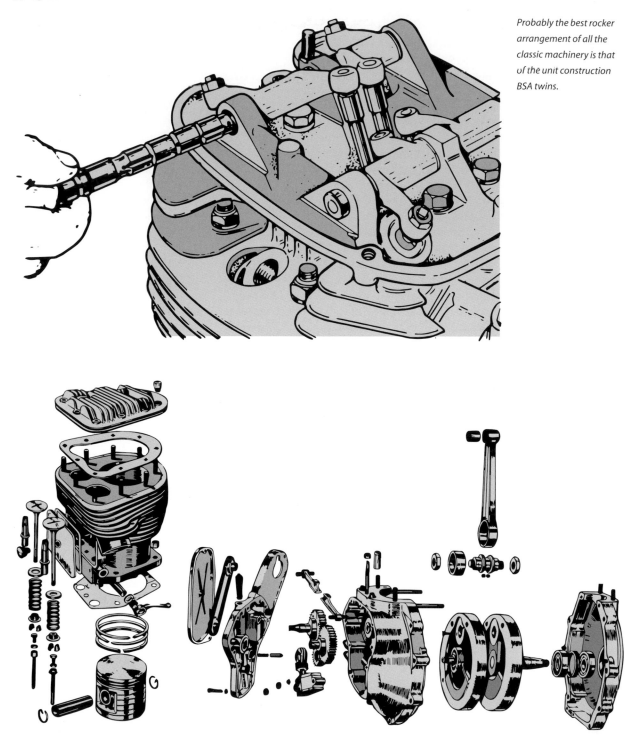

Probably the best rocker arrangement of all the classic machinery is that of the unit construction BSA twins.

Exploded diagram of the Norton side-valve engine.

that they don't fall out when you place the cover into the engine storage box. In the case of Triumph, the rocker cover is secured by means of studs in the cover, which poke through the head and are secured by nuts, so all you have to do is screw the nuts back onto the studs before you put it away.

With the cover off, you'll see the pushrods. Lift them out, give them a wipe with a rag and mark them so you'll know which one went where when it comes to reassembly. With a single, it's easy to wrap a bit of insulation tape around one and make a note in your book, for example, that it's the exhaust pushrod. With a twin's four pushrods, you can mark the timing side rods with a strip of tape, the exhaust of which can be identified with two strips. Provided you make a note, you'll get them back in the right place. To be fair, it's not that critical, but they'll have been running in their associated positions for years

and years and will have worn into each other's rockers and tappets accordingly, so it makes sense to reunite them eventually.

Now you can remove the cylinder head itself. Some machines have a straightforward means of fixing, such as Norton singles with four hexagon-headed, tubular sleeve nuts, which poke through the head onto four corresponding studs reaching up through the cylinder barrel from the crank-

A little bit of insulation tape and a note in your book can make refitting parts in their rightful place so much easier.

than pushing it down. The only problem with BSA's system is that spanner access to these nuts is very limited and can be problematic if the hexagon head has been rounded or damaged, for there is insufficient room to apply grips. In such cases, it may be necessary to use any way possible to free off the stud. One way is to drive onto the nut a spanner that is slightly too small and then attach a length of tube to it to increase the working fulcrum, thus increasing pressure on the stud. The stud will be steel, so bear in mind that if it's screwed into alloy, heat will be a big help and possibly avert potential breakages.

Like the rocker box, the cylinder head will probably be stuck. If it's iron, then a few clonks with the rubber hammer should free it, but beware the alloy head. Do not hammer against individual fins, simply because they may snap off – and do not under any circumstances be tempted to prise a screwdriver into the head-barrel joint.

BSA's screw up-pull down system works well enough but can be problematic with limited spanner access and tight studs.

If you have to hammer at all, then place a bit of soft wood against the side of the head and tap against the wood – that way at least the alloy fins will share the load of the applied shock. An old wrinkle is to feed some string into the plug hole, which sits on top of the piston and applies pressure to the underside of the head when the piston rises, thus lifting the head. As the string compresses slightly, it causes no damage to either the combustion chamber of the piston crown, though success is not always guaranteed.

case. Others, such as BSA singles for example, have a bizarre but perfectly satisfactory system where the sleeve nut has an external thread and slides upwards along the crankcase stud, through the barrel and into the underside of the cylinder head, in effect pulling the whole assembly down, rather

Be careful if you need to use the hammer; try to spread the load with a piece of wood across the fins otherwise this may occur.

Sometimes fins can be welded back into place if access for the welding equipment is available. Luckily this was the top fin.

With a solid copper gasket, it can be heated up to cherry red and then plunged into cold water to anneal it, and is then suitable for reuse.

Early post-war Triumph twins used an alloy chaincase with a removable steel plate to gain access to the primary chain and alternator.

Norton, however, persevered with the hopeless 'oil bath' pressed steel cover until the dawn of the Commando. This one is designed for the alternator engine.

The head can then be lifted clear. There should be a gasket or remains of one, though not always. Norton singles, for example, work on a spigot and socket principle so a gasket is not required, but flush-fitting twins will have either a copper gasket, which can be annealed and reused; or a composite – part metal, part asbestos or some such approved compressible material – which must be disposed of and replaced with a new one.

If you're so minded you can also now remove the cylinder barrel. A cast iron cylinder barrel is not light, and with regard to lifting the engine from the frame, every little helps. The barrel may be loose now and so can merely be lifted, or it may have a handful of securing nuts around its base, which obviously will have to be undone first. Lifting the barrel will probably bring the piston with it, so a second pair of hands is always useful to turn the engine and keep the piston at the bottom of its stroke. Bear in mind when the piston is free of the barrel, it will flop to one side, so minimizing its travel also minimizes potential damage.

In the case of a pre-unit engine, the primary drive must be dismantled in order to free the engine from the gearbox, whereas a unit engine, once the engine mounting bolts are removed, can be lifted straight from the frame.

Remove the rear brake pedal and its fitting to the rear wheel, as it will be in the way of the primary cover. Most manufacturers used a cast alloy primary cover, which is attached to an inner cover via a number of screws. These will be of varying length and often varying thickness too, so it will pay you to make a sketch in your book and annotate which screw is which length in which position. This is most useful, if for example, come reassembly, you decided to replace the old slot screws with their chewed up heads with new allen screws, because the allens may come at a set length so you may have to cut them down to appropriate lengths.

Norton, however, stuck with their pre-war design of a pressed steel cover, fixed by means of a single central nut around the footrest fitting and pressed against a thick rubber band. They called it the 'oil-bath', which it was, but the band was pretty ineffective as a seal and leaks were plentiful. Amazingly this archaic system prevailed right up into the 1970s, when the last of the Dominator range, the 650cc Mercury, was in production alongside the new Commando.

With the cover off, it's advisable to loosen the nut that holds the drive sprocket on the end of the crankshaft. With the clutch and primary chain still in place, it's possible to lock the engine against loosening pressure on the nut by putting the gearbox into gear and holding it by the rear wheel. The clutch centre nut can be undone in the same manner.

The primary chain will have a split link, so removal is simple – remember to reassemble the link within the chain before storing. The clutch will have a series of springs – three, four or six – all of which are adjusted by a nut and a locking nut. With the nuts undone, the springs can be released along with the cups in which they sit. Then the outer plate can be removed. This is the pressure plate, the one that is pushed out by the clutch pushrod when the lever is activated, thus allowing the plates to separate and disengage engine drive.

With the pressure plate removed, the pushrod can be withdrawn from the hollow mainshaft and then the inner plates, alternately a plain steel and a 'cork' plate. The latter has several cutouts within it that are filled with segments of fibrous material, which give grip. These were originally cork, then asbestos and now some form of approved, environmentally friendly medium. Undo the clutch centre nut and remove the chain wheel – that's the whole body in which the plates are housed and around which the primary chain runs. There will be a bearing in the centre of the basket. Loosely reassemble the clutch assembly and wire it all together in its correct sequence before storage.

With the drive sprocket removed, the inner case can now be removed. This may be bolted directly to the crankcase. There may also be an oil seal arrangement in the inner plate where the gearbox mainshaft passes through it.

Any engine mounting plates between the engine and the gearbox

Norton's oil bath on a pre-alternator engine.

Ariel, if nothing else, made their castings very shapely. Look at the curves in the primary cover.

The Matchless-Norton hybrid P11 range used neat Matchless primary covers grafted onto Norton Atlas crankcases and it looks great.

The basics of the clutch, from left: clutch body and pressure plate, clutch basket with integral sprocket, adjustment screws, clutch centre with bearings, cups and springs, plates plain and inserts.

will now be plain to see, so it's just a case of undoing the nuts and drifting out the studs and lifting the engine from the frame. Then, with the clutch cable already having been removed from its fitting on the gearbox, and the secondary drive chain removed via its split link, it's a repeat performance to remove the gearbox as a whole along with its associated mounting plates. Now you have a rolling chassis, which is comparatively light, movable and much easier to lift.

WHEELS

Removal of the rear wheel is simple enough. On one side there will be a nut, which screws on to the main axle, with an integral hexagon head on the other side. If the bike has a swinging arm with open ends, simply pull out the wheel; if it has closed loop ends, then remove the axle completely and slide out the wheel. Don't forget to undo the brake torque arm and the operating rod or cable. Reassemble and put to one side.

The front wheel is pretty much the same, though its fixing to the forks may be by the axle sliding through, akin to the rear, or by bolt-up clamps at the bottom of the fork sliders.

The forks can be removed as individual legs or as a whole with the yokes. At this stage it would be as well to remove them as one. Dismantle

the central steering damper arrangement, if one is fitted. This runs through the frame headstock to an adjustable friction damper arrangement under the bottom yoke, which is fixed to the frame by a lug and a screw. Again, take note of which order the various friction washers go and wire them all back together in the same order before you store them up. Then remove the handlebars from their clamps, and any clocks that may be fixed to the top yoke, and then undo the two large hexagon-headed fork top nuts. This will free the forks from the top yoke but they will still be held firmly in place within the bottom yoke by pinch bolts. Undo the central nut arrangement and then the top yoke will come off with a tap from the rubber hammer.

A second pair of hands is useful here because when the top yoke comes free, so will the bottom yoke come free from the headstock along with the forks. This will disturb the cup and cone bearing arrangement and greasy ball bearings will drop onto the floor. Count up the number of balls top and bottom and make a note in your book – the manuals have been known to make mistakes. Give the balls a wash in the degreaser and put them in a matchbox. New ball bearings are readily available and cheap but having a few spare, even if they are old ones, is always handy in case one makes a successful bid for freedom while you are reassembling.

Slip the cones over the bottom yoke stem and refit the top yoke loosely, then store up.

REASSEMBLY

So that's it, you're down to a bare frame and the only way is up. Now comes a dilemma, for no matter how easily things came apart, there will be odd parts, which for some unknown reason, do not go back together anything like as easily, and the odd easing and alteration has to be made. For example, engine mounting-plate holes do not quite line up with the engine and the frame; certain fittings, such as the aforementioned magneto mounting platform are found to be impossible to tighten up with the engine in place; chainguard mounting holes don't line up with the frame or the bolt is inaccessible to tighten up; these and countless more are all little things that are not noticed on dismantling and only come to light during reassembly.

It's for this very reason that professional restorers now undertake a 'dry build'. That is where all parts are prepared but not finished and the bike is completely reassembled, adjusted and run up before being stripped again for final refinishing and reassembly as the finished article. It's fair to say that when a customer is being charged by the hour, a restorer will have every

A/B series BSA forks from 1958, showing headlamp enclosure and the headstock bearing arrangement.

justification in doing this, but when it's your own machine you have to weigh up whether or not you deem such an exercise worthwhile in terms of time, inclination and required standard of finish. In the ridiculously cut-throat world of the serious concours d'elegance, a slight scratch or evidence of a touch-up will mean the difference between a trophy, a rosette or a complete thumbs down. What's more, the use of more efficient Allen screws as opposed to the correct cheese-head screws will render your bike ineligible, as will having the cheese-heads chrome-plated when they were originally cadmium-plated. It's all getting quite preposterous, and while some restorers still chase the trophies, many people have turned their backs on the show scene, preferring just to have a smart bike that runs well and that they can enjoy without fear of the odd road stone chip causing concours heartache.

Ariel, always fairly innovative, used the Anstey link system rather than the regular plunger system.

5   *the chassis*

THE FRAME

With the dismantling of the big bits all complete, it's now time to mantle, or to use a real word, reassemble – or at least start preparing parts to do so. So what to do about the frame? Well, if it's rigid then it's just about refinishing, if it's a plunger frame or swinging arm, then there's a bit more dismantling to do before the refinishing process begins.

Plunger Systems

The basis of the plunger system could be seen on early aircraft, decades before the motorcycle factories took up the idea. The plunger frame was adapted by several companies during the period from the late 1940s to the early to mid-1950s; it was essentially a stop-gap, and more importantly, a cheap exercise, utilizing adapted rigid frames with a C-shaped carrier casting at the rear axle position.

The rear wheel axle is connected to a pair of tubular sliders, which move up and down on guide rods secured at their extreme top and bottom to the frame casting. The movement of the sliders, or plungers as they are commonly known, is controlled by a pair of short coil springs – one compression spring above the axle lug and a smaller, lower rate rebound spring below, allowing the axle and thus the wheel itself a limited bounce up and down according to road conditions. The plunger, rod and spring assembly is all enclosed within a tubular, telescopic shroud, which makes for a separate spring box above and below the axle point. There is no damping other than what friction is generated between the moving parts.

By virtue of its very design and assuming that the springs either side of the wheel are equal to each other, the axle moves directly up and down, which in turn puts a large variation of

tension on the drive chain when the axle is at either extreme end of its travel. On the swinging arm arrangement, which superseded the plunger system, the rear axle prescribes an arc, or at least it should do, which is why manufacturers try to make the gearbox output shaft and the rear axle in the same line, in order to maintain something like consistent chain tension.

In an effort to alleviate the problem, BSA angled their plungers forwards on some models, and Norton even more so, though it is difficult to notice. Whilst this was marketed as a breakthrough in comfort, wheel travel was barely two inches and it increased the cost of the basic motorcycle at the time by anything up to £20 – a lot of money on a £185 machine.

BSA's design was basic and can be found on anything from the humble Bantam to the mighty Golden Flash 650cc sidecar hauler. Provided you keep it well greased on a regular basis,

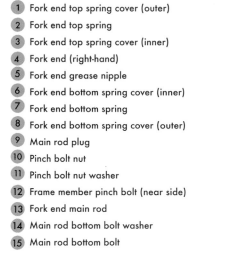

1. Fork end top spring cover (outer)
2. Fork end top spring
3. Fork end top spring cover (inner)
4. Fork end (right-hand)
5. Fork end grease nipple
6. Fork end bottom spring cover (inner)
7. Fork end bottom spring
8. Fork end bottom spring cover (outer)
9. Main rod plug
10. Pinch bolt nut
11. Pinch bolt nut washer
12. Frame member pinch bolt (near side)
13. Fork end main rod
14. Main rod bottom bolt washer
15. Main rod bottom bolt

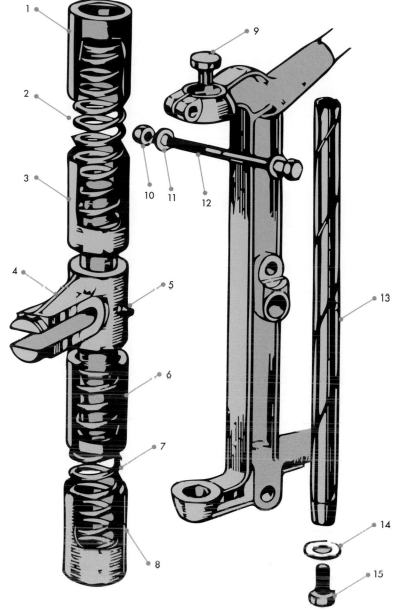

Norton plunger system.

certainly on the lighter models up to and including the 250cc side valve C10 and Ariel's 250cc ohv Colt, the system works adequately well. However, neglect it on a heavyweight at your own risk. You'll be able to tell if the bushes and rods are worn as not only would the bike handle poorly were it on the road, but also you'll be able to feel the play by waggling the wheel at the rim.

If your machine has been standing for a long time, particularly if it has been stored up in less than ideal conditions, then there's a good chance that damp or worse, water, has found its way into the spring boxes, and the guide rods will have seized into their

steel bushes at each end. The rods are just over 12½in long and the bushes just under 1½in long and pressed into the sliders. What's more you can bet the two outer shrouds will have worn away, the top one at its lower edge and the bottom one at its top edge, where they have rubbed against each other.

The guide rods are held in place top and bottom by split clamps secured by pinch bolts. Remove the pinch bolts, and, with the top nut undone at the top of the frame lug – the rod is threaded internally here and has a chamfer in it at the lower end to mate with the pinch bolt – the rod can be driven out from below. Now comes the tricky bit. Lever out the spring boxes carefully with a

long screwdriver until a long length of threaded studding can be inserted through the coil springs and then slip a couple of large washers over the ends of the spring, followed by appropriate nuts, and compress the spring. An alternative method is to get a helper to put their weight on the back end while you lever, then letting everything fly off in all directions when said helper removes their weight. It works for sure, but you can end up with a mouth full of spring and bits, not to mention possibly teeth all over the workshop!

Most BSA specialists can supply all you need to replace and repair the plunger system, including polished stainless steel shrouds, which will improve the look and resist the weather better than paint or chromium plate.

Norton dallied with the plunger system for a much shorter time. It reached the road models ES2 and International from 1947 and initially the Model 7 twin too, but in 1953 they made the sensible move and adapted the rigid frame to take a swinging arm conversion. The ohv Model 18, most side valves and the trials models all stayed with the rigid frame. The Norton system, while similar in principle to that of BSA, utilized, dare we say, a little more class in its parts. The axle lugs were alloy and the guide rods tapered at the bottom but it differs in that the only pinch bolt to slacken is on the top frame lug. The rods are threaded internally at the bottom and slotted at the top, so once the bottom securing screw is removed from the rod, it can be drifted out of its tapered housing.

There is a further system used by Ariel, which stayed with the heavyweight Square Four right to the end. A design by one Frank Anstey, not only does it have a flat rebound spring but also the stirrup link, which wraps around the spring box holds a dual role. One arm of the link carries the axle, while the other side is connected to the slider boss, through which grease is injected to the guide rod and bushes. The closed end of the stirrup is fastened to the bottom frame rail via short links.

The Achilles heel of this system is the fact that there are no fewer than six plain metal bushes on each side of the links, and they can wear very quickly. The only answer is to use the many grease nipples on the system on a regular basis. Because the Square Four never received a swinging arm frame, spares for the Anstey system are plentiful.

Ariel, always fairly innovative, used the Anstey link system rather than the regular plunger system.

THE SPRUNG HUB

Triumph went their own way with a similar system, actually fitting the plunger springs within a huge rear hub and slotting it into the rigid frame.

The sprung hub is no better than the plunger arrangement and is even more complicated and fiddly to work on. Indeed, the inner castings of the sprung hub carry a warning not to dismantle the mechanism without the proper tools. Though tried and tested pre-war, the sprung hub first appeared as an optional extra on the company's roadsters in 1947. The reasoning behind it was fairly obvious: to minimize unsprung weight and to give an element of suspension at minimum extra weight within the existing rigid frame. Designer Edward Turner achieved all three aims, with only an extra 12lb added to the overall weight of the bikes to which it was fitted. The downside, of course, was essentially the design itself, as it was, indeed still is, very tricky to assemble; furthermore, wheel support is – to say the least – a little dodgy, even before the parts begin to wear.

It's a large-diameter hub with detachable side plates, in each of which sits a hefty bearing. Integral with the hub is the brake drum and the drive sprocket. The hub and the bearings run on a central assembly, comprising two castings in which are held the springs and their guides. The actual wheel spindle

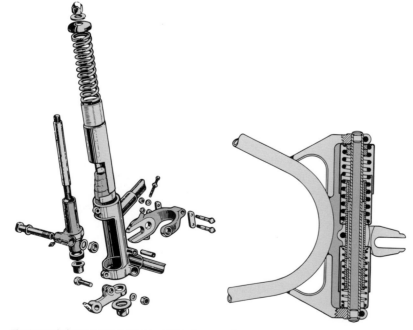

The Anstey link was a clever way around the plunger system.

American advert for the sprung hub Thunderbird.

Triumph's sprung hub, while an ingenious means of getting suspension into the existing rigid frame, is a complicated beast.

passes through a rectangular block and is located by a short arm keyed to one end with the opposite end mating up to a slot in the frame. The block is slightly curved to match the spring box castings and is positioned vertically. It's bored to accommodate the two lower compression springs, one inside the other, and a single upper rebound spring, which are tightly compressed. On either side of the wheel spindle is a slipper roller, which runs in either a convex or concave guide

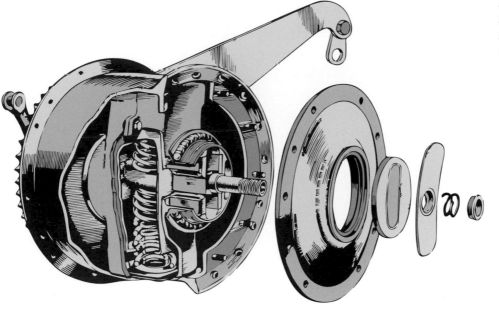

LEFT AND BELOW: The sprung hub only gave minimal springing and can be tricky to work on.

VIEW OF SPRING WHEEL SHOWING HUB MECHANISM

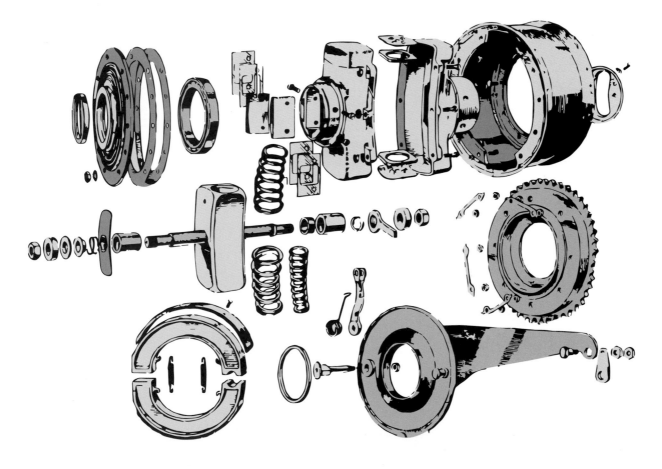

bolted to the spring box casting, which in turn are inside the bearing. These are curved to maintain the wheel's movement in an arc motion pivoting from the gearbox sprocket. Seals are fitted to keep out water and road muck.

In theory it was, relatively speaking, a good idea but in practice it can leave a lot to be desired. For example,

all possible adjustment, that is, shims to maintain a good fit of the rollers in their guides, is for fore and aft movement; the side-to-side movement is dependent on the fit of the spindle block in its housing, and any side-to-side slop, no matter how small, is magnified at the tyre, resulting in dodgy cornering. Wear and tear can also be uneven, so what

limited adjustment there is, when taken up on the loose side, will render the unworn side overly tight.

Triumph were acutely aware of the sprung hub's shortcomings and that many riders actually preferred the rigid frame as it was, so by 1954 their range was appearing with a twin shock sprung swinging arm frame.

By 1954, the sprung hub Thunderbird was being superseded by …

… the first of the swinging arm-framed versions.

Of course, the sprung hub has its place in history and many restorers will go to great lengths, and, potentially, equally great pains, to restore, fit and run a sprung hub in their Triumph. For the novice, however, the sprung hub is best avoided, though one advantage over the rival plunger frames is that the actual frame remains rigid, so it can be refinished, leaving the sprung hub rear wheel to be a separate entity for later perusal.

Both systems are, arguably, an improvement on relying simply on the saddle springs of the rigid frame, but when worn, the handling of the machine suffers and many classic enthusiasts prefer the rigid option.

Swinging Arm Systems

The swinging arm was a much better idea, though that too can cause serious handling problems if either the swinging arm bushes are worn or the shock absorbers are worn out.

Like the plunger frame before it, the swinging arm frame works on pretty much the same principle no matter which manufacturer made it. Essentially there is a horizontal tube across the lower part of the rear of the frame, invariably a steel lug of some form, as near as in line with the gearbox sprocket as possible, around which fits an H-shaped tubular steel subsection held together by a hollow axle running in bronze bushes. At the opposite end of this assembly there is the facility to connect the rear wheel axle, and this is supported on oil-damped shock absorbers to the rear of the frame proper.

There are really only two things to go wrong: the shock absorbers wearing out, and the hollow pivot pin seizing in the frame pivot. The former is usually down to age and wear and tear, the latter due to negligence. Somewhere along the length of the swinging arm there will be at least one grease nipple, often more than one, but if grease has not been regularly applied, the swinging action can cause the internals to seize together and the bushes can turn in their housing.

To remove the swinging arm, first remove the outer caps. In the case of early Triumphs, the open end of the swinging arm is closed off by a chrome-plated cap, through which runs a long, thin nut and bolt to secure the caps at either end. With these removed, it's a case of finding some form of drift that matches the diameter of the hollow pivot pin, and carefully knocking it through the swinging arm. Take care not to rough up the edges of the pin while doing this, so refitting doesn't cause any tight spots. This is why it is important to use a fairly blunt drift of the same diameter. This operation may be quite simple, or you may have to resort to the blow-lamp and copious amounts of penetrating oil and brute force. At worst, you may have to consider taking it to an engineering firm with a suitable press tool, though such instances are very rare. Removing the bushes can be done with the same method, drifting out the bushes from the opposite side. It's unlikely that the swinging arm pivot on either the frame or the swinging arm itself will be too badly worn, that is oval, but if so then it will be a case of having the pivot holes machined round again and fitting oversize bushes.

The bushes are usually made of a material such as phosphor bronze, or steel-backed phosphor bronze. Phosphor bronzes, or tin bronzes, are alloys containing copper, tin and phosphorus.

The addition of tin increases the corrosion resistance and strength of the alloy. The phosphorus increases the wear resistance and stiffness of the alloy.

Norton used a different type of bearing, called a Silent-Bloc bush, essentially a rubber tube sandwiched between an outer and inner steel tube. This arrangement was common to both the original single down tube swinging arm frame and the later Featherbed double-loop cradle frame, the swinging arm sitting either side of a lug on the former and between two lugs on the latter. BSA have a similar system on their duplex frames, but whereas the Norton has two Silent-Bloc bushes, separated by a central distance piece and all held together by a long through stud with a nut on either end, BSA use a pin with a tab on the head, which is then bolted to the frame, the other end being threaded to take a nut. Don't be too concerned, however, if your Norton does not have the centre spacer, as the 1957–58 Model 50, ES2 and 19S did not have them fitted. Why not? Who knows; perhaps Norton felt the singles did not have enough power to distress the swinging arm pivot during cornering, as the twins did. The question then arises, of course, were the spacers necessary at all?

Removing the Silent-Bloc bushes can be quite tiresome, to put it mildly, again especially if they've been neglected and have rusted into the pivot. Big heat and a big hammer is the only way to shift them. Fitting replacements can also be quite a job, as they have to be a tight fit and can be very difficult to push into place. Obviously, cleaning up the pivot, removing all corrosion and potential tight spots is imperative and then lubricating both the pivot face and the bush outer face before attempting to fit them together. All the manuals and handbooks will simply say something like 'press in the replacement bush until the outer sleeve is flush with the end of the tube' – oh, if it were only that simple! It can be a pretty tough job without specialist tooling but the regular method for the home restorer is to find a suitably strong length of reasonable-diameter studding and a series of strong washers, which will bear on the edge of the outer part of the bush. Holding one nut firm and using a long-handled spanner on the other, tighten the nut against the washers, which will then slowly push the bush into the tube. Heating the tube and chilling the bush will also help but this operation invariably follows refinishing of the frame and swinging arm and may cause damage to said finish, so it's a case of simply taking as much care as you can. Having said that, of course if your finishing method does not involve heat – for example, stove enamelling or powder coating – then a brushed or sprayed finish can be applied post bush work.

Norton's model 77 was a makeshift one, using up the old single downtube swinging arm frame and the 600cc Dominator engine. It did not sell well as the Featherbed was on the scene. Ironically it is now very sought after because it's so rare.

Basically the same machine albeit in a slightly higher state of tune, the Norton Nomad was an export model desert scrambler intended primarily for the American market. This model is now extremely rare on these shores and hence very expensive.

The wheel axle end of the swinging arm will be designed to suit the type of hub fitted: it could be an open end, as on Triumphs and Featherbed Nortons, or, as in the case of BSA, a slot within a closed loop. Though they look the same, the axle size of the full-width alloy Ariel hub, which BSA used in 1956 and 1957 (*see images in Chapter 2*), is not the same as the 1958-onwards iron hub, and they are not interchangeable as the slots in the swinging arms are correspondingly different.

Before you go for refinishing, have a look at your swinging arm and see if everything is there that should be there; for example, if your model could have been fitted with a fully enclosed chaincase, and you want to keep it that way, are the brackets present and if so are they undamaged and are the threads in the holes into which the chainguard securing screws fit in good condition? Will any welding be required, or threads to be drilled out and retapped?

THE STAND

Another thing to watch out for is the stand. Most classics were fitted with both a centre stand and a side stand, though many immediate post-war classics had a centre stand and the old-fashioned rear stand, which hoisted up the back wheel. The side stand should have a half-round lug welded onto one of the lower frame tubes, on which there are two protruding ears,

into which are tapped two threaded holes. This mates up with a matching half-round lug integral with the side stand's folding hinge assembly, which has two corresponding ears with blank holes. A couple of sturdy screws, or bolts, pass through the blank holes and screw into the threaded portion, securing the stand to the frame. There is a small 'tang' on the stand leg, around which the loop of a long spring hoops, and another one on the stand lug itself, so the spring holds the side stand tucked up against the frame tube. If you're lucky enough to obtain a bike with a side stand already in place, you'll often find that not only are the tangs missing from the stand and the

frame lug, but also one or both of the frame lug's ears have been somehow broken off. Count yourself lucky if you have a stand at all, because many people removed them as they could cause problems with ground clearance on corners.

If the ears are missing, but you have a stand, then there's little that can be done other than to have new ears made up and threaded and then welded into place. If you've no stand at all, then pattern items are available.

Leaning against, sitting on or starting the bike when it's on the side stand all add to stress on the stand, the lug, the bolts and the spring, so avoid the practice.

Lovely late Matchless twin utilizing its centre stand.

Typical side stand.

Norton centre stand.

Norton back stand.

The centre stand can suffer from a weak spring, in which case the stand will rock up and down when travelling, grounding on corners and maybe even clanging upward against the frame. Another problem may be that the mounting holes, where it mates with the frame lugs, may have worn slightly oval, giving the stand a sloppy feel and rendering it less stable than it could be when in use. Likewise, the tang, which projects outward of the frame to enable the rider to hook his foot beneath it, may have broken off, which can cause no end of problems when trying to park up.

A new spring can be readily sourced, but they are very strong and appear too short when trying to fit them over the appropriate tangs on the frame and stand leg. This is because they have to be at their tightest when the stand is up, so there needs to be an element of permanent pull on the fittings by the spring.

There is no hard and fast rule to fitting a centre stand spring. One suggestion is to force coins in between the spring coils to lengthen the spring but this is far from ideal as the coils are tightly bound and the more coins you squeeze in, the more out of shape the spring becomes and the more difficult it is to squeeze in any further coins. This is not really recommended unless you've only a millimetre or two to gain.

Another method is to fit the spring to the stand before fitting the stand to the frame. Again, it'll probably be a job for two pairs of hands as the strength of the spring will make lining up the stand and frame lugs difficult to fit the pivot pin. Hooking a strong screwdriver through one of the hoops and levering against another part of the frame will possibly achieve the desired aim but will also more than likely remove a fair bit paint, as it's highly unlikely you'll get the hoop to slip over the tang first time. The factories would have had some special tool, but essentially what is needed is a means of pulling the spring while maintaining enough space within the hoop for it to push over the pip, so it's a case of sourcing a length of wire that is fine enough not to prevent the hoop slipping onto the tang yet strong enough to withstand a seriously hefty tug. Safety wire, of the kind used to lockwire drilled bolt heads, sump plugs and so on to prevent them from vibrating loose, of diameter approx 0.030in (30 thou') will be pretty much the thickest that will fit. With a suitably long length attached, rig up some form of lever, the bigger the better, and with one end and the frame both firmly fixed, simply prise for all you're worth and let the second pair of hands push the spring into place. It's one of those jobs that differs from bike to bike, and from person to person and the facilities available to them. Fit the stand and spring early in the rebuild to take advantage of the space available around it. It can be even more difficult with the engine and wheels in place.

If the stand lugs and/or the mating lugs on the frame have worn oval, there is little that can be done other than to have them bored circular again and have an oversize pin made up, which is a job for an engineering shop.

Now's the time to get those repairs done, because you may have to hold the frame in the vice or something similar, which will damage the finish.

SHOCK ABSORBERS

As regards the actual shock absorbers themselves, unless they have lost their hydraulic damping action, through wear, neglect or damage, then they are quite restorable, at least aesthetically. For example, if they are fully shrouded, that is the springs are not exposed, new shrouds are readily available. The upper shrouds can be had painted, usually neutral black, or chrome-plated or even stainless steel, whereas the lower shrouds are usually chromed. However, there are some instances, like on Triumph's early Thunderbirds and Speed Twins, where the whole shock absorber is the same colour as the bike itself, in this case Polychromatic Blue or Amaranth Red. These colours are available from certain classic motorcycle paint specialists, such as John Crichlow, at MS Motorcycles, who has the original Triumph factory paint swatches and the appropriate recipes to make them up. It's not a

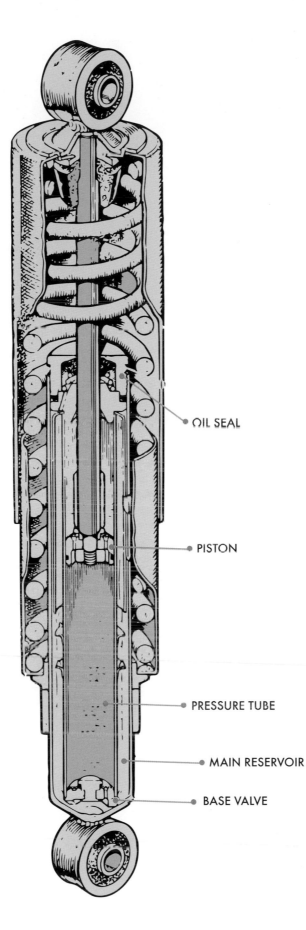

Section through a typical period rear shock absorber.

OIL SEAL

PISTON

PRESSURE TUBE

MAIN RESERVOIR

BASE VALVE

the top of the shroud there is a pair of semicircular collets, which, when the shroud is pushed down to compress the spring, slip into the neck of the shroud, and on release, butt up to the underside of the shock absorber's top fitting. The difficulty in compressing the spring on dismantling is the lack of bearing space on the top of the shroud for the tool doing the compressing. It's barely a quarter inch, and so unless you're using a specialist tool, which bears on two or three sides, then there is always the risk of whatever you're using slipping off the edge; this is generally all right unless you've removed the collets, in which case the spring and shroud will launch themselves into orbit, potentially via your face.

On the outside of the bottom part of the shock absorber, where the oil damping takes place, there is a peg, which, when the shock absorber is twisted, slips into one of three slots, each slightly higher than its predecessor, to give a soft, medium or firm effect. Before dismantling, ensure the spring is on its softest setting. It might even be possible then to compress the top shroud by hand, thus allowing a second pair of hands to pick out the collets.

Above the damping slots there is a crenellated ring in which a suitable C spanner can be applied if necessary to adjust the ride.

Cheaper, imported pattern shock absorbers often do not have this adjustment. What you use is up to you – you pay for what you get, at least to a certain extent.

If of course, your shock absorbers have to be of the exposed spring type and the existing springs are past their best, then a variety of spring lengths and diameters are available to enhance the appearance of your newly painted shocks. These springs are held in place in the same manner as the shrouds. Unfortunately, if the hard chrome damping rod inside the spring is less than ideal aesthetically, with a bit of rust here and there let's say, you'll have to think about what you want to do. Is it an 'oily rag' restoration, where the bike is complete and running but lacking in the spit and polish of the show bike? In this case, the shock absorbers, provided

difficult job to sand down the painted surface of an existing, or even a brand new, shock absorber and carefully spray it to the required colour.

To remove the shrouds is not difficult but does require care, for it is the pressure of the shock absorber spring itself that holds the thing together. At

ABOVE LEFT: AMC manufactured their own shock absorbers at one time. This 'fat' shock absorber was nicknamed the 'Jampot'. This one is on an AJS. Later versions were a little slimmer and called the 'Candlestick'. Eventually AMC bought in proprietary units like everyone else.

ABOVE RIGHT: This is the same in-house Jampot shock absorber as fitted to sister marque Matchless.

Velocette shock absorbers have a 'ride height' adjustment courtesy of the sliding bracket for the top fixing.

they work well enough, will be fine and not look out of place. However, if the new paint and polished alloy look smart, will leaving the shocks spoil the job for a ha'porth of tar and could you live with it? If you're on a tight budget, rather than buy new shocks, why not just go for new shrouds and cover up the rest – what the eye doesn't see, the heart doesn't grieve over!

Check also the condition of the Silent-Bloc bushes in the top and bottom eyelets. The rubber needs to be compliant but firm enough to prevent distortion of the mount, which will manifest itself in strange and potentially dangerous sensations when cornering. These bushes too are available from your local classic specialist. The bushes in the shock absorbers are pretty much the same as the bushes in the swinging arm, albeit smaller. They will have to be pressed or driven out. If they are to be replaced it doesn't matter if they are damaged on removal, but care must be taken when pressing new ones into place, with a suitably sized washer over the face of the bush to provide consistent pressure over both the outer and inner steel sections. It may be helpful to heat up the eyelet and chill the bush, but take care not to heat up the lower eyelet too much as it may damage the hydraulic action of the damping seals within the lower section of the shock absorber body.

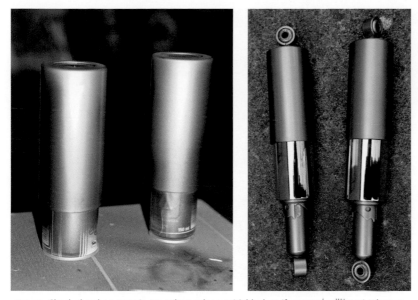

ABOVE LEFT: Shock absorbers come in any colour as long as it's black, so if you need a different colour, us for the Triumph Thunderbird, then you have to change the paint colour yourself.

ABOVE RIGHT: If you're patient and careful, a good job can be made.

Turning the base of the shock absorber onto the higher notches increases the loading on, and hence the stiffness of, the spring.

WHEELS, BRAKES AND TYRES

Before we get into the details proper, a word of advice. Wheel building from scratch is not the world's most difficult job but it does require some specific equipment, such as a means of supporting the wheel by its axle so it can spin, a dial gauge or two or at least some form of fixed pointer, a spoke spanner plus a barrowload of patience and not a little skill. Unless you really do

have a burning ambition to tackle the job yourself, farm it out to a specialist while you get on with something else in the meantime. What's more, if the specialist supplies tyres too, get them to fit a pair at the same time and do you a good deal on the whole package. The next time you see your wheels they will look fantastic and you'll be fired with another injection of enthusiasm. Indeed, you may well have the rest of the chassis prepared, so you can

simply fit the wheels and your project will straight away begin to look like a bike again – you'll not be able to resist sitting on the rolling chassis either!

Rims

In general, the majority of post-war classic motorcycles run on 19in-diameter wheel rims, though some have a combination of 19in front and 18in rear, or a pair of 18in, competition style. Late pre-war machines could have a 21in front and 19in rear, or even a 20in front; others, like Ariel's Arrow and Leader have a pair of 16in rims and mostly these were of chromium-plated mild steel from the likes of Dunlop, Jones and Palmer – all long defunct manufacturers. Sport bikes, like racing bikes, could be fitted with aluminium rims with deep, flat-sided flanges to give the lightweight material an improved strength but mostly the standard machine was fitted with steel rims. Again Dunlop was the British mainstay of alloy rims. After they ceased rim manufacture, it was down to the imported but nevertheless excellent Borrani, also gone, then Akront and today Morad, all pretty much the same quality and style.

With the improvements in metallurgy and technology, it also became possible to obtain a flangeless alloy rim, that is one that follows the same shape as the traditional steel rim without the strengthening flanges. Stainless steel rims are popular, albeit expensive, but they should last a lifetime.

With a restoration project, there is nothing to stop you from choosing a different-diameter wheel, or a different section either, should you wish, though certain things must be considered. For example, if you were to fit an 18in wheel to a machine normally fitted with a 19in wheel and that wheel drives the speedometer, then the speedometer will read slightly fast. The reverse applies the other way round, and in this case you may also find that the extra diameter will cause the face of the tyre to make contact with the underside of the mudguard over bumps, necessitating longer and stronger shock absorbers.

During the wilderness years, following the demise of the manufacturers and their suppliers and before the

When you have a rolling chassis is the first time you will actually realize you're making progress – and you'll not be able to resist sitting on it and scootering it around.

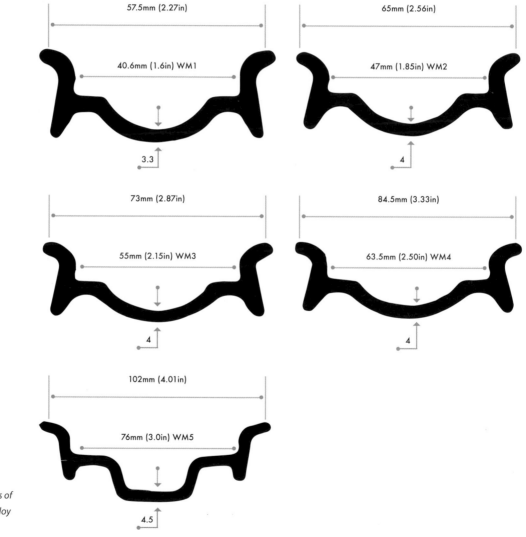

57.5mm (2.27in)

40.6mm (1.6in) WM1

3.3

65mm (2.56in)

47mm (1.85in) WM2

4

73mm (2.87in)

55mm (2.15in) WM3

4

84.5mm (3.33in)

63.5mm (2.50in) WM4

4

102mm (4.01in)

76mm (3.0in) WM5

4.5

Sections through sizes of traditional flanged alloy wheel rims.

growth of the classic industry, wheel rims were only available from abroad, and they were not particularly well made. If you can see a rather obvious weld mark across your rim, your wheel was probably changed in the late 1970s or early 1980s. Fortunately today there are British-made rims and also imported rims that are a very much higher, and perfectly satisfactory, quality.

Wheel rim widths are, or rather were, measured by a WM size, which gave an indication of the tyre size suitable to it. For example, WM0 was for 2.25–2.50in tyres, WM1 from 2.25 to 3.10in, WM2

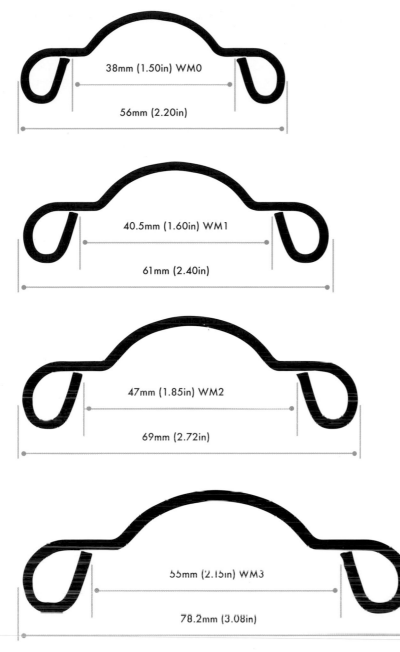

38mm (1.50in) WM0

56mm (2.20in)

40.5mm (1.60in) WM1

61mm (2.40in)

47mm (1.85in) WM2

69mm (2.72in)

55mm (2.15in) WM3

78.2mm (3.08in)

Sections through sizes of traditional steel wheel rims.

from 2.75 to 3.60in and WM3 from 3.00 to 5.10in, so as you can see the tyre and rim combination was fairly flexible, though obviously dependent on chain run and swinging arm width and so on. Today rims are measure by an MT rating, which is a different section shape, but for British classic motorcycles, all wheel builders still use the WM section.

Spokes

Most wheel spokes are made from plain, mild steel wire and finished with a protective coating. In the good old days it would have been cadmium or zinc but the health and safety police have outlawed many of the traditional coatings and processes because of the cocktail of chemicals used and the potential health hazard they present to long-term exposure, though chromium and nickel are still hanging on. New, approved, replacement coatings are available that give a similar appearance and an effective protection. Rustless wire was also used at one time, which turned black instead of going rusty, but these days stainless steel has taken over in the longevity stakes. Stainless steel could be quite brittle at one time and there was a question mark over its ability to withstand the required 45- or 90-degree bend. However, much development has taken place over the past few years and now stainless as a material for spokes is perfectly satisfactory. It's rare, however, that stainless nipples are used, for they

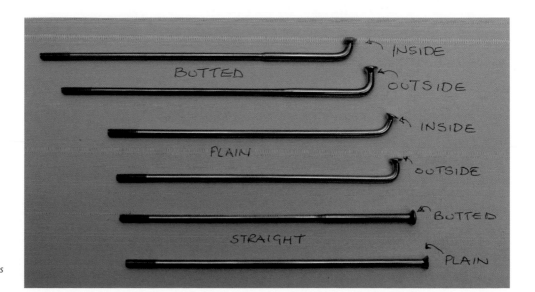

BUTTED
INSIDE
OUTSIDE
PLAIN
INSIDE
OUTSIDE
STRAIGHT
BUTTED
PLAIN

Spokes come in all shapes and sizes.

have a tendency to seize to the spoke and/or rim, so the majority of wheel builders still use the tried and tested nickel-plated brass nipple. It has been reported, in the case of road racing machines, that using stainless steel spokes with alloy rims can result in the spokes loosening due to the differentials between the two metals' characteristics. If you are considering this, please take advice from an experienced wheel building specialist first.

Spoke thickness depends on the size and power of your machine and its intended use. If merely replacing a wheel, then it's best to use a spoke the same as the one removed, so take it along to your wheel builder as a pattern.

As a rough guide, it's usually eight gauge for the rear wheel in machines 500cc or over, ten gauge for under 500cc. The threads on the spokes are rolled, with a specialist tool, rather than cut, as this tends to weaken the spoke, and the thread sizes are universal – 12g/52tpi, 10g/40tpi, 8g/32tpi, 6g/32tpi. As mentioned above, nipples are invariably plated brass.

Brakes

In the 'good old days' when your average Joe used a motorcycle as everyday transport, and for a good few years after too, the accepted medium for brake linings was asbestos-based.

It was an excellent retardant material but, like many other materials, its potentially hazardous qualities rendered it unlawful to use. For several years following its ban, numerous environmentally acceptable materials were tried, none of which came anywhere near asbestos, and it's fair to say that a few 'new old stock' linings of the outlawed material found their way from dusty boxes in the back of the store to various motorcycle drum brakes via the back door of many a local motorcycle repair shop. The manufacturers, particularly those involved in industry and heavy plant, were forced to develop better materials, which, fortunately for us motorcyclists, has led to a plethora of acceptable lining material available for any type of use – from the non-fade qualities of the classic road racer to the water-resistant requirements of the keen trials rider, and everything in between.

Linings were fixed to the shoes originally by means of half a dozen or so countersunk, soft brass rivets. When you were 'down to the rivets' you were due for some new linings. Nowadays chemical adhesives are generally used, though should you specifically require your linings to be riveted, most reputable lining specialists will oblige.

The shoes themselves are usually steel or alloy and can readily be

Traditionally riveted brake shoes. Modern adhesives have rendered the riveting process obsolete.

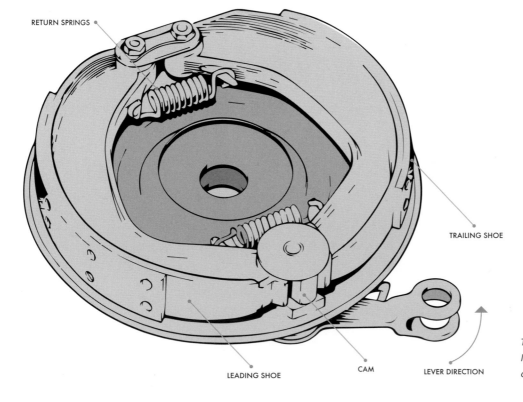

RETURN SPRINGS

LEADING SHOE

CAM

LEVER DIRECTION

TRAILING SHOE

The principle of the single leading shoe – one cam, one pivot point.

cleaned up by blasting, washing, wire brushing and so on, but take care to avoid the dust caused.

Most classic drum brakes are single leading shoe, where the two spring-loaded shoes are pivoted around a stop within the drum at one end and are prised apart by a cam, actuated from the external lever and cable attachment, at the other. That means the actuating cam inside the drum pushes forward one edge of the brake shoes, while the opposite end stays around the pivot point. Bearing in mind that the drum is turning, then one shoe 'leads' and the other shoe 'trails'. The leading shoe moves with the direction of the drum's rotation and exhibits a self-servo effect, that is, being dragged into the friction surface of the drum and thus achieving greater braking force. The trailing shoe moves against the direction of rotation, essentially being thrown off the friction surface and thus not being quite so effective in retardation. When moving in reverse, the role of the leading and trailing shoes swap over, with the forward motion leading shoe becoming the trailing shoe.

As machines grew ever bigger and faster, so the brakes became less effective, and following race practice, the twin leading shoe drum made an appearance on road machines. With a TLS both shoes are activated by their

Single leading shoe front brake on a BSA.

1. Brake-shoe retaining plate
2. Brake shoe spring
3-6. Brake-cam nut, washer, lever and spring
7. Brake-cam bush
8. Brake cam lock nut
9. Brake cam
10. Brake plate distance piece (inner)
11-14. Retaining washer, felt washer, pen steel
15-16. washer and bearing (brake side)
   Brake shoes, lining
17. Brake drum
18. Grease nipple
19-21. Bearing, distance piece and lock ring (plain side)
22. Speedometer gearbox
23. Shouldered distance piece
24. Distance piece
25. Sleeve nut
26. Brake drum attachment piece
27. Hub shell
28. Hub bearing sleeve
29. Hub spindle

A late 1940s/early 1950s, Norton single leading shoe drum brake.

own lever, connected by an adjustable rod, thus each is pushed into the friction area of the drum. When the bike is reversed, the brake becomes twin-trailing, with the rotation of the drum working against the shoes and creating the exact opposite of the self-servo effect, rendering the brakes virtually useless.

Vincent, however, had a slightly different idea and fitted single-sided, single leading shoe brakes on both sides of their wheel.

On the race track, with increasing speeds, the double-sided twin leading shoe drum appeared, which in effect was a four leading shoe. Dresda and CMA also marketed eight leading shoe brakes, with four leading shoes on either side. These, while looking exceptionally impressive, were a nightmare to set up correctly, were very big within the wheel and were heavy too. With

the arrival of the light and efficient disc brake, the big drums were instantly obsolete, though they are popular with the café racer crowd as they look the period part as well as being a better stopper than the original standard brake.

The classic brake drum is either single sided, or full width and made of either alloy or steel. Obviously, with a single-sided hub, the spokes will be longer on one side than the other, but otherwise the principle is the same. With the axle removed, there's a dust cover of some form on either side to keep the muck out and the grease in. This might be brass or alloy and screwed in by means of two recessed holes in the face of the cover into which a suitable peg spanner can be fitted, though more than likely these holes will be roughed up and oval at

least, where they've previously been removed by means of a hammer and punch. They'll probably also be left-hand thread. See if your manual mentions anything about it before you start walloping. The covers may simply be a push fit, in which case they'll have to be prised out and there's a good chance you'll damage them in the process, so make sure replacements are available before you wade in. If you're working on an alloy hub, use the blow lamp again here, because the press fit cover will probably be steel and should pull out easily enough, along with the bearing behind it, if heat is applied.

There will be a brace of ball bearings, one at each side, through which the axle passes, and as mentioned above, these should drop out with heat. In a steel hub, they'll have to be driven out with a drift of some form. As with all

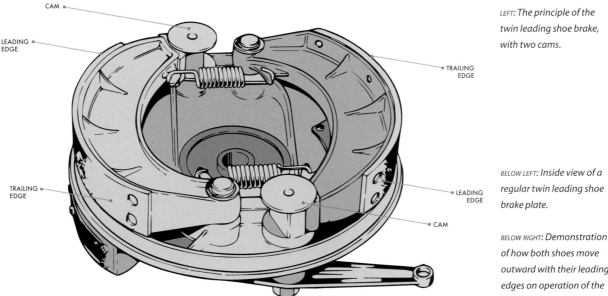

CAM • LEADING EDGE • TRAILING EDGE • TRAILING EDGE • LEADING EDGE • CAM

LEFT: The principle of the twin leading shoe brake, with two cams.

BELOW LEFT: Inside view of a regular twin leading shoe brake plate.

BELOW RIGHT: Demonstration of how both shoes move outward with their leading edges on operation of the lever.

The late 1960s/early 1970s twin leading shoe front brake plate used by Triumph and BSA group was an excellent brake.

Vincent's idea of a twin leading shoe brake was to fit the standard single leading shoe drum on both sides of the wheel.

bearings, unless you plan to junk them, do not drift on any part other than the edge of the outer race.

Tie all the hub internals, bearings *et al*, in their respective order along a length of wire and put in the box with the axle.

The Front Wheel

Assuming the tyre is to be replaced along with the rim, dig out those tyre levers and take off the tyre. Remove the valve and deflate the tube, then with the wheel rim on the floor, step on the tyre wall and let the edge of your foot break the seal between the tyre bead and the rim. Now hook the first tyre lever beneath the tyre bead and the next one about 8in or so around the rim, prise back and force the bead over the rim. Hook the first one under the spokes to prevent it slipping back then take a third and hook it further round still. Once this has brought the bead over the rim, the pressure on the tyre will have released and you may be able simply to drive the lever around the edge of the rim bringing the tyre bead with it; if not, then hook the levers under the bead as before.

Push the valve into the rim, then reach under the tyre and pull out the tube. Often, despite the tyre being old, the tube is quite serviceable and can be reused, especially if it's not festooned with puncture patches, or blebs, though new tubes are not expensive. Check if the rubber has perished around the valve neck.

Push, or prise using the levers if necessary, the tyre off the other side of the rim and put to one side for later disposal.

Now undo the securing nut for the brake plate and lift the brake plate from the drum. It may not have been removed for many years and thus could be stiff, so a squirt of penetrating fluid along the axle will ease its removal as you work it from side to side or round and round as you pull it off. If your chosen mount is an early 1950s Triumph with the alloy front brake plate with the integral torque arm, take care not to put too much pressure on the torque arm section itself when you're working the plate up the axle, as it may simply break off, then you'll have the job of trying to source a replacement – not an easy task. There again, it could be argued that if it is going to break, then better on the bench than while motoring along.

The next stage is important if you're having your wheel built elsewhere and imperative if you're going to have a go at it yourself. Measure the rim offset. This is the distance the edge of the brake drum face projects beyond the edge of the wheel rim. Lay the wheel on the bench and drop a straight edge as centrally as possible across the face of the drum, then measure the distance from the bottom of the straight edge to the edge of the wheel rim and make a note of it. Also make a note of the overall width of the rim itself, a simple task with a digital vernier, just in case the replacement rim is a different width to the original. Remove a spoke by undoing the nipple at the rim and then working it back through its hole in the drum. If you've a single-sided hub, remove one from either side. That way you have a record of the thickness, shape and size of the spokes required, to go with your drum to rim dimensions. Give all this information to your wheel builder.

If you're intending to do it yourself, then take a photograph and make a drawing of the pattern of the spoke lacing to the hub – that is, record which spoke goes where, through which holes and crosses over what. Make sure your notes or your photographs indicate which side of the wheel you were looking at, at the time (usually brake or non-brake), inside or outside, and clockwise or anticlockwise.

Should you have no further need for the spokes or the rim, you can find yourself some big cutters or use the angle grinder to cut the spokes in half, making it simple to remove them from both the rim and the hub.

Now remove the dust covers and bearings and you have a bare hub ready to be refinished as you wish. If it's a steel hub, a session in the blasting cabinet will have all the old paint off – take note however, that some of the enamel used in the factories was exceptionally good and takes a lot of getting off. Then you can prime and paint it, or take it away to be powder-coated or enamelled. Before you commence

LEFT: The four leading shoe brake was born on the race track but made – indeed still makes – an impressive road bike.

BELOW: A huge-diameter eight leading shoe drum, this example by Dresda, meant extra weight. It was a nightmare to set up correctly and was soon superseded by the much lighter and equally effective disc.

Early 1950s Triumph single-sided front brake.

Full competition style from AMC with the Matchless-Norton hybrid P11.

This Triumph brake plate broke while being worked over the axle in the process of removal. Luckily it broke on the bench rather than out on the road.

the rebuild, give it a very thorough wash and blow it clean with the air line to ensure you get rid of any lingering blasting medium.

Source a pair of good-quality new bearings. There may be nothing apparently wrong with the old bearings but if your machine has been motionless for many years, there is a good chance that the bearing may have suffered, though perhaps not visibly. If, once cleaned and lubricated, the old bearing spins freely with no discernible rough spots or side play, then it may be perfectly all right for a few more years. The choice is yours. Unmarked, cheap bearings from Asia are readily available but their longevity is questionable and in a wheel situation, a failure could be dangerous, so stick to regular brand names.

The bearings are a really tight fit, so if your hub is alloy, give it some serious heat and you'll find the steel bearings simply drop into place – it's even easier if you've had them in the freezer for a few hours – and you can ensure they're right the way home by merely tapping them with a hammer shaft. Of course if you have a steel hub then it's still a good idea to heat it up but the bearing may need to be driven home, in which case you'll have to find a drift that works on the outer edge only. A good tool for the job is an old bearing that has had a few thou' machined off the outer face so it's square in the hub but not too tight; that way you can use the old bearing to drift the new bearing all the way home and then simply tip the old bearing drift out of the hub recess. Make a note on it somehow, by a few spots of paint or something, to show that this is a drift and not a bearing to be used!

Before you remove the spokes from the hub and rim, put a trustable straight edge across the wheel and check and measure the offset, the distance from one face of the hub to the outside of the rim. In this case there is no offset measurement as the two edges are flush with each other.

If the dust covers are the screw-in type, you will need to assess whether the originals are serviceable based on what sort of standard you are hoping to achieve with your first restoration. Can they be seen? Will they look bad? Will they spoil the wheel's overall appearance? Are the holes too badly mangled to repair satisfactorily? Obviously, if they can be cleaned up to an acceptable standard, there is no reason why they cannot be reused. However, if new replacements are available, they will undoubtedly look better. If the covers are push-in, then you will inevitably have to fit new ones. Your favoured marque specialist will have them in stock. These will have to be tapped into place, so grease everything up well beforehand and use your rubber hammer to prevent damage.

Repeat the exercise on the opposite side too, making sure that there is an abundance of grease around the bearings, though often in single-sided hubs there is a grease nipple in the centre of the hub to keep the axle lubricated.

The brake plate will hold the operating arm to which the cable attaches. The brake shoe operating cam, on the inner face of the plate, projects through the plate, and the arm is secured to it with a nut and washer. The flat ends of the brake shoes rest either side of this cam and are held in place by a spring with a hook on either end. The opposite ends of the shoes have a horseshoe end to them, which usually wraps around a circular pivot pin, which in turn is bolted through the brake plate. Take a photograph of the various parts in their rightful positions before you remove them, though there should be an exploded diagram in your manual. If you are sending them to be re-plated, then trace round each piece in your book, and make a note of which part is which. That way, when it all comes back, you'll instantly know if there is any part missing, and if all parts are there, you'll know where they all fit. Take note, also, that while decorative chrome plate is only microns thick, it can make refitting a nut onto threads rather difficult, so either mask off your threaded parts before sending to the plating shop, or request that

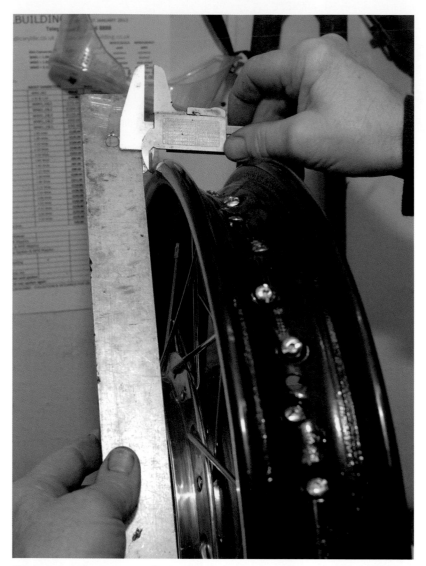

This rim has an offset, as measured by the calipers.

Measure the length of the existing spokes.

Measure the length of the spoke from its threaded end to the bend. That way you ensure that the new spokes are identical.

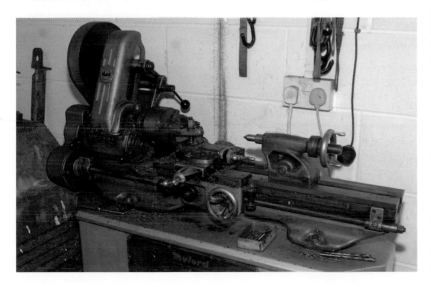

your plater does it for you – though don't be surprised if he charges for the service. What's more, chromium plate does not fill. If you send a part with a scratch on it, it will come back with a chrome-plated scratch on it. Like most things in restoration, it's the preparation that counts. If your plated parts still have a good amount of plate on them, let the plater do the work, for he can simply submerge them in a tank of chemicals that re-verses the plating process, that is, melt the chrome away. Then he will polish before re-plating, removing the pits, scratches and so on.

If the parts are rusty and have no discernible plate left on them, then you can prepare them yourself, via blasting and polishing, but it's a time-consuming operation and one for which the plater is better prepared equipment-wise. Again, the choice is yours.

With all the bits away at the plating shop, you can turn to the brake plate itself. Firstly, get it clean. Put it in the parts washer to remove all the muck and old grease, then, if it's an alloy plate, give it a good once-over with glass beads in the blasting cabinet. This gives a matt surface finish, which can be left, or used as the first step in the polishing process, which we'll deal with in a later chapter. Of course, if you have a full-width alloy hub and you're not particularly bothered about originality, or upsetting the purists, then why not go the whole hog and have the whole hub and brake plate polished. The alloy used by Ariel in their full-width hubs, for example, is excellent quality and will polish to a fantastic finish. If the plate is steel, then treat it to the same finish as the hub itself, making sure to keep openings and any threaded sections masked.

TOP LEFT: *Once you've logged your dimensions cut out the old spokes.*

ABOVE LEFT: *Keep a record of all your measurements and details.*

LEFT: *A lathe will come in handy for all sorts of things.*

Getting to the Hub of it

This genuine BSA Gold Star 190mm hub was in dire need of some TLC to return it to its former glory. With no rim on the hub, the rim offset for use in Gold Star forks was ascertained from the owners' club as $^3/_{16}$in when measured across the drum face. The first thing to do was to get it clean in order to see just what condition everything was in underneath the muck and grease.

Rusty steelwork, corroded alloy and generally in a bit of a state: time to dismantle.

The bearing cap-cum-dust cover was very tight in its thread and had to be driven loose bit by bit with hammer and punch, which didn't do the peg spanner holes in the brass a lot of good.

Eventually it came out, revealing the bearings.

The alloy part of the drum is fixed to the steel by means of allen screws.

Once the allen screws were out the hub came apart easily.

With the main steel section removed it was simple to secure the alloy in the vice to ease removal of the other bearing cap.

Then it was a case of removing the bearings. Heating up the alloy loosened the bearings, which were then tapped out.

Preparing the cook pot for an overnight soaking for the steel drum section in Flowliner rust-removing salts.

Flowliner Bio-Rust salts, from Wyldes of Leeds, are exceptionally good.

Once into the boiling water solution, the action begins immediately to remove rust and muck.

An overnight soak did the trick …

… followed by a good scrub in hot, soapy water.

How much better than that do you want?

Deal with it immediately, though, because the unprotected metal will soon begin to oxidize again.

So into the blasting cabinet for a quick once-over.

Then it was ready for a protective coat of cellulose primer.

A good covering prevents the onset of further rust.

Another coat about an hour later and the drum is ready for a top coat.

Smooth silver cellulose made for a tidy finish.

The brake shoes had plenty of lining left on them but were pretty grubby.

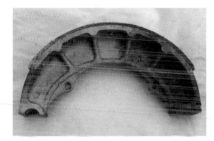

Brake shoe showing existing half and the blasted half.

Both shoes look fine now after a good seeing-to in the blasting cabinet.

The brake plate was sound but very greasy.

It went into the parts washer for a good degrease and a wash and brush-up.

Getting to the Hub of it *continued*

Five minutes later and it looked like this.

The operating arms were rusty too.

Again, they came up a treat in the blast cabinet and can now be prepared for re-plating.

The main alloy section was next up for the parts washer.

Clean and ready to reassemble.

The brake plate, though sound, had myriad signs of use. Often these brake plates were painted but BSA alloy was good quality and invariably polishes up a treat.

The first stage was to remove the scratches and marks with an abrasive mop and Satene.

Satene on the mop. This soft compound is applied to the mop and allowed to dry. It then turns into a soft grinding wheel.

The process was then followed by regular medium-coarse alloy polishing compound and then finishing compound, which brought it to the required mirror finish.

The main alloy then received the same treatment.

Reassembled and looking good, just awaiting new bearings.

A new stainless steel wheel spindle was purchased and the nuts were to be sent to the platers, ready for a new rim and a new lease of life.

Rebuilding the Wheel

Now your hub is ready to go again, there are a couple of things to bear in mind. First, if you're considering a second-hand rim – such as a genuine period alloy, for example – ensure the nipple dimples have been drilled in the correct manner for the hub to which you're intending to fit it. Think about it – with a single-sided hub, the long spokes will enter the dimple at a different angle from the shorter ones, so said angle will be incorrect for a full-width hub. What's more, unless you know the history of the rim, make sure you give it a thorough examination for cracks and other such damage. To be really sure, play safe and buy a new rim, for not only will it be damage- and stress-free, it will be specifically drilled to suit your hub.

With your new rim and your new spokes, nails (straight) – where the spoke is pushed through a hole in the hub that directly faces the corresponding hole in the rim and the flat head on the end of the spoke, like the head on a nail, holds it into the hub – and hooks (bent ends), you're ready to build your wheel. Take your drawing or refer to your photograph of your original wheel and examine the spoke pattern. Most wheels have either thirty-six or forty spokes and you'll notice that they're grouped together in little bunches of fours.

Let's work on the thirty-six-hole pattern as the example. There are eighteen spokes on either side of the hub and they are staggered, that is,

there's a spoke on the brake side, then a spoke on the opposite side, then the brake side again and so on, making thirty-six equally spaced spokes alternating from side to side. Notice that on the brake side every other spoke is outside and angled clockwise (like the first spoke). These alternate with inside ones angled anticlockwise.

Make sure you're looking at your wheel from the same side as in your photograph, and that you have a note of the rim offset. Now you're ready to assemble your new wheel. Give yourself plenty of space – a good 3ft or more – and lay on the bench surface an old blanket or towel to prevent any potential scratches; a single colour surface, the lighter the better, makes items easier to spot.

Set the flat side of the hub on the workbench and identify the spokes. If you've hooks then you'll have two patterns, as inside spokes have hooks with less angle than the outside spokes. Put the spokes into two piles, insides and outsides, and if you're working on a single-sided hub then further separate them into long and short. Now start threading the spokes into the hub, following your 1-2-3-4 pattern in the correct inside-outside orientation until all holes are filled, then arrange them in their clockwise and anticlockwise orientation as per your notes or photograph. Now lay the rim over the hub and spokes.

You'll see that the holes in the dimples are drilled to face one side or the other and to accept either clockwise or anticlockwise spokes. Rotate the

rim until the holes match the spokes' line. If they don't, you've probably got the rim the wrong way round, so flip it over. When properly oriented, start with the bottom spokes (those on the outside of the hub nearest to the bench). Put one spoke in its rightful hole in the rim and, with a dribble of light oil on the threads, loosely screw on a nipple.

Now skip four holes and fit the same spoke in the next group of four until you've got all nine (or ten if you have a forty-holer) spokes in place. Repeat the process until all bottom spokes are in place, followed by the bottom inside layer, then the top inside layer and finally the top outside spokes. Now you'll be getting excited because it will look like a proper wheel!

Make sure now that they're all in the correct orientation and tighten up the nipples to the extent that the hub is fairly firm in the wheel. Tighten them all to the same point so the wheel will be reasonably well aligned but do not torque them up yet. There's no hard and fast rule to this as spoke lengths obviously vary from wheel to wheel.

Now you've got to true up the wheel. Some form of wheel stand would be handy, though not essential, and is not difficult to make. Obviously if you're not intending to build wheels on a regular basis, the expense of a proprietary piece of specialist equipment would hardly be justifiable. A stand bolted up or welded together from 2in angle iron is perfectly

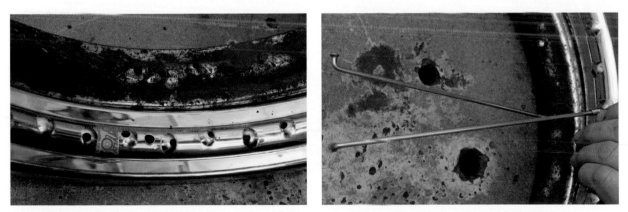

ABOVE LEFT: If you look closely at the spoke holes in the two rims, you will notice they are drilled slightly differently. The old rim had originally been drilled for a smaller hub and ideally should not have been laced to the full-width hub from which it was taken. The spokes did fit but were bowed due to the incorrect angle of drilling in the dimple.

ABOVE RIGHT: The difference in spoke angle between the correct drilling and the incorrect is very noticeable.

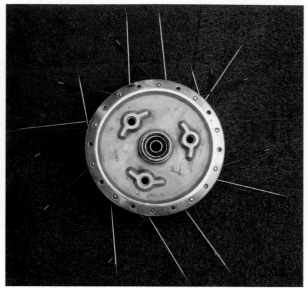

ABOVE: Begin the lacing with the inside spokes.

RIGHT: All inside spokes in place.

Now the rim can be offered up.

Feed the first spoke into the hole by the side of the valve hole in the rim, then move five spaces and temporarily fit an outside spoke to line up the rim with the hub.

All inside spokes in the rim. Now it looks like a proper wheel again.

Now fit the remaining spokes.

adequate and can be hung up in the roof space out of the way when not required. The drawing shown gives a basic idea.

Another way is to merely clamp the axle in the jaws of your vice so it can be spun to check for alignment. Either way, you must incorporate a guide that

can be positioned close to the rim to check for run-out as the wheel spins. It doesn't matter what it is as long as it's firm enough not to flex; a strong length

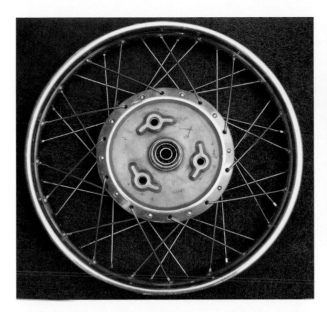

ABOVE: Tighten the spokes with a screwdriver.

LEFT: With all spokes in place, it's now time to tension them.

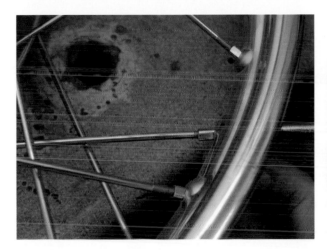

ABOVE LEFT: Tension until there are just four threads visible.

ABOVE RIGHT: Not the kind of tool usually found in the home workshop. This is a professional tool that instantly centres the hub with the rim.

RIGHT: Example of a perfectly adequate home-made wheel-truing jig.

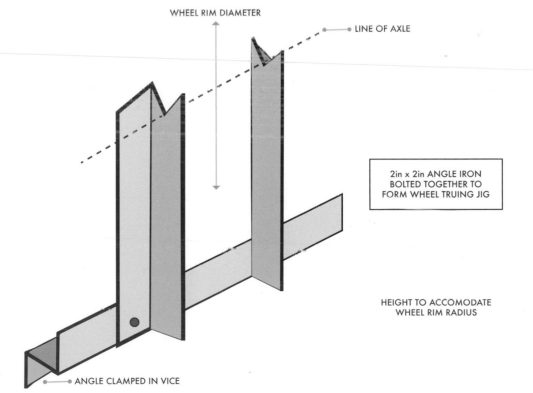

WHEEL RIM DIAMETER

LINE OF AXLE

2in x 2in ANGLE IRON BOLTED TOGETHER TO FORM WHEEL TRUING JIG

HEIGHT TO ACCOMODATE WHEEL RIM RADIUS

ANGLE CLAMPED IN VICE

of bent wire is more than adequate – just make sure it is firmly attached to the stand or vice.

Now it's time to test your skill and patience and to see if you can readily understand how tightening and loosening the spokes affects the position of the rim.

Bear in mind that the wheel can be out both side to side across the width of the hub and along its diameter too, running like an ellipse!

Let's say you spin the wheel slowly and you find a high spot on the left side of the rim diameter, so the rim has to move to the right at that point. Highlighting the actual high point, mark about a half a dozen or so spokes either side of the high spot and then loosen the corresponding dozen spokes on the right side. This allows you to then tighten the marked spokes on the left side, which effectively moves the rim across to the right of the hub.

To move the rim from side to side, tighten spokes on the side towards which you want the rim to move, loosening those on the opposite side. By repeatedly adjusting spokes you'll eventually get the rim spinning true. If you've managed to get it to within $\frac{1}{8}$in then you've done very well. This is where the offset measurement is required, so that the wheel runs central between the forks. The final stages can be very frustrating and laborious.

You'll know if the spokes are too loose because the wheel will flex when you're riding; but if the hub breaks then you've got them too tight! Like a guitar string, the tighter a spoke becomes, the higher pitch the ringing sound becomes when tapped with a screwdriver or spanner. A loose spoke will have a flat, dead sound. Once you're satisfied the wheel is true, tap the spokes and tighten them, one side then the opposite, randomly so the wheel isn't pulled out of line, a bit at a time until they ping like a champagne glass. If you find that tightening the nipples has indeed pulled the rim out of line, there is unfortunately nothing you can do other than simply repeat the previous process, albeit the spokes will be very much tighter. Once you've got it

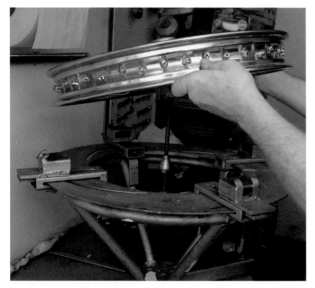

The wheel now goes onto the jig …

… and a turn of the handle centralizes everything.

ABOVE: *Now tension each spoke a little more …*

RIGHT: *… and the truing-up process can begin.*

ABOVE: Start with the ovality. A guide is placed across both edges of the rim.

RIGHT: As the wheel is rotated it shows high and low spots on the guide. At this point the rim is touching the guide …

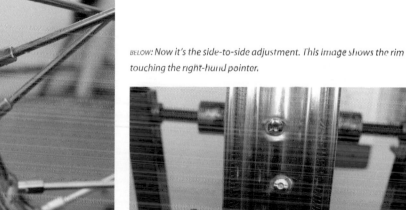

LEFT: … but a little further round there is a gap. So return to the high spot and adjust six spokes either side of it until there is a matching gap.

BELOW: Now it's the side-to-side adjustment. This image shows the rim touching the right-hand pointer.

running completely true, you may also find that some spokes have a considerably higher ping to them through necessarily having to be tighter than others.

If, on completion, you find that the spokes have poked through the nipples into the rim area, simply take them down to the nipple head with the grinder. Ensure you leave no sharp edges, which may poke through the rim tape and puncture the tube.

If you've done it right you can now allow yourself a pat on the back, but weigh up the time you've taken, the hair you've pulled out and the oaths you've brought forth, and assess what progress you could have made had you farmed the work out to the professionals. The choice again is yours.

Rolling the Spokes

Spoke manufacture is generally mechanized these days, albeit sometimes on amazingly old but perfectly acceptable machines that have been clonking away in the back of some factory for generations and will continue to do so for generations to come.

However, before the days of the specialist wheel-building companies, most motorcycle and cycle shops had their own in house craftsman who would build wheels as and when required. They would buy in blank spokes of the required gauge and the threads would be added manually in the workshop on a bespoke little machine as shown here.

This is a traditional, manually operated spoke-rolling machine.

The blank spoke is fed into the chuck, …

… secured into position with the butterfly nut and the chuck turned.

The rollers actually swage the spoke end, rather than cut into it, so there is no compromising of the spoke thickness.

Each roller is set for a specific gauge. Nowadays, the task is automated and there are specialists who produce spokes in such abundance that it is more economical to buy them in than to form them yourself.

A little further round, though, and the rim has moved away from it. So slacken six spokes on the cush drive side of the hub and tighten the corresponding spokes on the opposite side to pull the rim over. Put a mark on the rim where it is about right, then rotate the rim to a place where it is out and adjust in the same manner – six spokes either side. when the gap is pretty much constant all the way round, consistently tension the spokes and your wheel is complete. As the rim is tensioned, it may pull slightly out of true, so it's a case of painstakingly slackening and tensioning opposite sides to correct it.

This is a budget stainless steel rim, and on the seam where the rim was welded it has 'nipped' in slightly but there is also a slight high spot. In such as situation, split any difference across either side of the rim. It is quite safe and there will be no ill effects in its travel once in use.

Tyres

Like many aspects of the classic and vintage motorcycle scene, there is a much larger range of tyres available today than ever there was a couple of decades ago, or even in the days when these machines were in production. What's more, the tyre companies have recognized that there is an enormous market for period-style tyres, and many of the traditional patterns are now available in super-sticky modern compounds. Add to that good-quality, suitably period patterns in previously obsolete sizes, courtesy of Eastern European and Asian manufacturers, which are perfectly satisfactory performance-wise for the machines they are designed to fit, and there is a tyre available for practically any machine. Even the owners of pioneer machines with huge-diameter, spindly beaded-edge tyres are these days spoilt for choice.

Of course, there is no need to stick with the pattern of tyre with which your machine was fitted when it left the factory – more than likely Avon's ribbed Speedmaster front and Safety Mileage squarish section rear – for that very company has developed a range of classic tyres that resemble the covers on the top superbikes. Take a look at their Roadrunner, Venom/Super Venom and Roadriders.

Dunlop still have a terrific following for their TT100 tyre, so named after the late Malcolm Uphill used them, when first developed, to score the first ever 100mph Production TT lap on the factory Triumph, and so beloved of the café racer crowd.

A look through any tyre specialist's website will throw up names such as Mitas, Continental, Firestone, Michelin, Heidenau, Ensign, Cheng-Shin and Maxxis, the latter being a subsidiary of the massive Chinese Cheng-Shin Rubber concern. Not so many years ago, there was a stigma attached to using the budget-priced tyres from the Far East as they were regarded, quite rightly, as being of inferior quality and standard – with regard to grip and wear rate – to European and American concerns. This is not so any more – the investment, research and development that these companies have put into their products is mind-boggling and they now meet all current world standards while still maintaining a lower end, mass market price.

Do not be tempted by a good-looking, cheaply priced top-make tyre on an autojumble stall. You can bet your life, if it's 'new old stock' it'll be years old and as hard as hell and akin to riding on wooden rims, especially in the wet. Don't risk it – buy a new one. A new budget tyre is far superior to an old stock famous name. What's more, it'll be difficult to fit because the walls and beads will be age hardened and probably a darned sight harder to remove when it comes to finally replacing it. Most tyres today have a date stamped on them.

You're bound to have noticed the various letters and numbers on the walls of tyres, which give you the tyre specifications. Take, for example, a tyre stamped 130/90-18 67 H: 130 is the section width in mm, 90 is the aspect ration (90 per cent), 18 is the rim diameter in inches, 67 is the load rating and H is the speed rating. You may also see something like this: 5.00 H 18 4PR. In this case, 5 is the section width, H is the speed rating, 18 is the rim diameter and 4PR is the ply rating or casing strength. Another style you may see is like this: MT 90 – 18 Load Range B; here M is the motorcycle code, T is the tyre width, code 90 is the aspect ration (90 per cent), 18 is the rim diameter and Load Range B is the load range.

Fitting Tyres

If you watch an old school tyre fitter at work, you'll be amazed at just how easily he can get that tyre onto the rim and often without recourse to tyre levers, simply by 'walking' round the tyre and pressing it further onto the rim with his boots.

For those not so adept with their feet, there are the tyre levers. They're not so bad on chrome-plated mild steel or stainless rims but on a soft alloy rim they can cause damage if they slip or if too much pressure is used.

If you've had your wheel built professionally, then you've probably got a good deal on a suitable tyre, fitted to the wheel at the same time, so now it's ready to fit to the bike; but if you've done it yourself, then fitting the new cover is the next stage.

Let's assume it's a case of tyre replacement, in other words there's a tyre to remove first. Deflate the tube by removing the valve and unscrewing the locking ring. Lay the wheel on a suitable surface, which will not scuff, and break the seal around the bead and rim by 'walking' on it. Insert the first lever close to the valve area and prise the tyre bead over the edge of the rim. It might be helpful to insert a second lever a short distance away from the first to ease a larger extent of the bead over. Resistance should be fairly minimal unless the tyre is old and the walls and beads have hardened. Once this area is over the rim, it can be just a case of pulling the remaining

section over, or a little persuasion by the levers may still be necessary. Push the valve into the well of the rim and remove the tube. Then push the tyre over so that the side still on the rim is close to its opposite rim edge, and prise the tyre off.

Inspect the rim tapes – actually strips of rubber these days – which give an element of protection to the tube from the heads of the spokes in the deepest part of the rim well. They're not expensive so replace if they have perished or look dodgy. Make sure the hole in the tape coincides with the valve hole in the rim, then inflate the tube until it's just round and push it into the new tyre. Then lay the tyre on the rim at an angle, so that the tube valve can be pushed through the hole in the rim, and screw the locking ring on by a few threads – just enough to prevent the tube from slipping round. Then, starting at the side opposite the valve, push one of the tyre's edge beads over the rim into the well and then slowly work your way around the rest of the tyre bead. Sometimes a smear of household soap helps – the traditional books always suggested French chalk, but it's not so readily available these days. Avoid washing-up liquid if you can, for while it's an excellent lubricant for rubber on steel, it does contain salts, which will corrode the

inside of your steel rim. The final six inches or so of the tyre may need persuading over the rim with your levers, but take extreme care not to nip the inner tube.

Now repeat the exercise on the remaining bead, starting opposite the valve and ensuring it's straight in its hole in the rim. Again, the final few inches might need recourse to levers, so push the valve right in as far as it will go without losing it, in order to minimize the chances of pinching the tube and puncturing it.

With the new cover in place, inflate the tube and check the tyre seats correctly on the rim. There will be a fine moulded line around the tyre wall, just above the bead, and this line must be a constant distance from the edge of the rim all the way around it. If it's not, try either bouncing the wheel when the tyre is up to correct pressure, or inflating further to see if it will blow out into place, before of course deflating again to appropriate pressure. Screw on the dust cap and your wheel is ready to roll.

The Rear Wheel

The process for renovation of the hub and the rebuilding of the wheel, with new rim and spokes, is exactly as for the front wheel. The difference lies in the manner in which the rear wheel

Push the tube into the tyre.

Lightly inflate the tube when in the tyre to prevent twisting.

Place the rim inside the tyre as far as you can.

Then with the beads suitably lubricated, push the remaining part of the tyre over the rim.

Having ensured that the tube is not trapped, proceed to push the outside bead into the well of the tyre.

With the bead lubricated, it is not difficult to push most of the tyre onto the rim by simply 'walking' it on.

Sometimes, however, that last section can be on the tight side and needs a little tyre lever persuasion. Be careful not to nip the tube and puncture it.

That's your tyre fitted.

ABOVE LEFT: Inflate to more than required pressure until the tyre wall pushes out of the well sufficiently that the guide line around the tyre wall is visible and an equal distance away from the rim edge all the way round. Once it is, release the air to the recommended pressure.

ABOVE RIGHT: Your new wheel and tyre are ready to fit to your bike.

Typical speedometer drive for rear wheel.

fits to the motorcycle. Whereas front wheel removal involves little more than undoing the brake cable, the fork securing nuts and driving out the axle, the rear wheel carries both the brake and the drive sprocket and in many cases, the speedometer drive too.

QD is one of many abbreviations concerning motorcycles. It stands for Quickly Detachable and is a bit of a misnomer, because while it generally

means that the wheel can be removed from the frame leaving the drive sprocket and hence chain tension and wheel alignment undisturbed, it's hardly any quicker than a non QD system.

In the case of rigid and plunger-framed Nortons, for example, the actual wheel hub bolts to the combined drive sprocket and brake drum by means of three long-bodied sleeve nuts, access to which is via four suitably spaced

holes on the opposite side of the hub, through which an appropriately sized box spanner or socket can be slid.

Triumph and BSA gave buyers the option of a QD or a non-QD hub, the former being a superbly machined, fine splined arrangement, which meshed the sprocket/drum to the hub – and cost more than the basic wheel hub.

Though the design of the rear mudguard on many such immediate post-war machines of rigid, plunger and even early swinging arm-framed designs allowed for removal of the rear wheel, via either a removable or flip-up tail section, allied, certainly in the case of the two earlier designs, to the large rear wheel stand, it's difficult to imagine any rider actually undertaking such an exercise these days, were he to receive a rear tyre puncture in the middle of nowhere, invariably in foul weather in the dead of night! Having said that, of course what we now call classics were modern in their day, and electrical, ignition, tyre and brake technology was nothing like as reliable as today, so breakdowns of some form or another were regarded as a hindrance that could regularly be fixed by the roadside. These days we call the recovery van, courtesy of our classic insurance policies.

It's not often that there's a need to remove the drum from the frame once your new wheel has been built, unless of course you simply find it personally easier to remove the wheel as a whole than mess around with the QD system.

Once a new rim has been fitted and the spokes have been tensioned correctly, it is often the case that the brake drum has distorted slightly, and when the brake shoes are refitted, they do not grip the drum surface as flush as they once did. This will be quite apparent, because when you apply the brakes, not only will they not work as well as they did, but they will cause the wheel to feel like it's egg-shaped. The answer is to take the wheel to a reputable brake specialist who will mount the wheel on a lathe and skim the drum circular again. Your new brake linings can also then be machined to fit the new drum surface perfectly.

Obviously this process cannot be repeated indefinitely, as the removal of metal from the drum makes it thinner and there is a limit to how many times this can be done – or should need to be done – before the drum is scrap. Should said drum be irreplaceable, then it is possible to have the drum's braking surface built up by means of metal spraying and then machining round, but this is an expensive and very specialist operation.

Speedometer drive on the rear wheel of a rigid-framed Norton.

Drive side of the QD hub on a Royal Enfield; note the male projections.

Wheel hub showing rubber insert. Male hub projects into these slots to form the drive with the rubbers acting as a shock absorber.

The brake drum and sprocket remain undisturbed in the swinging arm.

RIGHT: The wheel as a whole pushes back into place and the axle is threaded into place.

BELOW LEFT AND RIGHT: BSA QD fine-splined rear hub.

CHAINS AND SPROCKETS

While the wheel is out of the frame, have a look at the teeth on the rear drive sprocket. If they're short, broken or hooked, then your sprocket is past its best and will quickly ruin a new chain if fitted to it.

In a case such as BSA or Ariel's full-width hubs, the sprocket fixes to the hub by means of four nuts on four projecting studs, so purchasing a replacement sprocket from your favoured specialist is the easiest option. However, if the sprocket is integral with the drum, then it might be necessary to browse the internet to see if you can find a firm that will machine off the existing sprocket teeth and shrink a replacement sprocket onto what's left. Again, this is a precise and potentially expensive operation. Often, on scramblers and trials bikes, you'll see the rear drum rebated to accepted any variety of bolt-on sprocket size. That's another potential route to go down, albeit involving some fairly precise machining, though of course it's dependent on there being enough metal in the drum to accommodate the exercise.

If you do replace the rear sprocket, it's wise to replace the gearbox sprocket at the same time, though in practice not everyone does – and they seem to get away with it.

Have a look at the chain too. It's probably the most obviously neglected part on a motorcycle. By virtue of its position and its job, it receives all the road water, grit, muck, winter salt and so on and still has to maintain a terrific strength as it whips in and out of tension, top and bottom run, as you accelerate and then shut off.

Traditional chains are simple but exceptionally effective – a couple of rollers, held together by a pin through each, the ends of which are burred over a solid figure eight-shaped side plate on either side. Like any roller, they work best when the fit between the pin and the hole it's in is close, clean and well lubricated. Everyone will have seen chains that are dry and rusty with several batches of links seized together – a legacy of simple neglect and a prime way of wearing out the sprockets too.

In a case like this, it's not enough to merely oil the chain. It must be removed, soaked in paraffin or diesel, or something similar that will penetrate the links with an oily residue, for a few days and then given a thorough scrub with a brush to remove as much muck and corrosion as possible. Work the links back and forth in the diesel until they all move freely, then give it a good degreasing and if you've access to a pressure washer, use that to blast out all the degreaser. You'll be amazed at how much muck still comes out. In the classic era, it was common to boil up your chain in proprietary waxes such as Linklyfe, which was a black wax you melted in a pot on your kitchen stove. You then dropped your chain in and let it set before excavating the chain from the mass. The wax was said to penetrate the links and the rollers. Since then various oils, waxes and other such chemicals have been developed, some of which don't show on the chain at all, other than as an initial wetness.

These latter substances are designed for the modern O-ring chain, where the link has a miniature O-ring between the side plate and the roller pin, thus keeping the muck out and the lubrication in.

Once you've cleaned and dried your rear chain, hold it out between outstretched arms and try and bend it into an arch shape. If it takes the form of a rainbow, then you've just wasted half an hour cleaning a worn-out chain. Wipe some oil over it and put it somewhere safe to be used again. If it's worn out, why keep it? These things 'always come in handy'. For example, an old chain is ideal to wrap around the gearbox sprocket and rear wheel sprocket temporarily to keep

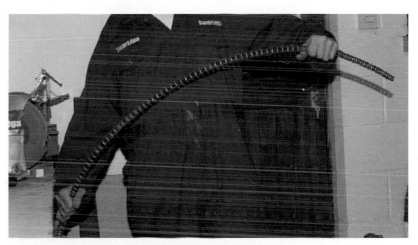

If you can do this with your chain, then it's time for a new one.

New chain with a split link.

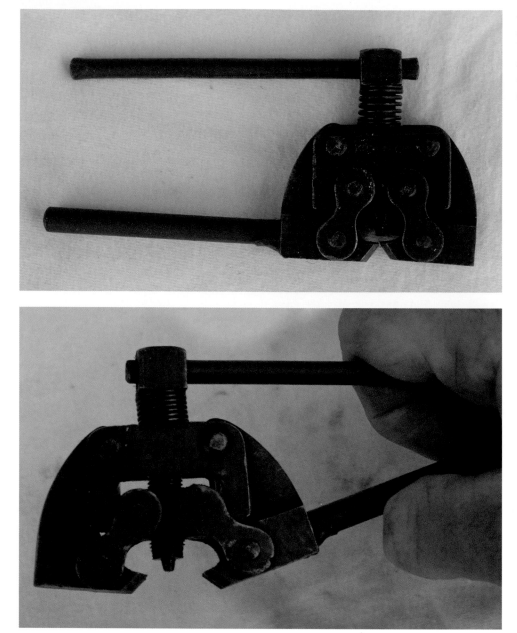

A good-quality link remover will last a lifetime. This one started life in the RAF in 1940s North Africa and is still doing sterling service today.

the former from turning when trying to undo it; it's useful as a form of puller, when perhaps something like an old nail or a nut and bolt can be used to hold one link through to the other to form a loop in order to prise something; and if for whatever reason you need to remove the new chain, say to give it a good clean, it's useful to fasten the old chain to it to run it off the sprockets, leave the old chain in place, then fasten the clean chain to it again to run it back onto the sprockets. You'll be amazed at how useful an old chain can be!

Always buy your chains from a reputable source. There are one or two specialist chain experts who advertise in the classic press and are regularly found at the major autojumbles. They will advise you on which is the best for your machine and give you options on cheaper chains, should you be working to a tight budget. Just because it looks right, does not necessarily mean it is right. For example, a mass of cheap chains appeared on the autojumble circuit a few years ago, which was snapped up quickly by less knowledgeable enthusiasts who soon began to wonder why their sprockets were wearing out so quickly. It transpired that the chain in question, while the correct size for many classics, was actually a drive chain for fork-lift truck hoists, which do not have rollers. As such, the fixed centre part of the link was 'rolling' on the sprocket itself and wearing it.

There is still the odd emporium where 'new old stock' ex-factory spares stock can be found, but in general, our everyday classics are well catered for by the marque specialists who ensure their remanufactured pattern parts are of exacting standards.

FORKS

Telescopic forks seem to hold a certain mystery about them, which tends to unnerve the inexperienced restorer, when in actual fact they're quite simple and don't contain that many parts. What they can be, though, is a bit awkward to work on.

Their make up consists of the sliders – the painted or polished tubes at

Norton's Roadholder forks were for many years the yardstick fork.

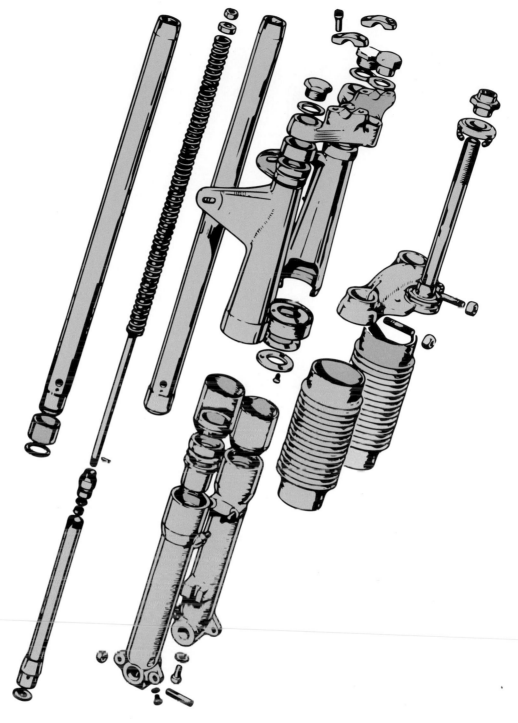

the bottom through which the axle pokes; the stanchions – the steel tubes inside; the bushes – the short bronze tubes that go over the stanchions but inside the sliders; the oil seal holders – the chrome-plated or painted tubes that screw down on to the top of the sliders; the oil seal – the rubber ring with a spring in it that sits in the oil seal holder and through which the stanchion passes; and the springs – the long coil springs that fit inside the stanchions and the steel top nuts, which hold the assemblies together

once they're in the yokes. The sliders will have some form of plug at their lowest point to allow drainage of oil.

The yokes, either steel or alloy, hold the forks to the frame. The bottom yoke is usually quite substantial and holds the head stock stem, the tube that fits up inside the headstock tube on the frame. The stem pokes up through the top of the headstock tube, and the top yoke then connects to it.

Traditionally, around the base of the headstock tube, on the upper flat face of the bottom yoke, is a cup,

essentially a steel ring with an outer face machined to the profile of a quarter circle, in which steel ball bearings of around a quarter-inch diameter are held in place by copious amounts of thick grease. This mates with an identical but handed cup inverted within the bottom of the headstock tube to form a track, which holds the balls in place but allows them to turn freely against each other. There is a matching cup arrangement at the top of the headstock stem too, and the bottom yoke is held in place at this point by an internally

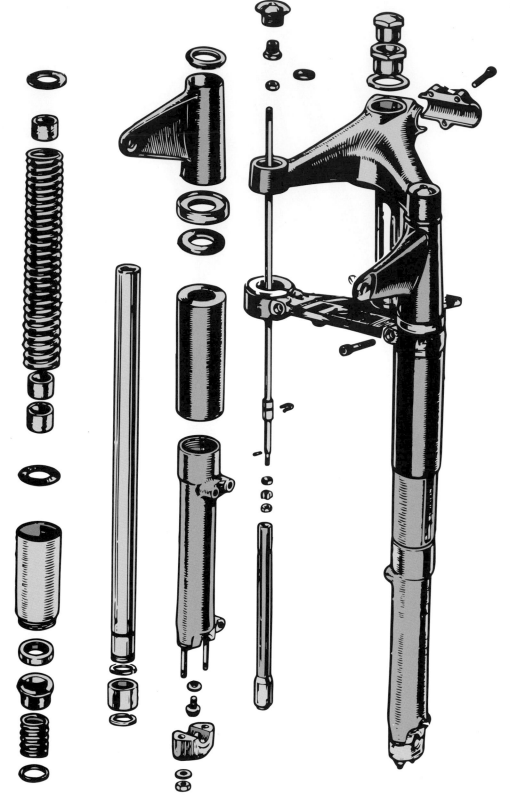

AMC's own Teledraulics were also an excellent fork. Indeed they were the first to be fitted to WD machines, making them the favourite machines of the despatch riders.

threaded nut through the top yoke centre hole.

The fork stanchions often have a tapered top, about an inch or so long, to aid their pulling up through the top yoke holes by the fork top nuts. When the forks are in position, they are held so by a pair of pinch bolts, which tight-en the slotted sections of the bottom yoke through which they pass, against the stanchion.

There's not a lot that can go wrong with the forks other than deteriora-tion caused by neglect, damage or simply wear. A bike that's been stand-ing for years may have stiffened up in the fork department through lack of movement and as such may need a bit of brute force to get them apart; likewise, if they've been run with in-sufficient damping oil, the springs will have seen better days. If they've taken a knock, they could be bent or the yokes twisted. You'll soon know,

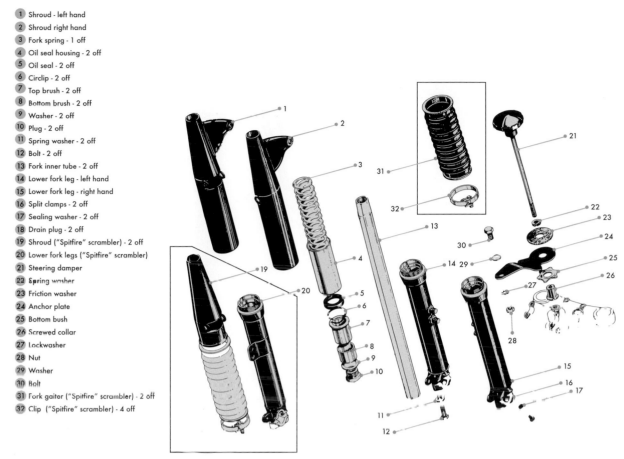

1. Shroud - left hand
2. Shroud right hand
3. Fork spring - 1 off
4. Oil seal housing - 2 off
5. Oil seal - 2 off
6. Circlip - 2 off
7. Top brush - 2 off
8. Bottom brush - 2 off
9. Washer - 2 off
10. Plug - 2 off
11. Spring washer - 2 off
12. Bolt - 2 off
13. Fork inner tube - 2 off
14. Lower fork leg - left hand
15. Lower fork leg - right hand
16. Split clamps - 2 off
17. Sealing washer - 2 off
18. Drain plug - 2 off
19. Shroud ("Spitfire" scrambler) - 2 off
20. Lower fork legs ("Spitfire" scrambler)
21. Steering damper
22. Spring washer
23. Friction washer
24. Anchor plate
25. Bottom bush
26. Screwed collar
27. Lockwasher
28. Nut
29. Washer
30. Bolt
31. Fork gaiter ("Spitfire" scrambler) - 2 off
32. Clip ("Spitfire" scrambler) - 4 off

BEARING

The BSA telescopic fork shows that the basic principle is the same as all the others.

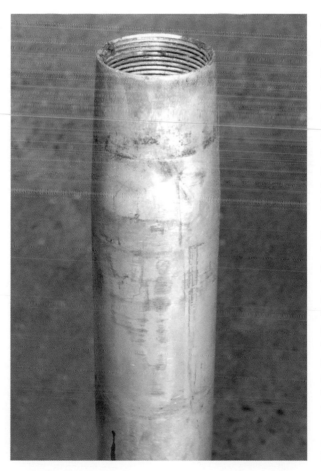

Fork stanchions usually have a tapered top section to make drawing into the top yoke easier.

though, by the effort needed to dismantle them.

Taking the worse case scenario, that is they're bent – and we're not talking visibly bent here, just a case of not quite straight – they can be straightened quite safely, albeit by a specialist. New stanchions are not expensive in the great scheme of things, however, so why spend almost as much having your old bent ones repaired? Again, it's your choice.

The most important aspect, apart from being straight, is the amount of wear between the bushes and the stanchion, an area in motion whenever the bike moves. If there's obvious wear and the bushes are sloppy, then, armed with your measuring callipers, compare the diameter of the area of tube where the bushes work to an unworn section of the tube; this will help you ascertain whether it's the tube that's worn, in which case new bushes will make no difference.

You then have two options: buy a pair of replacements or have the originals hard-chromed.

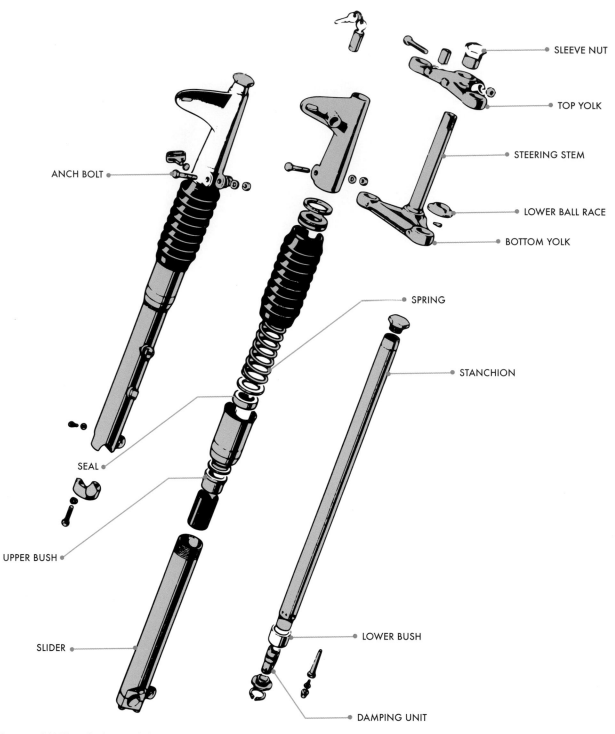

SLEEVE NUT

TOP YOLK

STEERING STEM

ANCH BOLT

LOWER BALL RACE

BOTTOM YOLK

SPRING

STANCHION

SEAL

UPPER BUSH

SLIDER

LOWER BUSH

DAMPING UNIT

Late-type BSA-Triumph telescopic forks.

If the fork stanchions are to run exposed between the yokes and between the bottom yoke and the top of the slider, then hard-chroming is a must – and even if they're not exposed, it's an excellent long-term treatment for the stanchions.

The specialist will first check the stanchion for cracks, damage and straightness, and, as mentioned above, if they are slightly bent, will straighten them on a press. Then an unworn section of the tube will be measured before the tube is ground down to remove all pitting and light damage. The stanchion will now be considerably undersize, so it is then immersed in a plating vat where a layer of chrome plate is applied to the surface. Unlike decorative chrome, hard chrome is a metal replacement and is applied to the stanchion in such a thickness that on removal from the vat, it is bigger in diameter than originally. It is then ground down to the size of the unworn section of original tube. It has a very smooth, but semi-matt finish, which, when allied to new bushes, makes for a super-smooth fork operation. It is also very tough, withstanding most everyday knocks, and is resilient in the face of bad weather and corrosion.

It's invariably going to be a more expensive exercise than buying replacements, so it's up to you. New bushes, oils and oil seal holders are all available

TOP: existing BSA Gold Star fork stanchions with bushes. BELOW: replacement hard-chromed stanchions with bushes.

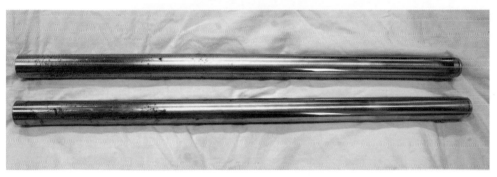

Fork legs before hard chrome-plating.

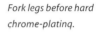

Fork legs after hard-chroming.

from your marque specialist. Removal of oil seal holders can be tricky, especially if they've not been disturbed for decades, but if they're rusty, don't mess around, get some big grips on them and make them have it. Once the slider is refurbished, make sure the threads are clean where the oil seal holder screws on, because sometimes, on pattern oil seal holders, the internal threads have a minute layer of chrome plate on them, which makes the thread just that little bit tight. Tighten them up as far as you can by hand then finish them off with a leather strap spanner

or a loop of rope – something that will turn them without damaging the plating. Don't forget the oil seal always has the spring side facing the oil it has to retain, so in the case of forks, it's spring down into the slider.

If you look at your fork stanchion, at the base you'll see a series of small holes and you'll notice that the bushes slide over these holes. This is the principle of the damping. The fork tubes contain oil, and as the forks compress, the oil is forced out of the tube into the slider; depending on the position of the bush, this may be restricted, thus

preventing the fork stanchion from bottoming. Insufficient oil or too thin an oil will result in minimal resistance – the fork will go straight to the bottom of its travel, under braking, with a clonk. Likewise, when stretched, say on a strong rebound, then the forks will 'top' in the same way.

Generally speaking, the spring pressure will be right, especially if they are still the springs fitted at the factory, give or take a few years of work. Heavier front springs are available when, for example, a sidecar is hitched to the bike.

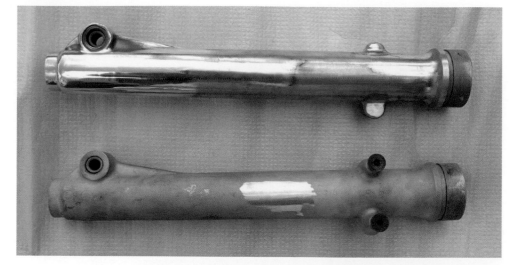

Alloy fork sliders post blasting and showing the area started to polish.

Fork sliders after polishing shows what can be done with the home buffer.

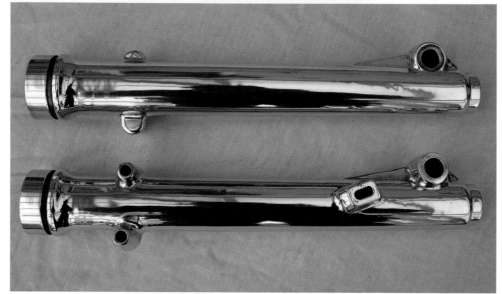

Typical brass bushes on a telescopic fork stanchion.

A good clutch makes riding so much easier. A high-geared machine like a BSA Gold Star can be especially hard on the clutch, so an aftermarket 'super' clutch like this NEB multiplate unit is a must.

6   *the engine*

If you haven't already, then the first thing to do is to put the engine somewhere where making a mess won't be an issue, and give it a thorough scrubbing with the degreaser, poking into all those little corners with an old screwdriver to get rid of the bulk of the muck and old oil. Then hit it for all it's worth with the pressure washer to get it as clean as you can and let it dry off.

The first step is to remove the primary drive to give access to the crankcases, which with a pre-unit engine you'll already have done to remove it from the frame. Norton stuck with their pressed steel and, it must be said, not particularly successful 'oil bath' system on all models right up to the launch of the Commando. It's an optimistic arrangement whereby the inner cover has a lip around its outer edge, onto which fits a thick, wide rubber band. The outer cover simply presses over the band and is secured via a single nut

that threads over the rider's left foot-rest fitting. It leaks – and always has, though there are better silicon-based sealants available these days if you're minded to use them.

An alternative is simply to run with the oil bath devoid of oil and use a proprietary chain wax on the primary chain, as you would on the main drive

chain. It does no harm occasionally to remove the cover and give the clutch bearing a squirt of oil, though, as it's only a five-minute job.

BSA, Triumph and most others use a screw-on alloy cover, a much better idea. Using the former as an example, remove all the screws from the outer cover, making a sketch and notes on

Before you do anything, get the thing cleaned up so you can see what you're doing (and you won't get so dirty).

which screw goes where in your book – most will be the same length but some will be a bigger diameter and others longer. With all screws out, tap the cases with a rubber mallet until the seal between inner and outer – probably years of undisturbed gasket cement and the remains of a paper gasket – breaks and the two halves can be separated. If they're reluctant, turn to the gas lamp to warm the cases up and soften the joint.

Inside you'll find the clutch, which will have to be removed, along with the primary chain and engine sprocket, to give access to the screws that hold the inner case to the crankcases; we'll look more closely at the clutch later.

It's a good idea at this stage to use some form of engine stand. It doesn't have to be anything elaborate – a few strips of angle iron bent to right angles and bolted to the crankcases will suffice, or you can invest in a fancy

LEFT: Norton's useless oil bath primary cover. Note the rubber band, which is supposed to seal the two pressed steel halves of the primary cover. It doesn't.

BELOW LEFT: BSA unit construction twin primary cover was as tidy as any.

BOTTOM LEFT: An engine stand, no matter how simple, can make life so much easier, as here with this Triumph.

BELOW AND BOTTOM RIGHT: Two suitably bent lengths of angle iron can make a perfectly good stand.

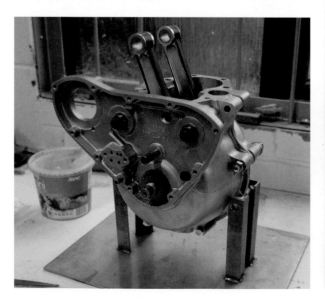

It doesn't matter what you use or how, as long as it works. The rear part of this engine stand was once helping to tie together two huge oak beams in the roof of a Tithe barn.

purpose-made job that not only holds the engine in place but also swivels so you don't have to keep turning the engine round in a complete lump on the bench, as long as you have some means of preventing the engine from rolling around.

THE TOP END

Hoist the engine up onto the bench and into its stand – be careful lifting here, even a single-cylinder engine is a heavy old lump. Apart from Norton twins, where the rocker cover is integral with the cylinder head, the rocker cover can be removed from the cylinder head simply by undoing half a dozen or so screws. Generally these screw downwards into the head. It's a good idea to remove the rocker cover inspection caps first, just in case there's a securing bolt hidden just inside, as inside the rear cover on BSA's A7/10 range.

Use a well-fitting spanner, preferably a socket – because you've room to do so – and expect the screws to be tight. If they seem overly so, don't be afraid to use the blow lamp. Heating up the job expands everything and can free up threads that are gummed up or rusted. Of course, there is always the risk that they will shear off, which naturally causes extraction problems later, but at least the rocker cover will come off. If the heads of the screws are rounded, that is the hexagon corners have been abused to the extent that the spanner will not grip, then as you'll be replacing them anyway, any means of loosening them is acceptable. If you have space to get some big grips

onto the head, fine; if not, then the best thing to do is find an open-ended spanner that is slightly too small and drive it onto the head with the hammer. It's crude but that screw will have to come out somehow. With the blow lamp having warmed up the case area where the threads are, use a long box spanner or some form of tube to gain serious leverage and let the spanner and the screw on which it's stuck have it. There's more chance it will free off than shear, so don't be afraid to apply some brute force.

Once the screws are all out there's a chance that the pressure on the one valve spring that is under compression may be sufficient to lift the cover off the head, but if not, do not, under any circumstances, try to prise off the cover with a blade or drive an old screwdriver between the mating faces of the cover and the head – that's asking for an oil leak. If it's stuck, again use the lamp to heat up the joint and then smack the cover with the rubber mallet. Try to hit a flat face rather than a lug, which may break. In most cases, the rocker gear is accommodated within the cover, apart from on BSA's unit twins, where the rocker gear sits on top of the head (akin to car practice), which makes it wonderfully accessible, and is protected by a simple alloy cover. Put the cover to one side and remove the cylinder head. Remove the pushrods one at a time, give them a good wash and then wrap a piece of insulation tape around either the inlet or the exhaust and make a note in your book as to which one is which. If you have a twin, then tape up both inlets, marking them one and two, and draw a little plan in your

book to show which is one and which is two, or use different-coloured tape, so they go back in the same place later.

Now, working in a kind of diagonal and opposite fashion, slowly loosen the bolts holding the head to the barrel a little at a time. If you have a dedicated service book or manual for your model it will show the correct sequence to loosen and tighten the head bolts. Make sure you have a look under the bottom fin too, for sometimes there's an odd fixing from underneath, which you may not notice at first but will baffle you when the head won't shift.

Some heads fasten down to the barrel, many have through bolts into the crankcases and some, such as BSA's pre-unit B range have fastenings that go up through the head to pull the rocker cover down. These latter fixings can be problematic if the corners of the hexagon have been worn because there is not a great deal of space for your open-ended spanner, and you may have to resort to driving on a smaller spanner as described above. (Be warned also that with the pre-unit BSA singles there's not enough room to take the rocker cover off with the engine in the frame, so it has to come in one with the head.)

With the screws/bolts undone, the head should free off its seat on top of the barrels. If it's stuck, try rocking it by hand, and if that doesn't shift it, put a soft piece of wood against it and tap the wood with the rubber mallet. Do not tap directly against the fins, especially if it's an alloy head, because they may break. If the bolts are different lengths, make a note on a diagram in your book about where each one fits. Move the engine on its stand to one side and bring the rocker cover into pole position on the bench, where the dismantling procedure can begin. You may well find, as you attempt to undo the nuts on the cover, that odd ones may be stuck to their studs, which duly unscrew from the cover. You have to be careful now not to damage the threads that screw into the cover, while trying to remove the nut from the other threaded section. If the nut is not overly stuck, then a pair of pliers on the plain section between the threaded sections will usually suffice. Alternatively, there's the age-old lock nuts method that involves screwing

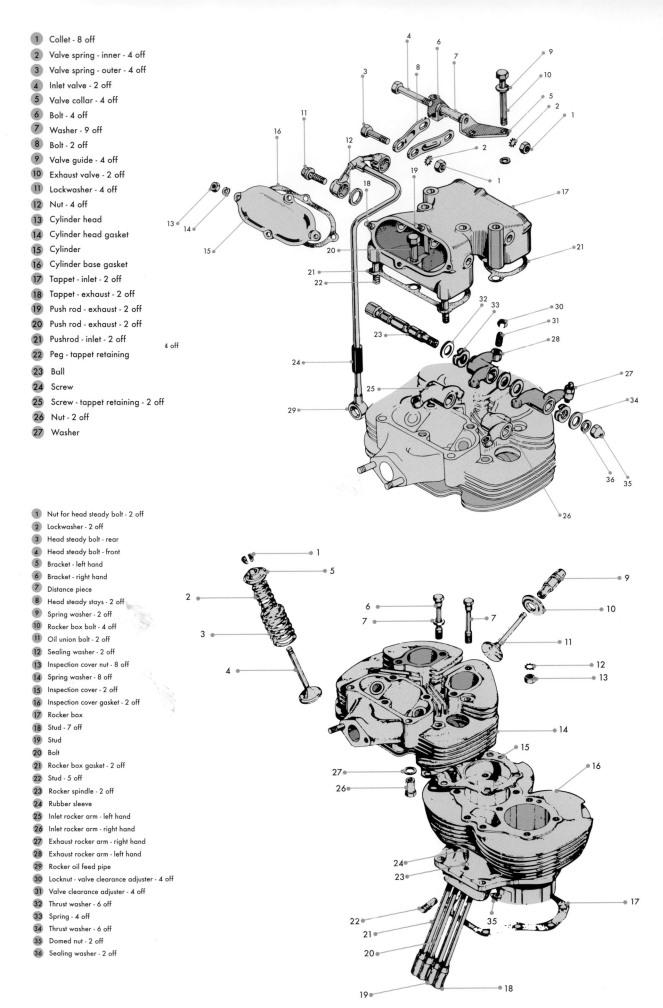

1. Collet - 8 off
2. Valve spring - inner - 4 off
3. Valve spring - outer - 4 off
4. Inlet valve - 2 off
5. Valve collar - 4 off
6. Bolt - 4 off
7. Washer - 9 off
8. Bolt - 2 off
9. Valve guide - 4 off
10. Exhaust valve - 2 off
11. Lockwasher - 4 off
12. Nut - 4 off
13. Cylinder head
14. Cylinder head gasket
15. Cylinder
16. Cylinder base gasket
17. Tappet - inlet - 2 off
18. Tappet - exhaust - 2 off
19. Push rod - exhaust - 2 off
20. Push rod - exhaust - 2 off
21. Pushrod - inlet - 2 off
22. Peg - tappet retaining
23. Ball
24. Screw
25. Screw - tappet retaining - 2 off
26. Nut - 2 off
27. Washer

1. Nut for head steady bolt - 2 off
2. Lockwasher - 2 off
3. Head steady bolt - rear
4. Head steady bolt - front
5. Bracket - left hand
6. Bracket - right hand
7. Distance piece
8. Head steady stays - 2 off
9. Spring washer - 2 off
10. Rocker box bolt - 4 off
11. Oil union bolt - 2 off
12. Sealing washer - 2 off
13. Inspection cover nut - 8 off
14. Spring washer - 8 off
15. Inspection cover - 2 off
16. Inspection cover gasket - 2 off
17. Rocker box
18. Stud - 7 off
19. Stud
20. Bolt
21. Rocker box gasket - 2 off
22. Stud - 5 off
23. Rocker spindle - 2 off
24. Rubber sleeve
25. Inlet rocker arm - left hand
26. Inlet rocker arm - right hand
27. Exhaust rocker arm - right hand
28. Exhaust rocker arm - left hand
29. Rocker oil feed pipe
30. Locknut - valve clearance adjuster - 4 off
31. Valve clearance adjuster - 4 off
32. Thrust washer - 6 off
33. Spring - 4 off
34. Thrust washer - 6 off
35. Domed nut - 2 off
36. Sealing washer - 2 off

The BSA A7/A10 cylinder head.

RIGHT: When the rocker cover is fitted to the A7 head there is no means of guiding pushrods into their rocker cups, hence the special comb.

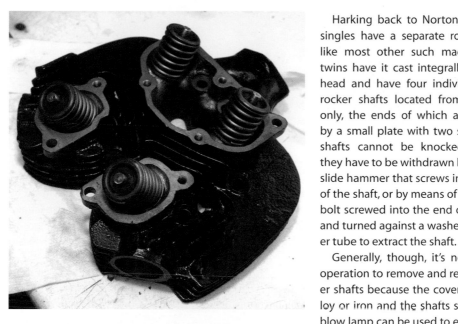

BELOW: The BSA A7A/10 rocker cover needs a special comb to align the pushrods into the rockers when fitting the cover to the head .

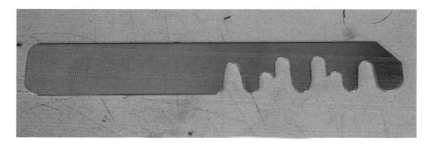

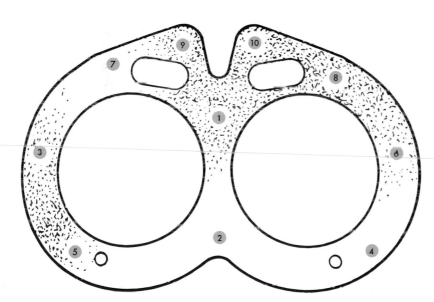

Typical sequence of loosening and tightening the Norton twin-cylinder head, as recommended by the factory to avoid distorting the alloy heads.

Harking back to Norton, while the singles have a separate rocker cover like most other such machines, the twins have it cast integrally, with the head and have four individual short rocker shafts located from one side only, the ends of which are covered by a small plate with two screws. The shafts cannot be knocked through: they have to be withdrawn by a special slide hammer that screws into the end of the shaft, or by means of a threaded bolt screwed into the end of the shaft and turned against a washer and spacer tube to extract the shaft.

Generally, though, it's not a major operation to remove and replace rocker shafts because the cover will be alloy or iron and the shafts steel, so the blow lamp can be used to ease removal by means of a drift. Don't hammer directly onto the threaded end – use something soft like a lump of brass or copper about the same thickness as the shaft hole, and hammer against that so you don't burr up the threads. As the shafts make their way out of the cover, the washers, and eventually the rocker arms themselves, will drop out – unless it's a Triumph twin, where there is a knack in getting them in and out of the limited access and they only go in one way. Again mark up which is exhaust and which is inlet.

The point of the rocker arm is to transfer the cam's lift to the valve via the pushrod, so one end has a cup into which the pushrod fits, and the other has a screw adjuster to give the required clearance against the head of the valve stem. These turn on the shaft and are allowed to float slightly sideways by virtue of Thackray washers; these are like flat springs with just a couple of coils, and bear against stock flat washers to prevent contact with the side of the cover itself. The shaft itself will have a spiral machined into it and a hole or two through from its hollow centre, through which oil passes to lubricate the rocker arms on the shaft.

Once out, it's just a case of giving them a thorough clean, making sure the shaft centre and its holes are clear and inspecting for wear, making sure the threads on the adjusters are in good condition and so on. The foot of the rocker arm, which swipes against the valve stem, is the area that will wear most. If it's badly worn, then it's a

two nuts tight up against each other on one end, which essentially locks the stud. It can then be placed in a vice and with the help of a little penetrating fluid, the stuck nuts can be readily freed off. A brace of spanners on the lock nuts undoes them and then once cleaned up, the stud can be replaced in its hole (duly cleaned out of course), secured with a dribble of threadlock and tightened into place by means of the aforementioned lock nuts on the other end. Once in place, the lock nuts are removed and the stud is ready to take on its normal role, in its normal manner.

ABOVE: B33 BSA project about to commence restoration.

LEFT: The cylinder head to barrel studs on a BSA pre-unit single.

case of either buying pattern replacements or having the foot built up with an appropriate metal and reground to the correct profile, which is obviously a specialist job.

The shafts fit into the cover metal to metal, so it's unsurprising that these areas have a tendency to weep oil. If it bothers you, ask your parts specialist about having a groove machined into the shaft into which a tiny rubber O-ring can be fitted prior to refitting. Now is the time, should you wish to do so, to have the rocker cover blasted and/or polished. It's not necessary, but a polished alloy cover on top of a black painted iron head always looks good. Don't forget to give it a thorough purging afterwards, though, to get rid of all the swarf. A domestic dishwasher does a terrific job but bear in mind that it uses salt, so make sure the cover is thoroughly rinsed afterwards otherwise it will soon be covered in a white corrosion. Then give everything a good blowing-through with the compressed air gun.

Reassembly is simply the reverse operation. Warm up the cover, oil the shaft and feed it through so far, fit the washers and Thackrays in the appropriate order, then the rocker arms, steadily tapping the shaft through until it's all the way home. Once in place, give the shaft a shot or two of oil and tip the cover on its side to allow the oil to run down and percolate around its regular route. As the rocker feed is at the end of the oil circulation system, invariably taken off the return pipe, it is one of the last places to get any oil,

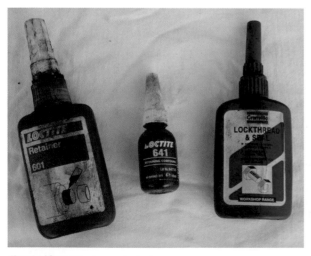

Chemical fasteners are amazingly strong.

The Norton twin rocker box has four individual rocker shafts, each accessed and withdrawn from beneath the cover plates.

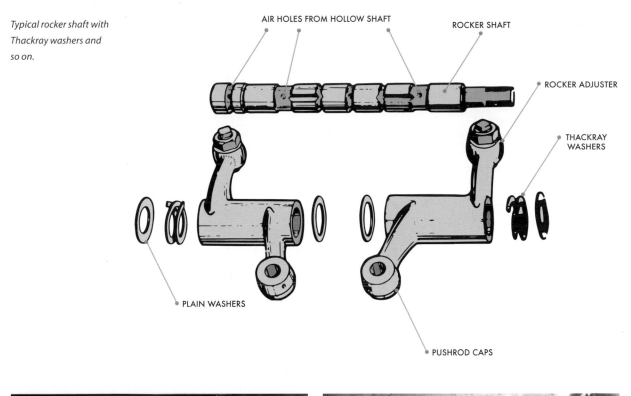

Typical rocker shaft with Thackray washers and so on.

AIR HOLES FROM HOLLOW SHAFT

ROCKER SHAFT

ROCKER ADJUSTER

THACKRAY WASHERS

PLAIN WASHERS

PUSHROD CAPS

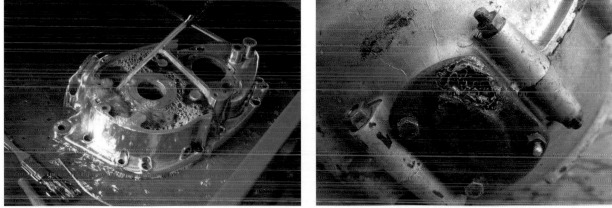

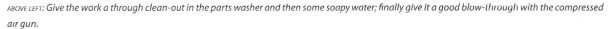

ABOVE LEFT: Give the work a through clean-out in the parts washer and then some soapy water; finally give it a good blow-through with the compressed air gun.

ABOVE RIGHT: These cases had stripped the thread of one or two screws and larger screws of the wrong thread had been forced in, making the holes even worse. The only answer was to have the hole welded up, re-drilled and tapped back to standard size (see the last picture in the Reassembly sidebar at the end of this chapter).

so it's wise to have some there on initial start-up, as it will have to look after itself for a few minutes before the circulating oil gets round to it. Something to remember when the engine is rebuilt – leave the rocker feed pipe off until you see the oil appear from it, so you know it's circulating around the rocker gear. Another little tip is, once the return pipe in the oil tank is squirting away merrily, put your finger over it for a few seconds. This will essentially pressurize the system and thus force the oil up the rocker feed pipe.

With regard to nuts, bolts, studs and so on, if the threads or the heads are damaged or in poor condition, then pattern replacements are available. If the threads, particularly those directly into the alloy – some alloy parts, such as cylinder heads themselves, have a bronze insert shrunk into the alloy to better accept the load on the thread – are damaged, it's a case of either drilling out the hole and tapping for a larger-diameter stud, at least at one end, or having the hole welded up and re-drilled and tapped to accept the new, standard-size stud.

Of course, if your chosen project is a side valve model then you have no rocker gear to deal with at all, just a flat cylinder head.

THE CYLINDER HEAD

With the side valve cylinder head, all there is to do is simply undo the nuts holding it down to the top of the barrel and lift it off. Iron or alloy, it's then just a case of cleaning out all the carbon from the combustion chamber and making sure the threads in the plug hole are sound. Job done.

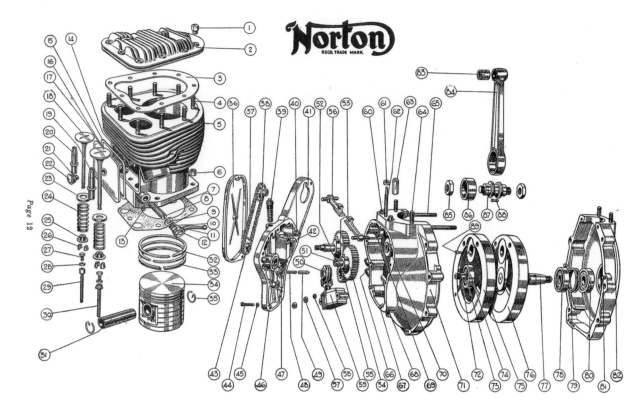

Exploded diagram of the Norton side-valve engine.

The overhead valve cylinder head is different, though nothing that should faze a first-time restorer, in that it contains the valves – hence its name. The valves are held in their seats, one exhaust, one inlet (or two of each in the case of a twin) by a tubular guide, a short coil spring, a cap and a pair of collets. The latter are essentially almost half-round section wedges, which push themselves into the central hole of the cap, around the valve stem and underneath a lip in the top of the stem. When the cam lifts the pushrod, it tilts the rocker arm, which in turn pushes down on the valve opening it; when the cam pressure is relieved, the spring closes the valve.

With a side valve machine, the valves are set into the barrel, alongside the piston, so the spring has to be compressed upwards to remove the valve from its seat; in an ohv machine they're in the head, so the spring has to be compressed downward. Hence different types of valve spring-compressing tool are needed, but the principle is exactly the same – squeeze up the springs, remove the collets and let the spring and the valve come out of their guide.

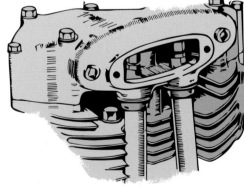

Access to tappet adjustment on side- and overhead-valve Norton engines.

The valve compressor is like a big G-clamp. The top end has a cutout in it, or has a couple of extended prongs to go around the valve stem, while the other end is an adjustable stop. Wind up the adjuster and the top cutout exerts a force onto the valve cap, which compresses the spring and allows the collets to be poked free. Once out, release the pressure, and the cap, spring and valve can be removed. Keep a note as to which valve is which if you're going to reuse them, especially if they're the same size – though it's fairly obvious, at least until you've spotlessly cleaned them, which is the exhaust valve.

The valve seats are a press fit in the head. They are a ring of hardened alloy, such as stellite, angled at 45 degrees, into which the valve head sits. This is a fairly general statement, as some tuned engines have two angles, even three, to maximize fuel flow.

Since the introduction of unleaded fuel in the UK, or rather the demise of leaded fuel, there has been much talk of valve seat recession. Essentially, the lead in the fuel acted as a cushion-cum-lubricant when the valve head beat down onto its seat. Without this cushion, it was feared that the seat would wear away – the valve head is a harder material – under the constant hammering. Should this happen, then the valve head would creep further into the port until clearance between the rocker and the valve is lost. This would in turn result in a loss of compression, power, incorrect contact between valve tip and rocker and potential damage.

In the event, it has been shown that this doesn't happen, and the panic that beset the classic and vintage movement was largely unfounded. That's not to say that should a machine be thrashed up and down a motorway at high revs for long periods of time, valve seat recession would not occur, it's just that in general, classic and vintage machines are not used overly hard and not for excessive periods of time. As such, unleaded fuel has not had the detrimental effect on cylinder heads that was originally feared, and those who rushed to dismantle their machines to have new valve seats suitable for use with unleaded fuel fitted, when their existing valve seats were perfectly serviceable, were proved to be rather hasty. Indeed, should valve seat recession ever occur over the long term, the cost advantage of buying stock unleaded fuel and waiting for the existing valve seats to wear out, over the immediate and continued use of 'special brew' leaded, or lead replacement fuels, will have easily saved what it costs to replace worn-out seats. Fuel additives are available, both in liquid and tablet form, which are said to help both lubricate and cushion the valves, as well as perhaps increase the octane rating of the low octane regular unleaded, so these are always an option, particularly for high-compression, high-performance classics such as BSA's Gold Star or the Velocette Venom.

Many later classics, such as BSA and Triumph twins and triples, Norton twins and similar, have unleaded-suitable valve seats fitted as standard, due to America's earlier introduction of the fuel. So, if the valve seats in your project cylinder head seem all right, leave them alone. If they're pitted, however, they can of course be cut back a little to remove the pitting. This can be done by hand, with a cutter that has a circular head with a series of 45-degree cutting edges and a central rod, which is inserted into the valve guide to centralize the cutter. It's then a case of laboriously turning the cutter until the pits are gone. Alternatively, if you don't fancy the effort involved, take it to a head specialist and let them do it on a machine.

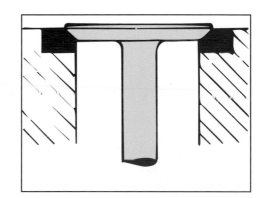

ABOVE: Central side-valve spring compressor flanked by a brace of ohv spring compressors.

RIGHT: Diagrammatic example of recessed and non-recessed valves.

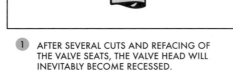

1. AFTER SEVERAL CUTS AND REFACING OF THE VALVE SEATS, THE VALVE HEAD WILL INEVITABLY BECOME RECESSED.

2. VALVE AS ORIGINALLY FITTED TO THE HEAD, OR WITH A NEW SEAT FITTED.

Then take the valve itself and pop it back into its guide, then with the traditional rubber sucker-headed wooden rod, stick it to the valve head and smear a little coarse grinding paste between the valve and seat faces, and spin the rod back and forth between the palms of your hands.

Once the seat and valve faces are consistent in finish, wipe clean and repeat with fine paste until they have a bit of sheen to them. That's really all that needs to be done, unless the seats and/ or valves are badly worn, in which case it's a job for a cylinder head engineering specialist. In this situation, you may as well invest in a set of new valve guides too and make a proper job of it. The guides are simply shaped tubes that are pressed into the head and through which the valve stem projects to 'guide' it in a straight line on and off its seat.

Valve guides in an iron head can be knocked out with a special tool, which is not difficult to make on the lathe. It's simply a strong steel rod, with one end machined down to a diameter that will fit snugly into the valve guide, the main diameter big enough to bear on the head of the guide. Hit it with the hammer to drift it out. If it's an alloy head, take care how you support it and rig up some form of pulling arrangement rather than driving with a drift. It can be done cold, as the expansion characteristics of the head metal and the guide metal are practically identical, for obvious reasons. Naturally, there has to be a clearance between the valve stem and the guide for the former to operate properly and this clearance will inevitably tighten up slightly as the engine gets to working temperature – which, in a combustion chamber, is mighty hot, often in excess of 1,000ºC – so at cold, there will be an element of slack. What may seem a lot to you, however, may in fact be about right, and when you change the guides there may be little if any difference between the new and the old.

Fuel additives come in various forms.

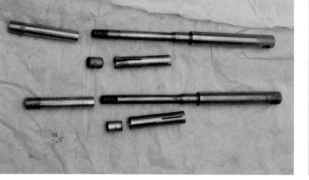

The component parts of the cutter guide.

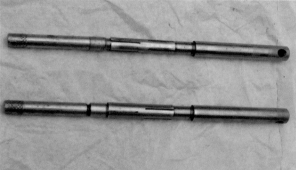

The cutter guide as it fits together.

The special tool for holding the Gold Star cylinder head at the correct angle for cutting while in the vice.

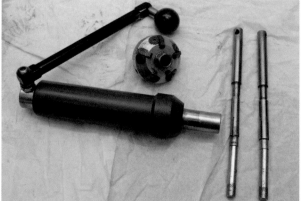

Cutter components, including guide.

Part of the cutter guide with an expandable end that fits into valve guide.

The main body of cutter guide is then inserted.

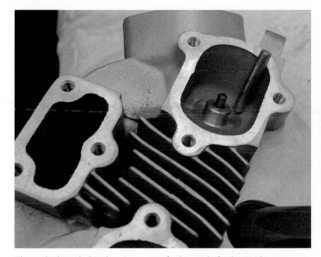

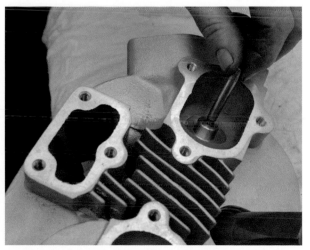

The male threaded end projects out of other end of valve guide.

The female end is screwed onto it, securing the guide true in the valve guide.

The cutter ready for action.

The cutter in place ready to cut a new valve seat face true, as it's lined up inside valve guide.

The cutter is turned manually until the seat is satisfactory.

The valve face is ground in to sit perfectly with its new seat face by hand.

Springs can, over time, compress a little, so stand them side by side on a flat surface and measure their height with a steel rule. Read up in the manual what the required length new should be. Unless there's a huge difference, give them a once-over and a good clean and reuse them.

A BSA A7 cylinder head combustion chamber showing the basic two-valve layout.

Note the inlet valve still has the original BSA piled arms logo stamped into its head along with 'in' for inlet and the part number.

With the head bare of its components, it can be blasted with any number of materials to clean it and give it the finish you require. If it's iron, a good dose of the sharp oxide will move any rust and get into those nooks and crannies; then it can be powder-coated, treated with a specialist heat-dissipating finish or merely given a few coats of the tried-and-tested cylinder black paint. Ensure all the threaded holes and the fins are clear of blasting medium – if you try to tighten down a stud into a hole that has muck at its base, it will eventually strip the threads, or worse, break the alloy around it. Poke them out with a piece of wire, wash them in the degreaser and then give them a good blast from the compressor. When they're clean, clean the threads out with an appropriate tap. If you haven't got one, ascertain what thread it is and then buy one, because you will find you'll use it over and over again (*see Chapter 3*).

Likewise, the exhaust valve still has its original marking on it. Obviously this head has not seen a great deal of use over the past half century.

A simple method of cleaning between the fins, or even polishing the top face of the fins on an alloy head, is to get a length of welding rod or similar and carefully cut a split into the end, into which you can wrap a length of emery cloth. Put the other end into your electric drill and you have an instant rotary tool.

Then it's simply a case of reversing the dismantling procedure valve by valve. Give the valve guide a shot of oil then slip the valve into it, fit any base bearing washer into place, then fit the spring or springs (some machines have a large-diameter spring with a smaller one inside it), place the top washer over the springs and use the valve spring compressor to squeeze

The Weslake eight-valve cylinder head and barrel was a regular conversion for Triumph twins. Dave Nourish of Nourish Racing Engines took over the manufacturing rights of the Weslake twin engines and these are still available in a variety of capacities.

Combustion chamber layout of the NRE Weslake four-valve head.

Four smaller-diameter valves actually allow in and out more charge than two larger valves.

Detail of the valve guide area from the top.

Valve layout from the top.

Tappet and pushrod layout is as per Triumph.

ABOVE: Four-valve combustion chamber devoid of valves.

LEFT: A finned rocker cover just adds a bit of sportiness to the head.

the spring enough to expose the collar at the top of the valve stem so that the collets can slip either side of the stem below the groove. On releasing the pressure, the spring will lift the washer around the collets and push them tight up underneath the collar to hold them in place.

A note regarding polishing of the head and rocker cover. Many feel that to polish an alloy head, rocker cover and, even worse, crankcase, detracts from its cooling capabilities. This is nonsense. Air still passes over and through irrespective of its finish; and even if it were the case, at least in the UK, our summer temperatures are rarely high enough to cause a problem, unlike say, on Australia's Gold Coast, where classic enthusiasts look forward to winter because their summers are simply too hot for air-cooled engines. Purists will tell you 'they never came out of the factory like that' and more often than not they'd be correct but that was down to economics of production: had you gone to the factory with a big wad of cash in your hand and requested that all your alloy be polished, your frame

RIGHT: The Commando exhaust screw can vibrate loose and damage the threads in the port.

FAR RIGHT: The iron head single works on the same principle but does not seem to suffer as much as the big alloy-head twins. Vincent also has the same system but they too do not seem to suffer.

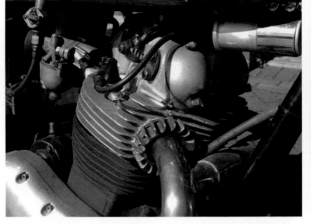

chrome-plated and everything else finished in bright pink, they would probably have been only too happy to oblige. So, if you want to polish, then polish and tell the detractors that that is exactly how you would have had your bike if you'd bought it new. After all, it is your bike.

Another point, which is particular to Norton, is the exhaust port screw. The exhaust pipe has a flange on the head end that pushed into the port up against a copper/fibre washer and is secured with a large-diameter rose, which screws into the inner face of the port. These can tend to work loose and the resulting vibration can damage or strip the threads within the port, making secure fixing of the pipe impossible. This is a common problem with big vibration twins, not so much so with the singles. New threaded units are available for the ports, but to remove the old and replace with new is a specialist job. Once renewed, or should your ports be in good condition, it is a good idea to tighten them fully and then drill a small hole in the rose and a corresponding hole in the nearest cylinder head fin and attach and tighten a length of lockwire to retain the rose in place.

Valve Guides

RIGHT: This Gold Star cylinder head combustion chamber looks like it's been running rich.

FAR RIGHT: The exhaust valve shows an unusual burn pattern.

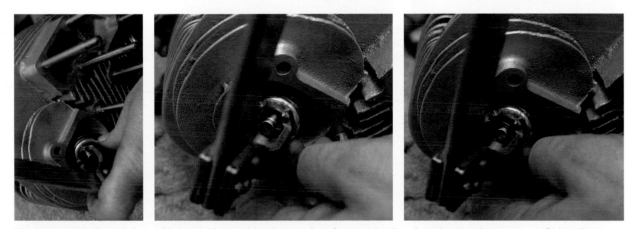

This shot was actually taken during the reassembly process but the procedure of compressing the valve springs to either remove or refit the collets is exactly the same.

Valve Guides *continued*

A lathe makes short work of cleaning up the valve.

On an iron head the valve guide can be drifted out, but with an alloy head it's best to pull it out, so first the old guide has a thread cut into it.

The outer section of the puller is pressed up against the head …

… while the centre part of the puller is screwed into the valve guide's new thread.

A nut is then screwed down the length of the centre section to put pressure against the outer section.

FAR LEFT: On tightening the nut, the centre section pulls the guide from its housing …

LEFT: … leaving an undamaged hole ready for a new guide to be fitted.

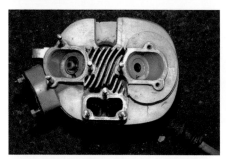

LEFT AND FAR LEFT: The alloy head is then seated on a gas ring to heat it up and expand the alloy, thus making the insertion of the new guide easier and a good fit when the alloy cools.

ABOVE LEFT AND MIDDLE: The new guide can be drifted into place.

The new guide in place.

The new guide will have 'nipped up' a little on being compressed into the head so will have to be slightly relieved internally with a smaller reamer.

The valve guide in place.

With the new guide fitted, it makes sense to ensure the valve seats are in good condition.

With the valve lapped into the seat using a combination of coarse and fine grinding paste, the face of the seat can now be examined for wear and tear.

The exhaust valve face has tiny pits and would benefit from a light refacing, so the cutting process follows as described in the text.

The valve is tried in its new guide during the reaming process until it moves freely, with adequate space for expansion.

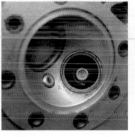

The valve is then lapped into a newly cut seat.

Valve guides and seats as good as new.

Time to refit the valve …

… the spring, collar and collets …

… job done.

Like new.

One fully reconditioned cylinder head.

Helicoiling a Plug Thread

Over years of use some threads become worn, and the spark plug hole in the cylinder head is a classic example: imagine how many times a plug has been removed and refitted over a life of fifty or more years. So, the answer is to fit a helicoil. These are spring-like items that act as a thread both externally and internally, that is the external thread screws into the hole and the internal thread accepts the stud, or in this case the spark plug. Let's go through the process with this Gold Star alloy head.

The plug hole with worn threads.

A suitable tap is inserted into the hole to cut a new thread to accommodate the helicoil.

The helicoil kit consists of various-sized helicoils, cutting tool and inserting tool.

The helicoil itself. The tang across the top is to aid the screwing into place and will be snapped off when the helicoil is in place.

The helicoil ready for insertion.

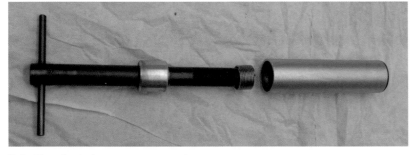

Helicoil insertion tool.

The helicoil is screwed to the base of the tool …

… and then screwed into the plug hole, the outer guide ensuring the helicoil goes in straight and true.

The helicoil in place; note the tang is still present.

Ensure the helicoil is all the way down to the base of the thread without protruding into the combustion chamber.

RIGHT: The tang is then snapped off with a sharp blow from the hammer and punch.

FAR RIGHT: The tang removed, helicoil fitted, plug hole as new.

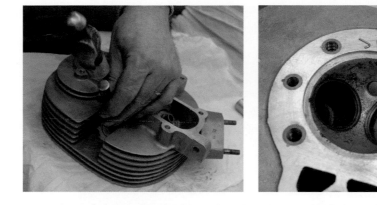

CYLINDER BARREL

With the head off the cylinder, you'll be able to see the crown of the piston and watch it move up and down the barrel as you turn over the engine – you can do this by turning the crankshaft nut on the end of the crank with a suitably sized spanner. If the piston crown is coked up with carbon, scrape it off carefully with something fairly blunt, such as the rounded end of an old hacksaw blade or a blunt screwdriver – anything that will not scour the alloy of the piston itself – until you can see the markings. Stamped lightly into the alloy should be something like STD, +10, +20 and so on, which represents the size of the piston – standard, 0.0010in, 0.0020in, the latter two being regular oversizes from standard and normally referred to as 10 thou' or 20 thou' (thousandths of an inch) over.

With all the necessary nuts and bolts removed, simply lift the barrel up off the crankcases. Again, a bit of heat or light persuasion may be required if they've been cosied up for several decades. The piston will lift to the top of its stroke along with it initially, then the barrel will slide up over the piston rings and free. Be careful here because the con rod, or rods if it's a twin or triple, will now flop to one side in celebration of their freedom within the crankcase mouth and the pistons will likewise flop sideways on their gudgeon pins. Turn the engine over so the piston is at its lowest position and cover it, or stuff an old towel around it. This not only protects the crankcases from entry of foreign bodies – not that it matters too much if you're intending to pull it apart further – but also gives it an element of support and protection.

The barrel on a single is simply that – an iron (or alloy) one-piece lump. On a twin it will contain the tappets, or cam followers.

These are exactly what their name implies, semi-cylindrical lengths of steel with a hardened, radiused foot, which transfer the rotary swipe of the cam into an upward-pushing motion to make the pushrod open the valve. These are usually located into their housing at the base of the barrel by a screw. In a single, they are usually like an inverted T shape, sitting within a guide in the top face of the crankcase. The hardened face against which the cam swipes can wear, and once the base metal is exposed the constant swiping action will eventually 'flatten out' the radius, causing valve timing and performance to be lost. If replacement tappets are unavailable, it is possible, as mentioned earlier, to have them refaced with hard material and ground to the correct profile. Speak to your favoured parts supplier, as he will know of a recommendable source. They are unlikely to wear along their sides, despite their restricted vertical action; the barrel housing in which they are fixed will be what wears, if anything. Unless they are ridiculously loose, it's not the end of the world – there'll be plenty of oil sloshing around them and the only real detriment will be perhaps a bit of a chittery rattle when running. A worst-case scenario will mean either replacement barrels or the fitting of a suitable sleeve – the latter being a fairly intricate and expensive engineering exercise.

Inside the barrel you may find one of any number of scenarios. If the machine has been stood motionless for a long time, the barrel's bore face may be rusty, and/or the piston rings may have stuck to it, there may be deep scores

With the cylinder head off, the piston crown shows the amount of carbon build-up.

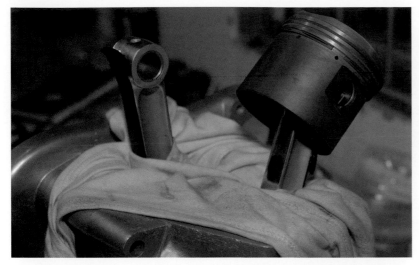

A rag stuffed in the crankcase mouth will save the heartache of stripping again on reassembly should something fall into the sump.

Triumph cam followers. The central follower is new, flanked by two worn items. Note the wear caused by years of swiping by the cam lobe.

Norton single cam followers have flat feet.

running the length of it, or, if you're lucky, it might just be nice and shiny. If it's the latter then feel around the very top and see if there is a distinct 'step'. If there is, or any of the other situations applies, then it's time for a rebore and a new piston or two. If, however, the step is only barely noticeable you may well get away with just a hone of the bore to 'glaze bust' it – essentially just roughing up the surface slightly – and a set of new piston rings. Find yourself a friendly engineer who has an internal micrometer and get him to measure the bore for ovality.

A piston, by the very nature of the crank's rotary motion, has a thrust face, that is where it is pushing against the cylinder wall on its way up. Eventually that face will wear, and as the bore becomes slightly oval the piston rings cannot maintain a perfectly circular seal and 'blow by' occurs – that's where an element of the unburned mixture escapes past the rings and when combustion gases and by-products are also allowed past the rings and into the crankcase sump, where they contaminate the oil. The exhaust will also blow out smoke when running. An element of ovality is acceptable, as piston rings can be very flexible in action, and most engines will run perfectly on anything up to 0.0005in – indeed Norton Commandos' maximum acceptable ovality is 6 thou'. It's very frustrating to find that an engine that has been motionless for years is perfectly satisfactory with regard to its ovality but has suffered damage where perhaps the pistons rings have corroded against the cylinder wall and eaten into it, thus necessitating a rebore, but that's the chance you take with a restoration.

The rebore procedure is quite simple, though not one which can be undertaken at home. It's a case of clamping the barrel into a suitable jig that holds it perfectly true and central to the cutter and then letting the cutter do its job.

The boring tool has a series of sharp cutting edges, and when turned within the cylinder, removes minuscule amounts of the bore's metal face. Before you go for the bore, ensure you can obtain the right-sized replacement pistons. If the rings have been stuck and damaged the bore or there's nasty-looking corrosion or a large step at the mouth of the barrel, let your chosen borer have a look at it first; his experienced eye will give you a better idea of just how much metal will have to be removed and hence what oversize of piston is required. Go armed with available sizes; so, for example, if your barrel is already 20 thou' oversize and it needs to go out another 10 thou' but only 20 thou' oversize ones are available, then you'll have to have the bore taken out a little more than would be preferred. Likewise, if the bore has already been taken out a good deal, say 40 thou' (1mm) then check to see if the next size out, usually +60, is available. If it's already out to +60, it's rare that a barrel will go out much more without the walls becoming rather thin, though +80 pistons are occasionally seen for Triumph. The best bet is to have the original cylinder lining removed and a replacement of standard size refitted, along with suitable pistons, which is another job for the precision engineer. At least that way, you'll also have a set of spare oversize pistons either to sell, to offset a little of the cost, or keep for years to come.

With regard to the pistons, if you can find genuine new, old stock then go for them. They may cost a little more than pattern replacements but you will be guaranteed that they were made in England during the period when the machine in question was in production, so will be dead right. It is often the case these days that original, almost household, brands have been bought by companies who then import Asian-made parts and sell them, quite legally, within the original company packaging, fooling the purchaser into thinking that the contents are as they were in the good old days. If you study your old piston inside and out, you'll probably see a name and a series of numbers here and there, which will not be on the patterns. That's not to say that said pattern pistons may not be of good quality, it's just that bad experiences with inferior products have been regularly recorded, and any piston that fails in operation invariably damages the barrel and may well cause considerably more damage if bits should drop into the crankcases. A cheap piston may not always be a bargain. Having said all that, if your regular specialist undertakes the bore, he will probably supply a perfectly satisfactory piston set, as his trading reputation depends on it. Indeed, there's nothing

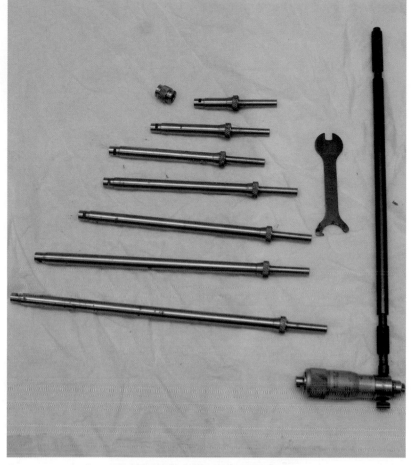

Component parts of internal micrometer for cylinders of varying diameters.

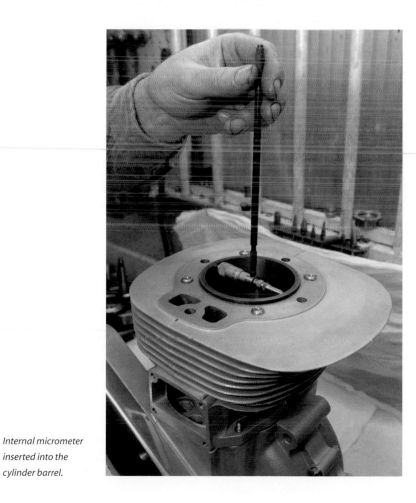

Internal micrometer inserted into the cylinder barrel.

When wound out, it will give a reading as to ovality.

The boring head is passed up and down the cylinder bore by hand to coincide with the unworn part of the bore. At this point the boring head has six self-centring feet known as cat's paws.

Gold Star alloy barrel with new iron liner ready to fit.

wrong with using a set of second-hand pistons, as long as they're sound and fitted with new rings.

Don't go mad with the compression ratio either. A slight raise in the pistons' rating, say from 7.5:1 to 8:1 or even 8.5:1 should see a slight power boost without detriment, but go much higher than this and you may find yourself with ignition troubles due to the only average quality of the fuels available at the pumps today. A really lumpy piston may have been happy in the 1960s with 5-star leaded petrol with a 101 octane rating, but today's grim, low-octane unleaded will give it a really bad time, resulting in pre-ignition, 'pinking', poor burning and eventually piston damage. What's more, it will be a darned sight more difficult to kick start and keep running evenly. A lower compression engine may not be able to cut it with the classic sports bikes but will be a sweet runner and a delight to ride. It is generally accepted that the cylinder heads of Norton twins, especially the Commando, have a perfectly shaped combustion chamber, which necessitates only a flat-topped piston to give an ideal flame path and excellent burn characteristics – hence good power – whereas Triumphs need a lumpy piston, which in turn causes a disturbed and much poorer flame path.

ABOVE: Refitting barrels. Note the piston ring clamps.

RIGHT: Pistons for a Triumph-based engine with NRE four-valve head. Note cutouts for the valves in the crown.

ABOVE LEFT: BSA Gold Star pistons from left, ranging from standard to high compression and, far right, racing.

ABOVE RIGHT: This Triumph piston would have been perfectly serviceable with regard to its cylinder ovality but luckily the hairline crack was spotted so the piston was discarded and a new pair sourced.

Reboring the Cylinder Barrel

While a fairly simple exercise for an engineer, the rebore process has an element of technical precision about it, which must be adhered to. In general, when your project machine was in manufacture, the company would strike a balance between longevity and performance when it came to considering the piston design and the choice of material for the piston itself and the cylinder bore material and the surface finish. Everyday engines do not normally have to suffer the stresses a competition engine does, therefore they run cooler, and quietness of operation is more desirable. New pistons normally come supplied with appropriate technical information and dimensions to enable the engineer to ascertain exactly what is required in the boring process. This information will give a specific bore size or a piston skirt dimension. So, if the piston measures 2.995in and the recommended skirt clearance is 0.005in, then the rebored cylinder diameter will be 3.000in.

Now, while it may appear round, a piston is in fact slightly oval; this is to accommodate thermal expansion and to take care of any deflection, which may arise from side loads. What's more, a piston does not have parallel sides, it is actually slightly tapered with a barrel shape. It is wider at the skirt (bottom), getting gradually narrower toward the crown, which will get so much hotter and therefore expand accordingly. In general, the measurement of a piston should be taken at the skirt and at right angles to the gudgeon pin.

With regard to skirt to bore clearance, if you have an original piston then the manufacturer's clearance data should be used; if it is a pattern piston, the metallurgy involved and the design configuration may be quite different so ignore the original maker's settings and work on those supplied by the piston manufacturer – if there are any.

Before you hand over the barrel to be rebored, ensure it is as clean as you can get it, as a left-over piece of gasket, a slight burr or any such deleterious matter may compromise the axis line of the cutter, resulting in a bore that is not straight.

Another small, but very important, point to consider is how the engineer will undertake the bore. If, for example, the engineer commences the bore from the cylinder head face downward to the skirt, there is a risk that, should the face have been skimmed to increase performance or perhaps alleviate slight unevenness or warping, then the axis line may again not be perfectly true. It is best if the bore is begun from the bottom flange to guarantee a true line.

It is general practice to rebore the barrel to 0.001in under the required finished size and then finish to the final size with a honing tool. This tool gives both the absolute correct dimension and the desired finish to the cylinder walls to maximize good bedding-in of the piston rings.

The honing head is made up of a number of abrasive stones held under light pressure against the cylinder wall and moved up and down its length. There are three aspects to consider when honing: the hone angle, the depth of cut and the surface finish. For an experienced engineer, the former two are assessed by eye, with

It is then inverted so measurement of bore is gauged against the unworn part of the barrel at the base.

The boring head showing three self-centring cat's paws and three angle single point cutter.

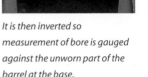
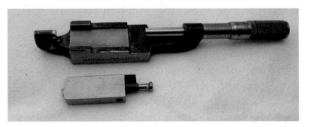

Bespoke micrometer to measure the exact length of cutter.

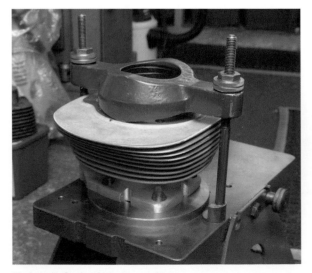

The barrel is fixed to the boring machine.

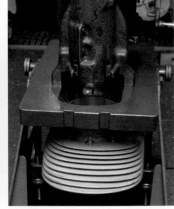

The boring head in place and ready to go.

The boring head at the bottom of its stroke.

cross-hatch patterns on the cylinder walls of around 35 to 45 degrees, which gives optimum oil retention. One set of hatch lines is created as the honing stones travel down the bore, the other on the upward stroke – the hone must rotate at a constant speed and traverse the bore at the same speed up and down. Abrasive levels of between 180 and 240 grit give a good balance of metal removal and surface finish.

Cylinder honing and glaze busting, while undertaken in the same manner, are quite different. The purpose of the former is to precisely finish a bored cylinder, whereas the latter is a means of removing the polished surface of a well-used cylinder.

Adjusting the honing tool to centre it in the cylinder.

The honing tool has plenty of length.

Bespoke jig for holding the Gold Star barrel in place in the vice.

The barrel clamped securely in its jig.

Another angle of cylinder clamped in the jig.

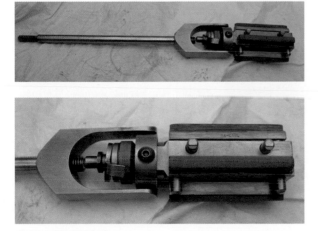

The actual honing tool.

Close-up of the honing head, showing its honing stones.

Always give the cylinder walls a through cleaning with a stiff brush, degreaser and even a pressure washer if need be, as the cross hatchings can harbour minute particles of abrasive loose metal and stone.

Reboring the Cylinder Barrel *continued*

Once back together, the piston and new bore must be run in. People have different views and opinions on whether an engine should be run in, and for how long and how hard. If the rebored surface has not been honed then the running in procedure must be undertaken very carefully, as there will still be minute high spots on the cylinder wall and the piston rings have to bed in with the new surface. It's usual neither to rev hard nor labour the engine for at least 500 miles, before gradually easing the engine to around normal use levels over the next 500 miles.

There are specialist running-in oils specifically designed to aid the bedding-in process, optimizing the lubrication and minimizing the effort. It would be wise to drain this oil at the 500-mile mark, as there are inevitably going to be elements of foreign bodies in it. It is also advisable at this stage to utilize a flushing oil to further cleanse the engine of any potentially harmful abrasives. Running-in oil is not designed to be used as a running lubricant, and instructions on its use must be carefully complied with. Fill up with the running-in oil again and undertake your next 500 miles before draining it away and refilling with your chosen regular, everyday oil.

Boring Equipment and Technique

The boring assembly pictured is a Van Norman Model 944, fitted with a rotary stand specifically for single-cylinder motorcycle barrels. The actual boring machine itself can be removed from the assembly and the rotary table revolved through 180 degrees. The barrel is then placed on top and aligned with the aperture in the rotary table before being clamped into place and the table reverted to its original position.

The boring machine is then placed over the barrel but not yet clamped into place, as it first has to be centralized in the bore. The boring head and shaft are passed down the bore by hand, to an area of unworn wall. The boring head has four self-centring fingers – known as cat's paws – that are then wound outward until they meet the cylinder wall, thus aligning the cutter dead central within the bore. It is then clamped firmly to the rotary table, the cat's paws retracted and the boring tool pulled back to the upper, start position.

The tool has a three-angle, single-point cutting tool, which cuts to the correct size using a special, integral micrometer, preset to the bore size required and no further.

The cutter is then set into operation and travels down the bore. The cat's paws are again extended, this time to support the overhang of the boring shaft. Depending on the amount of metal to be removed, it may be that more than one pass is necessary. Then the cutter is removed from the cylinder face and returned to the top of its travel before the exercise is repeated. Once the desired size is almost reached, the honing tool takes over for that final precise finish.

INTO THE CRANKCASES

With the barrel and head sorted, it's time to split the cases and see what lurks in the depths of the crankcases. While the engine is still in its support cradle on the bench, remove the timing cover; there'll be some oil in there, so be prepared to catch it when the cover to case seal is broken. Make a sketch of the cover in your book and then note how long each screw is and from where you remove it, so that when it comes to reassembly, you'll know exactly where the long ones and the short ones go. This is particularly useful if you choose to go with an Allen screw set, for example, which may not be quite the same lengths and may have to be cut to size.

Around the other side, you will already have had to remove the sprocket on the end of the crankshaft to enable you to remove the primary case. It will be located on a Woodruff keyway (a half-moon-shaped steel peg that fits its rounded bottom half into a cutout in the crankshaft and its square top half in a slot in the sprocket centre) and secured by a nut. Twins, and sometimes singles too, as in the case of the BSA Gold Star, often include a shock absorber on the crank too. This takes the form of a flat-faced spring that is tensioned up against the sprocket face, held in place by a castellated, dish-faced nut and secured by a split pin. This all assumes that the electrical system is powered by dynamo; on later machines the crank will carry a rotor, which spins inside the centre of an alternator fixed to the inner primary cover.

Though the principle is exactly the same and the layout very similar, depending on your make and model, there are a few differences. For example, with a Norton single, before you can go any further you have to remove the magneto timing cover, where you'll find two sprockets – one fixed to the end of the magneto, the other to the end of the crankshaft – over which runs an endless chain. Both sprockets are secured by nuts, but while the crankshaft sprocket is on a keyway, the magneto sprocket is on a taper. Do not under any circumstances try to prise these off their shafts because

Triumph bottom end. Note the markings on the crankcase to show that cams have quietening ramps – that is, the cam's profile has a less severe approach to the peak lift, thus making the movement less harsh and effectively quietening the operation.

the fairly thin alloy of the case will break. Draw on your patience and source a suitably sized puller for each.

Now you can remove the timing cover, but watch for the spring-loaded plunger, which governs the oil flow to the big end. Look out for a couple of countersunk screws inside the magneto drive case holding it to the crankcase, as well as the more obvious outer ones. You'll be faced with a nicely spaced out arrangement of pinions. There'll be a small one central toward the bottom, fixed to the end of the crankshaft, which is called a half-time pinion, then above it to the left and right there'll be two larger ones, one with the inlet cam on it and one with the exhaust cam on it. Right at the bottom will be the oil pump. This sits on two protruding studs and is secured by a couple of nuts; however, inside it is a worm drive, which mates with another worm, also on the end of the crank, so when the nuts are removed, the pump body has to be 'wound' off the studs on the worms.

The half-time pinion is so called because it conveys the crank's rotation to both cam wheels at once. It usually has a dash on it that corresponds with an identical dash on one cam, and a dot or similar mark, which matches one on the other cam; when these dots and dashes are all lined up, the valve timing is correct.

BSA's singles differ in that the magneto drive is by pinion rather than chain, so once the timing cover is removed access is gained to the cams, half-time pinion, oil pump and worm and an extra, large-diameter idler pinion that transfers the drive from the inlet cam pinion to the magneto pinion. It's called an idler pinion because it neither drives anything, nor is it directly driven by anything; it merely sits in a bush and acts as an intermediary, transferring rotation from one part of the engine to another, like Norton's chain. The oil pump drive, on the end of the crank, is a left-hand thread. While looking completely different to the

Norton oil pump, they are both gear pumps and work in exactly the same manner, only their means of drive is different.

The crankshaft sprocket, which drives and mates with the cam wheels, will need the use of a special puller to remove

With Triumph the cam wheels themselves have to be pulled off their cams, so again a special tool is required – and this is also necessary for refitting. The cam wheels also nestle in bushes.

Once removed, mark the wheels up 'EX' and 'IN' or similar with white correction fluid, or wrap a piece of wire or insulation tape around one and make a note of it in your book. You will see the cam followers, indeed with the cam wheels removed, they may actually drop out of their guides – again mark up which is which as it's imperative they go back in the same place, even if they've been refaced. Their guides are a tight fit in the crankcase and unless you're intending to have the cases blasted and/or polished, there's no harm in leaving them where they are. They can be drifted out if required, but be careful and get the cases as hot as possible to ease their exit because they will easily break. Again, remember to mark them up.

BSA and Norton twins, unlike Triumph, have a one-piece camshaft with four lobes on it; the BSA runs at the back of the engine, the Norton at the front. Inspection and removal

ABOVE: Magneto sprocket puller.

RIGHT: Magneto nut successfully removed.

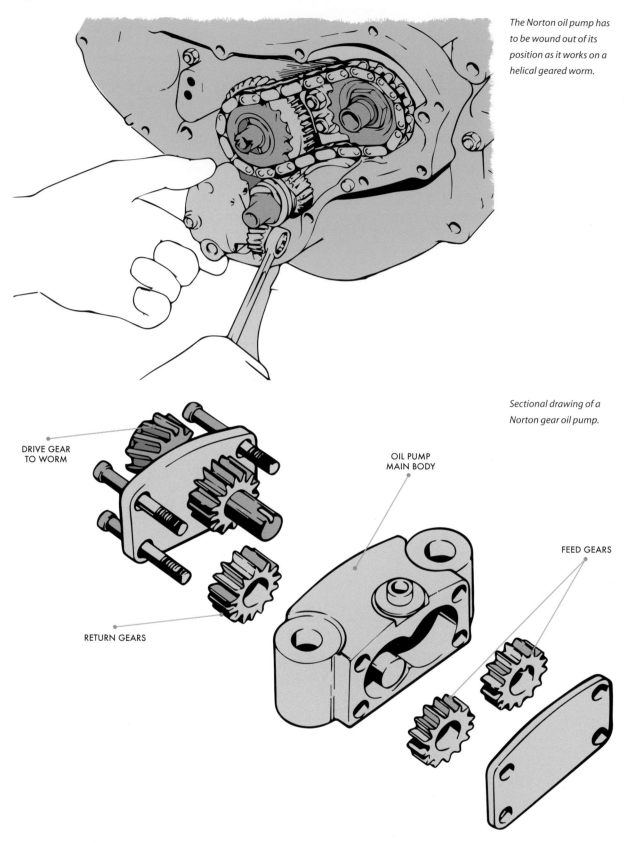

The Norton oil pump has to be wound out of its position as it works on a helical geared worm.

Sectional drawing of a Norton gear oil pump.

DRIVE GEAR
TO WORM

RETURN GEARS

OIL PUMP
MAIN BODY

FEED GEARS

is best undertaken when the engine has been split and you can work on the case half individually. If the crankcases have four long studs over which the barrel and head fit, they can easily be removed at this stage by the traditional locknut method. Screw one

nut down the thread so far, then add another above it and using spanners in the opposite direction tighten them together. Then with a spanner on the lower nut, turn it to undo. It will lock against the other nut and simply unscrew from the cases.

Now you can split the cases, so you'll have to remove your engine from its stand until reassembly starts. Make the usual drawing of both sides of the cases in your book and detail the length overall, head size, thread length and shank diameter of each

ABOVE: A universal puller is all that's required to remove crank pinions from a Norton single.

LEFT: A special puller tool is required to remove crank pinions on a Triumph twin.

BSA gear oil pump in its component parts.

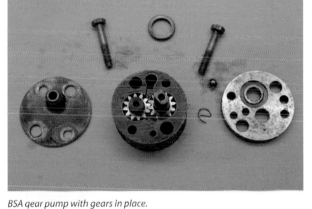

BSA gear pump with gears in place.

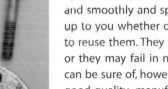

BSA gear pump with cover plate in position.

of wear, rust, pitting or the case hardening surface appears to be breaking up, then dump them. If they run cleanly and smoothly and spin freely, then it's up to you whether or not you choose to reuse them. They may last for years or they may fail in no time. What you can be sure of, however, is if they are a good-quality manufacturer's bearing, there's a good chance they'll be fine to refit. If you choose to buy new, then go for a reputable manufacturer, or take the advice of your local bearing factor. There are bearings on the market that will fit the bill and are very inexpensive but there's a likelihood they will have no manufacturer's markings on the outer race, though they should have a number. These will probably have been made somewhere in Asia, and while they may appear to be fine, who knows for sure just to what specification they have been made – if you fit them, you

bolt, nut, screw and washer and their place around the cases. With all bolts out, it's just a case of pulling the cases apart, though the bearings may have been in the engine since they left the factory decades ago, or they may have been changed.

Once they've had a thorough degreasing, study the balls and the race in which they run. If they show signs

ABOVE: Standard BSA gear oil pump and uprated race version.

LEFT: BSA gear pump assembled and ready to fit.

Triumph piston pump dismantled.

The Triumph crank pinion puller.

Triumph special tool to remove and refit cam gears.

may well be stripping your engine again rather sooner than you were hoping. Within reason, it's a case of you get what you pay for.

As regards the crank itself, a single is essentially a pair of flywheels with the con rod sitting on a pin, via a bearing, that joins them together. A twin is pretty much the opposite, with a central flywheel and a pair of con rods on a crank bolted to either side. All standard British parallel twins ran 360-degree cranks. That means both con rods and pistons go up and down together, firing 180 degrees apart. In other words, while one cylinder was compressing, the other was exhausting. A lot of Japanese twins ran a 180-degree crank, one up, one down, and lately it has become popular to built motorcycles with 90-degree cranks (or 270 degrees, whichever way you want to look at it), where one cylinder fires almost immediately after the other and then the crank has to turn through 270 degrees before they fire again. It is said to give the rear tyre a little more time to grip rather than being under constant drive, and therefore it is a popular configuration for racers of classic sidecar outfits. It also gives an uneven, Harley Davidson-esque chug to an engine, which is why, arguably, Triumph have used this configuration in their twin-cylinder cruisers and the Bonneville Scrambler – but this is getting beyond the remit of this book.

With a single, generally speaking, the con rod has a full-circle big end, that is, the con rod cannot be split, so once everything is cleaned, check for any noticeable up and down movement of the rod on its bearing – there should be none. Do not by misled by the inevitable side-to-side, rocking movement of the rod; it's just the up and down that's important. If it's sound, then leave it alone because that means the big end is sound. If you find that there is movement or the crank is in bad condition, then it's a case of having the flywheels split in order that a new bearing can be fitted to the crankpin/rod. This is pretty much a job for a specialist, or at least someone with past experience of such a task, mainly because it's quite difficult actually to split a crank without proper tools and even more so to reassemble once repaired, without the use of a hydraulic press. What's more, the complete crank assembly then has to be statically balanced to avoid excessive vibration. Without wishing to get too technical, this is where the combined weight of the con rod, its bearings and piston are balanced out by adding weights to, or by removing metal from the flywheel 180 degrees opposite. When in balance, the crank, when supported by its shafts on rollers, will stay exactly where it is positioned.

With a single, the crank's shafts are pressed into the flywheels. Sometimes one or more of these may be too slack, in which case machining may have to take place on the flywheel female part and the shafts may have to be built up, either with weld or by metal spraying,

Triumph cam gear.

BELOW LEFT: Norton cam gear showing timing dots.

BELOW RIGHT: Triumph cam gear with oil pump fitted – unit engine.

ABOVE: *A65 BSA new camshaft.*

LEFT: *Triumph cam gear oil pump fitted – pre-unit.*

Triumph cams – worn.

Triumph cams – new.

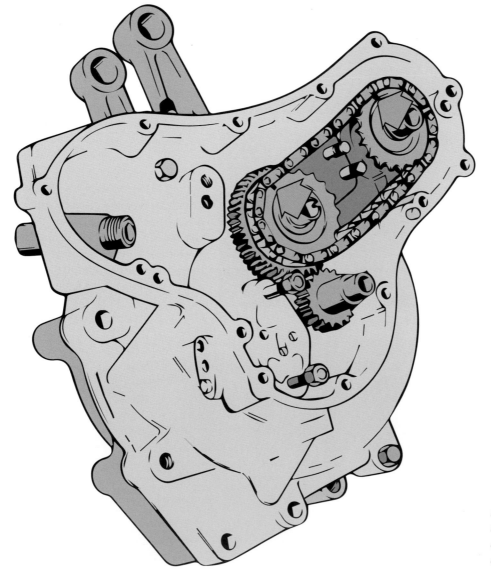

Norton twin: counting links between crankshaft and camshaft to achieve correct cam timing.

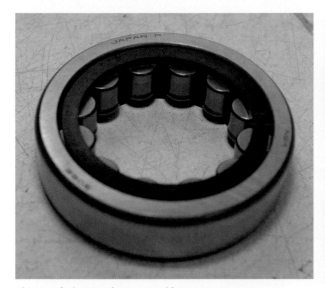

Always go for bearings from a reputable name.

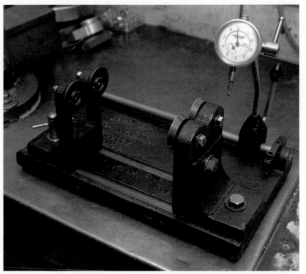

Crank balancing jig.

ABOVE LEFT AND RIGHT: Balancing jig with Gold Star crank assembly on board.

and then turned down to the appropriate size. Likewise with the big end, it may sometimes be necessary to machine down the shaft and fit a bespoke bearing. These are all fairly expensive exercises but in some cases there is no alternative.

If your machine is running prior to your restoration, you will know whether or not the big end is on its way out because as you put the engine under load, for example when accelerating uphill from a slow corner, you will hear a noticeable rattle or knock from the

bottom of the engine. Do not confuse this with the upper engine 'pinking' sound caused by the ignition sparking too early.

In the case of Triumph's early 350cc twins, for example, the con rods were as a single, that is full circle, and ran on white metal bearings, essentially a finish on the crankpins. Their later 350s and larger machines initially used split con rods but still incorporated the white metal bearing before changing to the bearing shell arrangement.

It is possible to have the crank machined and white metal reapplied but an easier solution is to have the crank machined and then fit later split con rods with shell bearings – that is, two detachable half-round bearings, which fit inside the con rod halves and make a whole when bolted up around the crank by the two halves. Make sure, of course, before you have the crank ground, that appropriate-sized shell bearings are available; you may have to grind a little more than absolutely necessary purely because of the availability, or lack of, bearing shells.

AMC's AJS and Matchless twins differed from the norm in that they had the dubious benefit of a third main bearing, central between the two rods, which was/is supposed to reduce the flex of the crankshaft. It does no harm, though can be rather fiddly to line up on reassembly, but whether or not it is any real advantage is debatable. It is a split shell bearing, more akin to a big end, unlike its outer two brethren. AMC pretty much always went their own way. For example, on early twins each cylinder had a separate barrel, but then again so did Royal Enfield with their twins and Ariel with their two-stroke Leader and Arrow which certainly makes it easier to fit a barrel over the piston on your own.

The large, central flywheel on Triumph, BSA and Norton twins bolts onto the crank and there are removable plugs in each end, through which access to the oilways can be gained. This is called the sludge trap and, like the name says, it collects most of the detritus that is picked up within the circulating oil over the years. Eventually this sludge builds up and will block the passage, thus restricting oil to the big ends, and engine failure results, so it is imperative that while the crank assembly is on the bench, the sludge trap is cleaned out. You will be surprised at the amount of muck that comes out. Once cleaned and flushed out, the tube and the plugs can be refitted, though make sure you incorporate a means of locking the plugs back into place, either by chemical means such as a proprietary thread-locking compound or by a punch to edge of the screw head. If a screw were to come loose while the engine was running, it would almost certainly result in a wrecked engine.

The standard oil filtration system is basic, to say the least, with a gauze covering the tank outlet and another gauze covering the scavenge pipe end in the sump, so to take a load off the sludge trap, you can always fit and plumb in an aftermarket oil filter kit. The tricky bit is finding a place to position the filter. As can be seen on p. 145 on this early A65 BSA, the filter is mounted between the engine plates.

Triumph con rods with original white metal bearings.

Triumph crank showing large central flywheel.

Norton crank with central flywheel.

As regards big ends, the single generally runs on a complete unit, where the bearing and the crankpin – the pin that squeezes into the two flywheels either side and is locked into place by a large nut – are as one, while the twin more often than not uses shell bearings with a con rod that has a removable bottom half, called the bearing cap. With the con rods removed, have a good close look at the surface of the crank journal and the shell bearings themselves; if they display no discernible wear then they can be refitted, though you will have already decided whether or not to touch them by checking the up and down movement mentioned above. Should there be wear, then the crank journal will have either scuffed or have simply worn slightly oval; either way it will need to be ground perfectly circular again. If you're unsure or have any doubts whatsoever, let your local precision engineer put his micrometer around the journals to ascertain whether or not they need grinding. It stands to reason that an undersize crank will need an oversize bearing shell, and these usually come in increments of 10 thou' at a time. Most cranks will stand a couple of grinds, depending on the severity of the ovality or the damage but grinding too far/too often will weaken the crank and it may break.

Grinds also depend on the availability of the shell sizes. If it's a rare crank – and, would you believe, AJS-Matchless 650cc cranks were, until very recently, virtually non existent, certainly compared to the 600 cranks – and you may have to resort to metal spraying in order to reclaim one. Indeed, the problem was such that the highly respected AJS and Matchless Owners Club commissioned a batch of new 650cc cranks to be manufactured using state-of-the-art materials and machining techniques. It pays to be in the know, so join your owners club.

When fitting new big end shells, give the journals a good smear of assembly lube beforehand. Any oil is fine, but as

Lightened and balanced crank for high-performance Triumph engine.

Triumph crank in the vice ready to split.

Crank webs unbolt from central flywheel section.

Once unbolted, the webs simply pull away from the flywheel.

As the web comes away the sludge trap tube is revealed.

Likewise the opposite side web also unbolts and leaves three separate pieces of the crank assembly.

Now the sludge trap tube can be removed from the web.

ABOVE: The contents of the sludge trap.

LEFT: More than overdue for a split to clean the sludge trap, this one was so blocked hardly any oil would have passed through it. A wrecked engine was imminent.

This aftermarket conversion to fit a screw-on cartridge oil filter fits nicely between the engine plates just ahead of the rear wheel.

Aftermarket sump plates also help if they have an integral magnet to attract any metallic particles. Note also the drain plug so the whole sump plug does not have to be removed to drain the oil.

sembly lube is thick and sticky and stays put, giving good lubrication to all moving parts before the circulating oil reaches them, when it dissolves into the oil.

Also, always fit new big end bolts to the con rod. When tightening these high-tensile bolts they have an in-built stretch quality, so do not reuse old bolts, and ensure that the new nuts are either self-locking items, are tabbed with a lock washer, and/or chemically locked in place. Tighten them to the approved torque settings in your manual. Once tight, make sure the con rod will spin freely on its journal; if it is stiff, then undo the

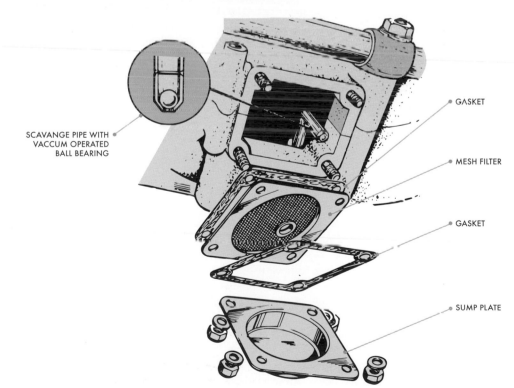

SCAVANGE PIPE WITH
VACCUM OPERATED
BALL BEARING

GASKET

MESH FILTER

GASKET

SUMP PLATE

Diagram showing the position of the scavenge pipe in a BSA sump.

New con rods for Triumph with removable big end shell bearings to replace the white metal originals.

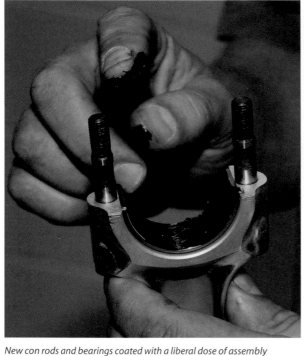

New con rods and bearings coated with a liberal dose of assembly lube to keep everything cool and smooth until the engine oil gets circulating fully.

Triumph crank, clean and tidy, clear sludge trap, flywheel bolted up with new bolts and the rods being fitted.

bolts and repeat the fitting procedure. If you hold the rod upright and let it go, it should flop down easily and you should be able to roll the crank assembly across your kitchen floor like a child's toy.

For many years there was a huge surplus of ex-WD big end assemblies for the likes of Norton, BSA, Matchless singles and so on, big ends that also fitted many other models in the companies' ranges, but these are now virtually extinct and it falls to specialist engineers to manufacture and supply such items. Be patient and speak to your fellow club members and to others with similar models and see who they recommend. You will probably find that in certain areas of the country there is a local engineer whose name crops up regularly and who will do a jolly good job for a reasonable price. Be wary of some specialists, especially those who blow their own trumpets in the club magazines. Do not go on self-recommendation. The author has had at least one bad experience with a so-called specialist with his own push-rod Norton single, so do bear in mind what other owners tell you and do not simply go on a single recommendation. New flywheels can be a costly investment, especially when they make them so that the crank won't turn in the cases.

Reassembly of the Bottom Half

RIGHT: With everything clean as a new pin, the cases can be warmed up ready for dropping in the new main bearings.

FAR RIGHT: With the cases too hot to handle, the bearings will simply push gently into their housing, especially if they have been in the fridge first.

All bushes are given a coating of assembly lube.

Likewise all bearing surfaces on the new camshafts are treated with assembly lube.

Then the crank is offered into one of the crankcase halves …

… followed by both inlet and exhaust camshafts.

Finally, the opposite crankcase half is offered up, and if everything is correctly positioned it should all go together well and spin freely.

Sump view of crankcases bolted up showing the scavenge pipe. The repair to the sump area mentioned previously is as good as unnoticeable.

The Connecting Rod

The con rod has a tough job, flying around the bottom of the engine from one side to the other, round and round and up and down too, being stretched one second, compressed the next. It's under colossal stress from these reciprocating loads and, while not wishing to drop into the realms of mathematics here, said loads increase to the square of the engine's speed increase, so it really does get a move on. Hence it's easy to understand why, when a con

rod fails (usually called 'throwing a rod'), the results can be catastrophic, as it all happens far faster than the rider can ever react. Most have seen at least photographs of engines with the broken rod poking through the side of the shattered crankcase, thus rendering the engine irreparable. A con rod can fail for numerous reasons – fatigue near a physical defect in the rod, such as a scuff or a cut; lack of lubrication in the bearing; failure of the rod bolts; inadequate or over-tightening; over-revving; or simply age.

Classic con rods are usually either a form of alloy or steel. For a high-performance classic such as the BSA Gold Star, it is wise to replace the con rod as a matter of course if the age of the existing rod is unknown. There are several manufacturers of high-quality performance rods for such engines, with a product specification – and invariably cost – higher than original. Your specialist will have his favourites, so speak to him to find out what's suitable.

The steel rods have a brass little end bush – that's the end of the rod to

147

which the piston fits – through which the steel gudgeon pin slips to hold the piston in place, via circlips, whereas most alloy rods have the gudgeon pin directly in the eye with no bush. Amazingly, and against all logical thinking, if any wear takes place in this latter situation, it is the steel that wears, not the softer alloy. The pistons will have a circlip groove in their gudgeon pin hole, into which the clip fits to prevent the pin from moving sideways.

On the subject of con rods, for those unfamiliar with the detailed workings of the internal combustion engine, it might be a good time to explain the difference between long-stroke and short-stroke engines.

The basics are quite simple. The stroke of the engine is the distance the crank pushes the piston – via the con rod of course – up and down the bore, the bore being the diameter of the cylinder. On a long-stroke engine, the piston travel is a larger figure than the bore diameter, while for a short-stroke the reverse is true. On an ES2 Norton for example, the bore and stroke is 79 × 100mm, so that's a long stroke engine, though nothing like as long a stroke as the early Model 1, or Big 4, side valve Norton engine, which was 82 × 120mm, later shortened to 82 × 113mm, along with the ohv version, Model 19. Later lightweight Nortons – the much-maligned 250cc Jubilee, the 350cc Navigator and the '400cc' Electra – all used short-stroke engines. The Jubilee sported a bore and stroke of 60 × 44mm, the Navigator 63 × 56mm and the Electra 66 × 56mm. Such dimensions are often classed as 'over-square' engines. A square engine is, for example, is Ariel's two-stroke Arrow, at 54 × 54mm.

The general rule of thumb is that a long-stroke engine will give good torque, that is will pull well from low speed or low revs, perhaps in a high gear without recourse to changing down, whereas the short stroke gives better power because of its ability to rev faster and higher, albeit with help from the gearbox to keep it spinning. In general, the British factories had their dimensions about right for the use to which their machines were put. For example, BSA'S A7 500cc twin, generally accepted as one of the sweetest-running motorcycles ever built, has dimensions of 66 × 72.6mm and Norton's Model 88 Dominator twin has exactly the same dimensions. BSA's 650cc A10 engine, from the all-iron, Golden Flash everyday machine to the super sports Rocket Gold Star, had a bore and stroke of 70 × 84mm, whereas Norton's 650SS Dominator had 68 × 89mm. Both gave a capacity of 646cc but the BSA engine had the shorter stroke engine. Triumph's Thunderbird used an even shorter stroke, 71 × 82mm, which stayed with the 650 range right to the end of the T120 Bonneville production. Their early 500cc range, however, was long stroke at 63 × 80mm, before being amended to a short stroke 69 × 65.5mm. Sunbeam's unusual, all-alloy, in-line 487cc S7/S8 twin used a short-stroke 70 × 63.5mm engine, Douglas's 350cc flat twin was almost square at 60.8 × 60mm and Velocette's 499cc MSS was square at 86 × 86mm (their 350cc Viper was 72 × 86mm, so they could use common cranks for both 350cc and 500cc models). Royal Enfield's 500cc twin was long stroke at 64 × 76mm but their super-sporty 250cc GT Continental had dimensions of 70 × 64.5mm. BSA and, later, Triumph's 250cc models were long stroke in comparison, at 67 × 70mm. When the company decided to build their Rocket Three and Triumph's Trident 750cc triples, they used the same dimensions, which for once made economic sense, albeit too little, too late.

KEEPING IT TOGETHER

Vintage and classic motorcycles vibrate, some more so than others. Unlike modern machinery with state-of-the-art, computer-aided tolerances and a host of balancing mechanisms, our motorcycles are crude in comparison – but are easy to work on. The British factories were, certainly in the latter years of the industry, never very adventurous; in fact they were downright complacent, preferring to slightly develop or upgrade last year's models rather than investing in something new. As such, even the last machines produced could easily trace their heritage back to immediate

ABOVE LEFT: Whoops! A con rod will always break when it's spinning and invariably at high speed, so as you can imagine, when the piston and the crank and valves all get in each others' way, the only way is out – and that means smashed crankcases and a totalled engine.

ABOVE RIGHT: A standard BSA twin con rod (left) with high-performance equivalent (right).

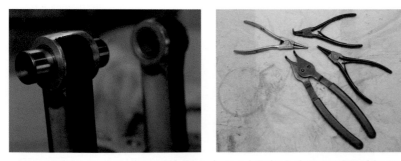

ABOVE LEFT: Gudgeon pins in the little end of a Triumph con rod. Circlips in the outer edges of the piston hold the pin in place.

ABOVE RIGHT: Circlips come in various forms so an equally varied set of circlip pliers is a must.

post-war, sometimes pre-war, designs. It's fair to say too that as the cry went up for more power and more speed, the old engines grew bigger and the inherent shakes grew bigger too. Indeed it's common knowledge that when Norton stretched the Dominator's 650cc to 750cc to satisfy the Americans' demand for more cubes, the resulting Atlas was a stretch too far, with vibration from the big 360-degree twin being just too much for both man and machine. Thus the isolastic-framed Commando was born, where the engine and gearbox were essentially isolated from the frame by means of ingenious rubber mounts, so keeping the huge vibes away from the rider.

However, when one considers, even with a medium-capacity single, that on one stroke the momentum of the rising piston is trying to persuade the engine to leap upwards out of the frame, then a millisecond later it's trying to do exactly the same out the bottom, it's inevitable that this rapid up-and-down movement is going to cause a vibration. Vibration can cause nuts to undo from their bolts, secure items to fall off, metal to fracture, bulbs to blow, electrical contacts to break and more besides. As there is little we can, or want to, do about the original design, the best we can hope for is to use some method to keep everything together.

About 85 per cent of the torque and effort of tightening a bolt is absorbed by the friction in the threads and under the head, the remaining 15 per cent is by clamp load. Therefore, high torque may be absorbed by high friction and not produce tension – that's why the threads don't strip. Now, strange as it may seem, and although it is always the first suspect in any case of something coming adrift, vibration is not capable of bolt loosening by itself. If vibration is violent enough to cause shifting of the threads then it will cause loosening, but vibration that violent is usually perceived as shock or impact. Towards the end of the loosening cycle, common vibration can and will rattle the fastener loose. This is why it usually takes full blame for loosening. The actual cause, however, is side-sliding or shifting of the threads. The empty space between the threads of a nut and bolt leaves room for movement that leads to self-loosening and loss

of clamping force. The friction in the threads and under the head of the nut or bolt is reduced to zero when the clamped parts and threads slide sideways to the bolt axis. Each time this happens it can unwind by itself. The loosening of a non-locking fastener starts with this first motion.

A mechanical means of security, which has long been used on race machines, is to drill through the nut and bolt, or whatever part is required to be secure, and insert a length of lockwire, or a split pin. There are numerous securing washers that can be placed beneath a nut to grip it, such as tab washers, star washers and spring (or split) washers, to name but three. The tab washer has a projecting ear, which, when the nut is done up to its desired tightness, is 'tabbed' over with a punch so that it sits flat against the hexagon sides of the nut, thus preventing it from turning. The star washer is a flat washer with small, star-like internal (or external, but internal looks better) projections, which are alternately curved outward and inward, so when the nut is tightened one set of projections is forced against the nut while the other is forced against the bearing surface, thus gripping both surfaces and forming almost a one-piece fitting. Obviously, a point to bear in mind with these is their use against a painted surface, where they will dig in and make a mark, so it's perhaps best to use either a 'nyloc' nut or a chemical lock fluid in that case – more on those below. The spring, or split washer is a flat washer, which has split in its circumference and is twisted up in a helical fashion, almost like a section cut from a spring. When the nut is tightened against this, the spring action applies pressure on both surfaces, which prevents the nut from turning.

In cases where a stock flat washer is used to spread the load of the nut any of the above can be used, though it can get a little unsightly, but another option is to use the aforementioned 'nyloc' nut or the chemical compound, either of which can also be used without a washer at all. Nyloc is in fact a trade name, though it has become a generic term along the lines of hoover, biro and jetski (the latter being a Kawasaki trademark), the correct term being the rather clumsy 'nylon insert lock nut'. It's a nut that

includes an integral nylon collar at the end and has an inner diameter is slightly smaller than the outer diameter of the screw. The insert deforms elastically over the threads of the screw, but, importantly, threads are not cut into the nylon, so the nylon insert locks the nut in two ways. Firstly, it forces the bottom face of the screw threads against the top face of the nut threads, increasing the friction between the two, while also applying a compressive force against the screw itself.

Another now pretty generic term is Loctite, again a trade name (part of Henkel Ltd), which has become synonymous with any form of thread-locking compound and has even developed into a verb, with restorers 'loctiting' things into place. Chemical threadlockers are anaerobic liquids that cure to a solid state when activated by a combination of contact with metal and absence of oxygen. The resulting cured material is a thermoset plastic that cannot be liquefied by heating, and resists most solvents. The purpose of thread-lockers is to lock threaded components without changing fastener or torque characteristics. They also have advantages over mechanical tightening such as lock washers, because thread-lockers find their way into minute thread imperfections and, as they cure, these imperfections become moulds for tiny plastic keys, which further resist fastener movement. What's more, because they fill all voids between threads they also prevent moisture from entering and thus corrosion is inhibited along with potential future seizure. They are graded by their various strengths and characteristics into distinct classification and are identifiable by their colour – low strength is purple, removable is blue, permanent is red, and the penetrating formula is green – and, of course, one size fits all, so the fluid that locks in a tiny screw is also suitable on a large bolt. The range of thread-lockers is comprehensive. In industrial applications it is important to consider shear strength, cure speed, gap-filling requirements, operating environment and removability potential but for general use, in our world of classic motorcycles, it's really not necessary to go into it so deeply and any form of thread-lock off your dealer's shelf will be more than adequate for external use on nuts and bolts.

Jubilee (foreground) and bigger-bore ES400, Norton's only production machines with unit construction engines.

transmission

THE GEARBOX

There seem to be two things that spook first-time restorers the most – one is the electrical system and the other is the gearbox. The former is indeed a black art to most but the gearbox really is nothing to be afraid of: it just has an imposing appearance through being quite a lot of moving parts in a fairly small space.

The principle of the average classic four-speed gearbox is pretty much the same across whichever marque you go for, and in some cases, such as Norton for example, while the outer covers may have changed shape, the main gearbox – which itself was derived from a truly vintage Sturmey Archer model – remained practically identical from the inter-war years right through to the Commando era.

Norton dallied with a unit engine – the unified twin as it's now called – but only ever got as far as a prototype and stuck with the archaic, though perfectly satisfactory, separate gearbox right to the very end of the reciprocating engine era and into that of the rotary – though, to be fair, despite its age, the Norton gearbox is a fairly bullet-proof piece of kit. Having said that, their 250cc Jubilee, its 350cc big brother the Navigator and the overbored, electric-start 383cc ES400 Electra all did have unit gearboxes, but it was a generally unloved and short-lived range, not to mention at the time unreliable. Typically, there is now a great following for these lightweights, which, with the advantage of modern technology, can be turned into very usable machines.

BSA and Triumph bit the bullet and went the way of unit construction in the early 1960s, which, by its very nature of being as one with the engine, did away with the fiddly job of having to adjust the primary drive chain by physically moving the gearbox.

Indeed, BSA with their early post-war models had a semi-unit arrangement, whereby the gearbox was bolted to the rear of the crankcases, all the while remaining a totally separate component. This alleviated the job of moving the gearbox to tension the primary chain, but for some reason they reverted to a completely separate gearbox with the introduction of the swinging arm frame before going the whole unit hog with the A50/65 twins, which were launched in 1962. By this time, their single-cylinder range had been unit since 1958, starting with the 250cc C15, followed shortly after by the 350cc B40 and so on.

Despite the big advance in development with the all-encompassing unit engines, the gearbox and transmission were still pretty much the same components that were used in the predecessor models, an archetypal factory move to keep costs to a minimum while increasing the retail price on the

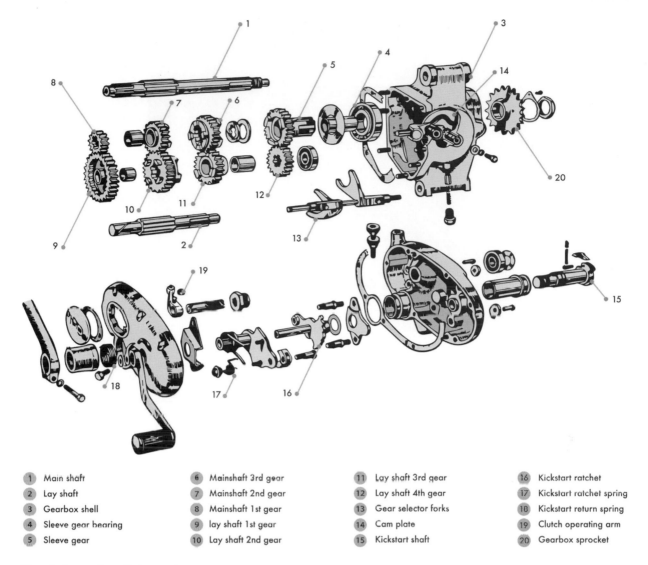

1	Main shaft	6	Mainshaft 3rd gear	11	Lay shaft 3rd gear	16	Kickstart ratchet
2	Lay shaft	7	Mainshaft 2nd gear	12	Lay shaft 4th gear	17	Kickstart ratchet spring
3	Gearbox shell	8	Mainshaft 1st gear	13	Gear selector forks	18	Kickstart return spring
4	Sleeve gear bearing	9	lay shaft 1st gear	14	Cam plate	19	Clutch operating arm
5	Sleeve gear	10	Lay shaft 2nd gear	15	Kickstart shaft	20	Gearbox sprocket

The swinging arm-frame Norton gearbox.

Unit construction Triumph engine.

basis that unit construction was the latest thing.

With a separate gearbox on the bench (or the unit cases), the first thing to do, as with the engine, is to get it clean, so put it into the degreas-er and a give it a good scrub so you can see what's what. Bear in mind that it should be full(ish) of oil and there's a good chance it will be old, black, sludge-like and full of bits, so when you begin to dismantle put it on some old newspaper and have a selection of rags handy.

So now it's nice and clean, let's look at what it's all about. Essentially it's a brace of shafts: the mainshaft, which carries four gear pinions and takes the geared turning movement to a sprocket to drive the rear wheel; and the other, the lay shaft, which is housed entirely within the gearbox shell and carries four corresponding gear pinions. These are moved into their various sequences by a pair of selector forks. These forks are C-shaped and run in a track on the back of some of the pinions. On the base of each fork there is a pip, which runs in a track cut out of the cam plate. The cam plate sits vertically on one side of the gearbox and turns with the movement of the gear lever, which in turn moves the selector forks, which in turn then moves the gear pinions along their

Unit construction BSA twin engine.

BELOW LEFT: P11 Norton-Matchless pre-unit engine.

BOTTOM LEFT: Pre-unit Ariel twin engine.

shafts to interlock with other pinions, thus changing gear. Throw in a couple of bearings and an oil seal and you've more or less got a gearbox. It's as simple as that really. Of course, while it's basically simple enough, care has to be taken to maintain the correct sequence of gears and that everything is located precisely, and there are times when not just two pairs of hands but three would be advantageous.

It's a good idea to study your manual as you begin to dismantle, because there are handy little wrinkles of which you'll not be aware, that can make life easier. For example, the kick-start lever is spring mounted, so it returns back up to where it began after you've given it a kick. The spring in question is like a big clock spring, winding round and round to gain tension and held in place by a peg within the gearbox case and by similar means on the kick-start shaft. Once the outer cover is removed from the main case, this spring can unload, spinning the shaft and losing tension. If the outer cover is to be polished, or needs repair, then this is not a problem, but otherwise a way to avoid this is to leave the kick-start lever on its shaft and turn outward the clutch-operating lever – the cable will of course have already been removed courtesy of the gearbox inspection eye – so that it fouls the kick start and prevents it from turning. This keeps the spring in tension and saves a lot of time, effort and aggravation when refitting.

The early BSA gearbox bolted to the back of the engine in semi-unit construction but still remained a separate gearbox.

ABOVE LEFT: BSA semi-unit bolt-up gearbox; the inside of the outer case showing speedometer cable drive worm gear, up and down return springs for gear change lever, clutch operating arm and kick start spring.

ABOVE RIGHT: Royal Enfield bullet gearbox.

ABOVE: Inside the pre-unit Triumph gearbox, showing kick-start spring, gear change quadrant and speedometer drive worm.

LEFT: BSA RRT2 close-ratio Gold Star gearbox.

With the nuts and screws undone, the outer cover can be removed. It may need some persuasion after been gummed together for years with some form of age-old jointing compound; use the blow lamp to soften it up and the rubber mallet to shift the case. What you must not do – and at times it's a difficult one to resist – is drive a screwdriver or blade between the cases, as this will certainly damage the faces and make oil-tight sealing more difficult. You may be forgiven perhaps using a fine Stanley-type blade to try and gently remove some of the jointing compound.

Once the cover is removed, inside the case you will see the aforementioned kick-start spring and its fixing points, the speedometer cable drive worm, the positive stop gearchange claw and spring assembly. Unless these are damaged or worn, they can be removed in as big an assembly as possible. As with the engine, take plenty of photographs and make sketches so you can refer to them on reassembly, just in case you can't remember which way up something fits. Likewise, if a component part has to be split, either rebuild it loosely once off the bike or link it all together on a wire in the order of its assembly before you put into the storage box.

Because the speedometer drive worm is helically geared and mates with its corresponding part on the inner case at 90 degrees, it must be 'unwound' to remove the case and 'wound' back into place on reassembly.

The gearchange claw just moves a short distance up and down on the gear pedal and interacts with what's called the selector quadrant. This is at 90 degrees to the claw and is pivoted within a slot in the inner cases. Both ends of the quadrant are toothed, the outer to mesh with the claw and the inner to mesh with a pinion integral with the cam plate. So, a lift or a press down on the gear pedal moves the claw, which in turn moves the quadrant, which in turn moves the cam plate and the pips on the selector forks and the gear pinions change partners accordingly.

Again, unless there is damage or wear, or the cover needs to be polished, there is no need to remove the quadrant from its slot. The inner cover will also have the corresponding drive worm for the speedometer, as mentioned above. Central in the inner cover is the kick-start ratchet assembly, which is on the end of the mainshaft and has to be removed in order to remove the inner case. The clutch pushrod resides inside the mainshaft and can simply be pulled out. The ratchet should be held in place by a normal right-hand thread nut and probably tabbed over with a securing washer. Once the nut is undone and the tab washer removed, the two composite halves of the ratchet pinion, its spring and associated bushes and washers can be pulled off the splines of the mainshaft. Keep them in the correct order. The inner case can now be removed – and the bulk of that old oil will manifest itself. The mainshaft is supported in the inner case by a ball bearing, which may be held

in place by circlip, so it's useful to have some suitable circlip pliers handy.

Now you can see inside the main case how the pinions interact courtesy of the selector forks and the cam plate.

The selector forks run along a shaft, sometimes with a threaded end that screws into a purpose-drilled and threaded hole in the case, sometimes just pushed into a blind hole and held in place by an external grub screw that mates up with a flat machined into the shaft. With the grub screw slacked and removed, the shaft can be unscrewed or pulled clear through the selector forks but leaving them in place. It's now possible to pull out the two shafts with the selector forks in place, having first ensured that their drive pegs are free of the cam plate. One selector fork has its drive peg in the lower part of the cam plate track and the other in the upper. Take some photographs again so you can refer to them on reassembly.

All that will be left in the main case by now is the mainshaft sleeve pinion, a big pinion that projects through the gearbox main bearing and oil seal, and the cam plate. The mainshaft sleeve pinion has a projecting 'tube', which pokes through any oil seal or washer and the bearing and is splined to match the gearbox sprocket. It also has a threaded end, onto which a nut is screwed to secure the sprocket. With the sprocket and so on removed, the pinion can be pushed into the gearbox shell and removed. You will notice that the outer edge of the cam plate has a series of notches; each one represents a gear position, plus a shallower neutral notch, and there is a spring-loaded plunger screwed into the gearbox main shell, which clicks into these notches to hold the cam plate in a fixed position while the gearbox is driving that particular gear. Releasing the plunger from the outside allows the cam plate to spin freely. Undoing an external nut will also release the cam plate. The sleeve gear pushes through the bearing and oil seal to be removed. Removing the oil seal can be tricky, but not as tricky as replacing it, as care must be taken not to damage the seal as you drive it into position. Some seals are rubber with an integral spring – with these, make sure the spring is against the oil to be retained; others have a metal face, and any deformation

of that face can result in a seal that doesn't seal. As before, it's often advantageous to heat up the case so that the seal can be drifted into place without recourse to excessive force. It is usually held in place by a circlip.

With everything laid out on the bench, examine the teeth on the pinions. A little wear is inevitable, but any badly worn edges, chips, or evidence of the case hardening beginning to fail – which will manifest itself as pits on the teeth face, or patches akin to peeling chrome work – mean the pinion must be replaced. Ideally its opposite number should be replaced also but in some cases it's not always possible and, to be realistic about it, with plenty of oil or grease in the box, the tolerances are loose enough to forgive putting a new, or at least replacement pinion, against an existing one.

Likewise, examine the dogs on the flip side of the pinions. These interlock with the corresponding female parts of the adjacent pinion and any serious wear on the edges could result in jumping out of gear, or not engaging, correctly. It's unlikely the splines on the shafts will have worn too badly, unless the gearbox has been run dry or similarly abused, but there may be some wear on the outer threads, where the sprocket nut has been taken on and off over the years, perhaps even evidence of the odd cross-threading. If it's a bit suspect, take it to your friendly neighbourhood precision engineer along with the nut, and let him refurbish them so they work smoothly together. Of course, with smaller threaded parts, a few moments running a tap or a die over the threads will often be adequate.

Reassembly

With the cases and the gearbox innards all in order and perfectly clean, reassembly is essentially the reverse procedure. It can be a bit fiddly trying to get everything lined up, and often a second pair of hands helps, especially with the limited room inside the main case when trying to ensure that the selector forks are mated with their correct pinions and their drive pins are in the cam plate track, but it's not rocket science and patience will prevail. Despite having dismantled all the parts and assembled them in the same order as they came out, it pays to obtain and refer to an exploded diagram of the gearbox in question because it has been known for previous spanner men to reassemble incorrectly, omitting the odd spacer or washer, or even fitting parts the wrong way round; and the last thing you want to be doing is repeating someone's mistake, only to have the gearbox fail or misbehave once your restoration is on the road. Take note also of the manual's recommended setting for the cam plate, that is, the position of the plunger in the notches, as this is imperative for the correct sequencing of the gears.

Again, once the shafts and pinions are in place, give everything a good squirt of oil and make sure it all turns smoothly. As with everything else, make sure the screw holes in the cases are clean all the way to their base, then, with the gasket medium in place, fit the central section of the gearbox to the main case. With the section in place, there is a slot through which the selector quadrant mates with the pinion affixed to the cam plate. On most machines there is some form of dot or dash on the quadrant, which must line up with a corresponding dot or dash on the gearbox central case. With the cam plate set in the right place – the handbook or manual will inform you if it needs to be in neutral or one of the gear notches – and loosely held by the spring-loaded plunger and the dot/dash lined up, the sequence of the gears should be correct, and it should be possible, by manually turning the mainshaft, to 'feel' all the gears into place, and neutral. Take note, however, if you are fortunate enough to have a machine with a reverse cam plate, such as a BSA Gold Star, then the dots and dashes do not correspond, and lining them up will result in the use of two gears only. In this case it's a case of trial and error, with the selector initially central in the slot.

The rest of the box can then be assembled. It all goes together fairly easily, but make sure you wind round the kick-start return spring so it remains under tension before refitting the outer case.

The clutch pushrod can at this stage be inserted from the sprocket side, as the clutch operating arm will probably prevent its access through the inspection eye in the outer case. Make sure the end of the rod is not cupped through wear – if it is, it should be replaced. An old wrinkle is to cut the worn tip off the rod and heat the new end until cherry red before dunking it immediately into oil; this will harden the tip and prevent it wearing rapidly in use. It will now be a little short of course, but a way round it is to cut the rod in half, harden each end and place a ball bearing between the two halves within the mainshaft. Do ensure though that the ball is big enough that the rod acts upon it centrally, but small enough to move freely within the mainshaft. Don't forget to adjust the cam plate plunger to its recommended tension setting. For example, on the swinging arm-framed BSA A/B series, the plunger is at its correct setting when approximately two threads are projecting beyond the lock nut. While it's not super-critical, any more will make it sloppy, creating the risk of gear selection problems, and any less will make the operation stiff.

Another feature of the BSA gearbox is the speedometer drive, which is integral, unlike many other marques, where the drive is taken from a separate unit fixed to the rear hub, or on earlier machines, from a drive attached to the brake plate of the front wheel. As the workings of the unit are inside the gearbox, which should be running in oil, it is not often that these fail.

THE CLUTCH

While the basic layout of a classic motorcycle clutch and primary drive assembly is the same, the details of the various marques and the period of their models differ enormously. However, they are all essentially a series of spring-loaded plates, which act as a means of neutralizing the drive between the engine and the gearbox and thus enabling smooth changes in gear ratio.

The plates are all housed within a drum, around the outside of which is a sprocket on which the primary chain engages from the engine sprocket. The drum runs on a bearing, which sits on the gearbox mainshaft projecting into the primary case. Secured by a nut on the end of the mainshaft is a clutch centre. Essentially a circular block, this engages onto the mainshaft's splines and has around its outer face a series of slots. It also has a number of threaded studs projecting from it onto which the securing nuts for the plates are screwed.

Plates are alternately plain steel and inserted; one is driven by square tangs that mate with corresponding female slots in the drum's inner face, while the others have a similar arrangement but with the slots in the clutch body.

The steel plate is simply that – a flat steel plate – while the insert is a steel plate with a series of cutouts into which fibrous inserts are fitted to grip the adjacent plain steel plates. Early machines used cork, but as more advanced combinations of insert material became available, these were utilized to give both better grip within the oily environment of the primary case and to be more durable and hard-wearing.

The number of plates can vary, but is usually around four or five, perhaps half a dozen or so of each as standard, though retro-fit, state-of-the-art clutches can have sixteen plates or more.

Holding the plates in place is an outer plate, often with a domed centre, in which there are several holes that locate over the centre's projecting studs. This is called the pressure plate as it receives the push from the pushrod. When in place, cups and springs go over the studs, within the holes, and they are secured by either self-locking nuts, a pair of locknuts or the proprietary 'nyloc' nut. These nuts tighten down onto the springs and form the adjustable pressure of the clutch operation.

The clutch is activated by a cable from the handlebar lever, which pulls against the actuating arm, sometimes on top of the gearbox, often inside it, with just a cable adjuster on the outside. This pushes against the pushrod within the mainshaft, which in turn pushes against the domed outer plate, taking the spring pressure off the rest of the plates and allowing them to separate and thus removing the drive. Some pushrods work directly against the outer plate, which will have a hardened centre to prevent the pushrod from drilling into it while others have a mushroom-headed, short, secondary pushrod to spread

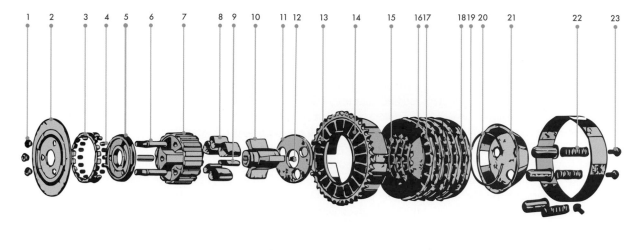

1 Spring-stud nut	7 Body	13 Sprocket	19 Outer plate
2 Backplate	8 Rubbers	14 Sprocket inserts	20 Spring clip
3 Roller cage	9 Rubbers (small)	15 Steel plate	21 Plate cover
4 Rollers (15 per set)	10 Shock-absorber centre	16 Friction plate	22 Spring
5 Race plate	11 Body front-cover plate	17 Friction-plate inserts	23 Spring screw
6 Spring stud	12 Cover-plate screws	18 Plate-retaining circlip	

Norton single three-spring clutch.

Mid-1950s Triumph four-spring clutch.

the load wider. There are aftermarket outer plates available, which have a kind of small spinner that can accommodate any rotation on the pushrod when it makes contact with the pressure plate.

For a smooth-operating clutch assembly, it is essential that all the plates are perfectly flat, and that all the tangs adequately fill their slots while remaining a loose sliding fit and have no hooked or ragged edges to them. Any of the above could result in an uneven lift and a poor or difficult gear change. An obvious sign of a worn or maladjusted clutch is the inability to find neutral when at a standstill with the engine running. Many is the time when the rider of such a machine will snick into neutral as he slows, just prior to standstill; otherwise he will be faced with having to hold the clutch in while the delay passes – which could be a long time if, say, he's at a railway crossing. If the clutch has uneven plates and doesn't lift straight and true, such a situation will cause the clutch to heat up and when attempting a getaway under engine load, it may result in slippage, where the engine revs rise but the plates slip against each other instead of gripping to deliver the required momentum.

Likewise, on a newly rebuilt clutch, slippage can still occur if the nuts are not tight enough and thus the spring pressure is too light, but this is easily remedied by tightening the nuts until slippage is eliminated. This will also manifest itself on the kick start, with the clutch slipping instead of turning the engine. If the spring pressure is too great, not only will the operating pressure be heavy at the handlebar, but the clutch may drag.

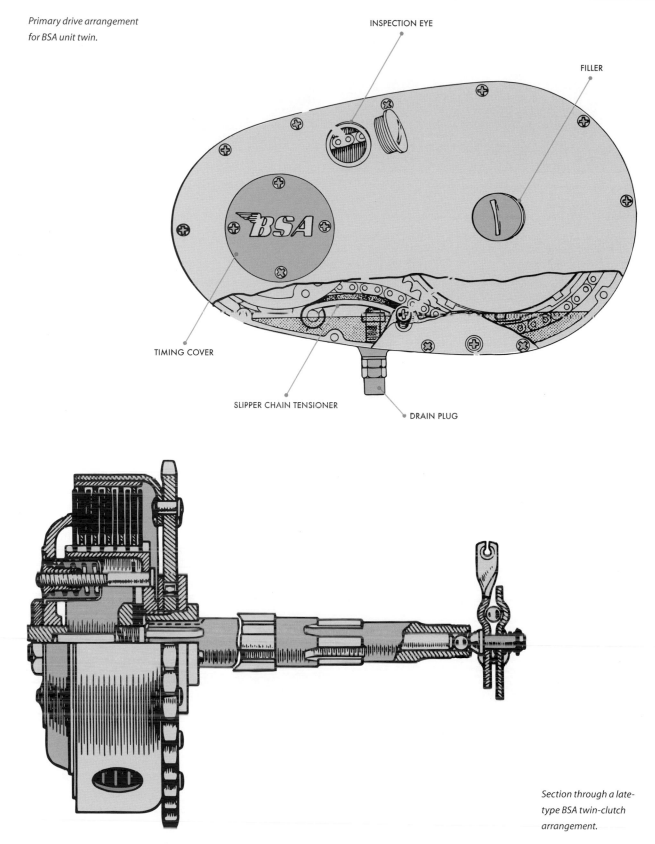

Primary drive arrangement for BSA unit twin.

INSPECTION EYE

FILLER

BSA

TIMING COVER

SLIPPER CHAIN TENSIONER

DRAIN PLUG

Section through a late-type BSA twin-clutch arrangement.

In other words, the bike will creep forwards despite the clutch lever being fully engaged. This will occur also if the springs have been unevenly and overly tightened, preventing the plates from lifting squarely. A slackening of the pressure will invariably cure the problem. It's a case of finding the right pressure to avoid both problems and give a sweet clutch action – simply trial and error.

A new clutch or new plates may also need to bed in, so after a few miles you may find it slips and you have to adjust the pressure to take up the slop formed by everything settling in together.

The part of the operating arm that acts on the pushrod within the gearbox has an adjustable centre piece, which can take up the slack in the

Clutch-holding tool for NEB multiplate clutch body.

Clutch tool made from an old plate and sundry lengths of metal to form the handle.

cable when the new unit beds down or the cable stretches a little.

Ensure there is always around $^1/_{16}$in of play at the handlebar lever before the operation begins to bite, otherwise the pushrod will be in constant contact with the pressure plate, overheat, lose its hardness and wear rapidly.

Also, to assist with good operation, always make sure the operating arm is lying parallel to the gearbox when fully engaged. This is easy with the BSA as the arm is on top of the case. Take note also of the run of the cable, keeping it as straight as possible with all bends being as wide a sweep as possible and making sure there are no tight angles.

One thing that many classic riders forget is to keep the cables well lubricated. This is pretty much a case of out of sight out of mind, but it is not uncommon for a rider to strip a clutch because of a problem only to discover that the dry, corroded inner cable run was to blame.

LEFT: Always ensure there is at least $^1/_{16}$in free play at the lever.

BELOW: NEB all-alloy, sixteen-plate clutch on a BSA Gold Star.

As machines developed and became more powerful, the poor clutch became a thing of much abuse. BSA's Gold Star and the Velocette Venom Thruxton were essentially clubman racers on the road and as such had a very high first gear. They needed a lot of revs and fair deal of clutch slipping to actually get them away from standstill and this naturally took its toll. The BSA's reputation was by far the worse and these days it's more likely to find some form of state-of-the-art aftermarket clutch hiding inside the Gold Star primary cover than the old BSA four-spring job.

Norton's pre-war three-spring clutch was used in most of their singles and twins up to the Commando, which used an extremely good, multi-plate unit of plain and insert plates, held under pressure by a car-like single diaphragm spring plate and in place by a large-diameter circlip. Unlike the traditional clutch plates, the steel plates do not have a series of large tangs, but an outer edge with lots of spline-like teeth, which give a better spread of load, and the inserted plates soon gave way to bonded, phosphor bronze-lined plates. These gave a good combination of both grip and a reasonable weight

Norton Commando clutch spring compressor.

Primary drive by toothed rubber belt.

of operation at the lever – though fairly stiff in comparison to modern standards. It could also be somewhat switch-like, either on or off. Be wary of the spring when removing the circlip; if you do not have the correct tool to compress it and allow its pressure to release steadily, it will fly out at great speed and under such circumstances that it would not be wise to find yourself in the way. These clutch compressors are readily available from your Commando specialist.

Whilst some purists will huff and puff about the use of non-standard parts on a classic, technology, materials and machining capability has increased to a massive extent and there are aftermarket parts available today that can make life so much easier on a classic – the clutch is a prime example. Why put up with troublesome parts and assemblies just because that's what the factory fitted at the time? After all, they only fitted said troublesome part because that was the best that was available to them at the time – in other words, had today's parts been available, the factory would have fitted them. So it makes sense to fit a new, state-of-the-art multi-plate clutch to your machine, especially if it's hidden behind a primary cover – who's going to see it and make judgements about not fitting an original? What's more, should you so wish, you can fit a belt-drive system and do away with troublesome oil leaks, or at least the worry about lubrication maintenance of the primary system. The café racer crowd like the belt drive because it means they can dispense with the full primary case and run a semi-exposed clutch system, or carve up the original case and fit gauze panels and so on.

If you retain your chain drive, despite the clutch itself not needing to run in the traditional oil bath, it is wise to give the primary chain a regular squirt of chain wax just to keep it running smoothly.

There are conversion fittings available that will allow, say, a Triumph clutch onto a BSA gearbox mainshaft (one BSA wrinkle is to fit a plunger-framed gearbox mainshaft into a later swinging arm-framed gearbox, which then allows the direct fitting of a Norton clutch without need for any converter or alteration), or a Norton clutch onto a Triumph and so on. There are certain specialists who utilize and convert modern Japanese clutches to suit classic British machines and there are others who specialize in a bespoke, multi-plate unit designed especially for your machine, often with the option of belt or chain primary drive. These are invariably made of tough but lightweight alloy, have twice the number of plates of the original and have springs that can simply be tightened up to a stop, thus guaranteeing perfect adjustment and alignment instantly – fit and forget and no more worries about finding neutral at rest, slipping, dragging or overheating. Some of these clutch assemblies were designed originally for speedway machines, where single-speed, 500cc, single-cylinder engines of around 75bhp demand terrific and instant acceleration, plus a high top speed, so they can cope effortlessly with the comparatively lowly output of even a normally temperamental Clubman Gold Star with its high gears; your humble slogger, even fitted with a sidecar, should have no problems. A good clutch is a worthy investment.

CHAINS AND SPROCKETS

A bit like the cables mentioned earlier, the poor old drive chain can often be a thing of much neglect, which is rather unfair on it because by the very nature of where it is positioned and the job it does, it receives about as much muck from the road as can be found. When you think about it, a gritty chain runs over the sprockets thousands upon thousands of times on even the shortest ride, each revolution acting as a minute abrasive wearing away that little bit more – then you wonder why your chain has gone slack. So, keep it clean and keep it well lubricated. It's a full-time job because an oily chain allows the road muck to stick to it, but an unlubricated chain will run hot and eventually break, as well as wear the sprockets.

If you take time to look into chains, you will be amazed at the number of different designs there are for their various purposes. Even for motorcycles, there are countless variations of length, width and shape, link types, simplex, duplex, triplex and so on. If you're unsure, just head to one of the classic motorcycle chain specialists and tell them which make and model you have; once they've determined the length required (by the number of links) they'll give you the option of a handful of manufacturers and prices, plus if you so wish, the benefit of their experience by advising which to go for depending on your type of machine and how you are intending to use it. For example, if you're just going to potter around steadily on relatively short journeys such as the odd vintage club run, then there is probably no need to go for the super-strong, high-efficiency chain and they'll sell you a perfectly satisfactory, less expensive item. If you're intending to go trials riding, vintage racing, scrambling or sprinting, however, then you'll be needing the toughest chain they have. The average sports classic, such as a Venom, Super Rocket or Bonneville, will be earmarked for something in between.

The roller chain has been around for a good few years, and while technology has improved the specification, the basic design has remained essentially the same since Hans Renold came up with the idea in 1879.

The roller chain can be identified by virtue of the size of certain elements of it:

Pitch The distance between the centre of the pins.
Inside width The distance between the innermost side plates.
Roller diameter Self-explanatory, the diameter of the roller.

Motorcycle drive chains are roller chains, but some primary chains, cam chains and dynamo drive chains are bush chains, which have no rollers that turn.

As mentioned earlier, on one particular occasion some years ago, in a less scrupulous quarter of the classic autojumble scene, lengths of correct-sized chain were being sold to the unsuspecting and inexperienced, naturally at a bargain price, that were totally unsuitable for motorcycle use. The chain in question turned out to be drive chain for the lifting prongs of a fork lift – with no rollers – and as such wore out the sprockets to which it was fitted in double quick time. The moral is: always buy from a recognized source.

Some modern chains are effectively sealed and come with terminology such as O-ring, X-ring and Z-ring, and

while most are for modern machinery, there are certain sizes available that can be retro-fitted to classics. In a nutshell, the O, X or Z represents the shape of the seal between the plates and the roller, which is designed to retain the lubrication inside around the roller. When the chain is at rest the seals are at their slackest, but as soon as the chain is put under load and the links are pulled forward, they close up and nip the seals. The O-ring squeezes up and the X and Z deform. It is an arguable point but the latter two are said to be better in that their deformation under load gives two sealing points either side – the top and the bottom of their respective shapes – whereas the side of the O just gives one either side. This is the marketing reason that the X and Z chains are so much more expensive than the O. Whatever your choice, the outer elements of the chain have to maintained, cleaned and lubricated as with any other type of chain.

With traditional chains, there are cranked links available too for many sizes, which enable an odd number of links to be achieved, along with split links and rivet links.

In 'the good old days', when the drive chain had stretched beyond the adjustable limits of the motorcycle, it was common practice to shorten the chain by removing a link or links in order to squeeze a few more hundred miles out of it. In practice, while this achieved its aim, it also helped to wear out the sprockets even quicker, as the odd number of stretched chain links did not run evenly across the teeth of the sprockets. Of course, this was in the days when tyres could be run down to the canvas and bicycle battery lights

often sufficed as night-time illumination, so don't do it. If your old chain can be bent sideways into even a shallow arc then it should be used only as a puller or something of that nature, and it's time for a new chain. Again, ideally, it's a good idea to change sprockets when changing chain but it can be expensive and often the sprockets are in good condition and quite serviceable to interact with a new chain. If, however, the teeth are hooked, worn down, broken or missing throw them away and invest in new replacements.

With the gearbox out too, it's a good idea to count the number of teeth on the various sprockets and make sure the gearing is correct. For example, if the bike has once hauled a sidecar, the gearbox sprocket may have less teeth than its solo equivalent and perhaps more on the rear wheel.

Just to clarify – chains don't really stretch, they simply wear at the bearing surfaces between the pins and bushes, and as the bushes elongate the pins move excessively, creating the effect of stretch over the length of the chain.

Chain length is measured by the number of pitches or rollers within it. So if your old chain needs to be replaced and it's the right length, despite having 'stretched', simply count the number of rollers in it, including the rollers on each end. If the number is odd, then it will have a half link in it. If the chain on your latest project is worn out and you know nothing about its previous history, assume that, sometime in its past, a roller or two will have been removed in an attempt to readjust it, in which case you run the risk of purchasing a new chain that is too short. If in doubt, it is always wise to buy a new chain that has half a dozen or so more rollers than the worn one.

There are classic chain specialists familiar to classic enthusiasts who have comprehensive websites to help you with your requirements, where you can calculate the required length of chain by the number of rollers. Take a length of string then divide its number of inches by the pitch for your chosen chain size, for example 65in divided by 0.625 (the pitch for $5/8$in chain) equals 104 rollers. Alternatively, your specialist can do it for you. They'll need to know the chain size, the number of teeth on both sprockets and the centre distance

ABOVE LEFT: A sprocket like this anywhere in the drive system will not only ruin a chain but also be quite dangerous – replace it immediately.

ABOVE RIGHT: New old stock can still be found if you know where to look. This gearbox sprocket is still in what's left of its original 1940s wrapping.

between the sprockets. Give them a call first, however, as they will probably have standard details already to hand on file.

Maintenance

Think about it. Every moving part of a chain is a steel-to-steel bearing face, so it is imperative a film of lubricant is constantly present to reduce friction, protect from corrosion and thereby extend the life of the chain. This minute film not only cuts down friction but also assists in cushioning the drive, essentially hydraulically. If your chain is fairly clean, that is not clogged up with a winter's road muck, then, generally speaking, the process of lubrication is more than enough to also clean it. If it's very dirty, it must be cleaned first. Wash it with an old tooth brush or paint brush, stiff enough to shift the muck and old oil but not abrasive like a wire brush. Use diesel or paraffin – both are oil-based and do not dry out the base metals in the manner that solvents or petrol do. Then give it a good blast with the compressed air gun. It's a dirty enough job with the chain on the bench, and can be even more so when on the bike, so take care to contain your mess as best you can.

Never use WD40 or similar freeing agent-type products to clean or lubricate a chain – they are not lubricants in the true sense of the word and contain solvents. They will also damage the rubber seals on an O-ring chain. For those who are unaware, 'WD' stands for water displacement. If the chain is stiff with corrosion, by all means use a freeing agent, but lubricate with proper chain lubricant. Incidentally, if

you are so minded, there are proprietary chain cleaners available. These are essentially a hollow block, the inside of which is covered with stiff bristles and through which the chain is run back and forth within the cleaning fluid.

Once clean, your chain can then be checked for wear. An acceptable rule of thumb is a maximum of $^1/_4$in 'stretch' per foot of chain length; beyond this it should be replaced. Lay it on a flat surface and secure one end so tension can be applied at the other end. Then lay a means of measurement, such as a rigid rule, next to the chain. If the chain is still on the bike, select bottom gear and rotate the back wheel in order to tension the upper strand of the chain and carry out the test on this tensioned sectioned.

With a new $^5/_8$in-pitch chain, sixteen pitches are 10in long, therefore the wear limit on a used chain of the same size would measure 10.197in. On a new $^1/_2$in-pitch chain, twenty-three pitches measure 11.5in, the limit being 11.732in. For a $^3/_8$in-pitch chain, twenty-four pitches is 9in and the limit 9.192in. Test several parts of the chain, as they can wear unevenly, causing 'tight spots'. These are regularly discovered when adjusting a chain; as the back wheel is turned, the bottom strand is first slack, then loose. Time for a new chain.

Ordinary, traditional roller chains are best lubricated with SAE 80–90 oil or with a specific chain lubricant. Ensure that any chain lubricant to be used on an O-, X- or Z-ring chain is 'O-ring friendly'.

Incidentally, even though sealed O-ring chains and X-ring chains are generally considered maintenance

free, they too need to be well lubricated, both the exposed outer metals, for obvious reasons, and the inner rubber seals. There are specialist aerosols available that apply wet and appear to dry quickly but leave a residue of PFTE or other such lubricating media that can reach into the seals. Use your common sense to decide how often to apply lubrication depending on weather conditions, but in general, a good squirt every 300 miles or so should do the trick.

Adjustment

It makes sense that correct chain tensioning is important for both efficiency and safety of a chain drive. Tighten up too much and additional, unnecessary, loading on the chain can cause loss of lubricant from the bearing surfaces causing premature wear and/or breakage, not to mention stress on the gearbox. Chains that are too slack whip violently during acceleration and deceleration, again applying unnecessary loading onto it. What's more, there's a good chance that it could jump off the sprockets, leading to serious damage, potentially locking the rear wheel and causing accident and injury.

Check over your new chain and re-tension if necessary after the first 60 or so miles and every 250 or so miles after that – though it's fair to say that most riders don't, instead giving it a cursory poke with their boot every now and again prior to a good once-over before the bike goes into winter hibernation. Obviously off-road bikes need chain checks before/after each event.

A basic method to assess tension is to get someone to sit on the bike to

A fully enclosed chaincase is not the sportiest-looking addition to any motorcycle but it does keep the chain free from damaging weather and road muck.

Royal Enfield rear wheel adjustment is by means of snail cams.

BSA wheel adjustment is by means of a bolt into the swinging arm with a locknut on it.

compress the suspension – that's if it's not a rigid frame of course – so that the front sprocket centre, the swinging arm pivot and rear sprocket centre are pretty much all along the same line. Then adjust the chain tension by turning the bolts or cams until the bottom strand has about half an inch up-and-down movement, while the upper strand is tight. Fasten everything up tight again and then recheck that everything is as it should be.

Joining Up

Most traditional chains are joined with a split link, where the side plate is a loose fit and secured in place by a horseshoe-shaped spring clip. The split link, in theory at least, is likely to wear at a faster rate than the rest of the chain due to the nature of the loose-fit side plate, because it moves more than the chain itself. This movement also creates flexion in its opposite fixed side plate, which over time may fatigue and break. In practice, however, such breakages are uncommon. Riveted or soft links are safer than split links when fitted properly, but are more of a specialist job. The two holes in the separate side plate are made to be an interference fit, that is, very tight, so after having fitted this over the two pins of the chain to the correct position and riveted over both pins, there is little likelihood of failure. The split link, however, has served motorcyclists extremely well from pioneer days and continues to do so.

CABLES

The two main things with regard to cables and their operation is to route them between their two points of connection in the straightest line possible and keep them well lubricated – this will make for a light and easy operation. There are a few cable specialists around who will have the original books from the likes of Romac, cable manufacturers of old, with the exact dimensions of the cables required for whatever purpose on your machine – for example throttle, front brake, rear brake, clutch – and therefore will be able to make them up for you with nothing more to go on than a make, model and year of machine. They will also have the required parts for you to make up your own cables should you so wish, with inner and outer cables, ferrules, nipples and so on. Traditionally, the inner cable would be a small-diameter wire rope made up of close-wound strings; once one of the strings breaks free of its soldered end or along its length, it's time to change it, as it will snag on the outer cable and prevent the cable from returning to its home. Today it is possible to buy cables with nylon inners, which are smooth and very reliable.

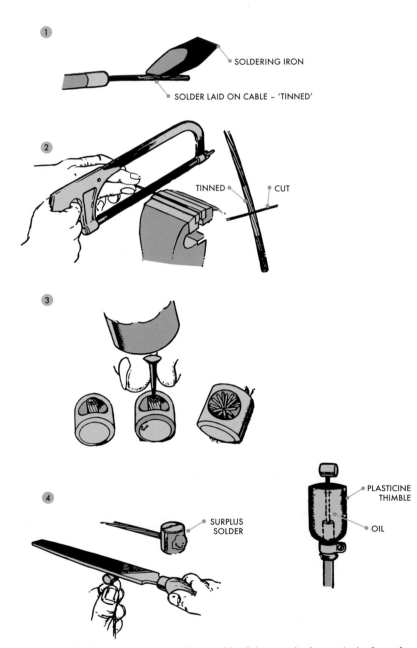

① SOLDERING IRON

SOLDER LAID ON CABLE – 'TINNED'

② TINNED CUT

③

④ SURPLUS SOLDER

PLASTICINE THIMBLE

OIL

Basic principles of securing a nipple soundly to a cable; all the controls rely on a nipple of some form.

The MC2 SU carburettor. This one has been refurbished by Amal Carburetters.

The MC2 SU carburettor on a Triumph Thunderbird.

the carburettor

The carburettor has come on in leaps and bounds during the post-war period. Practically all British motorcycles were fitted with Amal carburettors (you'll note on any Amal literature that they actually spell it carburetter, but we'll stay with the Queen's English). Amal – a trade name shortened from Amalgamated Carburettors Ltd, the overall company name of the merged Amac, Binks and Brown and Barlow carburettor manufacturers in the 1920s – came under the ownership of Imperial Metal Industries for many years, when the company increased its product range to more than just carburettors, to include twist grips, handlebars and so on. The name and manufacturing rights were sold in 1973 to Grosvenor works, who continued with the production of the most popular carburettors and associated spares. The 1980s and 1990s proved difficult for classic enthusiasts as there were no new Amal carburettors available, and a series of specialist restorers sprung up, machining out worn carburettor bodies and sleeving throttle slides, a useful service for many but even then not without its

difficulties as, for example, boring the body could block up the minute breather holes that are normally found in the internal face, thus causing unfathomable problems. Often it was a case of scouring the autojumbles or the old former British motorcycle dealers for their old stock jets, floats, slides and so on.

Some turned to other makes of carburettor, such as Dell Orto, and particularly the Japanese Mikuni, and found that the latter's multi-jet layout gave their old classics a breathing ability the likes of which they'd never previously experienced; but, while the bikes performed well, originality was still king and the fitting of a Japanese carburettor was almost seen as sacrilege.

Then in 2003, in a stroke of genius, Burlen Fuel Systems recognized this feeling within the classic marketplace and, having taken over the rights to the Amal name – to add to their SU, Solex and Zenith range – they made the brave move of remanufacturing the original Concentric carburettor as fitted to 1960s and 1970s British machines. These units were, and still

are, manufactured on state-of-the-art equipment with the best materials, and instantly proved an enormous success. The classic world breathed a sigh of relief as the newly manufactured Amal carburettors returned to the marketplace and relieved the pressure on owners having to decide whether to refurbish old carburettors or settle for a foreigner.

The success of the Mk 1 Concentric (the modern Mk 2 was already in production) inspired Burlen to remanufacture the Monobloc, followed thereafter by the GP, the TT, the 276 and the Mk 1½ plus a host of associated ancillary fuelling and related components. So, to put it simply, if your carburettor is worn, don't spend time and money trying to repair it, just buy a new one; then if your bike doesn't run quite right, at least you'll know it's not the carb. Another beauty of Amal's service is they can build your carburettor to the absolute exact specification for your machine. Most manuals or old handbooks have the part numbers and sizes of the throttle slides, main and pilot jets, jet blocks and so on, so if you supply them with that information, you'll know your carburettor is perfect for the job.

The dictionary definition of the carburettor is 'a device used in petrol engines for atomizing the petrol, controlling its mixture with air and regulating the intake of the air-petrol mixture into the engine.' In other words it's a mixing chamber, and that mixture ratio is critical in the correct running of the engine. If the amount of air is too great, when compared to the petrol, it runs weak. When there is too much petrol and insufficient air, it runs rich.

The carburettor body was originally made in brass but later in a less expensive zinc-alloy and it wears easily. Likewise, the slide that moves up and down inside the body also wears, and while this can readily be replaced with a new one, there is little point in trying to get it to work efficiently if the body is worn oval, as air leaks will still prevail. The jet block – the actual guts of the carburettor – can also wear, but usually only where the slide makes contact with it. Again, needles and needle jets can also suffer wear, and a sure sign of this is

over-rich running – black smoke from the exhaust, black, sooty spark plugs, high petrol consumption and poor starting when the engine is warm. Incidentally, a bent needle can also cause problems, so check it by rolling it across a flat surface. If it's bent, get a new one.

The float chamber is self-explanatory: it's the chamber in which the float is fixed to regulate the influx of petrol. The float was invariably brass, but nowadays improvements in plastics have rendered the brass float almost obsolete. It is 'hinged' within the chamber by means of two hoops fixed to the float through which a pin slides, the ends of which then fit into appropriate slots. This allows the float to move up and down, or 'float'. Central between the two hoops is a slot into which a 'float needle' rests. The petrol runs down into the bottom of the chamber from the tank via gravity, and as it fills, the float lifts up on its pin, which in turn pushes the needle downward and its tip then bungs the hole through which the petrol is drawn and the chamber is prevented from filling further. On the

The MC2 SU carburettor on a Triumph Thunderbird.

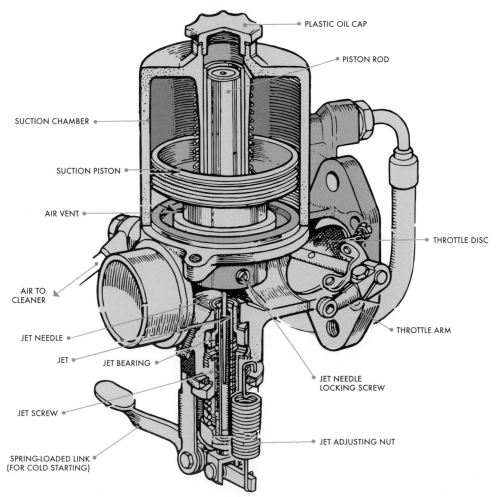

PLASTIC OIL CAP

PISTON ROD

SUCTION CHAMBER

SUCTION PISTON

AIR VENT

THROTTLE DISC

AIR TO CLEANER

JET NEEDLE

JET

JET BEARING

THROTTLE ARM

JET NEEDLE LOCKING SCREW

JET SCREW

SPRING-LOADED LINK (FOR COLD STARTING)

JET ADJUSTING NUT

Sectional details of the MC2.

top of the carburettor is a spring-loaded pin, a 'tickler', which, when pressed manually, makes contact with the float, pushing it down and allowing excess petrol to enter the chamber. This is called 'flooding' the carburettor and is necessary on many machines before initial start-up from cold can take place.

The carburettor (or carburettors if your bike is a twin or triple) more often than not bolts to the cylinder head via a manifold, again more often than not cast integrally with the head, but separate on some earlier models. It is imperative that all joints are sealed correctly, as the suction created by the moving pistons and opening valves will cause any leaks to admit air and thus mess up the correct air-fuel settings. However, a regular failing is in the over-tightening of the carburettor fixing flange to the manifold, which can result in a distortion of the flange and air leaks. While it's obviously necessary to keep the flange sealed and prevent the unit from falling off, the seal between the flange and the inlet manifold has only to withstand pressures of around 15 psi, so use a 'nyloc'-type nut or a dribble of chemical threadlock to keep the nuts in place while only applying sufficient pressure on them to make a good seal.

Assuming you've sensibly chosen a fairly everyday British classic as your first restoration then there's a fair bet the Amal carburettor on it will be a pre-Monobloc type with separate float chamber (immediate pre-war to 1955), a Monobloc (1955–66) or a Concentric (1966 to approx 1976). The good thing about all these is that they are all now available brand new off the shelf.

Burlen Fuel Systems/Amal Carburetters also manufacture and supply parts for the SU carburettor. In the early to mid-1950s, Triumph and their subsidiary Ariel dallied with the MC2 SU carburettor, essentially a miniature version of their regular car carb. Whilst an excellent unit, it was a little too expensive for Triumph and so they returned to the cheap, cheerful and quicker to wear out Amal. Amal do not presently manufacture the MC2 but they do supply a good number of parts for it.

If you don't know for sure if you have the correct type or specification of carburettor on your project, there are simple ways of finding out. The owners club will have details, often the handbooks and manuals dedicated to your marque model will have them listed, or you can simply contact Amal and tell them the make, model, size and age of your machine and they will be able to build a carburettor, or supply parts, to the exact needs of your bike. Do not waste time buying second-hand carburettors unless you know their history, and certainly not 'blind' from the autojumble stalls because you may finish up paying top money for an instrument that is no better than the one you already have. At least with a new one there is a warranty back up should something fail.

PRE-MONOBLOC TYPE 276 – THE STANDARD AMAL

You'll find two cables entering the top of the carb body, with screw adjusters. One is for the throttle slide, the other for the air slide or choke. With the top unscrewed, they will slide out on the ends of their cables, and if they need no attention they can simply be moved out of the way. The 276 has two types of fitting – stub and flange. The former is tubular and slides over a tubular inlet

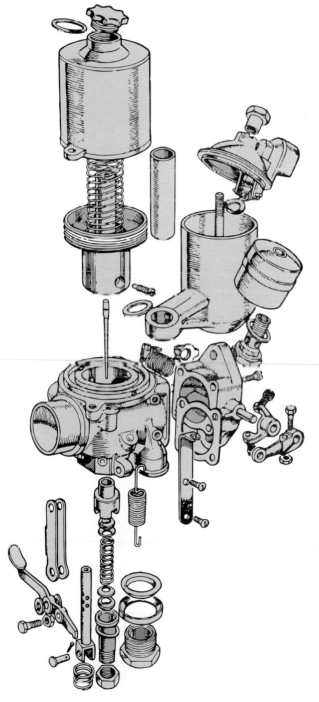

Exploded diagram of the MC2.

manifold, which in turn is screwed into the cylinder head. They are held together by a circular screw clamp. The latter is an egg-shaped flange with a hole on either end, which mates up with the same on the manifold.

To remove the throttle slide from the cable, compress the spring and allow the cable nipple to leave the hole in which it sits and the cable to pass through the slot to the larger hole through which the nipple can now pass, freeing it from the slide. To remove the needle from the throttle slide, remove the horseshoe spring clip from the top of the slide and allow the needle to drop out. The top of the needle has a series of grooves machined into it, into which the spring clip mates. Generally the middle of the grooves is the right setting; the lower the needle (that is, the higher the clipped groove), the weaker the mixture.

To remove the air slide, compress the spring and release the nipple from the end of the slide.

To remove the float chamber, unscrew the bolt at the base of the mixing chamber or main body. Take note – there are two fibre washers, one under the bolt head and one between the two chambers. Unscrew the float chamber lid, under which you will see the spring-loaded tickler, which simply presses down onto the float. To remove the float, simply compress the spring clip on the top of the float and lift the float out over the needle. Once the bolt is removed at the base of the float chamber, the needle will fall out. It's not critical on old brass floats, but it's often sensible to keep a note of, or mark, which is top. There are again two fibre washers. They can be reused if they're not too hard and worn but it's wise to replace them with new to save leaks.

In the base of the mixing chamber you'll be able to see the main jet, which can be removed from the needle jet. The main jet is the little hexagon-headed brass end piece with a tiny hole in the centre. Check the number stamped on it – you may need the magnifying glass. This screws into a longer hexagon-bodied jet – the needle jet – which in turn screws into the base of the jet block, the innards of the body. It is so called because the throttle needle runs up and down inside this jet. This too will have a number on it. Check the numbers against your details for

BELOW: Back in production and better than ever – the Amal 276.

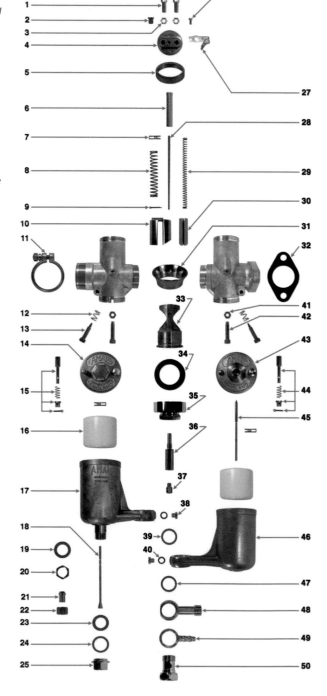

RIGHT: Parts list diagram for the Amal 276.

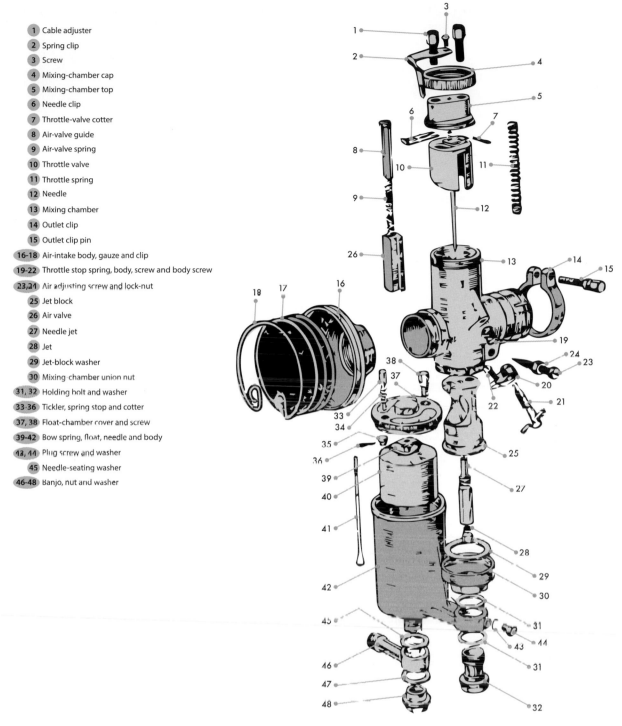

1. Cable adjuster
2. Spring clip
3. Screw
4. Mixing-chamber cap
5. Mixing-chamber top
6. Needle clip
7. Throttle-valve cotter
8. Air-valve guide
9. Air-valve spring
10. Throttle valve
11. Throttle spring
12. Needle
13. Mixing chamber
14. Outlet clip
15. Outlet clip pin
16-18. Air-intake body, gauze and clip
19-22. Throttle stop spring, body, screw and body screw
23,24. Air adjusting screw and lock-nut
25. Jet block
26. Air valve
27. Needle jet
28. Jet
29. Jet-block washer
30. Mixing-chamber union nut
31, 32. Holding bolt and washer
33-36. Tickler, spring stop and cotter
37, 38. Float-chamber cover and screw
39-42. Bow spring, float, needle and body
43, 44. Plug screw and washer
45. Needle-seating washer
46-48. Banjo, nut and washer

Exploded diagram of the Amal 276.

your particular model. If the jets are not the correct numbers, then buy the correct-sized jets from Amal, so that you'll know your settings are at least on the right baseline when it comes to fine-tuning your newly rebuilt engine.

To remove the jet block, the large union nut screwed onto the base of the mixing chamber must first be removed. There should be a large fibre washer in the base of the 'cup' of this union nut. With all ancillary adjustment screws removed from the chamber, the jet block can now be drifted out.

That is essentially all there is to a 276.

To reassemble, the jet block can be tapped back into position – there is a guide groove and peg so it's difficult to get it wrong – then the needle jet and main jets can be screwed into place. Refit the union nut, ensuring the fibre washer is intact and in place.

Fit the float needle through the base of the float chamber and drop the float over it, securing it at the top with the spring clip. There is only one groove so you can't get it wrong. Ensure everything here is spotlessly clean, as any little thing that detracts from the perfect operation of the float could cause flooding, high fuel consumption and very heavy running. Dirt on the needle, a bent needle, a worn needle, a punctured float, or even something silly like the carburettor being fitted out of plumb will all give those symptoms.

HOW TO TRACE FAULTS

There are only **TWO** possible faults in carburation, either **RICHNESS** of mixture or **WEAKNESS** of mixture, so in case of trouble decide which is the cause, by :—

1. **Examining the petrol feed.**
   - Verify jets and passages are clear.
   - Verify ample flow.
   - Verify there is no flooding.

2. **Looking for air leaks.**
   - At the connection to the engine.
   - Or due to leaky inlet valve stems.

3. **Defective or worn parts.**
   - As a slack throttle—worn needle jet.
   - The mixing chamber union nut not tightened up, or loose jets.

4. **TESTING WITH THE AIR VALVE** to see if by richening the mixture, the results are better or worse.

INDICATIONS OF :—

RICHNESS.	WEAKNESS.
Black smoke in exhaust.	Spitting in carburetter.
Petrol spraying out of carb.	Erratic slow running.
Four strokes, eight-stroking.	Overheating.
Two strokes, four-stroking.	Acceleration poor.
Heavy, lumpy running.	Engine goes better if :—
Heavy petrol consumption.	Throttle not wide open or
? If the jet block F is not tightened up by washer and nut E, richness will be caused through leakage of petrol.	Air Valve is partially closed.
	? Has air cleaner been removed.
	? Jets partially choked up.
? Air-cleaner choked up.	REMOVING the silencer or running with a racing silencer requires a richer setting and large main jet.
? Needle jet worn large.	
Sparking plug sooty.	

NOTE :

Verify correctness of fuel feed, stop air leaks, check over ignition and valve operation and timing. **DECIDE BY TEST WHETHER RICHNESS OR WEAKNESS IS THE TROUBLE AND AT WHAT THROTTLE POSITION.** See throttle opening diagrams, page 7.

PROCEDURE.

If at a particular throttle opening you partially close the air valve and the engine goes better, weakness is indicated ; or on the other hand the running is worse, richness is indicated. THEN YOU PROCEED TO ADJUST THE APPROPRIATE PART AS INDICATED AT THE TOP OF PAGE 7 FOR THAT THROTTLE POSITION.

FAULT AT THROTTLE POSITIONS
INDICATED ON PAGE 7

TO CURE RICHNESS.	↓	TO CURE WEAKNESS.
Fit smaller main jet.	1st	Fit larger main jet.
Screw out pilot air screw.	2nd	Screw pilot air screw in.
Fit a throttle with larger cut-away (§f, page 6).	3rd	Fit a throttle with smaller cut-away (§f, page 6).
Lower needle one or two grooves (§e, page 6).	4th	Raise needle one or two grooves (§e, page 6).

NOTE. It is not correct to cure a rich mixture at half throttle by fitting a smaller main jet because the main jet may be correct for power at full throttle : the proper thing to do is to lower the needle.

CHANGING FROM STANDARD PETROLS TO SPECIAL FUELS, such as alcohol mixtures will, with the same setting in the carburetter, certainly cause weakness of mixture and possible damage from overheating.

HOW IT WORKS AND PART NAMES

A.	Mixing Chamber.	O.	Needle Jet.
B.	Throttle Valve (see page 6).	P.	Main Jet (see page 6).
C.	Jet Needle and Clip above.	Q.	Float Chamber Holding Bolt.
D.	Air Valve.	R.	Float Chamber.
E.	Mixing Chamber Union Nut.	S.	Needle Valve Seating.
F.	Jet Block.	T.	Float.
G.	Cable Adjuster (*Throttle*).	U.	Float Needle Valve.
G1.	Cable Adjuster (*Air*).	V.	Float Needle Clip.
H.	Jet Block Barrel.	W.	Float Chamber Cover.
J.	Pilot Orifice (see page 6).	X.	Float Chamber Lock Screw.
K.	Passage to Pilot.		Tickler (to left of W.)
L.	Pilot Air Passage.	Y.	Mixing Chamber Top Cap.
M.	Pilot Mixture Outlet.	Z.	Mixing Chamber Lock Ring.
N.	Pilot By-pass.	Z1.	Security Spring for above.

The carburetter proportions and atomises the right amount of petrol with the air that is sucked in by the engine because of the correct proportions of jet sizes and the main choke bore. The float chamber maintains a constant level of fuel at the jets and cuts off the supply when the engine stops. The throttle control from the handlebar controls the volume of mixture and therefore the power, and at all positions of the throttle the mixture is automatically correct. The opening of the throttle brings first into action the mixture supply from the pilot jet system for idling, then as it progressively opens, via the pilot by-pass, the mixture is augmented from the main jet, the earlier stages of which action is controlled by the needle in the needle jet. The main jet does not spray directly into the mixing chamber, but discharges through the needle jet into the primary air chamber, and goes from there as a rich petrol-air mixture through the primary air choke into the main air choke. This primary air choke has a compensating action.

The carburetters usually have a separately-operated mixture control called an air valve, for use when starting from cold, and until the engine is warm ; this control partially blocks the passage of air through the main choke.

This design of carburetter offers perfectly simple and effective tuning facilities.

Fig. 3.
This section view does NOT apply if your carburetter has FOUR EXTERNAL primary air holes at the base of the mixing chamber. It is for carburetters with the primary air inlet in the main air intake.

Diagrammatic section of Carburetter showing only the lower half of the throttle chamber with the throttle a little open—and the internal primary air passages to the main jet and pilot system.

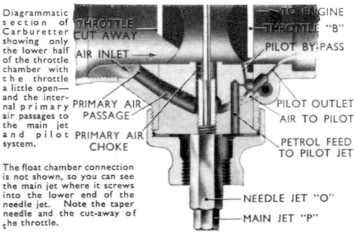

The float chamber connection is not shown, so you can see the main jet where it screws into the lower end of the needle jet. Note the taper needle and the cut-away of the throttle.

If the carburetter should flood whilst the engine is not running, the overflow from the main jet will run into the primary air passages and trickle out from there through a small hole seen at the side of the carburetter body.

TUNING TWIN ENGINES WITH TWIN CARBURETTERS
where each cylinder has its own Carburetter.

First of all, slacken the Throttle stop screws and put the Twist Grip into the shut off position to allow the Throttles to shut off ; there should be a slight back lash in the cables which back lash can be obtained, if necessary, by screwing in the cable adjusting screws on the top of the Carburetter. Then, with the Handlebars in the normal position, and with the Throttles closed, adjust the cable adjusting screws so that on the slightest opening of the Twist Grip, both Throttles begin to open simultaneously.

To set the Carburetters, follow the procedure as given on page 7 overleaf, and bear in mind these " Hints," which may be useful :—Main Jet sizes are of course selected by checking the effect of the Mixture on the Sparking Plugs after taking a run at full throttle over a straight piece of road ; the smallest pair of jets that give the best maximum speed is usually correct provided that the Plugs do not show any signs of excessive heat. It might be that for really critical tuning, one Carburetter might require a slightly different Jet size from the other.

For slow running, set the Twist Grip to make the Engine run slowly but just faster than a " tick over "; then gently screw in the Throttle stops to just hold the Throttles in that position, and return the Twist Grip into the shut position, leaving the Engine running on the Throttle Stops.
The next thing to do is to set each Carburetter according to paragraph 2, on Page 7, to obtain the idling by screwing down the Throttle Stop Screws and adjusting the Pilot Air Screws accordingly.

Regarding the setting of the Pilot Jets, a fairly satisfactory method is to detach one Sparking Plug lead, and set the Pilot Air Adjusting Screw on the other Cylinder as a single unit, and then reversing the process to the other Cylinder. It may be found that when both leads are connected to the Sparking Plugs, the Engine runs slightly quicker than desirable, in which case, a slight readjustment of the Throttle Stop Screws will put this right. It is essential that the speed of idling on both Cylinders is approximately the same, as this will either make or mar the smoothness of the get-away on the initial opening of the Throttle.

It is essential with Twin Carburetters that the Throttle Slides are a good fit in the bodies, and also that there is no suspicion of air leaks at either of the flange attachments to the Cylinder.
Regarding the lower end of the Throttle range, which is always the more difficult to set, one can only take excessive pains to make quite sure that the Control Cables are perfectly adjusted, without any excessive back lash or difference in the amount of back lash between one Carburetter and another ; otherwise one Throttle slide will be out of phase with the other, and so resulting in lumpy running.

To check the opening of the Throttles simultaneously, shut the Twist Grip back so that the Throttles are resting on the Throttle Stop Screws in their final position of adjustment ; then insert the fingers into the air intakes and press them on the Throttles and with the other hand, gently open by the Twist Grip and feel that the Throttles lift off their stops at the same time.

SERVICE ARRANGEMENTS

There are many AMAL Service Stockists in Great Britain and also in other countries where Motor-cycling is popular ; They have information about recommended settings for all standard machines and, you are strongly advised to purchase GENUINE AMAL SPARES through them, at our List prices.

The Main Jets for these Carburetters have a general type No. 4/042 and have interchangeable threads. All GENUINE JETS are stamped with the name AMAL and with the Calibration Number. They are made with orifice sizes and numbered from 30 to 500, going up in increments of 5 c.c. from Nos. 30 to 100 and thence by 10 c.c. : for example, 100, 110, and 120, etc.

The " number " stamped on the Jet is the number of cubic centimetres of petrol that will pass through the orifice under conditions of test by the AMAL Jet Calibrating machine. Never reamer a Jet out.
All GENUINE AMAL JETS have been tested before marking, and all genuine AMAL SPARES, as sold by our Stockists, are produced under the same conditions of Inspection as are the parts used in the production of Carburetters.

GUARANTEE.

AMAL

1

HINTS AND TIPS

LIST No. H294

for vertical, horizontal and inclined needle-jet carburetters with pilot jets

SINGLE LEVER   DOUBLE LEVER

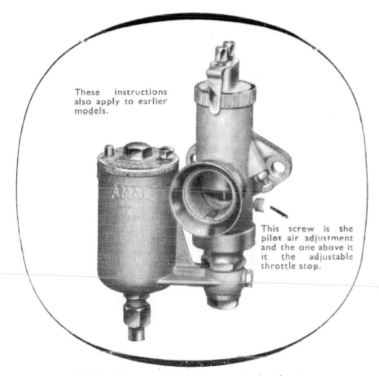

These instructions also apply to earlier models.

This screw is the pilot air adjustment and the one above it it the adjustable throttle stop.

FIG. 1—*Illustrates a double lever vertical carburetter with flange fitting.*

Printed in England. 25m./2/54. W.

AMAL LTD., HOLDFORD ROAD, WITTON, BIRMINGHAM 6, ENGLAND

'Phone : BIRchfields 4571.
(5 lines)

Telegrams : "AMALCARB, 'PHONE, BIRMINGHAM."

SECTIONED ILLUSTRATION of NEEDLE JET CARBURETTER WITH PILOT JET SYSTEM

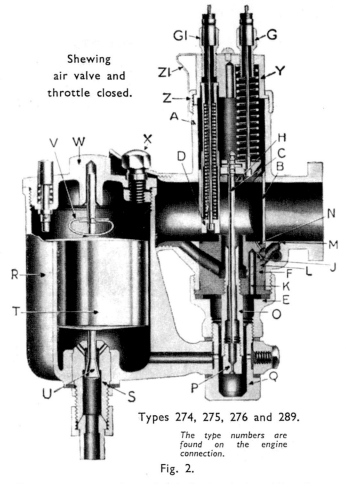

Shewing air valve and throttle closed.

Types 274, 275, 276 and 289.

The type numbers are found on the engine connection.

Fig. 2.

Your carburetter may be vertical, inclined or horizontal, but diagrammatically this view applies to all models, the variation being in the attachment to the engine and of the floatchamber.

TWO DESIGNS.

Fig. 2 above is the sectioned view of the Standard Ama. Carburetter as shown on page I, figure I.

This is the standard design where the primary air to the main jet and the pilot jet system comes in jointly through the main air intake, see figure 3, page 3. The type numbers are 274, 275, 276, 289.

An alternative design is made where the primary air to the main jet comes in through four visible ports around the base of the mixing chamber, and where also the air supply to the pilot jet system is separate. The type numbers of these carburetters are 74, 75, 76 and 89.

These tuning instructions apply to both the above designs.

HINTS AND TIPS

STARTING *from cold.* Flood the carburetter by depressing the tickler sharply three or four times, and close the air valve : set the ignition, say half retarded. Then shut the throttle and open it a little, *viz.*, about one-eighth open, see diagram on page 7 position 2, then kick-start. If it is too much open starting will be difficult.

STARTING, *engine hot.* Do not flood the carburetter but close the air lever. Set the ignition and close the throttle, then open the throttle about one-eighth of its travel and kick-start. If the carburetter has been flooded and wont start because the mixture is too rich—open the throttle wide and give the engine several turns to clear the richness, then start again with the throttle one-eighth open, and air lever wide open. Generally speaking it is not advisable to flood at all when an engine is hot.

STARTING, *general.* By experiment, find out if and when it is necessary to flood, also note the best position for the air lever and the throttle for the easiest starting (some carburetters have the throttle fitted with a starting position on to which the throttle must be shut down).

STARTING, SINGLE LEVER CARBURETTERS. OPEN THE THROTTLE VERY SLIGHTLY FROM THE IDLING POSITION AND FLOOD THE CARBURETTER MORE OR LESS ACCORDING TO THE ENGINE BEING COLD OR HOT RESPECTIVELY.

CABLE CONTROLS. See that there is a minimum of backlash when the controls are set back and that any movement of the handlebar does not cause the throttle to open ; this is done by the adjusters on the top of the carburetter. See that the throttle shuts down freely.

PETROL FEED, *verification.* Detach petrol pipe union at the float chamber end ; turn on petrol tap momentarily and see that fuel gushes out. Avoid petrol pipes with vertical loops as they cause air locks. *Flooding* may be due to a worn or bent needle or a leaky float, but nearly all flooding with new machines is due to impurities (grit, fluff, etc.) in the tank—so clean out the float chamber periodically till the trouble ceases. If the trouble persists, the tank might be drained, swilled out, etc. *Note that if a carburetter, either vertical or horizontal, is flooding with the engine stopped, the overflow from the main jet will not run into the engine but out of the carburetter through a hole at the base of the mixing chamber.*

FIXING CARBURETTER AND AIR LEAKS. Erratic slow running is often caused by air leaks, so verify there are none at the point of attachment to the cylinder or inlet pipe—check by means of an oil can and eliminate by new washers and the equal tightening up of the flange nuts. Also in old machines look out for air leaks caused by a worn throttle or worn inlet valve guides.

BANGING IN EXHAUST may be caused by too weak a pilot mixture when the throttle is closed or nearly closed—also it may be caused by too rich a pilot mixture and an air leak in the exhaust system ; the reason in either case is that the mixture has not fired in the cylinder and has fired in the hot silencer. If the banging happens when the throttle is fairly wide open the trouble will be ignition—not carburation.

BAD PETROL CONSUMPTION of a new machine may be due to flooding, caused by impurities from the petrol tank lodging on the float needle seat and so prevent its valve from closing. If the machine has had several years use, flooding may be caused by a worn float needle valve. Also bad petrol consumption will be apparent if the throttle needle jet "O" (see fig. 2) has worn ; it may be remedied or improved by lowering the needle in the throttle, but if it cannot be—then the only remedy is to get a new needle jet.

AIR FILTERS. These may affect the jet setting, so if one is fitted afterwards to the carburetter the main jet may have to be smaller. If a carburetter is set with an air filter and the engine is run without it, take care not to overheat the engine due to too weak a mixture ; testing with the air valve (page 5, §4) will indicate if a larger main jet and higher needle position are required.

FAULTS, read page 5. The trouble may not be carburation ; if the trouble cannot be remedied by making mixture richer or weaker with the air-valve, and you know the petrol feed is good and the carburetter is not flooding, the trouble is elsewhere.

RE-ASSEMBLING *after dismantling.* Note particularly that the mixing chamber nut E (fig. 2, page 2) is tightened up tight on to the washer that holds the jet block F (fig. 2, page 2), otherwise petrol will leak up. When replacing the throttle see that the throttle needle goes into the centre hole in the choke block and once in, note the throttle works freely when the mixing chamber top ring Z is screwed down firmly and held by spring ZI.

Float chamber lid. To remove, first loosen screw X (fig. 2). To remove float, pinch the bow V (fig. 2), and pull ; when replacing, slip over needle and slide down till bow jumps into the needle groove. Care required to avoid bending needle.

PARTS TO TUNE UP WITH

(a) This fig. 4 is two diagrammatic sections of the carburetter to show :—

1. *The throttle stop screw.*
2. *The pilot air screw.*

(b) **THROTTLE STOP SCREW.** Set this screw to prop the throttle open sufficiently to keep the engine running when the twist grip is shut off.

(c) **PILOT AIR SCREW.** This screw regulates the strength of the mixture for "idling" and for the initial opening of the throttle. The screw controls the suction on the pilot petrol jet by metering the amount of air that mixes with the petrol.

NOTE.—The air for the pilot jet may be admitted internally or externally according to one or other of the designs, but there is no difference in tuning.

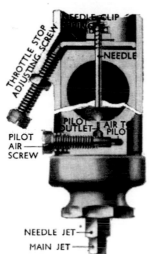

Fig. 4.

(d) **MAIN JET.** The main jet controls the petrol supply when the throttle is more than three-quarters open, but at smaller throttle openings although the supply of fuel goes through the main jet, the amount is diminished by the metering effect of the needle in the needle jet.

Each jet is calibrated and numbered so that its exact discharge is known and two jets of the same number are alike. NEVER REAMER A JET OUT, GET ANOTHER OF THE RIGHT SIZE. The bigger the number the bigger the jet. Spare jets ARE SEALED.

To get at the main jet, undo the float chamber holding bolt Q (page 2). The jet is screwed into the needle jet so if the jet were tight, hold the needle jet also carefully with a spanner, whilst unscrewing the main jet.

(e) **NEEDLE AND NEEDLE JET.** The needle is attached to the throttle and being taper—either allows more or less petrol to pass through the needle jet as the throttle is opened or closed throughout the range, except when idling or nearly full throttle. The needle jet is of a defined size and is only altered from standard when using alcohol fuels.

The taper needle position in relation to the throttle opening can be set according to the mixture required by fixing it to the throttle with the needle clip spring in a certain groove (see *illustration above*), thus either raising or lowering it. Raising the needle richens the mixture and lowering it weakens the mixture at throttle openings from quarter to three-quarters open (see illustration, page 7).

(f) **THROTTLE VALVE CUT-AWAY.** The atmospheric side of the throttle is cut away to influence the depression on the main fuel supply and thus gives a means of tuning between the pilot and needle jet range of throttle opening. The amount of cut-away is recorded by a number marked on the throttle, viz., 6/3 means throttle type 6 with No. 3 cut-away; larger cut-aways, say 4 and 5, give weaker mixtures and 2 and 1 richer mixtures.

(g) **AIR VALVE** is used only for starting and running when cold, and for experimenting with, otherwise run with it wide open.

(h) **TICKLER,** a small plunger spring loaded in the float chamber lid. When pressed down on the float, the needle valve is pushed off its seat and so "flooding" is achieved. Flooding temporarily enriches the mixture until the level of the petrol subsides to normal.

HOW TO TUNE UP

PHASES OF AMAL NEEDLE JET CARBURETTER THROTTLE OPENINGS

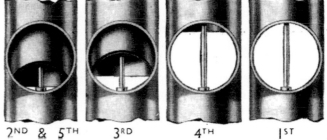

Up to ⅛ open	from ⅛ to ¼ open	¼ to ¾ open	¾ to full open
PILOT JET	THROTTLE CUT-AWAY	NEEDLE-POSITION	MAIN JET SIZE
2ND & 5TH	3RD	4TH	1ST

SEQUENCE OF TUNING

TUNE UP IN THE FOLLOWING ORDER ONLY, by so doing you will not upset good results obtained.

NOTE. The carburetter is automatic throughout the throttle range—the air valve should always be wide open except when used for starting or until the engine has warmed up. We assume normal petrols are used.

READ REMARKS ON PAGES 5 AND 6 for each tuning device and get the motor going perfectly on a quiet road with a slight up gradient so that on test the engine is pulling.

1st. MAIN JET with throttle in position 1 (§d, page 6). Test the engine for full throttle ; if when at full throttle, the power seems better *with the throttle less than wide open* or with the air valve closed slightly the main jet is too small. If the engine runs "heavily" the main jet is too large. If testing for speed work note the jet size is rich enough to keep engine cool, and to verify this, examine the sparking plug by taking a fast run, declutching, and stopping engine quickly. If the plug body at the end has a cool appearance the mixture is correct ; if sooty, the mixture is rich ; if however there are signs of intense heat the mixture is too weak and a larger jet is necessary.

2nd. PILOT JET WITH THROTTLE IN POSITIONS 2 AND 5. With engine idling too fast with the twist grip shut off and the throttle shut down on to the throttle stop screw, and ignition set for best slow running : (1) Loosen stop screw nut and screw down until engine runs slower and begins to falter, then screw the pilot air screw in or out to make engine run regularly and faster. (2) Now gently lower the throttle stop screw until the engine runs slower and just begins to falter, then lock the nut lightly and begin again to adjust the pilot air screw to get best slow running ; if this 2nd adjustment makes engine run too fast, go over the job again a third time. Finally, lock up tight the throttle stop screw nut without disturbing the screw's position.

3rd. THROTTLE CUT-AWAY with throttle in position 3 (§f, page 6). If, as you take off from the idling position, there is objectionable spitting from the carburetter, slightly richen the pilot mixture by screwing in the air screw sufficiently, but if this is not effective, screw it back again, and fit a throttle with a smaller cut-away. If the engine jerks under load at this throttle position and there is no spitting, either the throttle needle is much too high or a larger throttle cut-away is required to cure richness.

4th. NEEDLE with throttle in position 4 (§e, page 6). The needle controls a wide range of throttle opening and also the acceleration. Try the needle in as low a position as possible, viz., with the clip in a groove as near the top as possible ; if acceleration is poor and with air valve partially closed the results are better, raise the needle by two grooves ; if very much better try lowering needle by one groove and leave it where it is best.

Note, if mixture is still too rich with clip in groove No. 1 nearest the end—the **Needle Jet** *probably wants replacement because of wear. If the needle itself has had several years' use, replace it also.*

5th. FINALLY go over the idling again for final touches.

Fit the float chamber onto the base of the mixing chamber, not forgetting the fibre washers, and fit the holding bolt to secure the float chamber to the mixing chamber. Wherever there is a metal to metal fitting, use a fibre washer or petrol will leak out.

Fit the needle to the throttle slide with the spring clip in its appropriate notch of the five available. With the cable poked through the carburettor lid, feed the spring onto the throttle cable – positioned nearest to the cylinder head – and slip the nipple through its groove into its appropriate place of rest. Apply the same technique to the air slide. With a bit of light oil on the slides, slip them into the mixing chamber, taking special care when feeding the needle into the top of the needle jet. Often there is a little peg on the body and a corresponding groove in the slide to ensure correct fitting. Do not under any circumstances force it. If the slide will not go in easily there is a fault, which must be rectified. Once correctly fitted, the slides will operate smoothly, with the throttle slide making a firm clonk when it makes contact with the bottom of its housing under its spring-loaded return.

Mixture Adjustment

This is where it gets a bit complicated, or at least it sounds like it's complicated because of the terminology involved – in actual fact, with everything in order, it's fairly straightforward. There are three stages of air/fuel mixture control within the throttle opening: up to one-eighth throttle opening, it's controlled by the pilot air screw in the side of the carburettor body; from there to three-quarters open, the mixture is controlled by the needle inside

the needle jet; and from there to wide open it is the responsibility of the main jet. This is the reason race bikes and sportsters have a huge main jet: to get as much fuel into the combustion chamber as possible to get the biggest bang when flat out. Indeed the rule of thumb in vintage racing circles used to be find the biggest jet that will fit and then put a drill through it! However, for our purposes that is taboo. If you must experiment with jets, never tamper with the original; buy the size immediately above or below until you are happy with the result.

Slow-Running Adjustment

Start the engine and let it warm up to working temperature, then screw in the pilot air adjuster until it is all the way in, all the while slowly closing the throttle but balancing it so it does not stall. The engine should now be eight-stroking or hunting – like your car when it's on choke – which is essentially what you have done to your engine (choked it up). Slowly unscrew the pilot screw until the engine revs rise, continuing to close the throttle. Eventually you will find a spot where the throttle is on its stop and the engine is ticking over cleanly without hunting or spitting back. If it does then you've wound out the air screw too far and the mixture is now too weak.

Throttle Stops

Also in the side of the 276 carburettor is a throttle stop screw. This is a spring-loaded screw with a small T-section head to enable manual adjustment, which actually protrudes into the mixing chamber and makes contact with the base of the throttle

slide; its adjustment inwards lifts the slide off its stop, allowing the engine revs to increase on a closed throttle. Around it there is sometimes an adjuster clamp, which is useful for two reasons. When it's turned clockwise, it pushes the slide just off the stop, which lets the engine rev slightly higher than usual when first starting from cold; then, as the engine warms up and the revs rise even higher, it can be turned anticlockwise, returning the engine to its normal tick-over speed.

THE MONOBLOC

A very simple and effective instrument, the Monobloc's mixing chamber and side float bowl unit construction tidied up the construction of the 276 and all the potential leaks from its plethora of joints. The Monobloc came in three sizes, of identical design but different physical dimensions. Within the three sizes was also a variety of bore sizes, which made it suitable for engines from 125cc right through to 1,000cc and above.

These were the 375, the 376 and the 389 – and sizes ranged from the 375's $^{21}/_{32}$in to the 389's $1^3/_{16}$in.

The manufacturers of the day all worked hand in glove with Amal, as they did with, for example, Lucas electrics and Smith Instruments, so their different models had different-sized carburettors to suit their purpose. As mentioned above, these exact specifications are not difficult to find today.

The Monobloc recognition numbers always begin with the type of carburettor body size, that is 375, 376 or 389, followed by a further series of numbers, which translate into the exact specification. This is in theory, of course – there is no guarantee that your carburettor still fits this specification, as it may have suffered treatment in the hands of a less skilled home tuner in the past. Hence a check is necessary.

Having said that, many parts are common throughout the range and thus can be found in quite different carburettors; for example, main jet 376/100, holder 376/073, needle jet 376/072 and pilot jet 376/076 are regularly found. Indeed, another example is the mixing chamber fitted to BSA's B31 350cc single: it was also fitted to AJS

An original 276 still going strong. Note the throttle adjustment screw – this is set to the lowest tickover speed when engine is warm but can be turned to slightly push the slide off its stop when the engine is cold to help keep it running.

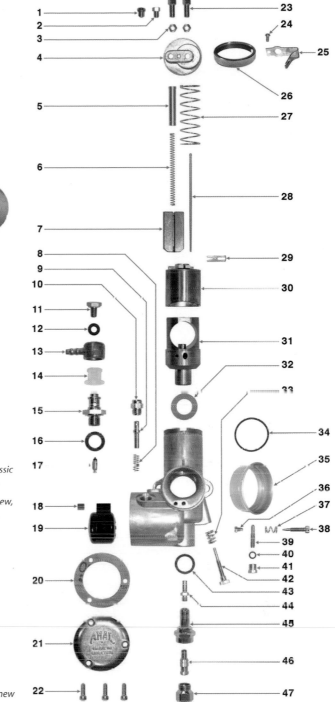

1 — 23
2 — 24
3 — 25
4 — 26
5 — 27
6 — 28
7 — 29
8 — 30
9 —
10 — 31
11 — 32
12 — 33
13 — 34
14 — 35
15 — 36
16 — 37
17 — 38
18 — 39
19 — 40
20 — 41
21 — 42
22 — 43
— 44
— 45
— 46
— 47

and Matchless 500/650cc twins, Norton's 500cc Dominator, Ariel's 500cc Fieldmaster twin and their 600ccVB side valve single, Panther's 350cc Model 75 and Royal Enfield's 350cc Clipper. These and many more like them can be found in Amal's specification sheets, but often the numbers change to suit the slightly different specification. For example, one carburettor could be identical to another apart from the slightly different size of the main jet – the higher the number the bigger the diameter of the jet's bore. The number represents the flow capable of passing through the orifice in cubic centimetres per minute.

If you buy new jets, then buy a new needle to go with them as wear occurs to both simultaneously. The standard size of needle jet is .106 and as such they are not usually stamped with a reference number, but alternative sizes invariably do have a number, such as .105, .107, .108. If yours is unmarked then it's a .106.

Needles are also often marked with a number, though it's pretty difficult to see. The letter B represents the 375/063 needle, C the 376/063 type and D is the 389/063.

ABOVE: Another classic Amal carburetter available brand new, off the shelf – the Monobloc.

RIGHT: Parts list breakdown for a new Amal Monobloc.

Of the five needle notches, number one notch is at the top, so obviously number three is the middle setting and five the bottom.

The throttle slides, often called throttle valves, have a cutaway on the outside, the air side. These create a depression over the fuel jets and the amount of cutaway is measured in sixteenths of an inch. The sizes are marked on the top of the slide, so for example a slide stamped 376/3 will be a type 376 slide with a cutaway of $^{3}/_{16}$in. The higher the

number, the bigger the cutaway and the weaker the mixture – that is, more air is allowed through.

If you think about what a slide does and the number of times it does it, there's little wonder they wear. As the slide is pulled up the mixing chamber, the machine accelerates, and as more fuel is demanded by the greedy engine there is a fierce suction from the cylinder on the carburettor, which inevitably pulls the slide toward the engine face of the carburettor body during its

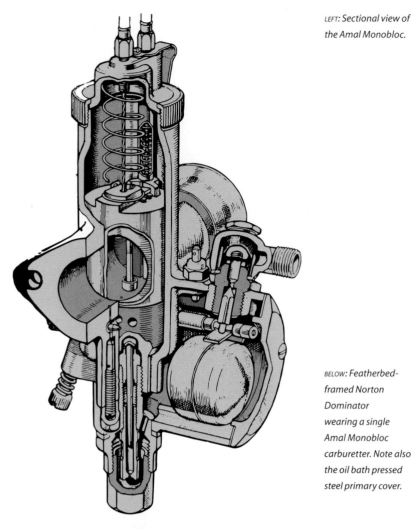

LEFT: Sectional view of the Amal Monobloc.

BELOW: Featherbed-framed Norton Dominator wearing a single Amal Monobloc carburetter. Note also the oil bath pressed steel primary cover.

with a new one. After a season's use, the newness will have worn off and it'll look as original as the original – and you can always polish up the worn-out original and use it as a paperweight or a mantelpiece ornament.

THE MK 1 CONCENTRIC

While the Monobloc was, without doubt, a very good carburettor, by the mid-1960s the motorcycle industry was putting pressure on Amal to come up with a cheaper version. Longevity didn't matter as long as it cost less. Amal came up with the Concentric. It did everything the Monobloc did but was smaller, more compact and cheaper to make, therefore cheaper to sell.

The Mk 1 Concentric is a much-maligned carburettor with the reputation of being a unit built of compromise; while the latter may be true to a certain extent, its reputation is unjust, for, all things considered, it is a perfectly good instrument of its time. There are other foreign carburettors available, which are more modern in design, more complex and can give excellent performance, but the Concentrics, which are available from Amal today – do not confuse them with similar, inferior Asian-built copies, identifiable because they do not have the Amal logo on the body – are now manufactured of improved materials on state-of-the-art machinery with much more precise tolerances. There has never been a better Concentric. Besides if it's the correct carb for your bike, it looks original and therefore right. The Mk 1 Concentric was first seen on motorcycles for the 1967 model year. The name comes from the float chamber surrounding the main jet, a design intended to reduce the effect of fuel surge in the float bowl under hard or inconsistent throttle conditions. It's currently available in two sizes: the 600 series (22mm, 24mm, 26mm and 27mm bore) and the 900 series (28mm, 30mm, and 32mm bore). The 1000 Series in 34mm, 36mm, and 38mm was discontinued during the 1970s. The larger sizes are now available in Concentric Mk 2 form. Mk 1s come in four-stroke and two-stroke configurations and can be left- or right handed depending on the position of the tickler mechanism and adjusting screws.

As the unit is so compact, it is easier to remove the carburettor from the

up-and-down motion. Therefore this side may wear more than the air side and the carburettor body may eventually become so oval that no amount of fine-tuning can overcome it. Again, the answer is buy a new one, complete with new slide, float, jets and all.

However, just because a slide has an appearance of wear, it does not necessarily mean it is past its best: as long as it remains a reasonably good fit within its housing, it will work satisfactorily. Many classics are still running with their original carburettors, which is testament to the basic idea of half a century ago and the quality of what was a mass-manufactured simple instrument subject to great deal of ham-fisted abuse.

Don't get sentimental over replacing the machine's original instrument

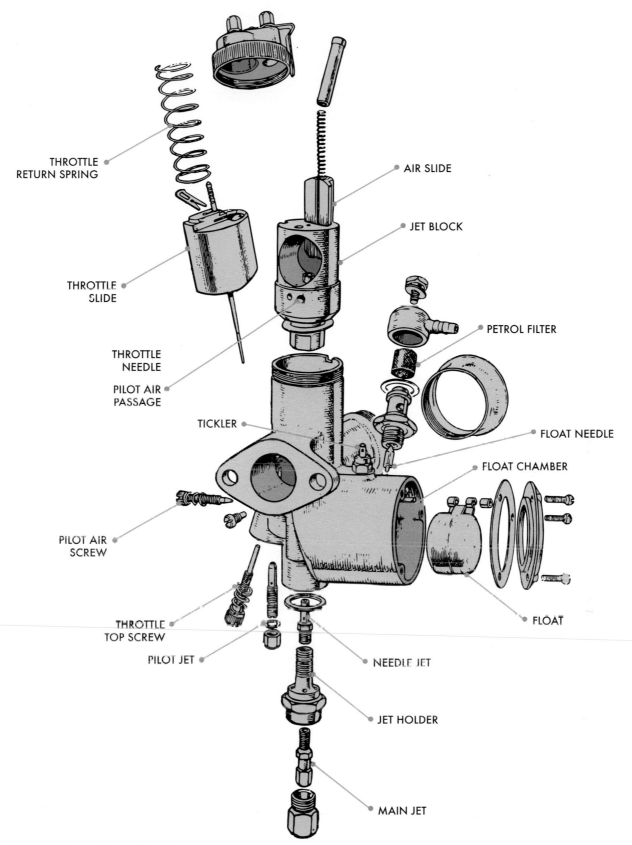

THROTTLE
RETURN SPRING

AIR SLIDE

JET BLOCK

THROTTLE
SLIDE

THROTTLE
NEEDLE

PILOT AIR
PASSAGE

PETROL FILTER

TICKLER

FLOAT NEEDLE

FLOAT CHAMBER

PILOT AIR
SCREW

THROTTLE
TOP SCREW

FLOAT

PILOT JET

NEEDLE JET

JET HOLDER

MAIN JET

Exploded diagram of the Amal Monobloc.

bike before working on it. Any fuel remaining in the float bowl can be drained by removing the drain plug in the base of the bowl. Remove the banjo bolts and the banjos and remove the mesh filter from within the banjo; clean it if necessary and keep it safe. If there are deposits that cannot be removed or the mesh is damaged, replace it with a new one. If there are rust deposits visible, there may be a petrol tank issue to deal with. Loosen the mounting nuts evenly, to avoid potentially warping the flange, then with them off, simply slide the carb off the studs.

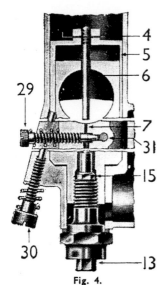

Fig. 4.

PARTS TO TUNE UP WITH

(a) This fig. 4 is three diagrammatic sections of the carburetter to show the throttle adjusting screw (30), and the pilot air adjusting screw.

(b) THROTTLE ADJUSTING SCREW.

Set this screw to hold the throttle open sufficiently to keep the engine running when the twist grip is shut off.

(c) PILOT AIR ADJUSTING SCREW.

This screw regulates the strength of the mixture for "idling" and for the initial opening of the throttle. The screw controls the depression on the pilot jet by metering the amount of air that mixes with the petrol.

FOR KEY TO DIAGRAM NUMBERS SEE PAGE 3.

(d) MAIN JET. The main jet controls the petrol supply when the throttle is more than three-quarters open, but at smaller throttle openings although the supply of fuel goes through the main jet, the amount is diminished by the metering effect of the needle in the needle jet.

Each jet is calibrated and numbered so that its exact discharge is known and two jets of the same number are alike. NEVER REAMER A JET OUT, GET ANOTHER OF THE RIGHT SIZE. The bigger the number the bigger the jet.

To remove the main jet unscrew the main jet cover, the exposed main jet can then be unscrewed from the jet holder.

(e) NEEDLE AND NEEDLE JET. The needle is attached to the throttle valve and being taper—either allows more or less petrol to pass through the needle jet as the throttle is opened or closed throughout the range, except when idling or nearly full throttle.

The taper needle position in relation to the throttle opening can be set according to the mixture required by fixing it to the throttle valve with the jet needle clip in a certain groove (see *figure 4 above*), thus either raising or lowering it. Raising the needle richens the mixture and lowering it weakens the mixture at throttle openings from quarter to three-quarters open (see *figure 5, page 7*). The needles are marked with the letters B, C, or D. B type are fitted in the 375 Carburetter, C type in the 376 Carburetter, and D type in the 389 Carburetter. The needles in some cases are marked with a number in addition to a letter.

(f) THROTTLE VALVE CUT-AWAY. The atmospheric side of the throttle is cut away to influence the depression on the main fuel supply and thus gives a means of tuning between the pilot and needle jet range of throttle opening. The amount of cut-away is recorded by a number marked on the throttle valve, viz., 376/3 means throttle valve type 376 with No. 3 cut-away ; larger cut-aways, say 4 and 5, give weaker mixtures and 2 a richer mixture.

(g) AIR VALVE is used only for starting and running when cold, and for experimenting with, otherwise run with it wide open.

(h) TICKLER, a small plunger spring loaded, in the float chamber wall. When pressed down on the float, the needle valve is allowed to open and so "flooding" is achieved. Flooding temporarily enriches the mixture until the level of the petrol subsides to normal.

ALCOHOL FUELS. When using alcohol fuels the following new components are necessary. Needle Jet 376/117, Jet Needle 376/116 or 389/088 according to type of carburetter, Needle Seating 376/118, Float Needle 376/161, Filter Gauze 376/093B, Banjo Washer 14/175, and possibly a double feed Banjo if not already fitted. The Main Jet must be increased for straight alcohol by approximately 150%. The final setting must be a question of trial and error according to the nature of fuel used. When using alcohol fuels it is advisable to err on the rich side to avoid engine overheating.

HOW TO TUNE UP

PHASES OF AMAL NEEDLE JET CARBURETTER THROTTLE OPENINGS

Up to ⅛ open PILOT JET	from ⅛ to ¼ open THROTTLE CUT-AWAY	¼ to ¾ open NEEDLE-POSITION	¾ to full open MAIN JET SIZE
2ND & 5TH	3RD	4TH	1ST

SEQUENCE OF TUNING

FIG. 5.

TUNE UP IN THE FOLLOWING ORDER.

NOTE. The carburetter is automatic throughout the throttle range—the air valve should always be wide open except when used for starting or until the engine has warmed up. We assume normal petrols are used.

READ REMARKS ON PAGES 6 AND 7 for each tuning device and get the motor going perfectly on a quiet road with a slight up gradient so that on test the engine is pulling.

1st MAIN JET with throttle in position 1 (fig. 5).
If at full throttle the engine runs "heavily" the main jet is too large. If at full throttle by slightly closing the throttle or air valve the engine seems to have better power, the main jet is too small. With a correct sized main jet the engine at full throttle should run evenly and regularly with maximum power. If testing for speed work ensure that the main jet size is sufficient for the mixture to be rich enough to keep the engine cool, and to verify this examine the sparking plug after taking a fast run, declutching and stopping the engine quickly. If the plug body at its end has a cool appearance the mixture is correct : if sooty, the mixture is rich : if however there are signs of intense heat, the mixture is too weak and a larger main jet is **necessary.**

2nd. PILOT JET (fig. 5) with throttle in positions 2 and 5.
With engine idling too fast with the twist grip shut off and the throttle shut down on to the throttle adjusting screw, and ignition set for best slow running : (1) Screw out throttle adjusting screw until the engine runs slower and begins to falter, then screw pilot air adjusting screw in or out to make engine run regularly and faster. (2) Now gently lower the throttle adjusting screw until the engine runs slower and just begins to falter, adjust the pilot air adjusting screw to get best slow running : if this 2nd adjustment make engine run too fast, go over the job again a third time.

3rd. THROTTLE CUT-AWAY with throttle in position 3 (fig. 5).
If, as you take off from the idling position, there is objectionable spitting from the carburetter, slightly richen the pilot mixture by screwing in the air screw sufficiently, but if this is not effective, screw it back again, and fit a throttle with a smaller cut-away. If the engine jerks under load at this throttle position and there is no spitting, either the jet needle is much too high or a larger throttle cut-away is required to cure richness.

4th. NEEDLE with throttle in position 4 (fig. 5).
The needle controls a wide range of throttle opening and also the acceleration. Try the needle in as low a position as possible, viz., with the clip in a groove as near the top as possible ; if acceleration is poor and with air valve partially closed the results are better, raise the needle by two grooves ; if very much better try lowering needle by one groove and leave it where it is best. If mixture is still too rich with clip in groove No. 1 nearest the top—the **needle jet** probably wants replacement because of wear. If the needle itself has had several years' use replace it also.

5th FINALLY go over the idling again for final touches.

TUNING TWIN ENGINES WITH TWIN CARBURETTERS

where each cylinder has its own Carburetter.
First of all, slacken the Throttle stop screws and put the Twist Grip into the shut off position to allow the Throttles to shut off ; there should be a slight back lash in the cables which back lash can be obtained, if necessary, by screwing in the cable adjusting screws on the top of the Carburetter. Then, with the Handlebars in the normal position, and with the Throttles closed, adjust the cable adjusting screws so that on the slightest opening of the Twist Grip, both Throttles begin to open simultaneously.

To set the Carburetters, follow the procedure as given on page 7, and bear in mind these " Hints," which may be useful :—Main Jet sizes are of course selected by checking the effect of the Mixture on the Sparking Plugs after taking a run at full throttle over a straight piece of road ; the smallest pair of jets that give the best maximum speed are usually correct provided that the Plugs do not show any signs of excessive heat. It might be that for really critical tuning, one Carburetter might require a slightly different Jet size from the other.

For slow running, set the Twist Grip to make the Engine run slowly but just faster than a " tick over " ; then gently screw in the Throttle stops to just hold the Throttles in that position, and return the Twist Grip into the shut position, leaving the Engine running on the Throttle Stops.

The next thing to do is to set each Carburetter according to paragraph 2, on Page 7, to obtain the idling by screwing down the Throttle Stop Screws and adjusting the Pilot Air Screws accordingly.

Regarding the setting of the Pilot, a fairly satisfactory method is to detach one Sparking Plug lead, and set the Pilot Air Adjusting Screw on the other Cylinder as a single unit, and then reversing the process to the other Cylinder. It may be found that when both leads are connected to the Sparking Plugs, the Engine runs slightly quicker than desirable, in which case, a slight readjustment of the Throttle Stop Screws will put this right. It is essential that the speed of idling on both Cylinders is approximately the same, as this will either make or mar the smoothness of the get-away on the initial opening of the Throttle.

It is essential with Twin Carburetters that the Throttle Slides are a good fit in the bodies, and also that there is no suspicion of air leaks at either of the flange attachments to the Cylinder.

Regarding the lower end of the Throttle range, which is always the more difficult to set, one can only take excessive pains to make quite sure that the Control Cables are perfectly adjusted, without any excessive back lash or difference in the amount of back lash between one Carburetter and another ; otherwise one Throttle slide will be out of phase with the other and so resulting in lumpy running.

To check the opening of the Throttle simultaneously, shut the Twist Grip back so that the Throttles are resting on the Throttle Stop Screws in their final position of adjustment ; then insert the fingers into the air intakes and press them on the Throttles and with the other hand, gently open by the Twist Grip and feel that the Throttles lift off their stops at the same time.

WHEN USING A REMOTE FLOAT CHAMBER. The fuel level should be set in line with the raised point below the name Amal on the side cover of the mixing chamber. This level is indicated externally on types 510 and 504 Float Chambers by a line. The type 302 level is 1 $\frac{1}{16}$" below the cover joint face. This setting must take place when the machine is not on its stand and on level ground.

SERVICE ARRANGEMENTS

There are many AMAL Service Stockists in Great Britain and also in other countries where Motor-cycling is popular : They have information about recommended settings for all standard machines and, you are strongly advised to purchase GENUINE AMAL SPARES through them, at our List prices.
ALL GENUINE JETS are stamped with the name AMAL and with the Calibration Number.

GUARANTEE.

The Company take all possible reasonable care in the manufacture and the quality of their products. Purchasers are informed that, any part proved to be defective in manufacture or quality, and returned to the works within six months of its purchase new, will be replaced.
The Company must respectfully point out however, that its responsibility and that of its agents, stockists and dealers, is limited to this Guarantee, and that they cannot, under any circumstances, be held responsible for any loss or for any contingent or resulting liability arising through any defect.
The conditions of sale and use also apply when the Company's products form part of the original equipment of machines purchased new.

50,000/9/66. W.   Printed in England.

HINTS AND TIPS
for
AMAL MONOBLOC CARBURETTER
Types 375, 376 and 389
Needle-jet Carburetters with pilot jets

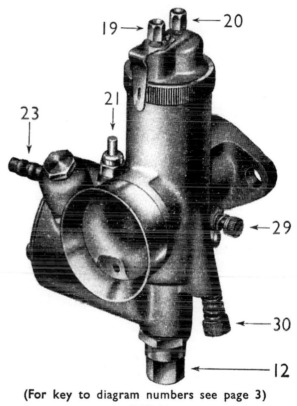

(For key to diagram numbers see page 3)

INDEX.

IMI Amal Ltd, *a subsidiary of IMI plc*
Holdford Road, Witton, Birmingham, B6 7ES
England
Telephone: 021-356 2000 Telex: 335959 IMICOM G

IMI

Sectional illustrations of Carburetters. Types 375, 376 and 389

(For key to diagram numbers see page 3).

Fig. I—Section through **float** chamber.

Fig. 2 — Section through mixing chamber, showing air valve and throttle closed.

HOW IT WORKS & PART NAMES

The carburetter proportions and atomises the right amount of petrol with the air that is drawn in by the engine because of the correct proportions of jet sizes and the main choke bore. The float chamber maintains a constant level of fuel at the jets and cuts off the supply when the engine stops.

The throttle control from the handlebar controls the volume of mixture and therefore the power, and at all positions of the throttle the mixture is automatically correct. The opening of the throttle brings first into action the mixture supply from the pilot jet system for idling, then as it progressively opens, via the pilot by-pass, the mixture is augmented from the main jet, the earlier stages of which action is controlled by the needle in the needle jet. The pilot jet system is supplied by a pilot jet which is detachable for cleaning purposes and which when assembled in the carburetter body is sealed by a cover nut. The main jet does not spray directly into the mixing chamber, but discharges through the needle jet into the primary air chamber, and goes from there as a rich petrol-air mixture through the primary air choke into the main air choke. This primary air choke has a compensating action in conjunction with bleed holes in the needle jet, which serve the double purpose of air compensating the mixture from the needle jet and allowing the fuel to provide a well outside and around the needle jet, which is available for snap acceleration.

The carburetters usually have a separately operated mixture control called an air valve, for use when starting from cold, and until the engine is warm ; this control partially blocks the passage of air through the main choke.

This design of carburetter offers perfectly simple and effective tuning facilities.

1—Mixing Chamber Top.	19—Cable Adjuster (Air).
2—Mixing Chamber Cap.	20—Cable Adjuster (Throttle).
3—Carburetter Body.	21—Tickler.
4—Jet Needle Clip.	22—Banjo Bolt.
5—Throttle Valve.	23—Banjo.
6—Jet Needle.	24—Filter Gauze.
7—Pilot outlet.	25—Needle Seating.
8—Pilot by-pass.	26—Needle.
9—Pilot Jet.	27—Float.
10—Petrol feed to pilot jet.	28—Side Cover Screws.
11—Pilot Jet Cover Nut.	29—Pilot Air Adjusting Screw.
12—Main Jet Cover.	30—Throttle Adjusting Screw.
13—Main Jet.	31—Air to pilot jet.
14—Jet Holder.	32—Feed holes in pilot jet.
15—Needle Jet.	33—Bleed holes in needle jet.
16—Jet Block.	34—Primary Air Choke.
17—Air Valve.	35—Primary Air Passage.
18—Mixing Chamber Cap Spring.	36—Throttle Valve Cutaway.

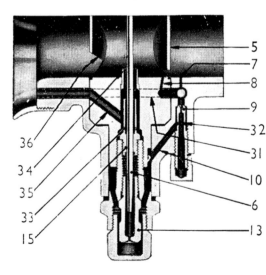

Fig. 3.

Diagrammatic section of Carburetter showing only the lower half of the throttle chamber with the throttle a little open— and the internal primary air passages to the main jet and pilot system.

FOR KEY TO DIAGRAM NUMBERS SEE ABOVE.

HINTS AND TIPS

STARTING *from cold.* Turn on fuel supply, set ignition (if manually operated) for best slow running, depress tickler to flood float chamber, close air valve, open throttle slightly and start engine. When engine starts open air valve and close the throttle ; if engine begins to falter, partially close the air valve until engine is warm, then set in fully open position.

STARTING, *engine hot.* Open throttle slightly and start engine. It should not normally be necessary to flood the float chamber or close the air valve when starting a warm engine.

STARTING, *general.* Experience will show when it is necessary to flood the carburetter or use the air valve and also the best setting of the throttle valve. If the carburetter has been over-flooded or strangled, which would result in a wet engine and over-rich starting mixture—fully open the throttle valve and air valve, give the engine several turns to clear the richness, then start again with the air valve fully open and the throttle valve slightly open.

STARTING, SINGLE LEVER CARBURETTERS.   OPEN THE THROTTLE VERY SLIGHTLY FROM THE IDLING POSITION AND FLOOD THE CARBURETTER MORE OR LESS ACCORDING TO THE ENGINE BEING COLD OR HOT RESPECTIVELY

CABLE CONTROLS. See that there is a minimum of backlash when the controls are set back and that any movement of the handlebar does not cause the throttle to open ; this is done by the adjusters on the top of the carburetter. See that the throttle shuts down freely.

PETROL FEED, *verification.* Later models are fitted with a filter gauze at the inlet to the float chamber. To remove the filter gauze unscrew the banjo bolt (22), the banjo can then be removed and the filter gauze withdrawn from the needle seating. Ensure that the filter gauze is undamaged and free from all foreign matter. Before replacing banjo turn on petrol tap momentarily and see that fuel gushes out. Avoid petrol pipes with vertical loops as they cause air locks. *Flooding* may be due to a worn needle or a damaged float, but nearly all flooding with new machines is due to impurities (grit, fluff, etc.) in the tank—so clean out the float chamber periodically till the trouble ceases. If the trouble persists, the tank might be drained, swilled out, etc.

FIXING CARBURETTER AND AIR LEAKS. Erratic slow running is often caused by air leaks, so verify there are none at the point of attachment to the cylinder or inlet pipe—check by means of an oil can and eliminate by new washers and the equal tightening up of the flange nuts. On later models a sealing ring is fitted into the attachment flange of the carburetter. Also in old machines look out for air leaks caused by a worn throttle or worn inlet valve guides.

BANGING IN EXHAUST may be caused by too weak a pilot mixture when the throttle is closed or nearly closed—also it may be caused by too rich a pilot mixture and an air leak in the exhaust system ; The reason in either case is that the mixture has not fired in the cylinder and has fired in the hot silencer. If the banging happens when the throttle is fairly wide open the trouble will be ignition—not carburation.

BAD PETROL CONSUMPTION of a new machine may be due to flooding, caused by impurities from the petrol tank lodging on the float needle seat and so prevent its valve from closing. Flooding may be caused by a worn float needle valve. Also bad petrol consumption will be apparent if the needle jet (15) (see fig. 2) has worn ; it may be remedied or improved by lowering the needle in the throttle, but if it cannot be—then the only remedy is to get a new needle jet.

AIR FILTERS. These may affect the jet setting, so if one is fitted afterwards to the carburetter the main jet may have to be larger. If a carburetter is set with an air filter and the engine is run without it, take care not to overheat the engine due to too weak a mixture ; testing with the air valve (page 5), will indicate if a larger main jet and higher needle position are required.

EFFECT OF ALTITUDE ON CARBURETTER. Increased altitude tends to produce a rich mixture. The greater the altitude, the smaller the main jet required. Carburetters ex-works are set suitable for altitudes up to 3,000 feet approximately. Carburetters used constantly at altitudes 3,000 to 6,000 feet should have a reduction in main jet size of 5 per cent., and thereafter for every 3,000 feet in excess of 6,000 feet altitude further reductions of 4 per cent. should be made.

RE-ASSEMBLING

RE-ASSEMBLING *after dismantling.* See that the washer on the bottom of the jet block is in good condition, otherwise fuel will leak across its face causing rich erratic running, if the washer is faulty it should be replaced by a new one. When replacing the throttle see that the jet needle goes into the centre hole in the jet block and once in, note the throttle works freely when the mixing chamber cap (2) is screwed down firmly and held by spring (18).

When re-assembling the float see that the narrow leg portion of its hinge is uppermost, as this operates the needle. Care should be taken to see that the joint faces of the side cover and body are not damaged or bruised and that the joint washer is in good condition, otherwise difficulty will be experienced in making a petrol tight joint.

On certain rod controlled air valve operated carburetters both the air valve and rod are screwed to enable adjustment for various bores. It is important to ensure that when reassembling in the carburetter the air valve fully closes when the click spring is engaged in the groove of the air valve rod.

HOW TO TRACE FAULTS

There are only two possible faults in carburation, either richness or weakness of mixture.

INDICATIONS OF :—

RICHNESS.	WEAKNESS.
Black smoke in exhaust.	Spitting back in carburetter.
Petrol spraying out of carburetter.	Erratic slow running.
Four strokes, eight-stroking.	Overheating.
Two strokes, four-stroking.	Acceleration poor.
Heavy, lumpy running.	Engine goes better if :—
Sparking plug sooty.	Throttle is not wide open or Air Valve is partially closed.

If richness or weakness is present, check if caused by :—

(1) Petrol feed.   Check that jets and passages are clear, that filter gauze in float chamber banjo connection is not choked with foreign matter, and that there is ample flow of fuel.
Check there is no flooding.

(2) Air leaks.   At the connection to the engine or due to leaky inlet valve stems.

(3) Defective or worn parts.   As a loose fitting throttle valve, worn needle jet, loose jets.

(4) Air cleaner being choked up.

(5) An air cleaner having been removed.

Removing the silencer or running with a straight through pipe requires a richer setting.

Having verified the correctness of fuel feed and that there are no air leaks, check over ignition, valve operation and timing. Now at throttle position shown on page 7, fig. 5, test to see if mixtures are rich or weak. This is done by partially closing the air valve, and if engine runs better weakness is indicated, but if engine runs worse richness is indicated.

To remedy, proceed as follows :—

	To cure richness.	To cure weakness.
Position 1.	Fit smaller main jet.	Fit larger main jet.
Position 2.	Screw out pilot air adjusting screw.	Screw pilot air adjusting screw in.
Position 3.	Fit a throttle with larger cutaway (para. F, page 6).	Fit a throttle with smaller cutaway (para. F, page 6).
Position 4.	Lower needle one or two grooves (para. E, page 6).	Raise needle one or two grooves (para. E, page 6).

NOTE. It is not correct to cure a rich mixture at half throttle by fitting a smaller main jet because the main jet may be correct for power at full throttle : the proper thing to do is to lower the needle.

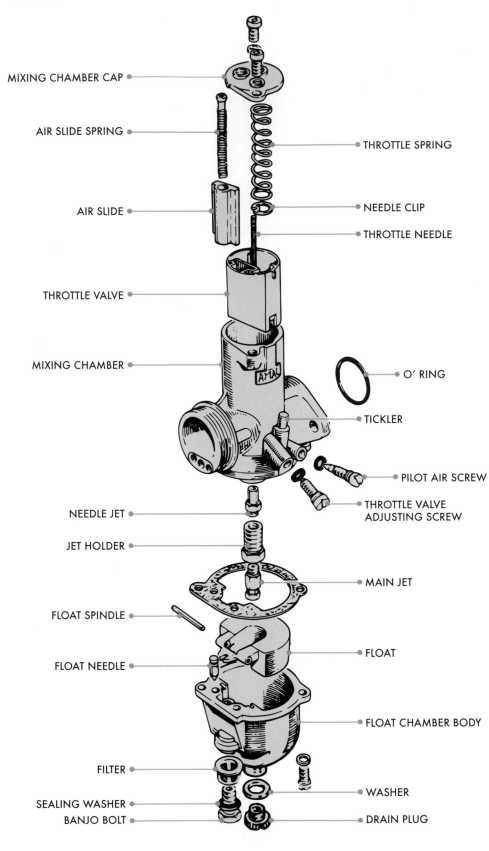

MIXING CHAMBER CAP

AIR SLIDE SPRING

THROTTLE SPRING

AIR SLIDE

NEEDLE CLIP

THROTTLE NEEDLE

THROTTLE VALVE

MIXING CHAMBER

O' RING

TICKLER

PILOT AIR SCREW

THROTTLE VALVE ADJUSTING SCREW

NEEDLE JET

JET HOLDER

MAIN JET

FLOAT SPINDLE

FLOAT

FLOAT NEEDLE

FLOAT CHAMBER BODY

FILTER

SEALING WASHER

WASHER

BANJO BOLT

DRAIN PLUG

Like all other items to be dismantled, give the carb a thorough clean with spirit and a stiff little brush to get rid of muck and old fuel residue. Indeed, should you so wish, the unit can be cleaned ultrasonically, both internally and externally and at a reasonable price, by specialist companies. Once clean, undo the two screws to release the mixing chamber top and slide out the throttle slide and needle on its cable. Compress the throttle spring and draw it out of the slide; then holding the spring and top, remove the needle and its spring clip, then unhook the cable from the slide once the needle is out of the way. Similarly, compress the air slide and unhook the cable to release the slide, spring and brass tube.

Sectioned diagram of the Amal Concentric.

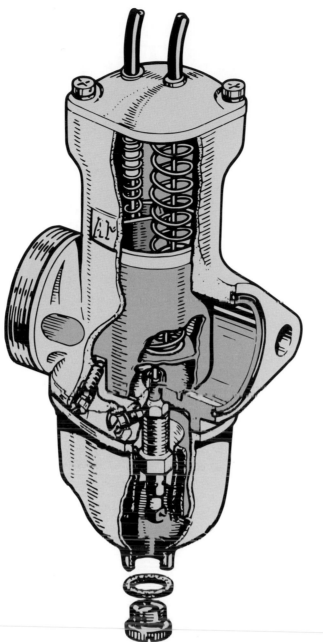

cause float operation problems. Allen screws are a popular modification but are easy to over-tighten, which in turn can warp the lugs and cause an air leak within the float chamber into the idle circuit. If the lugs are bent, replace the float chamber. Ensure the two galleries in the casting are thoroughly clean.

The float needle has a pointed tip to it, which mates up against a funnel-shaped seat at the bottom of the brass seating bush. The fuel flows upward through this until the float reaches its required level and in turn pushes the needle down into the funnel, cutting off the fuel supply. If the seat is damaged the float chamber must be replaced. Early Concentrics had plastic float needles, which should be replaced as a matter of course with the current Viton-tipped ones. To check the float, submerge it completely in fuel for 15 minutes then shake it to see if it has taken any on board. If it has, then dump it and treat yourself to one of Amal's new StayUp assemblies. Check the float tab to make sure they're not distorted or damaged, and check that the float spindle rotates easily in the float with no stiffness or tight spots.

The StayUp float is a great improvement as it's ethanol-resistant, is height adjustable and is made of a military-specification, closed cell construction, making it puncture proof. The ability to adjust the float arm allows for quick and easy minor alterations to float levels where required, something that has previously been impossible with the Concentric. Having said that, the optimum fuel level is determined during manufacture by the position of the float needle valve seat and generally should not require adjustment. Due to changes to the float chamber since its introduction and because you don't know what may have been altered by a previous owner, measuring the fuel level is the best way of setting up the float chamber. The correct fuel level for all Mk 1s is 0.21in plus or minus 0.040in below the top edge of the float bowl. Therefore, when the needle valve is being held closed by the tangs of the float, the level of the fuel should be between 0.17in and 0.25in (4.33mm–6.35mm) from the top of the bowl.

Float Chamber

Undo the two screws securing the float chamber, but keep it level so the float assembly does not fall out. You may have to twist or tap the chamber slightly if the gasket is stuck. Lift the float assembly from the chamber and slide the float needle out of its securing ears, then slide the float spindle out of the float. You will notice the drain plug in the base of the chamber. It's not necessary to remove this unless there's a reason to do so, such as a deformed screwdriver slot or the plug having hardened with age, for example. Early versions of the Mk 1 had no drain plugs fitted but had a

brass mesh sleeve filter fitted around the main jet. Replacement with the later type of float chamber is recommended, and they are completely interchangeable.

Inspect the gasket surface of the float chamber – it should be perfectly flat. Light damage and irregularities, such as scours from a previous owner using a blade to separate the chamber from the body, can be remedied by dressing the surface with fine abrasive paper on a flat surface, or fine grinding paste on a plate of glass or flat steel. Do not remove much, though, because if the surface is reduced too far, the depth of the slot for the float spindle will become too shallow and

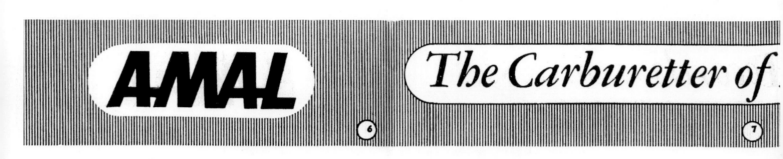
PARTS TO TUNE UP WITH

THROTTLE ADJUSTING SCREW (26). Set this screw to hold the throttle open sufficiently to keep the engine running when the twist grip is off. An "O" ring is fitted to the screw to hold this adjustment by friction.

MAIN JET (29). The main jet controls the petrol supply when the throttle is more than three-quarters open, but at smaller throttle openings although the supply of fuel goes through the main jet, the amount is diminished by the metering effect of the needle in the needle jet.
Each jet is calibrated and numbered so that its exact discharge is known and two jets of the same number are alike. NEVER REAMER A JET OUT, GET ANOTHER OF THE RIGHT SIZE. The bigger the number the bigger the jet.

To remove the main jet, remove the float chamber, the exposed main jet can then be unscrewed from the jet holder (28).

NEEDLE AND NEEDLE JET (22 and 24). The needle being taper either allows more or less petrol to pass through the needle jet as the throttle is opened or closed throughout the range except when idling or nearly full throttle.. The taper needle position in relation to the throttle valve can be set according to the mixture required by repositioning the jet needle clip in any of three positions thus raising or lowering it. Raising the needle richens the mixture and lowering it weakens the mixture at throttle openings from one quarter to three-quarters open (see fig. 5, page 7). The throttle needles are marked with a single groove around the top diameter for use on the 600 series carburetter, the 900 series carburetter needles are identified by three grooves around the top of the needle.

THROTTLE VALVE CUT-AWAY. The atmospheric side of the throttle is cut away to influence the depression on the main fuel supply and thus gives a means of tuning between the pilot and needle jet range of throttle opening. The amount of cut-away is recorded by a number marked on the throttle valve, viz., 622/3 means throttle valve type 622 with No. 3 cut-away ; larger cut-aways, say 4 and 5, give weaker mixtures and 2 a richer mixture.

AIR VALVE (3) is used only for starting and running when cold, and for experimenting with, otherwise run with it wide open.

TICKLER (25), a small plunger spring loaded, fixed in the carburetter body. When pressed down on the float, the needle valve is allowed to open and so "flooding" is achieved. Flooding temporarily enriches the mixture until the level of the petrol subsides to normal.

ALCOHOL FUELS. When using alcohol fuels the following new components are necessary. A metallic banjo preferably double feed if not already fitted, banjo bolt washer 13/163, needle jet 622/100, jet needle 622/099 or 928/099 according to type of carburetter, filter gauze 376/093B and banjo washer 14/175.
The main jet must be increased for straight alcohol by approximately 150%. The final setting must be a question of trial and error according to the nature of fuel used.

When using alcohol fuels it is advisable to err on the rich side to avoid engine overheating.

HOW TO TUNE UP
PHASES OF AMAL NEEDLE JET CARBURETTER THROTTLE OPENINGS

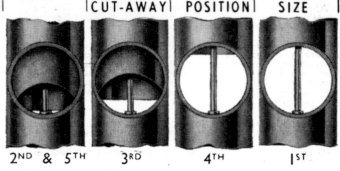

Up to ⅛ open	from ⅛ to ¼ open	¼ to ¾ open	¾ to full open
PILOT JET	THROTTLE CUT-AWAY	NEEDLE-POSITION	MAIN JET SIZE
2ND & 5TH	3RD	4TH	1ST

SEQUENCE OF TUNING

FIG. 5.

TUNE UP IN THE FOLLOWING ORDER.

NOTE. The carburetter is automatic throughout the throttle range— the air valve should always be wide open except when used for starting or until the engine has warmed up. We assume normal petrols are used.

READ REMARKS ON PAGES 6 AND 7 for each tuning device and get the motor going perfectly on a quiet road with a slight up gradient so that on test the engine is pulling.

1st. MAIN JET with throttle in position 1 (fig. 5).
If at full throttle the engine runs "heavily" the main jet is too large. If at full throttle by slightly closing the throttle or air valve the engine seems to have better power, the main jet is too small.
With a correct sized main jet the engine at full throttle should run evenly and regularly with maximum power.
If testing for speed work ensure that the main jet size is sufficient for the mixture to be rich enough to keep the engine cool, and to verify this examine the sparking plug after taking a fast run, declutching and stopping the engine quickly. If the plug body at its end has a cool appearance the mixture is correct : if sooty, the mixture is rich : if however there are signs of intense heat, the mixture is too weak and a larger main jet is necessary.

2nd. PILOT JET (fig. 5) with throttle in positions 2 and 5.
With engine idling too fast with the twist grip shut off and the throttle shut down on to the throttle adjusting screw, and ignition set for best slow running : (1) Screw out throttle adjusting screw until the engine runs slower and begins to falter, then screw pilot air adjusting screw in or out to make engine run regularly and faster. (2) Now gently lower the throttle adjusting screw until the engine runs slower and just begins to falter, adjust the pilot air adjusting screw to get best slow running : if this 2nd adjustment make engine run too fast, go over the job again a third time. Both the throttle adjusting screw and pilot air screw have an "O" Ring fitted to hold the adjustment by friction.

3rd. THROTTLE CUT-AWAY with throttle in position 3 (fig. 5)
If, as you take off from the idling position, there is objectionable spitting from the carburetter, slightly richen the pilot mixture by screwing in the air screw sufficiently, but if this is not effective, screw it back again, and fit a throttle with a smaller cut-away. If the engine jerks under load at this throttle position and there is no spitting, either the jet needle is much too high or a larger throttle cut-away is required to cure richness.

4th. NEEDLE with throttle in position 4 (fig. 5).
The needle controls a wide range of throttle opening and also the acceleration. Try the needle in the lower position, viz., with the clip in the groove at the top ; if acceleration is poor and with air valve partially closed the results are better, raise the needle by two grooves ; if very much better try lowering needle by one groove and leave it where it is best. If mixture is still too rich with clip in groove No. 1 nearest the top —the **needle** jet probably wants replacement because of wear. If the needle itself has had several years' use replace it also.

5th. FINALLY go over the idling again for final touches.

TUNING TWIN ENGINES WITH TWIN CARBURETTERS

where each cylinder has its own Carburetter.

First of all, slacken the Throttle stop screws and put the Twist Grip into the shut off position to allow the Throttles to shut off ; there should be a slight backlash in the cables which backlash can be obtained, if necessary, by screwing in the cable adjusting screws on the top of the Carburetter after releasing lock nuts. Then, with the Handlebars in the normal position, and with the Throttles closed, adjust the cable adjusting screws so that on the slightest opening of the Twist Grip, both Throttles begin to open simultaneously, then reset lock nuts.

To set the Carburetters, follow the procedure as given on page 7, and bear in mind these "Hints," which may be useful :—Main Jet sizes are of course selected by checking the effect of the Mixture on the Sparking Plugs after taking a run at full throttle over a straight piece of road ; the smallest pair of jets that give the best maximum speed are usually correct provided that the Plugs do not show any signs of excessive heat. It might be that for really critical tuning, one Carburetter might require a slightly different Jet size from the other.

For slow running, set the Twist Grip to make the Engine run slowly but just faster than a "tick-over" ; then gently screw in the Throttle stops to just hold the Throttles in that position, and return the Twist Grip into the shut position, leaving the Engine running on the Throttle Stops.

The next thing to do is to set each Carburetter according to paragraph 2, on page 7, to obtain the idling by screwing down the Throttle Stop Screws and adjusting the Pilot Air Screws accordingly.

Regarding the setting of the Pilot, a fairly satisfactory method is to detach one Sparking Plug lead, and set the Pilot Air Adjusting Screw on the other Cylinder as a single unit, and then reversing the process to the other Cylinder. It may be found that when both leads are connected to the Sparking Plugs, the Engine runs slightly quicker than desirable, in which case, a slight readjustment of the Throttle Stop Screws will put this right. It is essential that the speed of idling on both Cylinders is approximately the same, as this will either make or mar the smoothness of the get-away on the initial opening of the Throttle.

It is essential with Twin Carburetters that the Throttle Slides are a good fit in the bodies, and also that there is no suspicion of air leaks at either of the flange attachments to the Cylinder.

Regarding the lower end of the Throttle range, which is always the more difficult to set, one can only take excessive pains to make quite sure that the Control Cables are perfectly adjusted, without any excessive back lash or difference in the amount of back lash between one Carburetter and another ; otherwise one Throttle slide will be out of phase with the other, and so resulting in lumpy running.

To check the opening of the Throttle simultaneously, shut the Twist Grip back so that the Throttles are resting on the Throttle Stop Screws in their final position of adjustment ; then insert the fingers into the air intakes and press them on the Throttles and with the other hand, gently open by the Twist Grip and feel that the Throttles lift off their stops at the same time.

SERVICE ARRANGEMENTS

There are many AMAL Service Stockists in Great Britain and also in other countries where Motor-cycling is popular : They have information about recommended settings for all standard machines and, you are strongly advised to purchase GENUINE AMAL SPARES through them, at our List prices.
ALL GENUINE JETS are stamped with the name AMAL and with the Calibration Number.

GUARANTEE.

LIST No. 117/3 (issue No. 3)

HINTS AND TIPS
for
AMAL CARBURETTER
Series 600 and 900

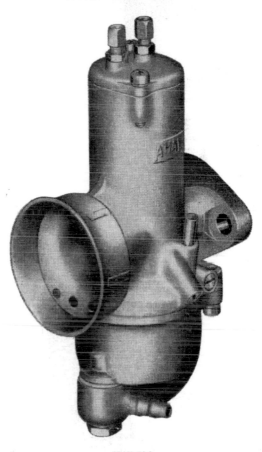

INDEX

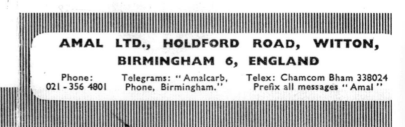

AMAL LTD., HOLDFORD ROAD, WITTON, BIRMINGHAM 6, ENGLAND

Phone: 021 - 356 4801   Telegrams: "Amalcarb, Phone, Birmingham."   Telex: Chamcom Bham 338024 Prefix all messages "Amal"

SECTIONAL ILLUSTRATIONS

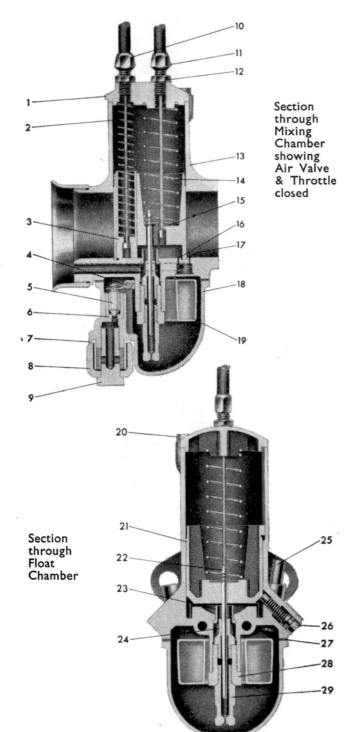

Section through Mixing Chamber showing Air Valve & Throttle closed

Section through Float Chamber

HOW THE CARBURETTER WORKS

The carburetter proportions and atomises the right amount of petrol with the air that is drawn in by the engine because of the correct proportions of jet sizes and the main choke bore. The float chamber maintains a constant level of fuel at the jets and cuts off the supply when the engine stops.

The throttle control from the handlebar controls the volume of mixture and therefore the power, and at all positions of the throttle the mixture is automatically correct. The opening of the throttle brings first into action the mixture supply from the pilot jet system for idling, then as it progressively opens, via the pilot by-pass the mixture is augmented from the main jet, the earlier stages of which action is controlled by the needle in the needle jet. The pilot jet system is supplied by the pilot jet (30) which is detachable on removal of the float chamber. On certain other models no pilot jet is fitted but a pilot bush is inserted in the continuation of the pilot air adjusting screw passage. The main jet does not spray directly into the mixing chamber, but discharges through the needle jet into the primary air chamber, and goes from there as a rich petrol-air mixture through the primary air choke into the main air choke.

The carburetters usually have a separately operated mixture control called an air valve, for use when starting from cold, and until the engine is warm ; this control partially blocks the passage of air through the main choke.

This design of carburetter offers perfectly simple and effective tuning facilities.

1—Mixing Chamber Top.
2—Air Valve Spring.
3—Air Valve.
4—Float Spindle.
5—Float Needle.
6—Needle Seating.
7—Filter Gauze.
8—Banjo.
9—Banjo Bolt.
10—Cable Adjuster (Air).
11—Cable Adjuster (Throttle).
12—Cable Adjuster Locknuts.
13—Carburetter Body.
14—Throttle Valve Spring.
15—Jet Needle Clip.
16—Pilot By-pass.
17—Pilot Outlet.
18—Float Chamber Body.
19—Float.
20—Mixing Chamber Top Screws.
21—Throttle Valve.
22—Jet Needle.
23—Choke Tube.
24—Needle Jet.
25—Tickler.
26—Throttle Adjusting Screw.
27—Float Chamber Washer.
28—Jet Holder.
29—Main Jet.
30—Pilot Jet.
31—Pilot Jet Feed Passages.
32—Feed Passage from Pilot Jet.
33—Pilot Air Feed Passage.
34—Pilot Air Adjusting Screw.

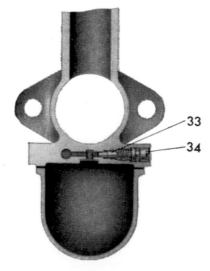

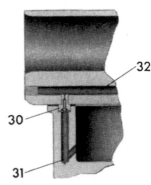

Section showing Pilot Jet and Pilot Jet Feed Passages.

HINTS AND TIPS

STARTING *from cold.* Turn on fuel supply, set ignition (if manually operated) for best slow running, depress tickler to flood float chamber, close air valve, open throttle slightly and start engine. When engine starts open air valve and close the throttle ; if engine begins to falter, partially close the air valve until engine is warm, then set in fully open position.

STARTING, *engine hot.* Open throttle slightly and start engine. It should not normally be necessary to flood the float chamber or close the air valve when starting a warm engine.

STARTING, *general.* Experience will show when it is necessary to flood the carburetter or use the air valve and also the best setting of the throttle valve. If the carburetter has been over-flooded or strangled, which would result in a wet engine and over-rich starting mixture—fully open the throttle valve and air valve, give the engine several turns to clear the richness, then start again with the air valve fully open and the throttle valve slightly open.

STARTING, SINGLE LEVER CARBURETTERS. OPEN THE THROTTLE VERY SLIGHTLY FROM THE IDLING POSITION AND FLOOD THE CARBURETTER MORE OR LESS ACCORDING TO THE ENGINE BEING COLD OR HOT RESPECTIVELY.

CABLE CONTROLS. See that there is a minimum of backlash when the controls are set back and that any movement of the handlebar does not cause the throttle to open ; this is done by the adjusters on top of the carburetter, after releasing the adjuster locknuts. See that the throttle valve shuts down freely, then reset locknuts.

PETROL FEED. A filter gauze is fitted at the inlet to the float chamber, to remove this gauze unscrew the banjo bolt (9) the banjo and filter gauze can then be removed. Before replacement ensure that the filter gauze is both clean and undamaged and check fuel supply by momentarily turning on fuel tap. Vertical loops in petrol pipes must be avoided to prevent air locks. Float chamber flooding may be due to a worn float needle but nearly all flooding and blockage of the filter gauze with new machines is due to impurities from the tank. Periodically clean out filter gauze and float chamber until the trouble ceases or alternatively the tank may be drained and swilled out, etc.

FIXING CARBURETTER AND AIR LEAKS. Erratic slow running is often caused by air leaks, so verify there are none at the point of attachment to the cylinder or inlet pipe. A sealing ring is fitted into the attachment flange of the carburetter. Also on old machines look out for air leaks caused by a worn throttle or worn inlet valve guide.

BANGING IN EXHAUST may be caused by too weak a pilot mixture when the throttle is closed or nearly closed—also it may be caused by too rich a pilot mixture and an air leak in the exhaust system ; The reason in either case is that the mixture has not fired in the cylinder and has fired in the hot silencer. If the banging happens when the throttle is fairly wide open the trouble will be ignition—not carburation.

BAD PETROL CONSUMPTION of a new machine may be due to flooding, caused by impurities from the petrol tank lodging on the float needle seat and so prevent its valve from closing. Flooding may be caused by a worn float needle valve. Also bad petrol consumption will be apparent if the needle jet (24) has worn ; it may be remedied or improved by lowering the needle in the throttle, but if it cannot be—then the only remedy is to get a new needle jet.

AIR FILTERS. These may affect the jet setting, so if one is fitted afterwards to the carburetter the main jet may have to be smaller. If a carburetter is set with an air filter and the engine is run without it, take care not to overheat the engine due to too weak a mixture ; testing with the air valve (page 5), will indicate if a larger main jet and higher needle position are required.

EFFECT OF ALTITUDE ON CARBURETTER. Increased altitude tends to produce a rich mixture. The greater the altitude, the smaller the main jet required. Carburetters ex-works are set suitable for altitudes up to 3,000 feet approximately. Carburetters used constantly at altitudes 3,000 to 6,000 feet should have a reduction in main jet size of 5 per cent. and thereafter for every 3,000 feet in excess of 6,000 feet altitude further reductions of 4 per cent., should be made.

RE-ASSEMBLING

When replacing the valve assembly see that the jet needle goes into the holes in the choke tube, needle jet and main jet and that both the throttle and air valve spring locate correctly in the mixing chamber top.

When refitting the float, engage the float needle recess in the horseshoe section of the float and fit in float chamber. Check that the needle jet (24) jet holder (28) and main jet (29) are fully tightened together before screwing assembly into the body.

HOW TO TRACE FAULTS

There are only two possible faults in carburation, either richness or weakness of mixture.

INDICATIONS OF :—

RICHNESS.	WEAKNESS.
Black smoke in exhaust.	Spitting back in carburetter.
Petrol spraying out of carburetter.	Erratic slow running.
Four strokes, eight-stroking.	Overheating.
Two strokes, four-stroking.	Acceleration poor.
Heavy, lumpy running.	Engine goes better if :—
Sparking plug sooty.	Throttle is not wide open or
	Air Valve is partially closed.

If richness or weakness is present, check if caused by :—

(1) Petrol feed.	Check that jets and passages are clear, that filter gauze in float chamber banjo connection is not choked with foreign matter, and that there is ample flow of fuel. Check there is no flooding.
(2) Air leaks.	At the connection to the engine or due to leaky inlet valve stems.
(3) Defective or worn parts.	As a loose fitting throttle valve, worn needle jet, loose jets.
(4) Air cleaner being choked up.	
(5) An air cleaner having been removed.	

Removing the silencer or running with a straight through pipe requires a richer setting.

Having verified the correctness of fuel feed and that there are no air leaks, check over ignition, valve operation and timing. Now at throttle position shown on page 7, fig. 5, test to see if mixtures are rich or weak. This is done by partially closing the air valve, and if engine runs better weakness is indicated, but if engine runs worse richness is indicated.

To remedy, proceed as follows :—

	To cure richness,	To cure weakness.
Position 1.	Fit smaller main jet.	Fit larger main jet.
Position 2.	Screw out pilot air adjusting screw.	Screw pilot air adjusting screw in.
Position 3.	Fit a throttle with larger cutaway (page 6).	Fit a throttle with smaller cutaway (page 6).
Position 4.	Lower needle one or two grooves (page 6).	Raise needle one or two grooves (page 6).

NOTE. It is not correct to cure a rich mixture at half throttle by fitting a smaller main jet because the main jet may be correct for power at full throttle : the proper thing to do is to lower the needle.

It's a bit tricky, but the fuel level can be checked by removing the float chamber and observing fuel running into it. Obviously the flow should be sufficient to hold the needle valve off its stop until the float rises and duly closes it. Insufficient fuel flow will cause the needle valve to shut under its own weight before the float rises far enough to press it shut. The level of the fuel can then be measured down from the top surface of the float chamber. Another method, not requiring so many hands, is to attach a piece of clear tube to the bottom of the float chamber. A plastic drain plug can be modified to mount a suitable spigot to attach the tubing. Route the tube in a vertical position alongside the float chamber. Open the petrol tap and fill the float chamber with fuel. If the fuel level is in the correct range the fuel will rise in the tube to a point between 0.17in and 0.25in below the top edge of the float bowl, as mentioned above. If possible, start the engine and ensure the fuel level remains within these parameters. The StayUp float has stainless steel tangs, which can be bent to alter the fuel level.

ABOVE: The brand-new Amal Mk 1 Concentric. Do not be fooled by Asian-made copies – if it doesn't say Amal on it, it's not an Amal.

RIGHT: Parts list diagram for the Amal Mk 1 Concentric.

Jets

Be gentle with the jets – they're brass, therefore quite soft and easy to damage. A $\frac{5}{16}$in BSF or $\frac{1}{4}$in Whitworth spanner is required to remove the jet holder from the bottom of the carburettor body. There is a special Amal tool available – part number 622/104 – but a suitably sized ring spanner will suffice to remove the main jet and the needle jet from the jet holder. If there is a pilot jet fitted into the base of the mixing chamber, remove this carefully with a screwdriver. If your carburettor was working well before dismantling, then on the outer body, screw the pilot air screw all the way in, making a note

The new premier version of the Mk 1 Amal Concentric.

Hard Anodised Throttle Slide

New precision engineered Idle Circuit

Ethanol resistant, puncture proof StayUp Float

of how many turns were required. That way, you'll be able to return your carburettor instantly to its previous satisfactory setting on reassembly. Remove the screw then unscrew and remove the throttle stop screw.

If the age of the jets within the carburettor is unknown, it's always a good idea to replace the needle jet, along with the needle, because they are the most susceptible to wear with only 0.001in between sizes, and a worn jet will cause the mixture to run rich between one-quarter and three-quarter throttle opening. Likewise, if the needle shows any sign of damage, distortion or corrosion, swap it for a new one and make sure the spring clip is in equally good order. The main jet is pretty tough but, again, if it shows signs of age or wear, play safe and treat yourself to a new one, as the slightest imperfection can readily affect its fuel-flow characteristics. Sensibly, in 1966, Amal standardized the 376/100-type jet for use in Monobloc, Concentric, GP and TT carburettors. The groove machined across the hexagon of the jet on the right indicates that it incorporates the modifications. New jets without the groove are not genuine Amal and should be avoided, as they are often found to be extremely inaccurate. It goes without saying that on reassembly you should ensure that the gasket and O-ring are in good serviceable condition.

Bear in mind also, that while the manufacturer's original standard carburettor settings are listed in the Amal catalogue and website, these relate to the machine as it left the factory, that is with or without air filters and with a stock exhaust system, so if your bike now runs with a bell mouth on the carburettor and an open pipe or megaphone exhaust, changes to the carburetion settings will be necessary.

Needle Valve

If your Mk 1 has a brass needle valve, it may be closing under its own weight before the float has risen far enough. This manifests itself as taking a long time to tickle, hesitation on pick-up, and an unreliable and inconsistent idle. A Viton-tipped aluminium needle valve is now available that overcomes this problem. It is a standard fitting in all new Mark 1s.

Mixing Chamber

Check and clean all threads in the mixing chamber. If no choke is fitted, seal the cable entry hole with a bolt, part number 4/137A. Replace worn screws and ensure they are fitted with spring washers. Check the manifold flange against a flat surface to determine if it has suffered distortion. A worst-case scenario resulting from, for example, over-tightening, can be the throttle slide jamming when the carburettor is bolted to the manifold. Replacement is the only

answer. Replace the O-ring if there is are any signs of hardening or damage.

The free length of the throttle spring should be 3in. These springs are pretty hardy considering what they have to do but if yours is damaged or compressed, get a new one. Likewise, inspect the air slide components for excessive wear or damage, and the throttle slide. If the wear pattern on the engine side of the slide is visible as a series of furrows or waves in the metal, or the step or groove at the top of the slide on the engine side has been worn away, replace it. As mentioned above in the Monobloc section, eventually the mixing chamber body will also wear, to the point where the amount of air leaking around the throttle slide prevents accurate tuning; at this point it's time for a new carburettor. Wear to the instrument in general will be much reduced by ensuring that an effective air filter is always fitted. Check the tickler mechanism to ensure it moves smoothly. A new version with a bigger head is available to convert earlier ticklers.

Pilot Circuit

Mk 1 Concentrics are equipped with two types of pilot jet. Two-strokes use a removable pilot jet, which should be replaced if it is damaged or shows signs of oxidization. Four-strokes generally use a pressed-in bush pilot jet, in the gallery behind the pilot air screw. Fuel residues, particularly modern unleaded, which has a poor shelf life, and oxidization can cause problems with the pilot circuit, especially in bikes that have been standing with fuel in the carburettor for a long time. It may be sufficient to purge the pilot circuit with an aerosol carburettor cleaner, but take care to inspect the two pilot circuit outlet holes either side of the slide location slot in the bottom of the carburettor bore. If regular cleaning methods fail, the pilot bush can be cleaned by removing the pilot air screw and using a No. 78 or 0.016in drill, held securely in a suitable extension and rotated lightly in the bush to remove encrusted deposits. However, it must be stressed that such a measure is a last resort and, as mentioned previously, heavy deposits can usually be purged by the ultrasonic submerging method.

Pilot Jets

Initially all Concentrics had a detachable pilot jet screwed into a threaded hole in the bottom of the carburettor body. It remains for two-strokes, but from 1968 it was replaced by a bush pressed into the gallery behind the pilot air screw on four-stroke units. The detachable jet caused problems with certain four-stroke engines. The distance of the jet from the two pilot outlet holes caused starting and idling problems on bikes with lower manifold vacuums, and could cause stalling during deceleration due to a weak mixture. The introduction of the pilot bush moved the pilot jet nearer to the outlet holes, overcoming these problems. The bush has a flow rate equivalent to 20cc/min. Carburettors fitted with a bush retain the threads originally used to fit the removable jet. The removable two-stroke pilot jet is stamped with a number from 15 to 200, indicating its flow rate in cc/min.

Carburettor Identification

The numbers on the raised pad on the side of the carburettor can be used to identify it. 'R' or 'L' indicate a left- or right-handed unit. The letter 'B' originally indicated that the carburettor was fitted with the upgraded needle and needle jet parts. The three digit number beginning with a 6 or a 9 indicates the series and bore size; for example, 624 indicates a 24mm 600 series carburettor, 928 indicates a 28mm 900 series carburettor. The number below the three digits identifies the jetting and the original machine to which the unit was originally fitted; for example, 930/62 is a 30mm 900 series carburettor for a 1971–72 BSA 50SS.

Interchangeable Parts

It's important to ensure that all the component parts in your carburettor are correct for the engine. The original Concentric used the same components for both four-stroke and two-stroke, and carburettors can often be found today with a combination of mismatched parts. For example, take a look at the spray tube – the little brass tube you can see poking up as you look through the carburettor – as they can be very different indeed.

Generally the spray tube is the give-away clue between a two-stroke and a four-stroke carburettor. Four-stroke spray tubes are cut off straight, two-strokes are cut off at an angle sloping towards the mounting flange. Some later 850cc Norton Commandos use a spray tube with a square cutaway step, while Triumph triples use an angled spray tube cutaway from the mid-point of the tube rather than right across as in the two-stroke version. Incidentally, two-stroke and four-stroke bodies are not interchangeable and will not run correctly if used on the other engine.

Needle Jets

In 1969 a new needle jet, jet holder and needle designed specifically for four-stroke carburettors were introduced to improve low to mid-range performance.

The differences between the parts are:

	New part	Old part
Needle	$2^{21}/_{32}$in (67.4mm) long with two identifying rings	$2^{9}/_{32}$in (57.9mm) long with one identifying ring
Needle jet	$^{13}/_{16}$in (20.6mm) long cross-drilled	$^{11}/_{16}$in (17.4mm)
New jet holder	$^{7}/_{8}$in (22mm) long	$^{3}/_{4}$in (19mm)

Check to ensure that the parts in your carburettor are a matched set; if you have the older set-up, an update conversion kit (622/235) is available. Two-stroke and four-stroke needle jets have their sizes stamped on them in inches, from 0.105 to 0.125. Four-stroke needle jets have an air bleed hole drilled through the hexagon, but two-stroke jets don't.

The Concentric's needles have inscribed rings or letters stamped at the head of the needle above the clip grooves. All needles use a constant diameter down to the head of the tapered section. The taper helps to manage the transition from the needle jet to the main jet and varies according to the type of engine or fuel:

One inscribed ring (622/063) is for the two-stroke 600 series.

Two inscribed rings or the stamp U1 (622/124) is for the four-stroke 600/900 series.

Three inscribed rings or the stamp X (928/063) is for the two-stroke 900 series.

Four inscribed rings (928/104) is for the Norton 850 Commando.

Five inscribed rings (622/099) is for Triumph's T160 Trident.

Y and Z markings are for alcohol fuels.

Throttle Slides

Throttles slides are stamped with their identifying size on the bottom surface. Typical markings will be either 622 for a 600 series slide, 928 for a 900 series slide, an MB number (a foundry mark) and a stamped number from 2 to 5 indicating the height of the cutaway. The angled cutaway on the slide manages the transition from the pilot circuit to the needle jet when the bike is running. Smaller cutaways will enrich the mixture, larger cutaways weaken it. Full details of available slide sizes and cutaway variations are on the Amal website.

Throttle slides have a variety of cutaways and are recognizable by number.

Reassembling the Carburettor

1. Fit a new O-ring to the throttle stop screw and install the screw.

2. Fit a new O-ring to the pilot air screw. Screw the screw fully home then back it out between 1¼ and 1½ turns for an initial setting, or to your previously noted position.

3. Install the needle jet in the top of its holder and tighten but take care not to over-tighten it.

4. Screw the main jet into the bottom of the needle jet holder and tighten.

5. Install the complete assembly into the base of the mixing chamber and tighten. (The recommended torque setting, if you want to be exact, is 10ft lb.)

6. Two-strokes: screw the pilot jet into the bottom of the chamber at this stage.

7. Assemble the spindle, needle valve and float, and position in the float chamber.

8. With the new gasket in place, secure to the base of the carburettor body with the two screws, checking that no part of the gasket fouls the float. Ensure the float chamber is the correct way round and the pilot jet (if fitted) aligns with the recess in the float chamber. Then tighten up and fit the drain plug together with a new fibre washer.

9. Slip the choke cable through the carburettor top – don't forget to fit the adjusters first – and hook it up to the air slide through the spring in the brass choke tube, then fit it into its position within the throttle slide. Then carry out essentially the same operation to hook up the throttle slide with its cable.

10. Line up the needle and its clip by the appropriate groove, compress the throttle spring, move it to one side, fit the needle into its central hole in the slide and the clip in its recess, clip them together then let the spring back into its place.

11. Carefully fit the slide into the body, ensuring the needle enters the needle jet. There is a lug on the slide and a corresponding slot in the body to ensure correct fitment.

12. Fit the carburettor top with the side tab pointing to the rear of the carburettor and tighten, then adjust the throttle stop screw so that it just begins to engage against the slide when the slide is closed.

13. Fit a new O-ring into the manifold recess.

14. Check the throttle slide operation to ensure it moves smoothly and returns sharply when the throttle is released.

Main Jets and Refitting

Main Jets are calibrated and numbered according to the rate of flow in cc/min, which is stamped on the side to identify them. Jets cannot be reamed but must be replaced if a larger size is required.

Check the manifold flange and any heat-reducing spacers for flatness, and dress accordingly if any distortion is discovered. Fitting to a distorted face can distort the actual carburettor flange or body. Mk 1 Concentrics are not designed to bolt up tight to the intake flange and easily distort if over-tightened. It is only necessary to compress the O-ring to ensure air tightness. When correctly tightened, the carburettor flange and engine manifold should be just touching. 'Nyloc' nuts are preferable and should be tightened to a maximum of 4ft lb.

With a stub-fitting carburettor, ensure the rebated section of the stub, onto which the carburettor fits, is a good snug fit and not sloppy, as this may cause air leaks and mysterious poor running. Over the years, it's inevitable that wear will have occurred on the mating faces, so it may be the case that the stub has to be machined down and a sleeve fitted over it in order to gain a good seal when the clip is tightened. Note also that the area around the carburettor, where it fastens to the stub, has factory-cut slots in it so that they can compress when the clip is tightened. Hairline cracks can often be found around this area, which may also be the source of air leaks. If your carburettor has such cracks, invest in a new one, or suffer potential problems with poor running and idling.

Ensure both cables have the simplest and most direct route from their levers to the carburettor. Lubricate the cables fully and when the fuel tank is fitted make sure that they are not snagged or their operation compromised and that they are not affected when moving the handlebars from side to side.

Air Filter or Bell Mouth?

It's common sense really – the air filter keeps out more everyday dust and abrasive material and thus, over time, will reduce related wear of the engine's top end. Having said that, sports bikes invariably run with bell mouths, or velocity stacks to give them their correct terminology. The science behind this is that the bell mouth accelerates the air heading into the carburettor, giving a more powerful charge. It's an

No self-respecting café racer, especially one fitted with twin Amal GPs, should have anything less than long bell mouths.

Medium-length gauze-covered bell mouths don't look out of place on a standard machine.

arguable point, but longer bell mouths have no advantage over shorter ones except for their appearance.

For everyday machines the factory carburettor settings would have been for use with an air filter, usually a corrugated paper element tucked away between the oil tank and the toolbox and connected to the centrally mounted single carburettor by a rubber hose.

It's not entirely necessary to have this system, should, for example, your machine be missing essential parts, for there are alternative air filters available, which clip directly to the carburettor mouth. Indeed, later classics such as Triumph's Bonneville, were fitted with chrome plated pancake filters, which served the same purpose and overcame the filtration problems of running two carburettors. These filters are readily available, some with a central hole and others with an offset hole for where space is limited. You can also find smaller, conical filters.

If, however, your machine's carburettor has a bell mouth fitted, check the jet sizes within it. Thinking about it logically, the air filter is bound to restrict the amount of air available to the carburettor in comparison to a gaping bell mouth, so the latter will be gulping more air, therefore weakening the mixture. As such it is regular practice to increase the size of the main jet by one, often two, sometimes more sizes to allow more fuel through to compensate for the increased air. Likewise, if you revert to an air filter from a bell mouth, the jetting must be reduced accordingly. If you're unsure then move slowly, one size at a time. If you know someone of long experience, ask their advice too.

On regular settings, the general rule of thumb is, if the carburettor spits back, the mixture is too weak, that is, too much air is getting in. If the fuel consumption is heavy, the exhaust sooty and running lumpy, it's too rich, that is, there's too much fuel, not enough air.

Take a 'plug chop' – warm up your engine, then take it for a ride out to an area where you can open it up for a reasonable length of time, essentially to give it a good clear-out. Then, while opened up, cut the engine and freewheel to a stand still. Remove the plug – carefully because it'll be hot – and check the colour of the electrode area. If it's sooty, then try a smaller jet, if it's white, try a bigger jet and repeat until you get the plug to its correct colour. Most manuals have colour images of plugs in various stages of poor running and the correct colour for which to aim. It's a fiddly job and you may finish up with a little box full of sundry Amal jets, but that tots up to a lot less expense than a holed piston.

Short bell mouths are fine too but, being open, do run the risk of sucking in foreign bodies.

ABOVE LEFT: *A 1955 Triumph Thunderbird air filter restored.*

ABOVE RIGHT: *A 1955 Thunderbird restored air filter in place between the oil tank and tool box with a tube to connect to SU carburettor by rubber hose.*

P11 has both carburettors breathing into a combined pan air filter, necessary as a minimum in its original guise as a desert racer.

If space is at a premium, a small filter like this is perfectly good.

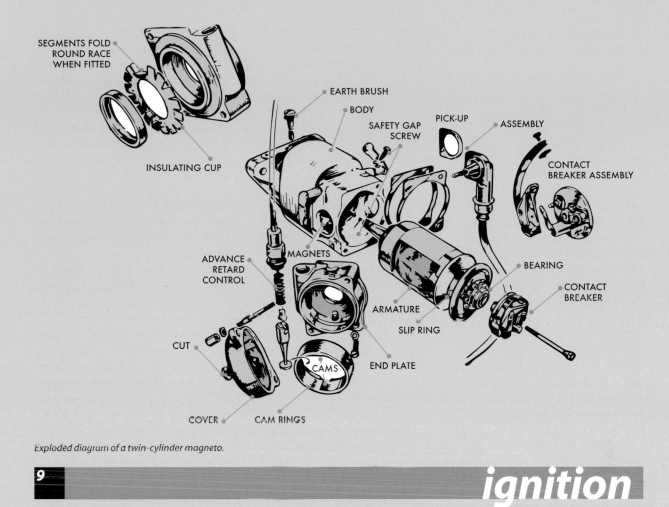

SEGMENTS FOLD
ROUND RACE
WHEN FITTED

INSULATING CUP

EARTH BRUSH

BODY

SAFETY GAP
SCREW

PICK-UP

ASSEMBLY

CONTACT
BREAKER ASSEMBLY

ADVANCE
RETARD
CONTROL

MAGNETS

BEARING

CONTACT
BREAKER

CUT

ARMATURE

SLIP RING

CAMS

END PLATE

COVER

CAM RINGS

Exploded diagram of a twin-cylinder magneto.

9

ignition

Before we get deep into the various component parts of the ignition systems, let's just have a quick look at what the ignition process involves in order to get a better understanding of some of the complicated physics of it.

Obviously, the correct timing of the spark is imperative to getting the optimum capability from your engine. So, we need to understand a little about why the timing of the spark changes and how it's changed during the engine's running. It's generally thought that when plug sparks, the mixture in the combustion chamber instantly explodes and that's what forces the piston downward, spinning the flywheel and creating a momentum to keep repeating the process. Whilst that's not incorrect, it is only part of the story, because if the compressed mixture did actually explode all at once, then there's a good chance that the top end of the engine would follow its example and disintegrate like a bomb detonating.

Let's now move into editorial slow motion and examine the process in the milliseconds it takes to complete its cycle.

In an ideal world, the most efficient combustion progression would be timed to perfection, in order to produce the optimum cylinder pressures in complete harmony with the piston's movement and position relative to the con rod and crankshaft/flywheel rotation.

Combustion does not happen instantaneously – it works in a progressive manner from the spark. The spark ignites the mixture gas closest to plug's electrode and then proceeds to burn outward, away from the plug in a spherical pattern. This is referred to as the 'flame front'. The design of piston and cylinder heads, and the spark plug placement are combined in such a way as to obtain the best flame front possible. It is generally considered that Norton's twins, with their hemispherical combustion chambers and flat-topped pistons, are not far short of the perfect example of good flame front design, whereas Triumph, especially with high-compression, 'lumpy' piston crowns, are poor in comparison as the flame front has a convoluted path to take around the piston hump. The time it takes for the mixture to combust varies with fuel/air mixture ratio, density (temperature), fuel octane, volumetric efficiency (how well the cylinder fills), the 'charge' turbulence inside the cylinder, compression ratio, the physical shape of the combustion chamber and piston crown and the spark plug position in the head.

Here's a very basic example comparing timing to process on an engine running around 3,000rpm:

1. At 34 degrees before top dead centre the spark occurs.
2. At 24 degrees btdc, combustion pressure overtakes normal cylinder pressure (without ignition). This 10-degree lag period is known as 'ignition delay'. (Normal cylinder pressure without ignition is called the 'compression line'.)
3. At 5 degrees btdc the cylinder pressure is around double normal.
4. Between 5 degrees btdc and 15 degrees atdc, combustion is rapid.

5. Between 10 degrees and 20 degrees atdc, peak cylinder pressure occurs.

6. Between 20 degrees and 25 degrees atdc, the combustion process is complete.

The rise in cylinder pressure, known as the pressure gradient, is technically called flagregation – not to be confused with a similar word referring to beatings! It makes obvious sense to have the combustion process occurring during the down stroke and the maximum pressure point to be when the point of leverage for the rod to crankshaft angle is at its best position to offer least resistance and hence spin the flywheel. To achieve this, the combustion process must start earlier. Hence the need for variable advance. As revs increase, the spark must occur earlier or the combustion process will complete later in the power stroke – in other words it will be retarded.

You will no doubt have heard people speak of their engine 'pinking' or 'knocking' – well this is a phenomenon, known as 'detonation', that occurs when the timing is too advanced. While not advancing the timing would result in power loss and overheating, advancing the time too far is much worse, for if the spark occurs too early then the combustion, and the resulting peak cylinder pressure, occur before top dead centre while the piston is still on an upward motion. Essentially this is attempting to force the piston back down as it's on its way up and the result will quickly be evident as your engine dies to a standstill with a hole burned in the piston crown. You will be able to hear a disconcerting tinkling noise and the clonking of the bottom end as you put the engine under sudden load, as when accelerating from a slow corner. Do not ignore it as the piston is steadily banging itself to pieces!

Do not confuse detonation with pre-ignition, though they are related. Pre-ignition is less to do with incorrect timing and more to do with some other aspect that causes the charge to ignite too early. The most common causes include poor-quality or too low an octane fuel, a 'hot spot' on the piston crown, a heavy carbon deposit on the spark plug end, or perhaps the incorrect heat rating for the plug itself,

allowing it to run too hot. In modern vehicles, the timing is often automatically variable, so the problem seemingly doesn't exist, but in older vehicles the timing can be adjusted, invariably retarded, to get round the problem, which was common when low-octane unleaded fuel first became the norm on UK forecourts, especially on sports engines or older vehicles designed to run on higher-octane fuel. Once it was a common sight, particularly with cars and vans, to see a vehicle pull up, the owner switch off the ignition and walk away from it, with the engine still turning itself over, in a series of disconcerting clonks, due to pre-ignition. Fortunately, what with cleaner fuels, better oils, a whole host of fuel additives and technological advances in ignition systems, this bizarre phenomenon is now rare.

THE MAGNETO

In those heady, pre-electronic days of 6v lighting and mechanical, repairable components, the magneto and contact breaker ruled the roost for decades. Eventually, it was superseded by the battery and coil, which also served the contact breaker assembly before technological advances gave us electronic ignitions, which rapidly became more efficient and ever smaller. There is, however, nothing much wrong with a magneto, providing it's in good condition, along with its associated allies, the leads, the points and the plug. That said, the power of the magneto, being essentially a mechanical device, depends on the power of your legs – that is, the bigger the kickstart effort, the faster the spin and the bigger the spark. How many times have you seen the owner of a Gold Star or a Thruxton Velocette sweating profusely as he adjusts the air lever on his GP carburettor and the ignition lever of his magneto, in an effort to harmonize them sufficiently to make the spark fire the mixture and not to keep whacking the back of his leg or the underside of his foot as the stubborn beast prefers to kick back rather than start? One advantage is of course the ability to run without lights; this is why on any single-cylinder machines you will see the dynamo riding piggy-back on the magneto, in an arrangement

called the 'mag-dyno'. So, let's have a look what the magneto is all about.

All the main component parts of the magneto have to work in a constant state of high speed, from the bearings to the contact breaker points and unless you're either a natural electrical wizard or a seriously technical enthusiast, then little more than a general idea of how a magneto works is necessary, as there are specialists available who can refurbish or convert the units, allowing you to get on with something within the scope of the home workshop.

It's all about creating magnetic fields. The principle behind the magneto is the opposite of an electromagnet. Whereas an electromagnet uses electricity passing through a coil to produce a magnet, a magneto uses a magnetic field around a coil, in our case the armature, to produce an electric current. The magneto is essentially made up of three main parts: the armature, the magnets and a contact breaker. The armature has a primary coil of thick wire and a secondary coil of thin wire wrapped around it in layers. This is driven round inside the magneto body, in the sides of which are two strong magnets, which duly create a magnetic field around the armature. As it revolves, the contact breaker (along with a capacitor) disrupts this electromagnetic field and directs the resulting electric current away from the magneto to where it is needed, that is, the spark plug. To produce the required power, either the magnets (in the form of a flywheel, often seen on two-strokes or industrial engines when combined with a cooling fan) or the coil (armature) must spin one around the other. This is the reason you see people in early American films winding their telephone before yelling at the operator – they were essentially creating electricity using the magneto within the telephone. On each rotation, an electromagnetic field is built up inside the coiled wires of the armature, and when this field is disrupted it creates an electrical voltage in the primary coil. The high tension of the secondary coil compared to the primary coil increases this voltage as it is directed to the spark plug along the high-tension (HT) lead, that is, the plug lead. The cam within the contact breaker then forces the points apart, which breaks that contact with the armature and the electromagnetic field regenerates for a new pulse of electricity. The entire process takes milliseconds.

Of course, the spark alone is no use unless it coincides with the moment the piston reaches top dead centre with the cylinder filled to capacity and compressed to extreme temperature, whereupon it ignites the mixture and the reciprocating combustion process of the engine is underway. In some engines, a distributor is used to time the electrical charges to each plug. In a 360-degree twin, for example, the sparks need to be delivered alternately, 180 degrees apart; similarly a triple at 120 degrees, or a four at 90 degrees.

On later singles, such as BSA's B31/33 or early unit singles, such as Norton's ES2/M50, which used an alternator and coil ignition instead of a mag-dyno, a distributor was also used. This was somewhat odd as there was only the one cylinder to which the spark needed distribution, but it's simplicity itself to time up, or to adjust the timing. With the engine running, it's a case of merely loosening the securing clip that holds the distributor in place and turning the distributor as a whole either clockwise or anticlockwise until the engine ticks over and revs up to your satisfaction; then tighten up again and job done.

A favourite trick of the experienced old hand is to get some unsuspecting sop to hold onto the spark plug, when it's removed from the cylinder head but still on its HT lead, to check to see if there is a spark, while he then hoofs the kick start for all his worth, sending a serious bolt of electricity up the arm of the unfortunate novice. It's pretty painful but an invaluable lesson never to be forgotten.

Dismantling

If your project has been standing for a long time, particularly in poor conditions, then there's a pretty strong chance your magneto will have no apparent spark. However, this may simply be due to damp or perhaps corrosion and does not necessarily mean an expensive refurbishment is necessary, so strip it and clean it and then see if it can be persuaded to spark.

Remove the spark plug leads and the advance and retard cable if fitted – some magnetos have an automatic system in the form of a gear wheel on the end of which are spring-loaded bob weights, which are in the retarded position at rest; but by virtue of centrifugal force, once the engine starts and the fitting spins, these weights fly open, advancing the ignition as necessary. If a cable is fitted, it will have a nipple on the magneto end, which is secured inside a small captive, spring-loaded, round flat-headed ferrule, which interlocks with the face cam in order to pull it back and forth. This nipple has to be released before the main cable fitting can be unscrewed from the body. The drive sprocket or pinion in the timing cover has to be removed before the unit can be removed from the engine and this will necessitate the use of a puller of some kind. If there is adequate space behind the pinion to allow access for the feet of a three-jaw puller then fine; if not, it may require the acquisition of a bespoke sprocket puller from your parts supplier. (Do not be tempted to try and prise it off using a brace of screwdrivers or tyre levers, as this will invariably lead to broken cases and much heartache. If you can't remove it initially, let patience prevail until you obtain the right tools.)

If you've a mag-dyno, remove the piggy-back dynamo by first detaching the horseshoe clip, which holds the D and F terminals into the face, then unscrewing the hexagon securing nut on the opposite side. With the securing strap to the magneto loosened, simply slide the dynamo out of its cradle.

With the mag-dyno, as with the individual magneto, use the correct puller to remove the drive pinion. Another point, which is often skimmed over in certain manuals and handbooks, is where it states something in simple terms along the lines of 'remove magneto from its platform'. With something like a BSA Gold Star this is fine because the magneto simply stands on the platform, with four small pegs in four corresponding slots in the platform held in place by a pull-down strap, which keeps the magneto and the dynamo in place; in other cases such an exercise may not be quite so straightforward because often the magneto is secured to its platform by four flat-headed screws that screw up

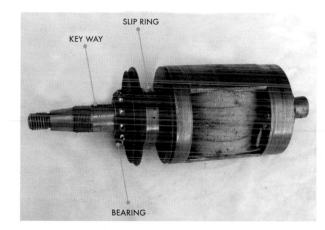

The magneto armature.

Distributor fitted to a 1953 Triumph Thunderbird.

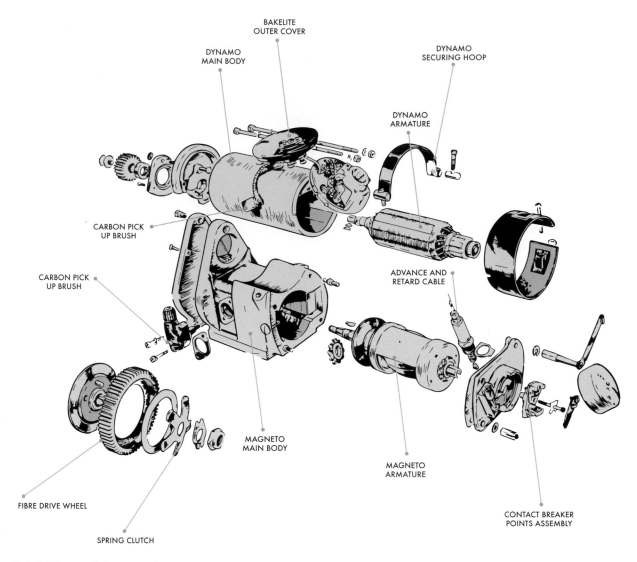

BAKELITE
OUTER COVER

DYNAMO
MAIN BODY

DYNAMO
SECURING HOOP

DYNAMO
ARMATURE

CARBON PICK
UP BRUSH

CARBON PICK
UP BRUSH

ADVANCE AND
RETARD CABLE

MAGNETO
MAIN BODY

MAGNETO
ARMATURE

CONTACT BREAKER
POINTS ASSEMBLY

FIBRE DRIVE WHEEL

SPRING CLUTCH

Exploded diagram of a Lucas mag-dyno.

into the base of the magneto from the underside, and these can often be very difficult, if not impossible, to access without serious dismantling of surrounding parts. It may be simpler and easier to remove the platform with the magneto still attached and separate on the bench.

The magneto cannot be stripped before the fibre gear wheel is removed, which means that the gear assembly has to be locked in order to prevent it turning when the centre fixing nut is turned. Do not under any circumstances hold or wedge the points assembly on the opposite side, as when pressure is exerted on the nut, the points assembly will break. The fibre gear wheel is either gear- or chain-driven and incorporates a five-fingered, spring-like clutch, which is preloaded to slip at peak shock loading. It is necessary to form, or acquire, a U-shaped sprag, the ends of which fit into appropriately placed holes in the magneto body. It's also possible to jam up the unit by means of a purpose-made wedge. The centre nut should be secured by a tab washer.

The contact breaker assembly works on the face cam system, where the cam is on a plate behind the assembly, or cam-ring system, where the cam is on the inside of a ring that runs around the outside of the assembly; both work on the same principle, with a stationary cam and a rotating tappet.

The latter runs around the face or ring until it reaches the cam, where-

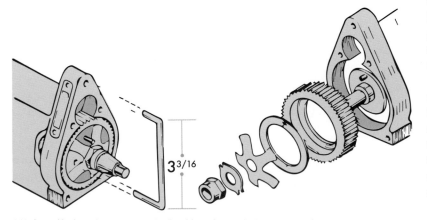

$3^{3/16}$

A U-shaped locking device is needed to be able to dismantle the magneto clutch.

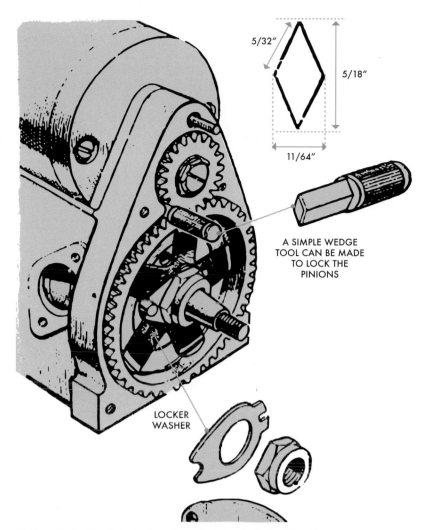

5/32"

5/18"

11/64"

A SIMPLE WEDGE TOOL CAN BE MADE TO LOCK THE PINIONS

LOCKER WASHER

An alternative locking device is a bespoke wedge to jam the teeth of the pinions.

RIGHT: The magneto clutch assembly.

BELOW: The face cam contact breaker assembly.

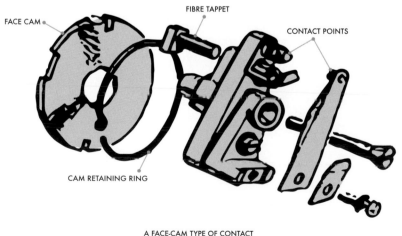

FACE CAM

FIBRE TAPPET

CONTACT POINTS

CAM RETAINING RING

A FACE-CAM TYPE OF CONTACT BREAKER PARTIALLY DISMANTLED

upon it rises up the contour and separates the contact breaker – opens the points – hopefully at the right moment. The assembly is keyed to the end of the armature shaft and retained by a hexagon nut. The whole assembly forms part of the general circuit and is live with low-tension voltage. In later magnetos, with cam-ring operation, there is an earthing cutout facility, which often can be identified by a button projecting from the points cover; this impinges on the bolt head and cuts the ignition and hence stops the engine. On mag-dyno single-cylinder engines, the engine is stopped by virtue of lifting the valve lifter lever.

Access to the centre fixing bolt of the face cam system is prevented by the rotating arm itself, but this is not difficult to dismantle. Unscrew the outermost screw and remove the washer and double backing spring – note this is correctly assembled when the lip of the backing half is facing outward. The moving arm, along with the moving fibre tappet, fit into a keyway on the end of the armature spindle and is secured by the fixing bolt, which can now be unscrewed. The cam ring is located in its correct position by a screw at the base of the end plate, which allows a set amount of movement for advance and retard; likewise, movement of the face cam is provided for by a slot in the periphery wherein the head of the cable ferrule engages the face cam plate. Much of the work so far undertaken can be done with the magneto still fixed to the bike, but for any further work, it would be better now to remove it and head for the bench.

To remove the armature, unscrew the points housing, which acts as an end plate and locates a bearing for the armature shaft. Unscrew the pickup, or earthing brush, and remove it from its slip ring track. It should then be possible to pull the armature clear of the magneto body. It's unlikely that the bearings will need to be replaced but if so, ensure you use some form of extractor or puller rather than trying to prise with screwdrivers.

Wash the bearings with degreaser but try not to get any on the armature windings as it may seep into them and be thrown out at a later date, causing problems.

The windings can be checked by replacing the contact breaker screw in the shaft and running a wire from it to an ammeter and then on to the positive terminal of a battery. Another wire should then be run from the negative terminal to the shaft track. If all is well with primary windings, a reading of some 4 amps should be seen. To check secondary windings, leave the positive where it is but then twist a wire around the slip ring and position it about a quarter-inch from the armature body. Take the lead from the negative terminal and flick it against the shaft – there should be a big fat spark leap from the coiled wire to the armature body. If there isn't, then there may be trouble with either the condenser or the HT windings; either way, specialist refurbishment is the answer.

Essentially, that's about as much as you can do at home. When reassembling, make sure all bearings are well greased again, check that the carbon pick-up brush or brushes have a good flush fitting face with the slip ring and make sure that the armature spins freely on the bearings. Likewise make sure the contact faces of the points are as flush as can be. If they're pitted, they can be faced up with small file or stone but heavy pitting or burned contacts should be replaced. On the mag-dyno, reload the dynamo drive clutch, torqueing the lock nut to 10ft lb.

COIL IGNITION

What is an ignition coil? It's essentially an induction coil that transforms the battery's 6 or 12 volts to the thousands of volts necessary to create a spark

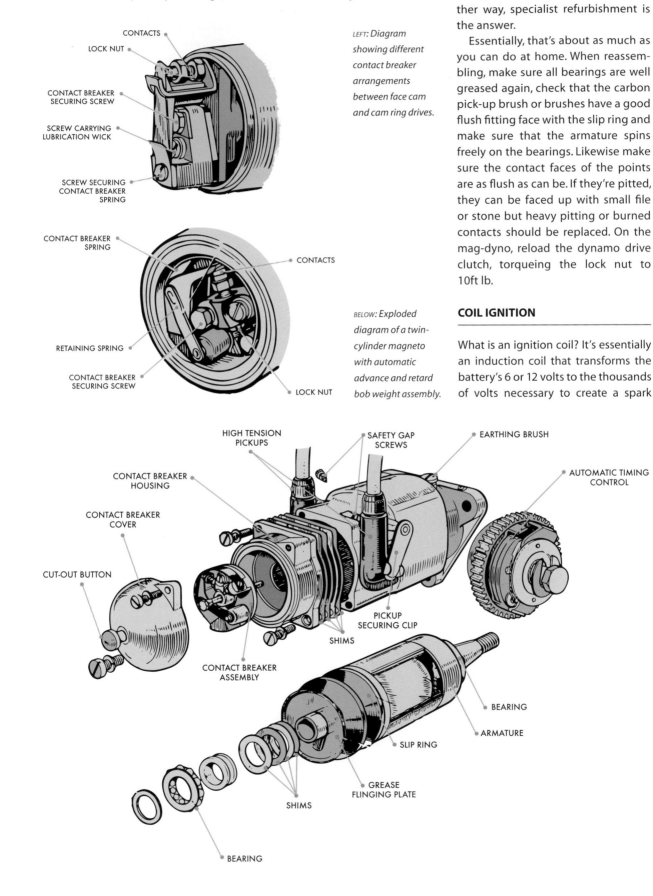

LEFT: Diagram showing different contact breaker arrangements between face cam and cam ring drives.

BELOW: Exploded diagram of a twin-cylinder magneto with automatic advance and retard bob weight assembly.

across the electrode of the spark plug. To prevent a massive overload of volts through the coil, some have an internal resistor, whereas others simply have a resistor wire or an external resistor to limit the flow of current. Some machines, singles, twins and multis like Ariel's Square Four, with coil ignition, are fitted with a distributor. Inside the distributor cap there is a rotor arm, which spins and makes contact with the appropriate connections to send the volts to the required cylinder's spark plug at the right time during the firing sequence. The leads from the distributor to the spark plugs are called high-tension leads, or more commonly plug leads. Originally, all coil ignition systems worked via mechanical contact breaker points and a capacitor (condenser). Electronic systems use a transistor to provide pulses to the ignition coil, doing away with the points, but more on that later.

There's really no need to understand the construction of the components in a coil ignition system, just what is what and roughly what each part does. However, for those who are interested, in layman's terms, an ignition coil is basically an iron core surrounded by two coils of copper wire, a primary winding and a secondary winding. It has an open magnetic circuit – that is, the iron core does not form a circuit loop around the windings and the energy that builds and is stored in the core's magnetic field is the energy that sparks the plug.

The primary winding is of heavy wire and has a number of turns but the secondary winding consists of thousands of turns of smaller wire, insulated against the colossal voltage it develops by means of an enamel coating on the wires and layers of oiled paper insulation. The coil is fitted into a tubular metal can, or on more modern machines in a plastic case, encapsulated with resin, with insulated terminals for the high- and low-voltage connections. When the contact breaker (points) closes, it allows the current from the battery to build up in the primary windings to produce the magnetic field in the core and in the air surrounding it. Once the current has reached its maximum level, the points open. Now it gets a little bit complicated, because as the core has a capacitor connected across it, the pri-

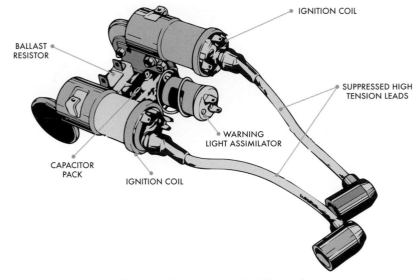

The coil arrangement usually positioned beneath the tank and the mainframe spine tube on a Norton Commando.

BALLAST RESISTOR

IGNITION COIL

SUPPRESSED HIGH TENSION LEADS

WARNING LIGHT ASSIMILATOR

CAPACITOR PACK

IGNITION COIL

mary winding and the capacitor form a circuit, and as the stored energy flip-flops between the inductor (the coil and the capacitor), the core's changing magnetic field induces a much larger voltage in the secondary winding. Naturally, this has to coincide exactly with the piston approaching top dead centre and the fuel-air mix being compressed to its maximum.

The main problem with the coil system, when compared to the magneto, is that the former relies on a battery, and if the battery is dead you have no ignition. On the other hand, if the battery is in order then the coil has a great advantage over the magneto in that the primary voltage generated by a magneto at low revs is low, therefore the quality and strength of spark is low, whereas a coil has a constantly high voltage irrespective of revs. Thus coil ignition can give better starting – providing the battery is good. What's more, while the magneto is an enclosed system, the component parts of the coil system are all separate, giving a maintenance advantage too in that individual parts can be replaced without recourse to a partial engine strip. The only moving part of a coil arrangement is the contact breaker, but the system is not foolproof: it does consist of several wiring connections and for each connection there is a further risk of breakdown.

While coils and condensers can fail, if your sparks cease it is just as likely to be something else within the system, such as an old HT lead – the central

core on old leads can turn to ash, simply through years and years of carrying high voltages and can give frustratingly intermittent starting problems, invariably when you've an audience – so replace with a new one for peace of mind. Don't forget the simple things like the spark plug: just because it's brand new doesn't necessarily mean it isn't a dud. What's more, just because it shows a healthy spark when outside the cylinder, do not take it for granted that it behaves the same inside the cylinder when subject to serious combustion pressures, so give yourself the option of a couple or three to choose from. Does the ammeter work? Has the fuse blown? There are several potential problem areas to check out.

If you have a multimeter and know how to use it, this is where such an instrument pays its way. If you don't, see about finding a friendly auto electrician.

If the system's circuit seems in order, switch on the ignition and turn the engine over until the contact breaker points are fully closed, then hold the HT lead close to the cylinder or some other good earthing point and flick the points open. In theory, a good strong spark should 'click' across the points – and while it'll probably make you jump, it should not give you an electric shock. If there is no spark, the secondary windings in the coil may be faulty and thus a replacement coil should be tried.

Keep the distributor and the points area clean, likewise the bullet, spade or screw-on connections, and apply a

Triumph distributor on dismantling – pretty grubby.

The Triumph distributor having been cleaned and restored, ready for reassembly.

little light grease on them to prevent corrosion. Lubricate the cam and the point pivot and, if you can get to it, the distributor shaft, with thin engine or machine oil. Be frugal, though, as over-lubricating can cause poor running or ignition failure.

ELECTRONIC IGNITION

The beauty of electronic ignition is that it has fewer moving parts and relies on electronics rather than mechanics. It is invariably self-regulating with regard to advance and retard and, in theory at least, should not need adjusting once set up correctly and therefore should guarantee perfect starting every time. Of course this also depends on the other parts of the machine, such as spark plug, carburetion and so on being in good condition and correctly adjusted.

Of course, like everything else, it is not designed to last forever. You will be familiar with other electronic devices, particularly in the domestic environment, such as vacuum cleaners and washing machines that are often cheaper and simpler to replace when they fail rather than invest in the electronics that may be required for repair, if they are not already obsolete. Computers are another classic comparison. Early ignition systems were known to suffer from component failure, and because of that pioneering companies such as Lucas won an undeserved reputation for being unreliable. Solid state components are particularly sensitive to heat, vibration, moisture and power surges – indeed, pretty much everything they'll get on a motorcycle – so we have to try and place

them somewhere where they'll be out of the wet weather but in the cooling wind, within a sensible distance of the engine and seated upon a cushion. Today's aftermarket systems come with heat sinks and cooling fins, resin- or rubber-encased components to keep out the wet, separate ignition modules for each plug so a single failure won't kill the whole engine, and are generally heavier duty to withstand the heat and vibration.

Once again, the actual physics of the electronic system is complicated and technical and, to be quite frank, is for the vast majority of classic enthusiasts something to simply buy, fit and forget about without necessarily understanding why it works.

The first benefit of the electronic system was the replacement of the mechanical contact breaker points with a solid state (meaning completely self-contained and often sealed within a block of resin with nothing more than contacts or wires protruding) semi-conductor switch, called a transistor. Its advantage is that it can conduct up to some 500v, is extremely accurate, fast (nanoseconds rather than milliseconds) and can withstand a long time in the extreme conditions (heat and vibration) of the engine. This switch, however, has to be triggered, and the main systems that have evolved over the years to do this are Hall effect, magnetic and optical. There are other systems but these three are the most common.

Hall Effect This is the most widely used type of ignition sensor, certainly in the automotive industry. Named after the American physicist Edwin Herbert

Hall, it involves a current being passed though a silicon wafer. When exposed to a magnetic field, the current flow is disturbed and distributes more 'potential' on one side of the wafer to the other, which is then amplified to trigger the ignition module. Most Hall Effect rotors involve a stationary Hall switch and stationary magnet. What rotates is an 'interrupter blade.' When the blade passes between the sensor and the magnet it blocks the magnetic pull on the switch. When the blade is open, the magnetic field switches on the Hall sensor. This system must be externally powered. The Hall Effect ignition system came to prominence in the world of motorcycling when it was used by Brian Crighton on his rotary-engined Norton race bikes in the late 1980s.

Magnetic This is still very common because of its ruggedness and durability, plus it does not have to be powered like the Hall system does, so it can be used in self-powered magneto ignition applications, such as mowers, mini tractors and stationary engines. A coil sensor is used to detect the magnet's field when it passes close by. The problem with the magnetic system is that at high revs the sensor may have trouble seeing 'teeth' close together on the magnetic rotor (called a reluctor). Magnets also tend to eventually lose their strength when subjected to vibration and heat.

Optical This the system most commonly used in aftermarket classic motorcycle applications, essentially because it's fairly simple to adapt to most applications. An infrared sensor triggers when a rotor blade blocks the light path. Although accurate, the sensor is sensitive to dirt and dust.

Modern Electronic Ignition Modules

You may have heard certain terminology during motorcycle conversation, such as CDI or TCI. These are capacitor discharge ignition and transistor controlled ignition. Both systems use a sensor to trigger a transistor switch (in place of the contact breaker points).

The Kettering design of induction ignition is a classic example of TCI. The coil is used as a power store (inductor) for the spark. This stores up to 30,000v and unleashes them when the coil collapses (when the power supply is cut off). An advantageous feature of this system is the slightly longer spark duration while the coil collapses. This helps when starting and for igniting lean or high-compression mixtures at high revs. This system requires a special induction ignition coil, with a higher resistance than CDI coils. Induction ignitions are simpler in design and accordingly less expensive, and are often used on less sophisticated motors, such as our classics.

Commercial development of CDI exploded in the mid-1960s when the Japanese motorcycle industry perfected it, though it was initially pioneered by Bosch. A CDI module has 'capacitor' storage of its own and sends a short pulse of around 250v through the coil. The coil then takes on the role of transformer and multiplies this voltage anything up to 100 times – so a typical 250v CDI module output becomes 25,000v at the coil. In some cases claimed coil output can be vastly more than this. It gives a powerful and accurate spark, albeit of very short duration, which is better at high revs but not so good for starting.

Choosing a System

Before you take the plunge, ask around your club colleagues, or owners at a gathering, or your local parts specialist, and see what they've fitted and their opinions on the system. There are systems, such as those available from SRM Engineering, which can now convert your Lucas mag-dyno system magneto to electronic operation, along with solid state rectifiers and so on to upgrade the system to 12v from 6v.

BT-H have a Lucas magneto looka-like system, which uses a self-generation set-up so no battery is required. For later classics with points in the cases, there are several excellent systems available from Boyer Bransden; if original appearance is unimportant, Pazon have a very tidy, compact magneto replacement system; and if you want to go completely compact, then the likes of Rex Caunt Racing have self-generating systems that fit directly on the end of the crank. All these options and more besides invariably come with fitting instructions. They comprise of very few parts and are simple to fit, though when fitted they do invariably have to be timed up with a strobe. If your magneto is past its best, or has parts missing, you can choose either to have it refurbished at quite a cost, or go for an electronic system. It's all down to personal preference.

Like all solid state equipment, the electronic ignition system cannot be tuned. It either works or it doesn't work. You can ensure all contacts are clean and connected properly, the spark plug is good, the coil is good, the battery is good, but if it doesn't work, the only thing you can do is try and isolate where the problem might be with your multimeter. Some

manufacturers have excellent trouble-shooting directions on their website, but otherwise you'll have to dismantle it and return it to the manufacturer to be checked and for replacement parts, or a new system completely. As technology races on and systems become ever smaller yet ever more powerful, electronic ignitions benefit both in efficiency and in miniaturization and thus the ease in which they can be hidden away to maintain that original look. Furthermore, as such systems become the norm, the price becomes more competitive. Once you have an idea what you want, have a shop around the internet for the best package and best deal.

SPARK PLUGS

The spark plug is essentially quite simple, yet its variations for different engines are legion. It forces electricity to arc across a gap. As we've discussed previously, the electricity must be at a very high voltage in order to travel across the gap and thus create a good spark, anything from 40,000v to 100,000v. The plug has an insulated passage down which this voltage travels to reach the electrode, where it jumps the gap and is then conducted into the engine and grounded. The plug also has to withstand the incredible heat and pressure present inside the combustion chamber while preventing a build-up of carbon and other by-products of the combustion process on it.

Spark plugs use a ceramic insert to isolate the high voltage at the electrode, ensuring that the spark only happens at the tip of the electrode and nowhere else on the plug. Ceramic is a conductor of heat, so the plug body gets exceedingly hot when in use and this also helps to burn off any potential deposit on the electrode.

There are three types of plug: hot, normal and cold. A classic example is the Champion N3, N4 and N5. The basic rule of thumb is to use a cold plug on a hot-running engine and vice versa. A spark plug must operate between temperatures between 470°C and 960°C and this is regulated by the length of the insulator around the electrode, which governs the amount of heat absorbed into the plug.

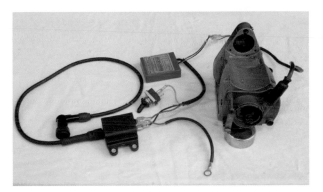

SRM Engineering do a superb mechanical magneto conversion to electronic using Boyer Bransden internals.

Most British classics use 14mm diameter plugs but the length of the threaded portion varies. With an alloy cylinder head, for example, a plug needs to be long enough to provide strength in its housing, thus the ³/₄in 'long reach' plug is used instead of the ¹/₂in short reach regularly used in pre-war and iron heads. A long-reach plug used in place of the correct short reach may cause pre-ignition and in a worst case scenario actually hit the piston. Equally, a short-reach used in place of the correct long-reach leaves a pocket between the electrode and the combustion chamber, which may make for poor starting and/or poor running.

A hot plug, also known as a soft plug, has a ceramic insert with a smaller contact area to the metal part of the plug, which reduces the heat transfer from the ceramic, making it run hotter and thus burn away more deposits.

By contrast, a cold plug, also know as a hard plug, is designed with more contact area, so it runs cooler.

High-performance engines naturally generate more heat, thus they need colder plugs. Think HC = high compression = hard/cold. This is why, on occasion, a race bike engine will fluff on its getaway from the line if it is insufficiently warmed up – and why sometimes an engine is warmed up on hot plugs before having the plugs changed to colder plugs for the race. If the spark plug gets too hot, it risks igniting the fuel before the spark fires, or indeed continuing to fire the engine after it is turned off, akin to pre-ignition as mentioned previously. This phenomenon is primarily a car, or at least multi-cylinder, problem.

There is no strict ruling on the plug gap; most manuals will state that the gap can be between 0.015in and 0.020in, so a well-fitting feeler gauge of around 0.018in will be perfectly adequate, though a little more or a little less will be of no consequence.

To quote a well-known phrase – the plug is the window to your engine. However, before you can 'read' the plug a simple basic must be observed and that is the tightness of the plug in the cylinder head. If it's too loose it will overheat and give an incorrect reading. Plugs invariably come with a washer these days and this washer must be flattened, the rule being finger tight plus half a turn with the spanner.

If, let's say, your engine is not running as well as it should be at low speed, cruising speed or high speed, to get a correct reading of what's happening at the plug, it must be removed from the cylinder head during the period when the engine was running at its problematic stage. The 'plug chop' works as follows. Run the engine until it is up to working temperature, then find a straight stretch of quiet road and run at the problem speed before pulling in the clutch to freewheel to a halt, while simultaneously killing the engine. Remove the plug and review what you see. Of course, this is all assuming that ignition timing and carburetion is spot on. In a nutshell, if the plug end is brown to light grey, it's fine, if it's sooty and coked up, it's too rich, if it's white and the ceramic is blistering, it's too weak. However, there is much more to this to be absolutely sure of the problem. Therefore an obligatory part of any classic motorcyclist's workshop library is a little booklet compiled by Stan Dibben, entitled *Spark Plugging the Classics* (available from Panther Publishing). Stan has been involved with the motorcycle (and car) industry since 1950. He worked for Norton and partnered Eric Oliver to the sidecar world championship, he was part of Sir Malcolm Campbell's all-conquering Bluebird teams and for twenty-five years was a major part of NGK's British spark plug business. No one knows more about the technicalities and intricacies of the spark plug than Stan. It's an A5 paperback of just twenty pages

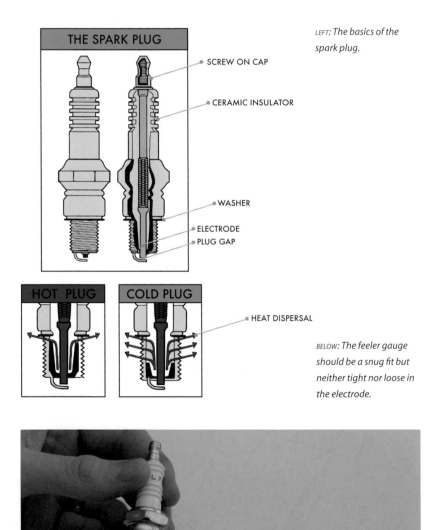

THE SPARK PLUG

- SCREW ON CAP
- CERAMIC INSULATOR
- WASHER
- ELECTRODE
- PLUG GAP

HOT PLUG   COLD PLUG

- HEAT DISPERSAL

LEFT: The basics of the spark plug.

BELOW: The feeler gauge should be a snug fit but neither tight nor loose in the electrode.

but contains all there is to know about spark plugs.

PERFECT TIMING

Contact Breaker Points

Let's look first at an ignition timing system where there are contact breaker points. As mentioned previously, the points are opened by means of some form of cam over which the heel of the assembly runs. First adjust the points gap to, say, 0.018in, by means of the feeler gauge blade of that thickness. It should be possible to 'feel' both faces of the points on the blade and it should be a sliding fit without recourse to pushing and thus forcing the points open. The faces of the points should be flat and fit squarely and fully flush together when closed. Often they may have run previously slightly offset and have developed a small 'pip' on one face with a corresponding burn hole in the other. It is easy enough to take off the pip with a small, fine file or oil stone but be careful as the points are usually finished with a very thin, hardened surface, which renders the points useless if broken through, so don't file them too much. In many cases, just a light dragging of some fine wet and dry or emery cloth between the faces is enough.

The points are adjusted by means of a adjustable nut that winds the fixed points face in or out, and is locked in place by an equivalent-sized locknut. These are very small and it is wise to have access to a set of 'mag spanners' (a fold-up selection of maybe half a dozen or so small, fine spanners de-

signed especially for the job). These are available from specialist magneto and ignition supplies.

Now it is necessary to find top dead centre of the piston's travel, that is, when the crank throw is at the very top of its upward stroke. Remove the spark plug and lift the bike so that the rear wheel is off the ground and can turn freely. If you insert a wooden dowel, like a long pencil, into the plug hole, put the bike into top gear and gently turn the rear wheel forwards, you will feel the piston rise in its bore. When it reaches the top there will be a short period when the rear wheel will turn but the piston does not seem to move, then it will start to move back down. This delay is the few degrees when the crank turns from just before to just after top dead centre during its normal travel. It's at the very centre of this back-and-forth rocking period that top dead centre is found.

The timing figures in your manual are always quoted at full advance, so set the ignition advance and retard lever to the fully advanced position. Mostly this has the lever at its closed point, where the cable is at its slackest and the cam ring against its advance stop. This is known as a slack wire advance. Some magnetos work the opposite way round, with advance being when the lever is pulled fully back, which is called the tight wire advance. Full advance is achieved when the cam is rotated in the opposite direction to the direction of the rotation of the points. If your magneto has the automatic advance and retard spring-loaded bob-weight mechanism, then the bob weights must be wedged wide open.

Some machines have their timing settings measured in so many parts of an inch before top dead centre, others have it measured in degrees. With the former, which is not as accurate as using a degree wheel but is more than adequate for the type of machine for which the method is advocated, it is all a matter of a keen eye and a steady hand. In both cases, the timing is measured on the compression stroke (inlet, compression, fire, exhaust being the four strokes of the cycle, of course), when both inlet and exhaust valves are closed and the piston is on its way up the barrel. If you expose the valves or at least the tappets/pushrods, you can easily work out and count the strokes to ensure you're on the right one. If you time up your engine on the wrong stroke, you'll never get it to start as the plug will be sparking when the engine is exhausting.

Because of the backlash within the gear trains of the engine – the slight back and forth slack as the teeth move within their appropriate partners with which they're meshed – and the 'slop' of the crank and other engine parts, ensure that the rear wheel is turned in the direction of travel to take up all this movement. If you go past your required position, do not simply wind the wheel backwards to the spot, take it well past and bring the engine back up again. If you merely take the engine back down to the correct position, it will have to turn through this slop before it begins to work, so will be several degrees out of time.

So, with your dowel in the plug hole and your rear wheel having been turned forward to take up the slop, proceed to turn the wheel until you feel the piston rise to the top of its stroke. At this point, using a straight edge flat against a common surface, such as the fins by the plug hole, or across two constant nuts or bolt heads, make a mark on the dowel. Remove the dowel and make a second mark above the tdc line corresponding to the distance before tdc required in your manual (above because the dowel will be sitting on the piston crown when it is lower, so before tdc). For example, the ohv Model 18 Norton is $5/8$in, whereas the side-valve 16H and Model 1 (Big 4) is $7/16$in and the 350cc Model 50 is $9/32$in, while the International models and the twin-cylinder range are all measured in degrees.

ABOVE LEFT: Mag spanners: an obligatory and essential part of the classic motorcyclist's toolkit.

ABOVE RIGHT: Simple but effective, a wooden dowel in the plug hole and a measured mark on it for top dead centre and another for the required distance of piston travel preceding it makes for an adequately timed engine.

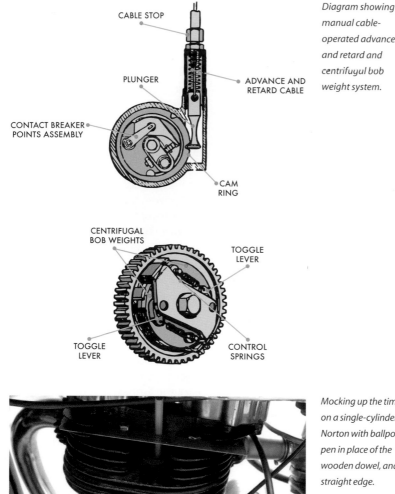

CABLE STOP

PLUNGER

ADVANCE AND
RETARD CABLE

CONTACT BREAKER
POINTS ASSEMBLY

CAM
RING

CENTRIFUGAL
BOB WEIGHTS

TOGGLE
LEVER

TOGGLE
LEVER

CONTROL
SPRINGS

*Diagram showing
manual cable-
operated advance
and retard and
centrifugal bob
weight system.*

*Mocking up the timing
on a single-cylinder
Norton with ballpoint
pen in place of the
wooden dowel, and a
straight edge.*

*The BSA Gold Star
needs a little more
accuracy, so a degree
wheel is used.*

Using a degree wheel, while more accurate, is also much more of an exercise because it means removing the primary cover to get to the crank. Any part of the engine that turns can be used – it doesn't have to be the crank – but bear in mind any gearing involved. For example, the camshafts work at half engine speed so any degrees measured on the cams must be doubled up to compensate – a certain recipe for forgetting and making a mistake, thus wasting time and patience. So let's stick with the crank. On a simple engine, especially one with no alternator to get in the way, it's quite easy to undo the engine sprocket nut and fit the degree wheel over the shaft and secure it with the nut. Then find a piece of wire that is stiff enough to stay in position but soft enough to bend manually. Form a hoop on one end and fasten it underneath a close by crank case stud nut, then bend the other end over and down so it almost touches the degree wheel, thus making a pointer.

To find tdc exactly, a special tool must be used. Many folks drill out a spark plug and make up a graduated central shaft, which projects down into the cylinder, but there are proprietary tools available that are well worth a small investment, as they will last a lifetime and be used over and over again. With the engine set approximately to tdc on the compression stroke – this can be found with your dowel – zero the timing disc on the pointer. Turn the engine backwards anything up to 40 or so degrees before tdc, then screw the tool into the plug hole and adjust the length of the central section until it just touches the piston crown. If it doesn't, bring the piston up 5 or 10 degrees until it does. Then turn the engine back and bring it forward again until it touches the piston crown, when the piston will obviously come to a stop. Note the reading on the timing disc. Now turn the engine backwards, right through its stroke until the piston comes up and touches the stop again, and then note the timing disc reading again. Take the difference between the two readings and divide that figure by two. Then, without moving the crank, move the disc around until the pointer aligns with the figure calculated. With the disc secured again, if you turn the crank back round until the piston touches the tdc finder again, then the reading should be the same at the other side. You will note that the disc does not go from 0 degrees to 360 degrees but from 0 to 180 degrees in either direction. Remove the tdc-finding tool from the plug hole and turn the engine forwards until the pointer aligns with the zero on the disc – this is true top dead centre.

So now your engine is at top dead centre, your points gap is set at the required width and your magneto is set at full advance. Now it's a question of determining just when the points are beginning to open, which is something so fine that using your eyes alone will probably result in being a long way out with your timing. In the true classic manner, the 'fag paper' was the best way to ascertain when the points opened. The fine silver foil found in cigarette packets, or the actual paper used for rolling your own, is still useful, in that with a strip of paper stuck between the closed points, the points can be turned until the paper can be freed with light pressure – this is the exact position when they begin to open.

A more technical method is by a proprietary magneto static timing indicator. This has an integral battery, a small 9v PP3 type, which avoids the nuisance of having to use an external power source. One lead must be clipped to the movable points arm and the other to the base assembly so that a circuit can be made and broken. It makes life easier if the points are set up fairly close to

their opening position; that way there is not too much rotation for the leads to have to deal with. The good thing about these tools is that not only do they have a light that turns from green to red when the circuit is broken – that is, the points open – but they also have a sounder, which means you can keep a close eye on the degree wheel and not have to keep watching the indicator because you'll hear when the points open. This tool can also be used on coil ignitions and rotating magnet magnetos as found on two-strokes. When the buzzer sounds, the whole ignition system can be tightened up and that's the job done – points just beginning to open on the correct stroke, just at the right time before top dead centre, in readiness for the combustion process to begin.

Electronic Systems

Assuming the points have been removed and replaced with the rotating pick-up unit and the engine is set at the required number of degrees before top dead centre on the compression stroke, then the stator plate can be loosely bolted into place. It has slotted fixings to accommodate any adjustment required. There will be at least one hole in the stator plate, which should align with a suitable marking, usually a red dot, on the rotating pick-up. This will be the fully advanced position. If you are working on figures from an original manual or handbook, then deduct a degree or even two degrees from the full advance position as those

figures would probably have been for the better-quality, four-star petrol of the period. When the system is bolted up, this is the basic starting point for the timing and now it has to be fine-tuned with a strobe.

Before you go any further, check all the wiring is correct and tightly connected, that there is a good earth to the frame and the battery is fully charged. Start the engine in the usual manner and warm it up. With the strobe fitted to the power source and the plug lead, have someone rev up the engine while you point the strobe at the timing disc. As the revs rise you should see the pointer move to the top dead centre position, dropping back as the revs fall. The revs must reach at least 3,000rpm – indeed it is recommended on fitting electronic ignition to a Norton Commando that the timing be strobed at 5,000rpm, at which point the bike is trying to make its own way out of your workshop, on its stand, by itself! If the timing is slightly out, stop the engine, loosen the stator plate and turn slightly in whichever direction until the strobe shows the correct settings, then tighten up. It should then be a case of fit and forget, with good starting, running and fuel consumption from thereon in.

THE POWER BOX

The power box is a self-regulating rectifier with an internal current and voltage storage capacitor. Connecting directly to the alternator, the output is around 15v with no current being drawn, and around 14.5v with some load. These figures are ideal for either charging a battery or running the electrics direct. The unit is designed using the latest state-of-the-art semiconductors to provide a stable direct current from standard permanent magnet alternators. There are three types

Special top dead centre-finding tool.

Red means points open.

Green means points closed.

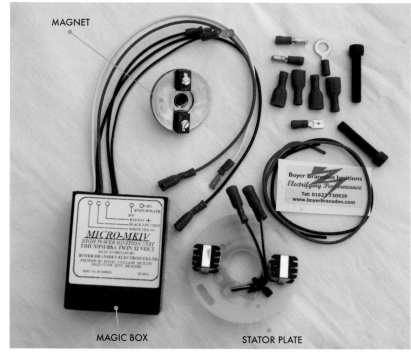

MAGNET

MAGIC BOX

STATOR PLATE

Micro Mk IV ignition system – aka the Black Box System. Boyer Bransden's range of analogue Micro units have been upgraded to the present Mk IV version but remain fully interchangeable with early Mk Ia and Mk III units. They have been further developed to improve timing stability while starting an engine on a very low battery voltage. The advantage of this system is that the engine functions best with a retarded spark for starting and low revs but needs ignition advance to run at high speed. The Mk IV simply advances the spark at a set rate from fully retarded to maximum advance as engine speed rises from zero to 4,000rpm. Like all Boyer units it is contactless, vibration-, water- and oil-resistant, and can also be incorporated into a totally battery-less arrangement when used in conjunction with the power-box alternator regulator.

available: single phase, bi-phase and three phase. The first two control 200 watts and the third controls 300 watts. In general, single-phase power boxes are suitable for most pre-1975 British machines fitted with either a two- or three-wire alternator. Bi-phase will suit most Italian machines and the three-phase will suit some post-1975 British iron with three wire alternators and Japanese three-wire alternators.

It is wise to convert to 12v operation if considering this route as most 6v alternator systems do not have a regulator to control the voltage output. If the battery becomes faulty or disconnected, the output of the alternator will rise to over 200v and the rectifier and ignition unit may be destroyed. Converting to 12v provides more stable electrics as well as giving brighter lights. A typical alternator at 2,000rpm will put around 8 amps into the battery (48 watts – volts × current). If the battery is replaced with a 12v unit, the current then drops to 6 amps, giving 72 watts. In reality this is closer to 84 watts as the battery voltage on charge is nearer 14v. At just under 15v, the battery is fully charged. At this point with no regulator the

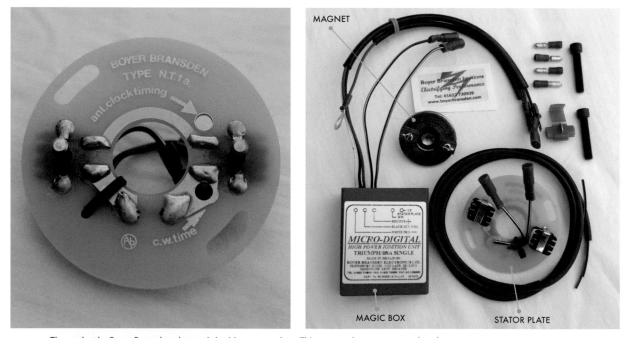

MAGNET

MAGIC BOX

STATOR PLATE

ABOVE LEFT: The works: the Boyer Bransden electronic ignition stator plate. This supersedes your contact breaker system.

ABOVE RIGHT: Micro Digital ignition system – aka the Red Box System. While doing everything that the Mk IV analogue can do, the Micro Digital contains a miniature computer, the size of a postage stamp, which can make a million ignition decisions per second – thus it constantly monitors engine speed and times the spark precisely. It also controls the coil energy, starting speed, tick-over stabilization and rev limits. It is designed to use the original coils where possible – the time these coils are switched during the ignition cycle is programmed into the microchip. With our older machines, the coils have a high primary resistance and require a long switch-on time, so if the coils are replaced, it is important that coils of a similar resistance are used.

Micro Power Ignition System – aka the Blue Box System. This is similar to the Red Box but timing is controlled in bands of 50rpm across the whole rev range, so this then gives the ability to programme any firing angle required. To help engine power at idle, the timing can be advanced on and below the idle speed, which stabilizes and reduces the chance of stalling. It is designed to work only with Boyer Bransden's special digital power ignition coils – type 00007 single output, or 00008 dual output. Up to four such coils can be run from one ignition box, providing very high energy sparks for single or twin plug cylinder heads. Everything is monitored and controlled by the microchip and total current is reduced by more than half with spark energy increasing. Average current consumption is less than 1.5 amps at max revs. The units have a very low primary resistance and a very high-quality iron core. The HT cables are detachable and the primary connections are by spade terminal. As these coils are controlled by current input not voltage, up to four coils can be run in series from one ignition unit.

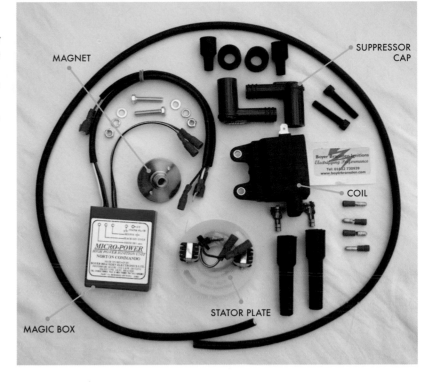

current is no longer stored by the battery and is lost as heat. The battery would eventually boil dry and explode – but not with a power box in place. What's more it's possible to start the bike with a flat battery.

All details on how to convert to 12v operation are available from Boyer Bransden with the appropriate unit. There is also available a power box dynamo regulator, which replaces the mechanical voltage regulator and cutout – or aftermarket electronic units. The regular two-brush dynamo is designed for 6v systems, but when connected to a power box dynamo regulator it will charge 12v at over 120 watts without placing undue load on the dynamo windings.

The power box dynamo regulator unit can be hidden beneath the cover of the original Lucas mechanical regulator box to maintain original appearance.

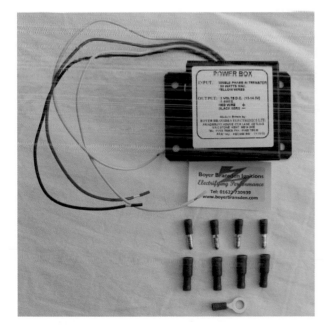

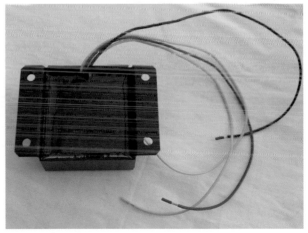

ABOVE: *The Power Box is a sealed unit – just fit and forget.*

LEFT: *The Boyer Bransden 'magic' Power Box.*

A translucent shell allows the electrolyte level to be easily spotted.

10   *the electrical system*

THE LOOM

Apart from gearbox internals, the thing that most spooks classic enthusiasts is the electrical system. You either get electrics or you don't. If you're fortunate enough to fall into the former category then you'll know your way around a multimeter, you'll know the difference between a rectifier and a regulator, you'll understand all about wave patterns, high frequency, low frequency, ohms, watts, volts and what items with strange names like Zener diode all do. Classic motorcycle electrics are fairly basic, but nevertheless, even when armed with a proper wiring diagram, there's a good chance that if you fall into the latter bracket then after all your painstaking and thorough work, when you turn on that switch, nothing will happen, which is even more aggravating because the former lot will do exactly the same and their efforts will be rewarded with

glorious sound and vision first time! It's a good job they're there, so that those of use who lack the magic touch with the black art of electrical logic can turn to them for assistance.

Indeed, there is a highly recommendable motorcycle electrician who goes by the rather salubrious name of 'Ferret'. He travels the country in his fully kitted out mobile workshop van and will undertake rewires at your home, at your convenience. He is one of the aforementioned wizards who actually understand the black art and uses nothing but the best materials, in the right manner and is guaranteed to make a perfect job in a fraction of the time it will take you. In the meantime you can be getting on with something else productive, safe in the knowledge that your motorcycle electrics will work when you need them to. *See* the Useful Contacts at the end of the book.

If your project machine has any wiring on it, before you do anything

or make any decision about it, have a good look around it. Are the connections a mix and match combination of all sorts of different fittings, are they green with corrosion, are there any bare wires, are they hanging on by a flimsy thread of copper core wire, and so on? Remove the headlamp lens (if there's one on), have a good look inside and see if there is a series of different coloured wires that don't match what's on the wiring diagram, or worse, if what's there is held together with the regular domestic plastic chocolate box type connector block or multicolours of insulation tape. If it is, you can bet that somewhere in the system there will also be a bit of domestic wire or even cooker wire. If so, don't think twice – rip it all out and put it to one side. Don't throw it out because a bit of wire always comes in useful, if not for making a short length of the right colour then for making a bulb connector as a tester, for example.

Making a Connection

Using a good professional wire-stripping tool makes for an easy, neat job.

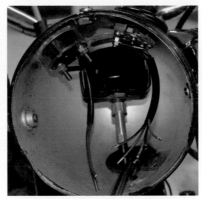

Wires stripped to consistent length ready to accept bullet connectors.

Good-quality bullet connectors and a professional crimping tool.

The tool holds the connector in the correct position, allowing the wire to be threaded into the bullet.

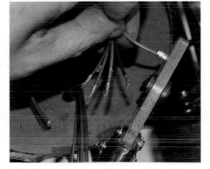

With the wire in the connector at the correct length, the tool is closed to make the crimp.

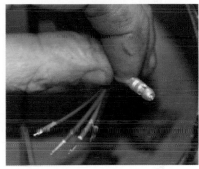

Bullet connector crimped and ready to fit.

ABOVE LEFT: All wires and connectors crimped up. A neat job well done.

ABOVE MIDDLE: There's not a lot of room to work in a headlight shell so the bullet connectors allow for parts to be quickly detached, making access much easier.

ABOVE RIGHT: Bullet connectors regularly found on the high street and the DIY crimping tool (see p. 209), which leaves the dimple shown on the fitting, are adequate but frowned upon by professional auto electricians.

In the heady days when your bike was in manufacture, the factories would have any number of people, usually women, seated at tables whereon there would be a pattern to which they would work laying wires together to form the loom, or harness, for the appropriate machine to be built. These wires would all be the correct length and fitted with the correct end connectors for their required purpose. On the assembly line, the fitters would have their set routes for the loom and all the wires would essentially fall into place at the correct length and simply be fitted up to the dynamo, ammeter, headlamp, tail lamp, horn and so on; then once that was secured to the frame, it would be on to the next one coming along the line.

Half a century later of course, it's unlikely that original wiring has survived unscathed, having passed through any number of ham-fisted previous owners who have abused it with a variety of Heath Robinson fixes in order to keep the lights working long enough to get them home, for example. So, if it looks the least bit suspect, then replace it. You can do it two ways – you can make up the wiring loom yourself or you can buy one ready made. Today there are many specialists who can supply a new loom tailored to fit your specific machine. What's more, most are generally of adequate quality too, whereas not so many years ago, a new loom off the shelf would probably be of poor quality, made in Asia, potentially have the wrong size or type of fitting on the ends – if it had any at all – and quite possibly no match to the colours of your original wiring diagram, which led to guessing what went where by virtue of its approximate length.

The issue with the colour of the wires is a problem you may still come across. If you come up against this, contact your supplier, who then should either make up a loom to your diagram or supply a diagram to suit his colours. The former would be preferable obviously, as if this is to the original factory diagram then many other such books and manuals will have the same colours on their printed diagram, and should you part with the machine, then you are not passing on the confusion.

Another bit of confusion, rather than a problem, is the possible presence of superfluous wires. Norton's Commando is a classic example, where the loom may contain wires suitable for the Interpol police machine with its blue lights and nee-noo horns. You will find, however, that should you request the services of the likes of Ferret, he will not use a replica loom, preferring the guaranteed nature of his own wiring combinations, so do not buy a pattern loom if you're considering outsourcing the job.

As mentioned above, generally speaking the classic wiring diagram is pretty simple, covering headlight, pilot light, horn, dynamo/alternator, brake light and tail light – and maybe indicators. Your manual will have the correct diagram so the first thing to do is either redraw it to a larger size or enlarge it to around A3 size on a photocopier, then go over the wires with the appropriate coloured crayon so it's obvious at first glance what colour you're looking at.

It's quite an impressive sight to walk into someone's workshop and witness a home-made lightweight gantry, over the front of the bike being restored, with a series of small rolls of different coloured wire on a cross-member axle all leading to various parts of the bike. Original wire size for general use was/ is 14/0.3, which equates to 14 strands of 0.3mm diameter, giving a cross sectional area of 1mm². Main circuits and charging output used 28/0.3, giving 2mm² cross-sectional area. The former is rated at 8.75 amps and the latter at 17.5 amps. These wire types were discontinued in the late 1990s and superseded by a thin-wall cable, which has a much higher current rating for the same cross-sectional area.

The appropriate colours are all available either in small rolls or by the foot or metre. It's advisable to buy the full roll, which is probably a little more expensive in the initial capital outlay, around £5 for a 6m roll, but you can then be confident that you'll have enough to do the job and have plenty left over for the next job too. If you choose to buy it by the length, measure up first and then buy twice as much because that way you'll cover your mistakes – imagine being almost there on a bank holiday weekend when you realize that you're six inches short of purple wire and instead have two feet of red wire surplus. What's more, when you make up your own loom you can be absolutely certain of the workmanship and quality of materials used, you can add or remove certain items should you so wish, such as increasing security with a little secret switch somewhere, you can upgrade the insulation and weather protection with state-of-the-art wraps and, when it all works fine, you can sit back in smug satisfaction that you achieved it all by yourself. One little thing that is often overlooked, especially by the electrical novice, is the earth. If you've had your frame painted, enamelled or, worse, powder-coated, ensure that the earth connection can get through the finish to the metal of the frame. Powder coat especially makes a good insulator and thus prevents a decent contact.

If you go down the DIY route then use the Lucar flat spade-type connectors. They make a good connection and are also available with an integral

plastic sheath, which can be slipped over the connection.

While the wires can be stripped with side cutter and crimped onto the fitting with pliers, or even the vice, it pays to invest in a proper crimping tool, which combines both facilities. If you study the crimping tool you will notice it has a series of blade-edged holes of set size, which will grip and cut into the outer plastic covering of the appropriately sized cable so when you pull it one way and the crimping tool the other, it strips off the cover without damaging the inner wires, leaving a perfect length of bare wire for the fitting and a perfect edge to the cut cover.

Strip back about a quarter-inch or so of the cover to reveal the bare wires then insert or lay it into the female end of the fitting. Your crimping tool also has a series of male and female teeth into which the correct-sized cable and fitting can fit, which, when the tool is closed, squeezes them together to make the crimp. The fitting can of course be soldered as well as or instead of crimping. Pull back the portion of the wires that are projecting through the crimp into the fitting, flip them back over the crimp and splay them flat. Then add a little solder onto them and allow it to flow between the wires and possibly into the crimp itself. Don't forget to pull back the cover sheath when the joint is made. Don't forget, either, to slide your wires into the sheathing to keep them together on the frame before you fit the end connectors, otherwise it they may not all pass through the sheath.

There are several sheathing materials available, from the polyester, open-weave traditional type of cloth lookalike to the brilliant heat-shrink tubing. The latter is a lightweight loose tube, which comes in flat form on a roll through which you feed the wires; then simply warm it up gently with a heat gun and watch it contract to give a good tight seal around the cables. No only does this provide excellent support to the cables within but it also gives weather protection second to none and makes for an easy time when connecting to the frame. By it's very nature, however, it does show up all the 'varicose veins' within it, so in areas where the wiring has to be seen, it may be aesthetically better to use a

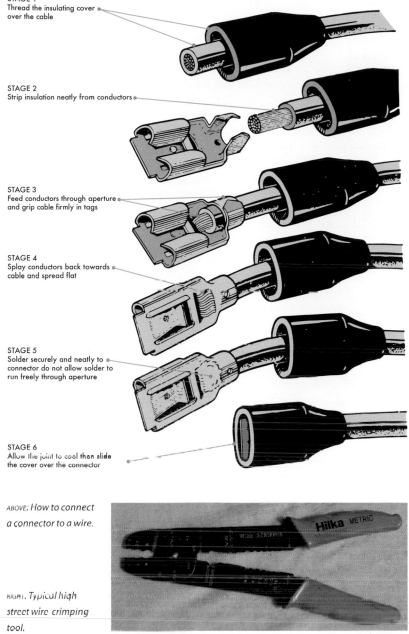

STAGE 1
Thread the insulating cover over the cable

STAGE 2
Strip insulation neatly from conductors

STAGE 3
Feed conductors through aperture and grip cable firmly in tags

STAGE 4
Splay conductors back towards cable and spread flat

STAGE 5
Solder securely and neatly to connector do not allow solder to run freely through aperture

STAGE 6
Allow the joint to cool then slide the cover over the connector

ABOVE: How to connect a connector to a wire.

RIGHT: Typical high street wire crimping tool.

this case, the dynamo, the anode will develop a covering of lead peroxide and turn a dark brown colour. The cathode will appear unchanged. When the terminals are bridged, for example to light a bulb, current will flow in the opposite direction, from the positive plates to the negative plates, and the bulb will light up. It will continue to glow until the anode (positive) has lost its covering and both plates are back to the same colour – that is, when the battery is flat. As such, the bigger the size and number of the plates within the cells, the stronger and longer the battery will operate.

To get a bit technical, the plates are actually a skeleton, a bit like an ice cube tray, filled with a lead oxide paste (negative) and lead peroxide (positive). The insulators are usually rubber or nylon.

By its very nature, the internals of the battery flip-flop back and forth from charge to discharge. The water content of the electrolyte – the water-acid mix – splits during discharge into hydrogen and oxygen. The oxygen acts on the spongy surface of the negative plates, forming lead oxide, which reacts with the sulphuric acid in the electrolyte to form lead sulphate and more water. This lowers the specific gravity of the mix. Then, at the positive, lead peroxide-covered plates, the hydrogen reacts to form lead oxide and even more water.

Finally, the sulphuric acid reacts with this additional lead oxide deposit resulting in even more water. So now there is water, water, everywhere. A sample of electrolyte drawn off into a battery tester (hydrometer) at this point is essentially little more than pure water and will not keep the test beads afloat in the hydrometer tube. You have a completely flat battery, so you put it on charge.

Now everything starts to go in the opposite direction. Hydrogen, instead of oxygen, now reacts with the negative plates' lead oxide to form sulphuric acid. At the positive plates, the oxygen, together with all the water, then combines with the lead sulphate to form lead peroxide and sulphuric acid, and your battery starts to come back to life.

In a fully charged state, electrolysed oxygen and hydrogen no longer react, as neither negative nor positive plates contain any lead sulphate.

plain PVC sleeve of adequate diameter. If there are some bare areas, then you can also use a brush-on insulation fluid, which dries in minutes and forms a flexible rubberized sealant. Of course, there is nothing wrong with good, old-fashioned impregnated cloth insulation tape or even PVC tape, in places where aesthetics are unimportant or the use cannot be seen.

Now let's have a look at the parts of the electrical system.

THE BATTERY

With fears over climate change and the potential exhaustion of oil, electricity generation has shot off in all sorts of different directions over the last few years; if nothing else, this has meant that battery technology has improved in leaps and bounds and it's no longer necessary to rely upon the traditional lead acid battery.

The Lead Acid Battery

The lead acid, or wet cell battery in its simplest form is a series of cells, in which there is a series of lead alloy plates immersed in a solution of distilled water and acid. One plate acts as the anode, or positive element, the other acts as the cathode, or negative element. When the battery is connected to its charging source, let's say in

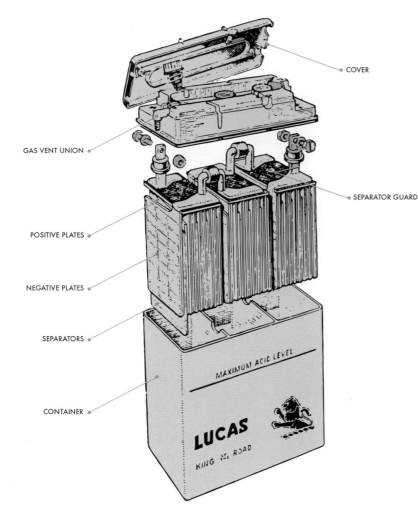

COVER

GAS VENT UNION

SEPARATOR GUARD

POSITIVE PLATES

NEGATIVE PLATES

SEPARATORS

MAXIMUM ACID LEVEL

CONTAINER

LUCAS

KING THE ROAD

ABOVE: Basics of the lead acid battery.

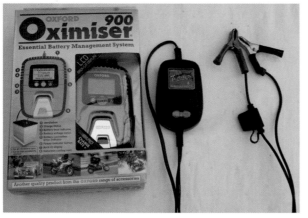

LEFT: A battery monitoring system is a worthy investment if you lay up your bike over winter.

this is invariably because one or more cells have failed through storage.

If a battery is to be stored up over winter, then a regulated trickle charger of some form is an excellent investment, as it will monitor the condition of the battery and cut in when required, cutting out when the battery is back up to full charge.

Size of course is a limiting factor on a motorcycle so it's always been a case of getting as much as possible into the little space available so the battery will fit into its shelf, usually behind the engine amidships of the toolbox and oil tank.

Some original batteries, especially on rigid and plunger-framed machines, would be hung on the side of the bike beneath the rider's thigh, and some were a special shape, such as the Lucas King of the Road T-shaped job, which had its own special support system. While such items were in production this was not a problem, but once obsolete and before the classic movement took off, there was no longer any call for anything but the basic box-shaped battery and it didn't matter what it looked like because it was just an old bike. However, as vintage and classic motorcycles gained popularity, aesthetics and originality began to play an important part, and restorers were faced with the question of what could be done about an obsolete T-shaped battery that was right for the bike but completely useless? Well, the answer was to carefully cut out the top, remove all the old dead plates and core out the remaining box to accept a new battery within it. At first, the only suitable 6v batteries were low-powered Asian items, intended mainly for mopeds and lightweights, but they were adequate and would last reasonably well if looked after. Nowadays there are better alternatives.

On coring out the box, you could then see how the battery was put together in order to maximize the space available. There would be a number of plates, obviously negative and positive, sandwiched together alternately and separated by tiny insulators with just enough room for the acid to circulate between them. The plate-to-plate connections are made in series and the individual cells are connected by a form of bridge, so that the capacity read at the terminals naturally represents the

However, if the charging continues, it is possible to 'boil' the battery, resulting in poisonous and inflammable gases bubbling from the electrolyte. Fluid can also be discharged, and if it does so on the bike then it invariably runs down the paintwork and onto the exhaust, stripping all before it and ruining the chromework. Obviously normal evaporation takes place, so it pays to keep a regular check on the electrolyte levels. Most modern batteries now have a translucent shell

through which the electrolyte level can be seen against the minimum and maximum markings on the outer case.

The best thing for a battery is to be used. A regularly used, well looked-after battery will give exceptional long-term service, but let it stand, for example over winter, and the lead sulphate, normally essential, becomes a destructive element and can 'kill' the cell. Often the battery appears to take a charge but once in the system fails instantly –

ABOVE LEFT: The King of the Road has to have its own mounting system.

ABOVE RIGHT: Careful work with the chisel cored out this original King of the Road of its useless innards.

A mini 6v battery from Burlen Fuel Systems can then be hidden away in the old case.

efficient in AGM batteries than in gel-type batteries, which have a liquid barrier between the plates.

Like with any battery, it is wise to try to keep a sealed battery fully charged at all times, especially when the battery is off the bike. If a battery is not kept charged, the plates will eventually sulphate, causing an increase of internal resistance, which prevents it supplying its maximum amount of cranking current and capacity. Letting a battery go flat through non-use or allowing it to discharge by being connected to a 'low-level parasitic drain current' such as a security device, can be damaging. Disconnect the battery if storing it up for a long time, for example over winter, and keep it hooked up to an appropriate monitoring charger. If a sealed unit is allowed to go flat, while it can be brought back, its performance will inevitably be compromised and it will never be quite the same again.

Take great care when charging as over-charging can cause pressure and heat to build up inside the battery, causing it to balloon and potentially explode. Of course, there may be circumstances where you will be unaware it is being over-charged, for example if the dynamo or alternator regulator fails, allowing the output voltage to rise and force too much current into the battery.

On the bench, or on the bike, make sure that the charger you use is compatible with AGM batteries. Boost chargers used to recover sulphated wet batteries should not be used on sealed units. Ensure the charger's maximum input is no more than 14v. Keep the battery away from heat too, for when a battery is hot, the chemical reactions within it occur at a much quicker rate, so it will accept a charge current at a higher than normal rate.

While they are invariably more expensive than their wet cell equivalents, the good thing about the AGM battery, and the Gel Cell (*see below*), is that they do actually store well and don't tend to sulphate or degrade as quickly as wet cell. Unless you over-charge, as mentioned above, there is little chance of a gas explosion. If you don't use your bike every day, then an AGM battery is likely to be a better bet as it will hold its charge through longer periods of inactivity.

battery as a whole. The case would have internal ribs to support the plates off the base of the case, so that when age or vibration forced the plates to shed lead fragments, the sediment formed built up in the base and did not bung up the plates. These ribs could then be carved out to accommodate the new battery. New, replica King of the Road T-shaped battery boxes are available, especially made to accommodate a smaller battery.

Sealed Units

Though also a trade name, the generic, traditional term for these was Varley batteries, as Varley Dry Accumulators Ltd were the pioneers of such technology.

The Varley system is again a lead acid battery but uses an absorbent glass mat (AGM) to separate the positive and negative plates. There are two main benefits to this. The first is the electrolyte (sulphuric acid) is absorbed onto the fibres of this mat, therefore there is little free fluid within the cells as only enough acid is used to achieve the required performance levels. The AGM retains the electrolyte ensuring that, if the battery casing is damaged, there is minimal risk of electrolyte leakage and subsequent damage. The AGM also allows gas flow to occur between the plates over a large area. This is important for a high level of gas 'recombination' to occur. Recombination is where chemicals within the battery are converted back into their original state during overcharge. This allows the battery to retain gases internally and thus be maintenance free. In order for recombination to occur, oxygen must flow from the positive plate to the negative plate and this is more

Gel Cell

These batteries are similar to the AGM as the electrolyte is suspended, but different in that the electrolyte in the Gel Cell has a silica additive that causes it to set. These are the most sensitive cells in terms of adverse reactions to over-charging, and if an incompatible charger is used on a Gel Cell, premature failure is certain. It is very common for the term Gel Cell to be used rather generically when referring in general to sealed, maintenance-free batteries, so you have to be careful if and when you buy a charger to suit a Gel Cell – your assumed Gel Cell battery might not actually be a Gel Cell battery at all.

Dry Cell

Referring back to the old Lucas King of the Road T-shaped battery, the arrival of the dry cell unit has been a boon, and many an original battery casing now sports a dry cell 6v unit within (or even a brace of sealed lead acid types). It's quite simple also to link two 6v units together to form a 12v battery, and as they take up little room when stood on their ends, they too can be accommodated within an old battery box. That is the main advantage of the dry cell, or to be correct, solid state battery: as it is completely sealed and contains no fluid, it can be positioned in any position without detriment.

A solid state battery has both solid electrodes and solid electrolytes. The electrical lithium-iron-phosphate chemistry of the system is a bit complex and rather unnecessary for us to explore, for all we need is a versatile battery, which will keep its charge for a good while. Nevertheless, solid state batteries have a very minimal self-discharge rate, which gives them an excellent shelf life, which in turn benefits the classic, which perhaps doesn't get used in poor weather conditions and hence spends much of the British summer in the garage! What's more they are easy to miniaturize, there is no electrolyte leakage risk and their performance does not tend to react to changes in temperature, though perhaps for our classics, a tad overkill.

THE SWITCH

There are any number of switch variations on classic motorcycles, from the basic on-off lever to the multi-point and multi-pain Lucas PRS8 combined lights and ignition unit. Essentially they all work on the same principle, using a rotor that touches a contact and directs power to wherever it's needed. The diagram shows the principle.

There is a central rotor, which is a non-conductive distributor, originally made of Bakelite but now some form of similar-looking plastic. Inset in the rotor is a brass strip (shown black on the diagram), which, when moved, connects two or more of the terminal posts, each of which has a spring-loaded contact that permanently touches the rotor. The diagram shows that the main supply from the battery is to terminal number two, and the switch is positioned so that current will pass along the brass section to terminals one and three to feed the head lamp and tail lamp. When the switch is moved clockwise, the rotor moves off terminal one, so the head lamp goes out, but it makes contact with terminal four, which then lights up the pilot light and the tail lamp. A further turn clockwise removes the contact from terminal two, the feed, and all lights go out – the off position.

There is often a second brass section on the opposite side of the switch, which also makes contact with terminals to bring in a combined ignition

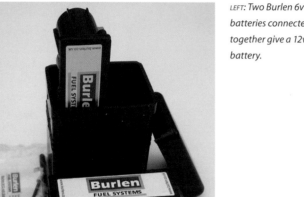

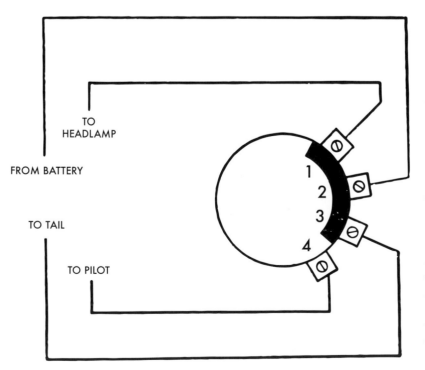

LEFT: Two Burlen 6v batteries connected together give a 12v battery.

BELOW: The basic principle of the switch.

TO HEADLAMP

FROM BATTERY

TO TAIL

TO PILOT

1
2
3
4

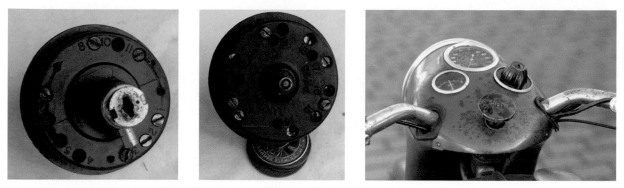

ABOVE LEFT: The uppermost side of the PRS8 combined ignition and lights switch, showing the key slot.

ABOVE MIDDLE: The underside has a number of connections and interconnections too, separated by an insulated washer.

ABOVE RIGHT: PRS8 was fitted to 1950s Triumphs such as this Thunderbird, as well as several other machines too.

arrangement, or, as in the case of the PRS8, a double-deck arrangement with several contacts above and below a sandwiched insulator, with many of the contacts interconnected.

As far as maintenance and repair is concerned, there is little that can be done with such a switch other than to ensure the contacts are clean and the ends of the wires are held securely in the slotted terminal posts by the screws. Occasionally the springs will need a little persuasion to retain their contact; indeed pattern switches can often suffer from poor contacts, so do not dispose of your old switch until you are satisfied with its replacement. Many are the times that a new pattern switch has had to have its internals replaced from an old, perhaps damaged original.

If your project has no switchgear, or has obviously got the wrong sort, it's easy to see what would have been fitted originally simply by looking at appropriate images, plenty of which will be in whatever book you should have referring to your particular model. Add to that a close look at the wiring diagram and you'll soon be able to deduce what you need, be it a PRS turn knob, a PRS4, or a PRS6 with integral ignition key, or a similar but more involved PRS8, or two individual turn knobs, or just a key switch. All are available as patterns.

On the inside, the actual switch area with its connections are marked numerically, so at least you can see which

RIGHT: The component parts of the PRS8 – the two halves and the insulated sandwich filling.

BELOW: PRS turn knob.

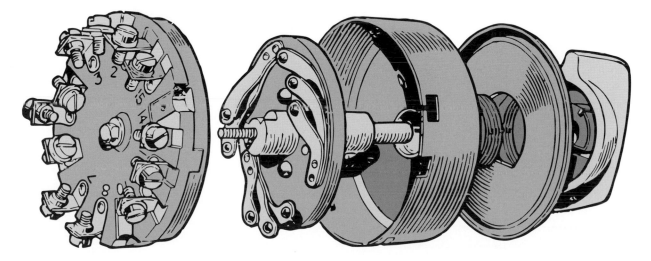

is terminal two, three, four and so on. The keys are pretty simple, just T-headed pieces of lightweight pressed steel, and it's not a big job to switch on the ignition with a screwdriver or penknife blade. Be careful with the keys when turning on the ignition, as sometimes, especially if the centre section has a rubber weather shield on it, the operation can be stiff and it's not difficult to damage the switch and even easier to twist or even break the key in the slot.

THE DYNAMO

Most dynamos found on a classic motorcycle will be 6v – but that doesn't mean they have to remain 6v, as there are ways of getting them to deliver 12v (more on that later). The dynamo has to be studied in conjunction with a voltage control unit of some form. As the dynamo – also known as a direct current generator – spins faster, it generates more current, much more than required for a 6v system, so its output has to be regulated or the bulbs would blow and the battery would boil.

If the dynamo is present on your project, remove it; on the bench, join the two contacts D and F as one, then lead a wire from them to the positive terminal of a battery. Then take a lead from the negative terminal and touch it against the body of the dynamo – if it's all right inside, the dynamo should

then 'motor' – that is, spin. If that occurs, then the armature windings are sound and there's not a lot wrong with your dynamo. If it doesn't motor, do not despair, simply resign yourself to the fact that it will have to be dismantled to see what's what inside.

Dismantling a dynamo is quite simple. A central screw can be undone to release the Bakelite end cover, under which will be the two connections to the D and F terminals. The D terminal is attached directly to the positive brush and the F terminal to one of the two leads emerging from the body of the unit. The other lead of this latter pair runs to the other (negative) brush lead on the commutator end bracket. If the dynamo has an adjustable steel cover band around the commutator area, this can also be removed, allowing complete access to the commutator, on the end of the armature. The two carbon brushes that run on the commutator are spring-loaded; the springs simply push out of their holding slots, which then allows the brushes to be removed from their contact with the commutator face.

Turning to the opposite end of the dynamo, unscrew the securing bolt and remove the tab washer. Using a suitable puller, remove the drive pinion from the end of the armature shaft. Prise the Woodruff key out of its slot on the shaft and keep it somewhere safe –

you'll be amazed just how easily these small but vital parts are lost. Undo and slide out the two long screws that pass through the length of the dynamo and mate with two hexagon-headed nuts recessed in the brush gear end. The alloy end plate contains a bearing through which the armature shaft passes and turns; this may well be a tight fit, and gentle warming of the alloy may be required to facilitate removal. That's more or less it.

Clean and degrease everything thoroughly using a medium that evaporates quickly, such as petrol, white spirit or a proprietary clutch, brake or contact cleaner. Clean out the gaps between the commutator segments using a broken hacksaw blade – which is exactly the right width – or a blunt knife to remove all remains of carbon dust. Check the size and face shape of the carbon brushes: if they are too worn for the springs to keep them pressed against the commutator face, then replace them with new ones. Inside the Lucas dynamo shell are fixed the magnets, or pole shoes. If we're being perfectly correct, the pole shoes are not actually magnetic, but do serve to increase the strength of the magnetic field created by the field coil. These can be unscrewed and removed but it can be difficult to replace them as snugly as they were fitted in the factory without the aid of an appropriate

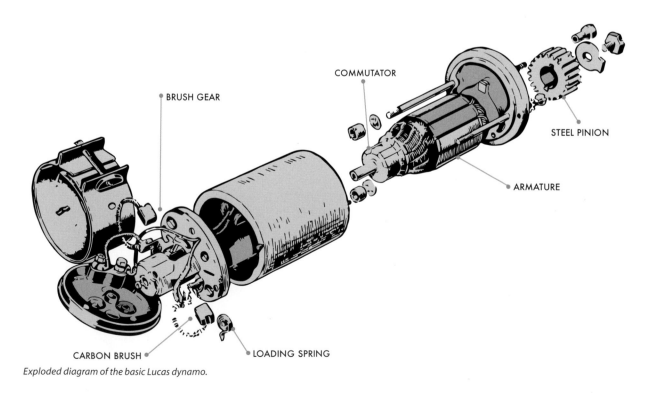

COMMUTATOR

BRUSH GEAR

STEEL PINION

ARMATURE

CARBON BRUSH

LOADING SPRING

Exploded diagram of the basic Lucas dynamo.

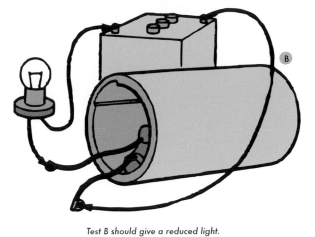

Field coil test. Using a 6 volt headlamp bulb, test A should give no light.

Test B should give a reduced light.

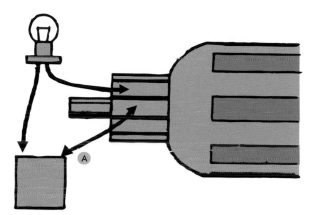

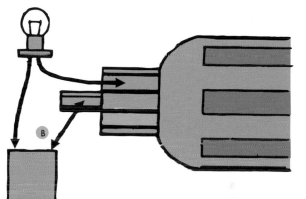

Armature test. Using a 6 watt 6 volt bulb, connect leads between each adjoining commutator strip (test A), this should light the bulb.

Test B – should give no light

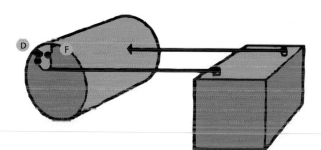

Bridge D and F terminals on the dynamo with a loop of wire and connect as shown. The dynamo will then act as an electric motor and spin.

Diagrams demonstrating various dynamo tests.

expanding, scissor jack-like tool. It is essential they do not touch the armature – there must be an air gap at all times.

A further test on the armature windings, now it's in pieces, is to touch the leads from a fully charged battery onto adjacent segments of the commutator: if the windings are good there will be a spark. Continue this segment test two by two.

To check if the fault is because some of the armature windings are actually touching the armature spindle, hold the

wire against each of the commutator segments and the other end onto the armature spindle. There should be no passage of current and therefore no spark.

If your machine has the Lucas type E3H or E3HM, then note there is a lubricator, usually a small felt washer, on the commutator end bracket, which would benefit from a little light oil every 1,000 miles or so. Most other Lucas dynamos have sealed bearings.

Reassembly is equally as straightforward – just ensure everything fits together correctly and the armature

spins freely. Once back together, repeat the test to see if it motors and note the direction in which the dynamo is turning, as it may have changed its polarity while apart. There's usually a direction arrow stamped into the body somewhere. If it spins in the wrong direction, it will need repolarizing.

The following advice regarding the dynamo is verbatim from Ferret:

The first thing I always do is determine the direction of the rotation of the dynamo when it's fitted

F = FIELD
A = AMMETER
D = DYNAMO
E = EARTH

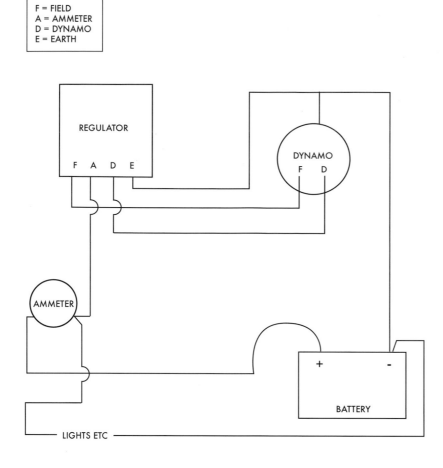

The basic charging system.

The dynamo armature.

Dynamo body showing the position of the magnets.

The dynamo dismantled.

to the machine. Then I check the direction of the arrow on the dynamo body, as there are no guarantees you have the original or even the correct unit fitted.

Electrically speaking, a dynamo and a DC motor are one and the same, so the best way to find out if the thing is any good is to carry out a motor test. Lightly clamp the unit in a vice and, having established or decided upon the polarity of your machine's electrical system – negative or positive earth – proceed as follows.

For Lucas dynamos, connect the D and F terminals together, then using an appropriate length/gauge of wire, connect them to the live side of a fully charged battery of the correct voltage. Now, using another length of wire, connect the other side of the battery to a clean unpainted part of the dynamo body (earth). You can do this by simply stripping the end of the wire and touching it across. There may be a spark as you make the connection, but fear not, you will not get a shock, and the dynamo should now rotate smoothly at a few hundred rpm. If it does this and in the correct direction too, your unit can be considered probably fit for service. It will also be correctly polarized.

For Miller, Bosch and most other dynamos, the procedure is the same in principle but slightly different in practice. The F terminal must be connected to earth (dynamo body) and only the D terminal connected to the live side of the battery. Apart from this the rest of the test is identical. It is easy to convert a Miller or Bosch to Lucas configuration and vice versa, but do seek expert advice.

If, after having carried out the relevant test, the dynamo does not turn at all, then either poor brush contact (remedied by cleaning commutator segments and brushes) or a defective field coil (best to send it away to a specialist) is most likely. If it does turn but only reluctantly, rough and slowly then the armature is probably the problem (again best outsourced). If all seems good but the direction of rotation is wrong, then remove the end cover and swap the field coil leads, carry out the motor test again and you'll probably find it motors the other way.

The wide choice of solid state electronic voltage regulators now available are a good upgrade and all are reliable, if properly installed, but it is vital to ensure that the unit purchased is of the correct voltage, polarity and for the right configuration of dynamo.

A 6v dynamo can be converted to 12v. Most 6v dynamos start charging at around 800 1,000rpm so they are geared to the engine to suit; however, a 6v dynamo used to power a 12v system may not begin to charge until perhaps 1,500rpm or more, therefore it's not ideal for slow-speed night riding or town work as the battery will simply run down. So if you want to upgrade then check out the specialists who will supply and fit a rewound armature to 12v specification, new field coils (magnets and so on inside the dynamo body), brushes, springs and

A typical solid state rectifier, sealed; simply fit and let the electronics inside do their work.

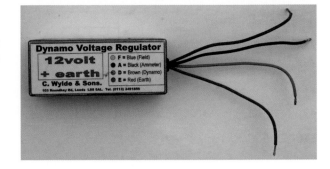

bearings to suit and a 12v sold state electronic regulator.

Most of the time, such a conversion allows an even lower than previous charging cut-in speed, which is a boon for low-revving machines or where the dynamo is crankshaft driven at engine speed. It's generally not a cheap exercise – prices will vary so shop around – but 80W output or more can be achieved and the dynamo runs a little cooler, so if you have to ride at night, at least you'll have considerably brighter lights. Of course, all bulbs will have to be changed to 12v, though you may get away with leaving your 6v horn, as it's an item rarely used for long periods,

though for peace of mind a 12v replacement may be the best bet. Having said that, a 6v horn with 12v passing through it will be loud and the pitch will be higher. Don't forget to add up all the wattages of your new bulbs – the tail, stop and headlight – which will be on all together at times, as they must not exceed the dynamo output.

VOLTAGE CONTROL UNITS

Also known as CVCs – compensated voltage control units – or generically as the regulator box (the MCR1 and later the MCR2). Essentially, these are electro-mechanical devices that allow

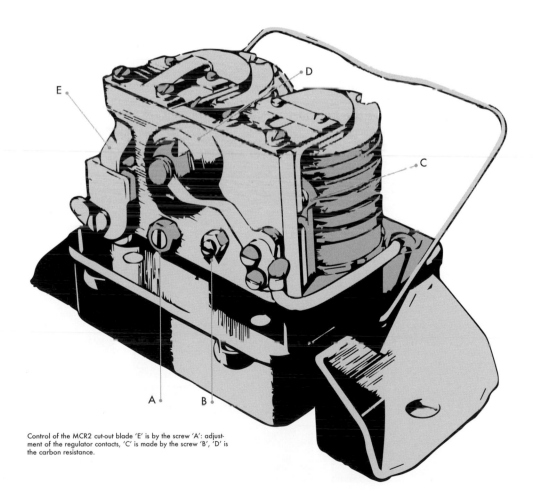

The Lucas mechanical voltage control unit. It's adjustable to allow more or less power through it as required.

Control of the MCR2 cut-out blade 'E' is by the screw 'A': adjustment of the regulator contacts, 'C' is made by the screw 'B', 'D' is the carbon resistance.

enough current to pass from the dynamo to the battery to keep it charged when not in use, but then cut off that supply when the battery fully charged. The unit should then allow a swift boost of current when there is a drain on the battery, such as when all the lights are on.

The MCR unit has two electromagnets, both of which can be manually adjusted to govern the flow of current and the point at which it cuts in and cuts out. One acts as a cutout, the other acts as a regulator by means of a set of points on top of the magnets. The gap between these points must be between 0.02in and 0.025in. However, as clever and as good as these units were, most are well into pensionable age and, as such, suffering from the ailments and frailties age brings, so forget them and fit a solid state electronic equivalent. There are several makes and styles, both in 6v and 12v, and some even have the option of both – you select which simply by flicking a switch or snipping a small wire.

The electronics are resin-encapsulated and all you see are the F, A, D and E wires projecting, so all you have to do is connect them up correctly into the system and mount the regulator somewhere safe, out of the weather and as insulated from vibration as possible. There are some versions available that take the form of the original MCR, so they can remain in their original positions on the bike and no one is any the wiser that inside the Lucas box is a state-of-the-art replica. There is no mechanical fiddling around or adjustment – just fit and forget.

LEFT: CVC from the front showing the contact points.

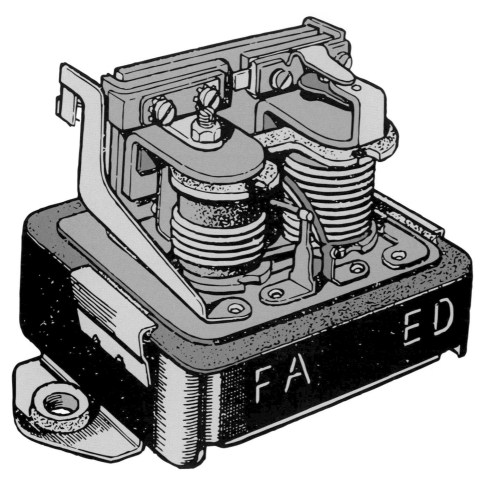

BELOW LEFT: A rigid-framed Norton CVC sits on brackets between the frame tubes under the front saddle.

BELOW MIDDLE: With the cover off, it exposes an electronic unit designed to look like the original.

BELOW RIGHT: Totally sealed with the four wires coming out the base, the CVC can simply be connected up and job done.

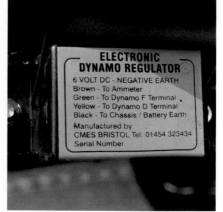

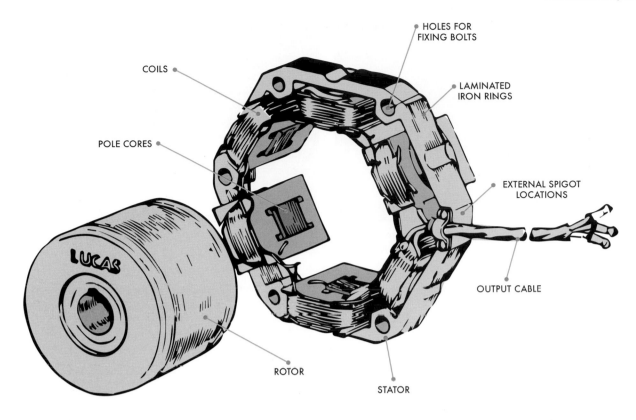

COILS

POLE CORES

HOLES FOR
FIXING BOLTS

LAMINATED
IRON RINGS

EXTERNAL SPIGOT
LOCATIONS

OUTPUT CABLE

ROTOR

STATOR

ABOVE: Component parts of the alternator.

RIGHT: The Lucas alternator features a fixed ring of up to six laminated copper coils wound onto a pole core, inside of which spins a magnetic rotor on the end of the crankshaft, all within the primary drive cover.

ALTERNATORS

Coil ignition and alternating current generators first appeared (not includ-

ing two-strokes) on the Triumph Speed twin in the early 1950s. The Lucas alternator features a fixed ring of up to six laminated copper coils

wound onto a pole core, inside of which spins a magnetic rotor on the end of the crankshaft, all within the primary drive cover. The air gap between the coils and the magnet should be between 0.014in and 0.016in. The crankshaft has to be longer than the dynamo-engined crank, to carry it. The six coils are coupled in series but connected in parallel for output. One side goes to a switch with three lighting positions that bring in to use when required one, two or all three pairs of coils. The current is AC – alternating current – so then has to be channelled through the rectifier to convert it to DC – direct current – in order to charge the battery.

The Lucas RM alternator, introduced in 1964, has its coils and wiring resin-encapsulated. Unlike the dynamo, which can be refurbished, the alternator, if it shows signs of wear and tear and has broken wires, is really not worth trying to repair as there are brand new ones available, plus higher output 6v systems, 12v versions and even 200W or more three-phase systems, which will simply bolt into place and guarantee you brighter lights and a more reliable charging system.

Discuss the options with your parts specialist or speak to some of the classic motorcycle electrical

The alternator rotor fits on the end of the crank with the stator around it, inside the primary cover. Here the clutch has yet to be built up.

Clutch plates and pressure plate in place, along with the primary chain. Now a converter kit can be fitted.

With the primary drive in place, the converter bracket can be fitted. Note the three long studs have been removed as the converter ring is secured by three flush-fitting allen screws.

The new rotor fits onto end of crank, over the Woodruff keyway, and is secured by a nut and washer.

Finally, the new alternator stator is fitted over the rotor and secured to the converter ring by three allen screws.

specialists – at least one of which will come to your home and completely rewire, refurbish and refit your classic's electrical system with the best components available.

Unless you're keen to retain as much specification originality as possible, if you've got to fit a new alternator then why not take the opportunity to upgrade to a 12v system. With a new bolt-on 12v alternator and rectifier kit, it's then merely a matter of changing the bulbs to suit – your lights will be a revelation – but like many other things, it depends on the preparation, wiring, switches and so on.

THE RECTIFIER

The clue is in the name – alternating current – and the original problem with using an AC generator, or alternator, to charge the battery in a DC manner was the phenomenon of half wave rectification. Draw a horizontal line through the centre of a wave pattern, with half above and half below. The top half, positive, would find its way to the battery, whereas the lower half would head to the negative side of the battery and essentially take away everything the positive had just brought. This negative wave was blocked off but that meant only a half wave would reach the battery and as such it would take a long time to charge and would not be able to keep up with demand on it should prolonged night-time running with lights on be required.

The rectifier effectively solved the problem by rerouting the negative wave to the positive side of the battery, thus giving a full DC charge. If you come across a completely unrestored machine you may spot a series of discs stacked, akin to 45s on a record player, secured on a central shaft albeit with cooling air gaps between them, usually positioned somewhere in the

ABOVE: The original selenium-coated rectifier on an unrestored 1953 Triumph Thunderbird is still working well after sixty years of service.

RIGHT: The selenium rectifier was superseded by the silicon bridge type shown here on a 1955 swinging arm Triumph Thunderbird restoration project.

When this 1955 Thunderbird was restored the silicon bridge rectifier was replaced with a state-of-the-art electronic version.

cooling air but away from the weather, for example under the single saddle. The original rectifier discs were metal discs coated in selenium, a low melting-point alloy conductor. However, selenium has a strange attribute in that it will allow current to pass from the metal base through the selenium but not the other way round. The opposite direction forms a high-resistance barri-

er, which can completely suppress AC flow. The way round this was to introduce a further disc into the circuit to allow the second half of the AC wave to pass through. In 1962 Lucas upped the ante with their No. 49072A silicon bridge rectifier. This did away with the selenium principle and incorporated an encapsulated silicon crystal (diode) in each of its four cooling fins and three

Lucar clip-on connectors. It also acted as a heat sink.

The rectifier can be tested with your multimeter switched to ohms, or with a battery and a bulb. Connect one lead to either of the input tags and the other to both the output tags, remember the fixing stud is also an output. Then reverse the leads and repeat the test. There should be a complete circuit in one direction and an open circuit in the other – the latter may manifest itself as a high resistance on your meter. If current flows both ways, dump it and get a new replacement.

Some older bikes have square rectifiers with rubber protection to the selenium-coated fins. These were superseded by the round silicon bridge versions, and while these, or at least replicas of the Lucas originals, are still available, it's simpler to buy a tiny solid state job. It's a little tin box, about an inch square, with resin-encapsulated

This is an old-style rectifier from the Westinghouse Bake and Signal Company, which changes the alternating current to direct current. These normally worked all right, albeit allowing a small back feed, which may cause the battery to go flat.

The old Westinghouse rectifier compared to the miniature solid state replacement.

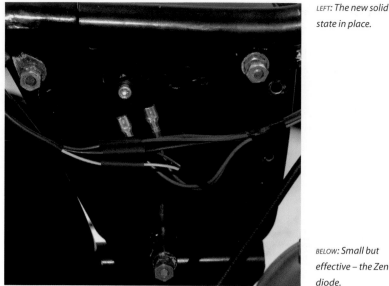

LEFT: The new solid state in place.

muck – where it can radiate its heat via its fixing. It's often found in a fanned alloy heat sink beneath the headlamp on Triumphs, or fixed to the large alloy footrest hanger plates on a Norton Commando. It works like a bypass valve for the rectified current and directs it to where it is needed and when. As the battery reaches its fully charged period, around 14v, the Zener diode, which until this time has blocked any passage of current, becomes partially conductive and provides an alternative path for a small amount of the alternator's output. As voltage rises further, the diode passes more, until at 15v the bulk of the alternator output is bypassed and power to an already full powered battery is shut off.

If load is then placed on the system, such as lights, the system will drop below the on-charge voltage of 15v, so the Zener allows a little back to the battery to keep it topped up, increasing the flow as the load increases and battery capacity begins to fall.

The Zener diode is only found on 12v machines and renders a switch such as the PRS8 redundant, as the switching in and out of various alternator coils is no longer necessary. Full alternator output is used all the time and the Zener diode dumps all excess current to earth – crude but effective. This is why 12v alternators only have two wires (except three-phase units).

THE HORN

Lucas's Altette was pretty much staple fare for most post-war 6v motorcycles and as such there are still plenty around. One dedicated specialist, appropriately known as 'Taff the Horn', has all the records and documentation to ensure that your hooter is the correct model for your bike, and that it has the correct bracket (of which there are very many), and he will also do either a service exchange or restore your existing hooter to immaculate show-winning standard – and it will also work like new. There are Asian-made replicas available too and a common dodge at one time was to have your old non-working Altette fixed in its correct place but have a tiny foreign job hidden away out of sight to 'peep' when 'an audible warning device' was required.

BELOW: Small but effective – the Zener diode.

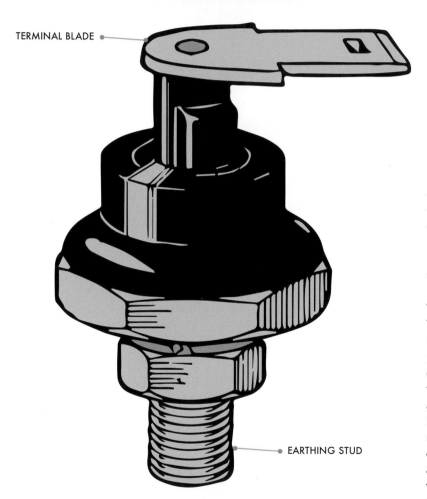

TERMINAL BLADE

EARTHING STUD

miniature electronics inside it and just four connectors protruding from it. Connect it up and forget all about it.

The Zener Diode

A further development of the Lucas rectifier was the Zener diode. Named after the man who developed the principle in 1963, it's a semiconductor that can be totally conductive in the reverse direction at a predetermined moment. It's an unobtrusive little button with a Lucar male connector on its end and is usually fixed to an area of flat metal, out in the cooling air – but preferably away from the worst of damp and road

While you may be able to have the bezel re-plated and paint the body, if the horn will not work no matter how you adjust the centre screw, you would be advised to let the expert repair it, as it is easy to do more harm than good. Clearhooters is another horn company who supplied the British bike industry, especially in latter years. Like the Altette, spares are readily available should yours need a full refurbishment.

BULBS

Massive advances in bulb technology over the past few years have fortunately filtered down to the classic motorcycle market, with the new technology available in older-style fittings. It is possible now to replace the traditional two-filament headlamp bulb with either one much more powerful or a halogen version. Likewise stop-tail light bulbs and pilot bulbs are now available as LED. The beauty of the LED ones is that they are high output but low input, thus not putting too heavy a load on your 6v system. If and when you should upgrade your bulbs, do bear in mind the capacity of your dynamo, or even your alternator. For example, if your dynamo has a maximum output of say 60W, then there's little point in going mad and fitting a 60W headlight bulb, because with the added tail light and horn, you will have the dynamo constantly working flat out; before long it will overheat and the melt the solder around the windings, leaving you without lights.

Of course, if you have upgraded to a new 12v high output alternator then you can increase the bulb wattages greatly.

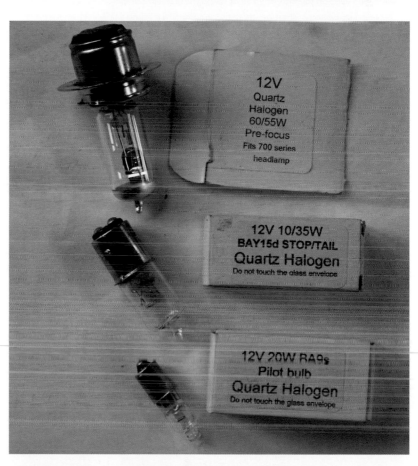

TOP RIGHT: *Fully restored Lucas Altette by Taff the Horn.*

ABOVE RIGHT: *State-of-the-art halogen 12v bulbs for classics.*

RIGHT: *A halogen tail lamp lets you be seen.*

How to Use a Multimeter

One of the most useful pieces of kit available for testing and finding faults on motorcycle electrics is a multimeter. In years gone by, a multimeter would have been akin to a car battery in size and weight but thanks to modern electronics, the same functions are now available in a compact meter, usually with a digital display and at a fraction of the price. Modern digital multimeters come in all shapes and sizes, and prices range from less than £10 up to £250. For general use in the home motorcycle restorer's workshop, a fairly good-quality 'budget' meter, around £20 or so, is perfectly adequate. The meters shown in the photographs include an electrical engineer's high-quality unit, which would have cost in excess of £100 over two decades ago and a regular high street version, available for around a tenner. The key to price variations is the accuracy and the number of features.

Multimeters come with probes and connecting leads and it's useful to have both types – one pair with pointed probe ends and one pair with clips on the end. The use of each type is obvious and can be seen in the photos. There are three probe sockets: a black one marked 'com' (common) and two others, invariably red, marked 'V/O' or similar, and 'A' or 'mA' or similar.

The electronics hobbyist will need all the ranges and functions, but for our purposes, we only need to know how make three measurements.

Checking Voltage

To measure voltage or resistance, the black lead is connected to the 'com' socket and the red lead to the 'V/O' socket.

As with all checks on motorcycle electrics, it helps if you have an idea of what the result should be before you connect the meter. So, for the example here, the voltage measurement on a 12v battery should give about 12v DC.

DC stands for 'direct current' – current that flows in one direction only, say from positive to negative, as from a battery through some sort of electrical system. For some unknown reason, voltage has always been known as DC not DV. On both meters, DC is represented by a symbol comprising a solid line with a dotted line below it. It is a graphic representation of a voltage above a base line.

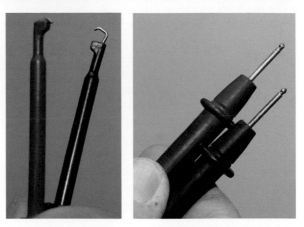

The meter ideally should have both spring-loaded claws, so one end can be hooked into place without having to hold it manually, and probes.

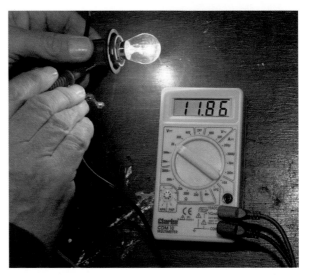

Measuring current passing through bulb. If you want to measure current, you will have to disconnect a wire from the bit of equipment in which you're interested and connect the meter between the wire end and the terminal from which the wire came. Check and recheck that you have the meter selector switch and the probes in the right positions.

A professional meter (left) and budget meter both set across the terminals of a 12v battery, showing difference in basic accuracy. Set the dial to volts and the prongs on the battery terminals tell that this battery, at 12.43v, is in good health. Note the red lead is to volt, black lead to common.

Amps measured through the bulb on a pro meter.

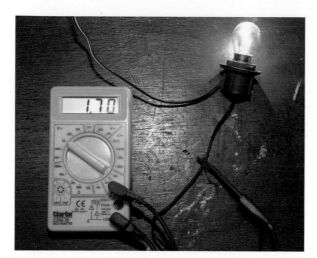

Amps measured through the bulb on a budget meter.

So, expecting a voltage of around 12v DC, select a range on the multimeter to suit. On the budget meter, that would be 0–20v DC and this is marked as 20 in the DC ranges. The professional meter has automatic range selection so only Volts DC has to be selected and the meter will look after the range.

Voltage is measured by connecting the black probe to a common point, typically an earth such as the bike's frame, and the red probe to the point that we want to measure. This might be a terminal screw, a bullet connector, or even a little bit of bared wire projecting from a terminal. Digital multimeters will be fine if connected with the polarity reversed, they will simply show a negative sign in front of the reading. However, it's sensible workshop practice, if you have a positive earth system, to connect the positive to earth and measure with the negative probe. The results of measuring a lead-acid battery voltage can be seen in the photo and it is plain to see that they are slightly different.

Checking for the presence of a voltage at a certain point within the bike's electrics is the most common task.

Checking Current

On the right-hand side of the budget meter there are current ranges, again marked with the symbol of a solid line above a broken line, and with the letter 'A' meaning amps DC. You can see that there are four ranges, which need clarification. The symbol '(μ)" means 'micro' or millionth. So the 200m range measures 0-200 millionths of an amp – no use for us, only for the electronics hobbyist. The other symbol '(μ)' means 'milli' or thousandth, and this might be used, for example, when measuring low current, through, say, a 1W bulb; 200 milliamps is the same as 0.2 amps.

The most useful range when measuring current is the 0–10 amp DC range. This is important, so when selecting a meter make sure it has a 10 amp range. You can see from the photograph that the red probe has to be moved to the third probe socket, marked 10A, in order to measure the kind of current flowing round the bike's system. A word of caution here. A 12v battery can punch out a surprising amount of current and, at this setting, if you connected the meter directly across the battery terminals, you will burn something out. A professional meter is fused to prevent this, but a budget job is probably not. Bear in mind, for example, that a motorcycle horn may well exceed 10 amps, so be careful when using the current ranges. Check and double-check that the probes are in the right position, that the right range is selected and that you are sure what it is you are measuring.

To measure the current flowing in a circuit, you will have to disconnect one wire from the item you are concerned about, and then connect the meter between the disconnected wire and the place whence the wire came. This is where probe clips come in handy. It is best to do this with the circuit 'off', to avoid the risk of accidentally shorting something out. On a negative earth system, the black probe should be connected to the place the wire originated and the red connected to the wire end.

A typical example of measuring DC current might be to ascertain the amount of charge going to a battery from the dynamo or alternator and to check the bike's ammeter.

Checking Resistance

Perhaps the most difficult part of understanding electrical theory concerns resistance. The analogy of a garden hose might help. The water pressure at the tap represents the battery voltage, and the flow of water from the nozzle represents the current. If you tread on the hosepipe, less water will flow from the nozzle because you have created a resistance to the water flow. It is the same in electrical circuits. Everything electrical has an inbuilt resistance to the flow of electricity through it. The higher the resistance, the lower the current flow. It is useful to be able to measure resistance for many reasons, for instance to check if the HT coil is defective; if there is a good earth; if the fuse is all right; if that wire goes from here to there without a break? The tricky bit is knowing what the answer should be before doing a test.

The unit of resistance is the ohm. It is calculated by using the other two main electrical units, the volt and the ampere. If you apply 12v DC to a bulb, and the resultant current through it is 2 amps, then its resistance is said to be 6 ohms, from the formula volts/amps = ohms (12/2 = 6). Obviously, this formula can be used to find any of the three variables if you know the value of the other two. This is known as Ohm's Law.

On the budget meter there are five ohms ranges. The higher ranges include the letter 'k', which means 'kilo' or thousands, so the 2,000k range measures 2,000 ohms multiplied by a thousand, or 2 million ohms. That's high and it's very unlikely to be needed. The range most commonly needed is 0–200 ohms. The multimeter is clever because it uses Ohm's Law to find out what the resistance of a bit of equipment is. If, for example, we connect the meter across a light bulb, the meter will apply a small voltage and measure how much current flows, then it will calculate the resistance and display it on the meter in ohms. For this reason, the resistance of something can only be measured in a dead (switched-off) circuit and the meter would be damaged if applied to a live circuit when set to measure resistance.

Budget multimeters fall down slightly when measuring resistance because they are not terribly accurate. The example budget meter specification quotes 0.8 per cent of reading plus or minus three digits, and that last bit is the killer. Say you measure the earth loop resistance of a motorcycle lighting circuit and the reading is 0.5 ohms. The ±3 digits means the reading could be between 0.2 ohms and 0.8 ohms, in other words, between 'fair' and 'pretty poor'. The way to get round this is to check the meter before you start, by selecting the correct range, and switching on. The meter will read simply '1' or OL (overload), which means that the resistance of the air between the ends of the probe is very high. With the probe plugs back in the original sockets, 'com' and 'vwma', connect the probes together firmly. The meter should show a short circuit, or 0.0 ohms. If it doesn't, as is the case with the budget meter, there is a zero error and in this case it's 0.4 ohms. This figure represents the resistance of the probe leads and the zero error on the multimeter and has to be deducted from any reading taken. So, with our example of the earth loop resistance

How to Use a Multimeter *continued*

ABOVE LEFT: 'OL' on a pro meter stands for overload. Air resistance between probes is high.

ABOVE RIGHT: Zero on the pro meter represents the resistance of the probe leads and the zero error on the multimeter. Compare this to the reading on the budget meter.

reading 0.5 ohms, when we deduct the reading we obtained with the probes shorted, we get 0.1 ohms, an acceptable reading.

The photographs show a simple loop resistance test of a light bulb, a bulb holder and the connecting wires. Be aware that the resistance of a light bulb increases dramatically when it gets hot in use.

All the other meter ranges are for transistor and diode testing for the electronics specialist and can be ignored. However, some of the slightly more expensive models have a sound tone on the diode testing range, which allows you to test for continuity on a wire between, for instance, the back of the bike and the front, and sounds a tone if there is continuity. This is useful when the meter is out of sight of the point where you want to measure. Pay a bit more still and you might get a bounce-proof housing and a stand fixed to the back of the meter, both of which are worth having. Make sure your probe leads are at least 4ft long – budget meter leads are only just over 2ft long.

The budget meter gives up a zero error of 0.4, and this figure has to be deducted from any reading taken in order to get to the true resistance value.

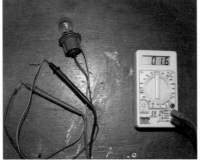

Now connect the probes across the item of interest and the meter will show the resistance in ohms. This shows the meter measuring the resistance of a 12v light bulb, the lamp holder and the connecting wires.

Note the difference in reading between the two meters. When the error of 0.4 ohms is taken from the budget meter reading it is practically the same reading as the pro meter.

Measuring the resistance across a stock 13 amp fuse.

This old battery gives a reading of 0.6v – it should read 6.4v, so it's time for a replacement.

Testing an old rectifier shows that it conducts electricity one way …

… and the other too.

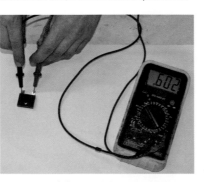

A new state-of-the-art miniature replacement passes electricity in one direction …

… but in the other direction it shows up a figure 1 – no passage of power.

THE AMMETER

The little clock up on the front of the headlight shell is a vital part of the electrical system: not only does it make up part of the circuit, but it shows you just what is happening to your battery. You will note it ranges from –8 amps to +8 amps. When the battery is in a fully charged state, the ammeter will show no reading, the needle resting quietly on the centre zero. However, flick on the lights and you will see it flip rapidly left to the –8 amp position in a full discharge situation.

If your dynamo and CVC system is working correctly, then on engine start-up the dynamo's charge will be allowed to pass through to the battery and the ammeter needle will rise up to the zero – and into the positive if the battery drain requires that little extra. As soon as the battery has enough charge to cope with the demand, the ammeter needle will revert to its centre spot because the CVC has sensed that there's enough life in the battery for what's required of it and until such time as the charge falls again, it will not allow further power to the battery.

Even without lights, for example, if your bike has been standing for a while, the battery may have discharged slightly and you will notice that on start-up the ammeter will temporarily move into the positive until, again, the battery is up to full capacity.

If you get the opportunity to look inside the ammeter, you'll see there really isn't much to it, but it is a fairly delicate device and does extremely well to take the vibrations and fork-induced road knocks that the bike hands out and will usually last a long time. Pattern replicas are available should yours be a dud but be warned, the needle on the cheap ones can shake and dance around a fair bit and they're not renowned for their longevity of service. Genuine Lucas items are still manufactured, and, while more expensive, they are stronger and much better quality.

A full –8 amp discharge here – better get some power to that battery quick.

A 1948 Norton chrome-plated tank with traditional Norton silver, red and black panels.

the cycle parts

If your restoration project has a fuel tank, oil tank, toolbox and mudguards, then you're in a good position because, if they're missing and you're looking to restore the bike to original specification, sourcing cycle parts such as these can be very expensive. The good bit of course is that pattern replicas are ever more available and in many cases – not all of course – the quality of the workmanship and the fit of the part is as good as, if not better than, the original. Most pattern parts are imported from India, where there is a booming metal-bashing industry hammering out replica parts for any number of classic British machines.

FUEL TANK

Let's start with the petrol tank, for after all, it is the focal point of the bike. You could have made the best job in the world on the rest of the bike, but if the tank is poor it will detract from the

overall job and will be the only thing that catches the eye. Conversely, if the bike is in average condition but the fuel tank is immaculate, all that would be needed is a quick once-over with the polish and the bike moves up several notches in as many minutes.

Apart from a brief period in the 1950s when the Korean War limited the imported supplies of raw materials and minerals from which chromium plate is achieved and all brightworks such as fuel tanks and wheel rims were painted, the fuel tank on many machines was partly chrome-plated.

For sure, it added a bit of class to the appearance, but by the 1960s the factories were cutting costs by painting their fuel tanks and perhaps adding a bit of bling by means of a screw-on plated tank badge.

The problem with chrome, or any plated finish come to that, is that it is microscopically thin and therefore the slightest scratch is an entry point for

bad weather, road salt and so on, which cause corrosion to set in on the base metal beneath the plate; eventually it lifts the plate and the process escalates. Having said that, a well looked-after tank may simply have its chrome plated surface worn away, say by years of riders' knees rubbing on its side. In this case, there's an extremely good chance that a re-plate will be an easy option.

In the days before the accountants ran the factories, the traditional chrome-plating procedure included at least one layer of copper, more often two, onto the base metal and several polishes before the chrome was applied, and this base make-up gave the part a strong, weather-resistant and deeply lustrous finish. Eventually it proved cheaper to plate directly onto the bare metal.

Often it is the case that if the tank has suffered from chrome corrosion, an owner may have decided to tidy up the job by means of a coat or two of

Norton tank top design.

Norton colours aped that of the race bikes but with added chrome. Coach lines are hand painted.

Knee grip rubbers were embossed with the company logo and were screwed into the tank.

A similar silver top panel but with red coach lines on chrome backing makes the BSA Gold Star tank immediately recognizable, especially with its 4in-diameter badges.

Again, not unlike Norton, Royal Enfield knee grips are embossed with the company name and screwed to the tank.

Hand-painted coach lines may wear over time but they have that natural imperfection that is so much more appealing than a sticker tape line.

FAR LEFT: The Royal Enfield design is not dissimilar to Norton except for different colours.

LEFT: The BSA Super Rocket tank is flamboyant in bright red with that Rocket transfer in your face so you don't forget you're riding one of the sports bikes of the day.

paint. Of course, paint will not adhere to a bright, plated surface, so said surface will have to be abraded. So, if your tank is coated with paint but seems, on the face of it at least, quite sound, set to with the paint stripper and the wire brush and get it down to bare metal again, because you may find horrors lurking beneath such as large dents containing even larger amounts of filler. At least that way you'll be able to see for yourself just how much abrasion has taken place. Is it simply a lightly abraded surface, achieved by emery cloth, or has someone taken a grinder to it and made a real ploughed field of it?

It's then a case of deciding if you want, or can afford, to have it refurbished; repaint it and make do; or treat yourself to a new pattern tank.

Let's say, once you've stripped the tank to bare metal, you've unearthed some dents. They may not be large dents but your options depend on where they are on the tank. Are they on the area that should be plated or are they on the painted section? If they're on the former, and if you want to have the tank restored to original specifica-

tion, there is no choice – the dents will have to be somehow knocked out; if they're on the painted area they can be filled and painted over.

Replacement pattern fuel tanks can be purchased in bare metal, plated or plated and painted complete with badges, again, it depends how much you want to spend and/or do yourself. Prices will vary accordingly and so it's worth taking your tank to a few specialist tin-bashers to gauge how much they will charge you to get the tank to the position required, then compare that cost against simply buying a replacement.

If the dents are many, or there are some large ones, it may be case of having to cut out the base of the tank, knock out the dents and then weld the tank base back into place – a very skilled and specialized job and quite time-consuming that costs accordingly. Even a small dent in a prominent position may be inaccessible without recourse to removing the tank base, so you see how the budget has to be a balancing act. There are any number of so-called specialists advertising in the classic press, but speak to others first,

ABOVE: In the 1950s Triumph moved away from plated tanks for a few years, going with all-over colours and the added bling courtesy of tank embellishments.

LEFT: A 500cc Matchless sports chrome tank with panels and rubber knee grips the standard of the day.

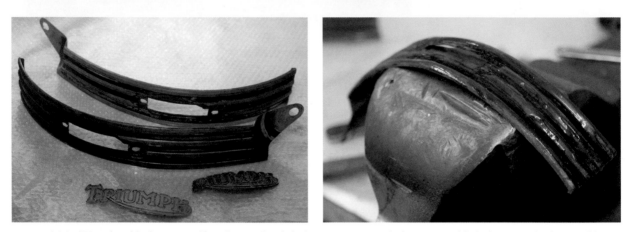

ABOVE LEFT: Original Triumph tank badges removed from the 1955 Thunderbird restoration project. The front section of the badge support hooks around the front of the tank, the rear portion goes beneath the knee grip rubber and is bolted to the tank bracket courtesy of the rubber-fixing screw. The Triumph logo badges then screw onto the badge support. Note that one has broken and will be replaced with a pattern.

ABOVE RIGHT: Paint stripper was preferred on the pressed tin badge supports as blasting was deemed too harsh.

club mates or people you meet at gatherings who have obviously had a tank job. There are some who have excellent reputations but actually do nothing themselves other than handle your goods; they outsource their tin-bashing, polishing, plating, painting, everything and merely add on a percentage for themselves at your expense. Once an outfit is recommended, go along with your tank and have a look at what they do on site and some of the work they have in hand. If they're worth their salt they will be only too pleased to show off their craftsmen in action.

Even if the dents can be removed, is there sufficient metal in the tank to polish out the abrasions without making the tank overly thin? If there is, then a refurbishment including dent removal, polish, plate and paint is feasible, albeit at a price. It has often happened that, in striving to get that perfect surface finish, the tank's old metal has become so thin it will not hold fuel and can be nothing other than a show tank, or that little extra effort has given the tank a hole.

Apart from the cosmetic appearance of the tank, the internal condition has to be considered too. For example, if the tank has been standing up with fuel in the bottom for years and for whatever reason it has not evaporated, then it's unlikely that the area where there has been fuel will have suffered internal corrosion. However, the area above the fuel, where there is just stale air, may well have suffered from years of condensation and be quite badly corroded. A peek inside with a light will give an idea of how bad it is.

An old method of removing rust and corrosion from the inside of a tank was to insert a big handful of old nuts and bolts, bung up the fuel tap holes and the filler hole, slosh in some degreaser, old fuel, or even hot soapy water and shake it around for all your worth. The idea was that the nuts and bolts would bang against the rusty internals and knock off the corrosion. Some even resorted to using a cement mixer, onto which the tank was fixed in order to give it a good old swill around for a long time while sparing the arm muscles.

This is fine for removing the heavyweight corrosion and big flakes but when it comes to the minute pores in which the corrosion will still lurk, you will need a chemical treatment. There are some excellent ones available that will remove the rust right back to bare metal.

These salts turn into acid when water is added, so this part of the project must be done prior to any painting or plating, for obvious reasons. The acid works best at a constant temperature, which is usually a little higher than

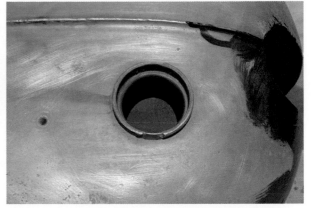

ABOVE: The inside of the Triumph tank came up like new with Flowliner salts.

LEFT: Flowliner salts are as good as anything for removing rust.

regular room temperature, so there has to be a heat source.

A portable ring hooked up to a gas cylinder is ideal. Source a metal container large enough to accommodate the whole fuel tank and fill it with water. With the various holes on the tank bunged up, add the acid to the tank and fill it. Then immerse the tank into the water bath until it's as good as submerged and bring the bath water up to the required temperature, before turning down the gas ring heat to keep it simmering overnight at the desired temperature. It's a bit involved but well worth it because the following day you will have a tank that inside is like new. Give it a thorough swill out and then squirt some light oil inside and slosh it around to prevent the corrosion from making a quick comeback. Obviously it's wise to do this in an area where, should there be a mishap, it will not cause damage or set fire to anything in the vicinity.

It may be the case that the internal corrosion has penetrated deeply, and when it comes to the polishing process, where metal is removed from the outer surface, it may manifest itself from the inside out and render the tank porous. For such a case there are sealants available to essentially form a solid liner within the tank, thus keeping the fuel away from the metal itself.

These sealants have been available for a number of years but with the increased addition of ethanol into everyday petrol, they have failed due to being attacked by the alcohol content of the fuel. This has resulted in the tank lining breaking up into large flakes and forming a residue in the fuel lines, taps, carburettors and so on – which have proved very difficult to remove once solidified.

The only answer has been to completely remove all remnants of the original sealant, clean the tank thoroughly and reapply an ethanol-resistant sealant. Many sealant kits come complete with suitable removal and cleaning chemicals as part of the pack. If your tank shows signs of having been sealed, it's a good idea to remove it before you start work, as the thickness of the sealant on the internal surface will give a false reading on the thickness of the tank overall.

Of course, if you have a painted tank, then a few dents will be of no consequence but have a close look at the badges if they're still on the tank. They'll probably be screwed on, and, as in the case of Triumph's early 1950s range, made up of a combination of parts, including a four-bar chrome pressing, which hooked around the front of the tank and was secured by a screw beneath the rubber knees grip, onto which the actual badge was screwed independently. Be careful with this as not only might the slots of the tiny screws be chewed up, the screws themselves will inevitably be seized in place and the 'monkey-metal' badges are very fragile. Likewise the four-bar trim is lightweight, easily deformed, dented and difficult to polish if re-plating is required. It may have to be a case of gently grinding off the heads of the screws to remove the badges and strip in order to be able to douse the screws with penetrating fluid, and/or applying some heat before trying to remove them with grips. Great care and infinite patience is the order of the day here. Be careful with petrol vapours when using a naked flame. Even an old tank that appears dry can contain enough vapour to explode – give it a thorough wash-out beforehand.

Once you've cleaned off the inside of the tank and stripped off the paint, bung the tap holes or insert the old taps and fill it with fuel.

Leave it overnight or for a weekend and then give it a close inspection to see if there is any evidence of pinhole leakage. If there is, then the sealant should take care of it. If there isn't, then it's up to you to decide if you deem a sealant treatment necessary. If in any doubt, then go for it; it's better to be safe than sorry as a pinhole leak in the tank will bubble up the paint like a big blister and you'll have no choice but to burst the blister, remove all the dead paint and have the tank refinished all over again. As with other aspects of the restoration, ask your club mates what experience they've had with various sealants before you make your choice.

As regards the filler cap, you'll probably find that apart from that bit of rust underneath the chrome or what's left of it, there's a perfectly preserved metal filler cap with the aforementioned copper plating showing through. Unless it's damaged, this is worth having re-plated rather than replacing, because it will be of superior quality and will come up a treat.

Triumph petrol tank in the blasting cabinet.

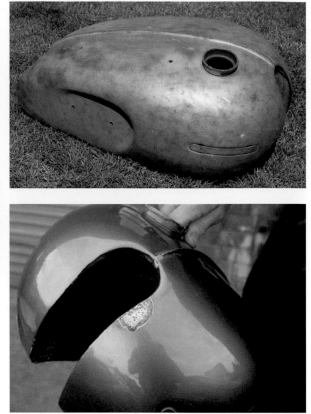

TOP: Triumph tank post blasting.

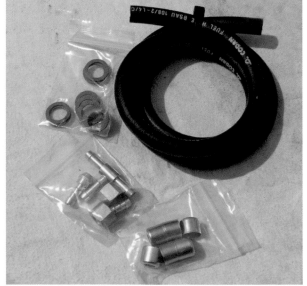

ABOVE: To discover a pinhole leak in your tank after it's been refinished is pretty disappointing.

FUEL TAPS

Again, pattern replacements are available but they're not cheap, and perhaps all yours need is a good clean and some new corks to seal them again. The little corks act like sealing washers either side of the flat section of the push-pull type, but without fuel they dry out and shrink. However, they do eventually swell again when the fuel is switched on, albeit after a few minutes' leaking, so don't instantly discard them if they initially leak like a sieve – it may just be that the corks that have dried out and shrunk, and after a few minutes of being soaked in fuel will expand again and be perfectly serviceable. New corks costs pennies but they may need to be slimmed down slightly in order to get your tap to reassemble. Also, soak them in fuel for a few minutes to allow them to swell before you fit them.

ABOVE: New corks are available to refurbish your old fuel taps but there come a point when new taps have to be purchased.

RIGHT: New fittings are readily available. Ensure you get ethanol-proof rubber pipes otherwise the alcohol in the fuel will perish the rubber.

Other taps can work on a metal-to-metal basis, and if they begin to leak there is little to do other than replace them with new.

Have a look at the condition of the filters integral with the taps. If they're damaged they will not stop any little bits of swarf from getting into the carburettor and it's amazing how a little grain of muck always manages to find its way right into the middle of a jet. In this case, fitting new taps is the answer.

OIL TANKS AND TOOLBOXES

More often than not, the oil tank and the corresponding toolbox were painted, with perhaps an oil level transfer on the tank. As such, a few dents and scratches can be cosmetically overcome with good-quality filler and a paint job.

The Oil Tank

It can be that oil tanks on machines that have been stood up for years suffer corrosion and pinholes on their upper half (exactly as described for petrol tanks above), where old oil has been sitting for decades in the bottom of the tank; it's been protecting the metal, but the upper reaches, where the oil mist and returning oil usually splashes around, have been neglected and over the years the oil has run down and left the inside surface open to condensation and the resulting corrosion. In this instance, if the pinholes are small they can be filled with an appropriate sealant from the inside, though ensure all feed, return and breather holes are kept free, and/or a suitably oil- and heat-resistant resin-based filler on the outside – have a word with your local bodyshop about this. If the problem is on the back of the tank and it's like the proverbial pincushion, then it may be better to have it cut away and a new section of metal welded into place. The joints will fill and paint over and it will be facing into the bike so should not be a problem.

If you go down the sealant route, then ensure the tank is thoroughly cleaned out. Get an old screwdriver down into the sludge and fetch it out, immerse it in degreaser overnight and flush it through over and over. Then turn it upside down and apply

some heat to the base of the tank to melt and free off all the sediment that has collected in the deep seam of the tank bottom. If you're so minded, once you've cleaned it thoroughly, you can treat the oil tank to the overnight acid bath too – you'll be amazed what still comes out.

Of course, if your oil tank was once and is still supposed to be chrome-plated, then if the holes are on the front there is very little you can do. It is possible at times to have each hole filled with weld or solder and then ground/sanded/polished flat to receive the appropriate plated finish; but in a situation like this it would be necessary to build up the surface with several layers of copper to enable a satisfactory polished finish to receive the final chrome. It can be done but it will be expensive. An alternative is to take it to a specialist who can cut up the tank and remake the affected area and weld it back into place, or indeed make a new tank from scratch, but both are very skilled and time-consuming exercises, which in turn equates to frightful expense.

Depending on the make and model of project, it may be that your marque specialist, or a general parts specialist, the owners club, the internet, ebay, an autojumble, or even a wanted advert in the VMCC journal may turn up another tank that is in better condition, or if expense is an issue then simply settle for a paint job, silver perhaps instead of chrome, and then keep your eyes open for a suitable replacement at your own convenience. It's amazing how word of

mouth spreads over time, so one is sure to turn up before long – just be patient.

Pattern replica oil lines, unions, filters and so on are all available, so if your drain-off knob is looking a little worse for wear and its integral filter is damaged, dump it and buy a new replacement. Likewise the filler cap, even if it's got the embossed lettering suggesting which oils to go for; these are available as patterns if yours has seen better days.

The Toolbox

The toolbox always seems to have a rough trip. Originally it would have been used to do exactly what it was designed to do and that's carry a few tools in a roll, such as plug spanner, screwdriver, spare bulbs and so on. Over the years it will have been opened and closed countless times and as such the hinge will be sloppy and the knob roughed up or even missing. With the original fitting being unlockable, a regular trick was to bend out the tang into which the original knob screwed, cut a slot in the toolbox lid so the tang projected through it and then hook up a little padlock. This in turn would rock back and forth against the lid, merrily fetching off all the paint.

If the lid is still sound (apart from the inevitable few dents and scratches) but it's suffered the padlock treatment, then the tang can probably be bent back into place and the slot patched up from inside, the scar filled and the whole job repainted – but you'll have

Royal Enfield utilizes one of its toolboxes as an air filter housing.

to source a suitable screw-in knob. Of course, if it's a simple mushroom or flat-headed shape, it will be a simple operation for a skilled lathe operator to turn one up for you and drill the core to take a suitable length of appropriately threaded studding.

As far as the hinge itself is concerned, if it's really bad, it may have to be a case of having another one made or sourced, and welded in; otherwise tidy it up as best you can because it's unlikely you'll be using it very often. This is an instance when a component intended for domestic use can be carefully and skilfully brought into service. Be aware also of the actual fit of the lid onto the toolbox itself. The toolbox edge will have a slight recess into which the lid fits so try to make their mating faces as even as possible, with no tight spots, because when they're painted they'll be even tighter of course and forcing the issue will inevitably crack off some of the paint. Keep the paint thickness on the recess to a minimum.

The toolbox body often doubled as a battery compartment too, as on early sprung hub and swinging arm Triumphs, or perhaps the mechanical regulator box. Over the years previous owners may well have drilled and cut holes to poke wires through or make a bracket when they've cobbled up the ignition with a big old 6v coil for a car, and any number of other similar make-do arrangements. The number and size of these, and the amount of rot or corrosion on the metal, will determine whether treatment is required or whether they can just be ignored.

If your project is missing these parts, patterns are available for most models with even a good deal of new old stock for certain more everyday machines, but make sure you get the right one for your model. For example, BSA made oil tanks and toolboxes with flat faces and rounded faces, the latter being found on the Gold Star as well as others, so amazingly every round-faced toolbox seen for sale now is, would you believe, ex-Gold Star, thus a premium price.

A little different but essentially the same in principle, BSA's unit construction C15 and B40 range have a central 'console' behind the carburettor, into which the oil tank on one side and the tool box on the other fit to make what appears to be a one-piece unit.

The centre section contains air filter, battery, switchgear, horn and so on, depending on which model. Later models from most marques did away with the toolbox altogether, using just a toolbox lookalike panel to shield the battery tray, the tool roll having its own little place under the seat.

Along with the oil tank, the ears on the toolbox, through which it is fitted to the frame, usually have some form of rubber buffer – often missing – to protect it from metal-to-metal vibration damage, be it a screw and locknut, which sandwiches a section of rubber tube, or a rubber grommet forming an eyelet through which the nuts and bolt fit. If the buffer is missing, it's quite simple to improvise with an appropriately sized off-cut from a rubber tube or a standard rubber grommet, but for most everyday classics, the part was standard across the range of both twins and singles, which used the same cycle parts, and will be readily available off the shelf at your favoured specialist.

MUDGUARDS AND CHAINGUARDS

Like anything else on a project, the mudguards are not necessarily going to be the correct shape, specification or even material for your model and year, so study form before you set about doing anything with them. Often it was the case that while most year models in a manufacturer's capacity range, for example BSA's pre-unit 350cc and 500cc singles and their 500cc and 650cc twins, shared the same cycle parts, a case example being the rear mudguard, the everyday 'cooking' models might have a deeply valanced, almost square section front mudguard while the more sporty versions would have a non-valanced rounded section. Some would be painted the same colour as the rest of the cycle parts, others would be treated to a bit of chrome plating. If your project has lightweight aluminium mudguards, take them off and sell them to help offset the cost of buying the correct steel ones. Alloy guards are always in demand for those who build café racers, or have an off-roader or trail-style bike.

What you can do with the guards obviously depends on their condition. The first thing to do is get rid of the old oil, muck and paint and see what state they're in when you're down to bare metal. Assuming they're to be painted, then if they're pock-marked from rust or even if there are a few small holes, these can be readily filled and smoothed over to give a first-class finish. If they're chromed then it all depends on the thickness of the remaining metal where the rust has done its damage because, as mentioned before, chrome does not fill: if you have a pock mark on your metal then it merely becomes a chrome-plated pock mark, so the mark has to be taken back to bare, flat metal. If the area is not particularly structural, that is, it's not around a securing fixing, then it's not the end of the world if the metal gets a bit thin; and if it's around an area that is pretty much hidden from view, then why worry about the pock marks at all – just get the rust out by blasting then have it polished a little and plate over the marks.

Of course, there is a limit. If the metal is essentially rotten and the valances are eaten away or falling off the main guard, then unless you really want to spend a lot of money having a sheet metal expert remake, refit and patch up that old guard, weld it, fill it and cover it in primer ready for the top coat, then go for a new pattern.

Most makes and models are now catered for in the pattern mudguard market and while the bulk come from Asia, there is little wrong with them: the metal is good, the various ridges, rolls and shapes are well replicated and the fit, in the vast majority of cases, is excellent too. As it will probably be a blank, you will have to temporarily hold the guard in place while you mark the appropriate places for drilling for the stays, but this is not difficult, especially if you have a second pair of hands and eyes. Once fitted and painted, no one knows, or cares, if it's an original or not and it fits well and looks great.

The same applies to chainguards. Generally speaking, the chainguard had a deep rear valance, which rolled over the top of the chain run and formed an open front but some manufacturers offered an optional fully enclosed chainguard – as in the case of BSA – which on their pre-unit models consisted of four pieces, a front, top, bottom and end section. Later unit models had simply a top and bottom, the end section being integral in the two halves. Rubber

Unless you're a tin bashing wizard and have the patience of a saint, this mudguard is destined for the scrap heap.

This pattern replica mudguard for Triumph fits really well and only needs drilling to take stays and rear number plate.

The mudguard in place.

grommets would bung inspection and lubrication holes for maintenance purposes. The fully enclosed chainguard is a bit of a rarity and when one does turn up for sale it usually commands a hefty premium. The choice is yours of course, and while aesthetic opinion is mixed, they do keep the road muck off the chain, especially if the machine is used in bad weather, and add a little quirkiness to the project, which is always a good talking point. On the other hand, most classics do not get used when the road salt is prevalent on the Queen's highway and what's more, if there is a chain problem, the whole unit has to be split to gain access, whereas the regular half guard is less work. So, if the project has one then fit it; if it hasn't, do you deem it a requirement?

Like with the other cycle parts, check out the condition. While the area that has had oil flung at it from the chain will be well preserved, albeit gummed up with old oil and muck, there may be areas that have suffered the ravages of the road and where rust and rot have taken hold. The principle is exactly the same as for other parts – if it's painted then a repair is possible, if it's plated it all depends on the amount of metal left. Pattern replacements are available for most machines, even if your project just happens to be that one year when an interim fitting was used – for example Triumph's early swinging arm twins used a chainguard that was different from the earlier sprung hub models, but which was soon changed for the 1956 onward shape, which in turn stayed in production for a long time. As such the correct 1954/55 chainguard is difficult to find and not available as a pattern. However, it is naturally very

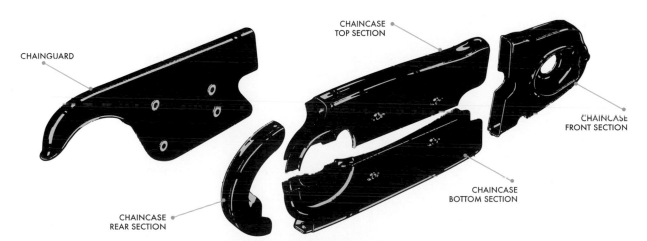

CHAINGUARD

CHAINCASE TOP SECTION

CHAINCASE FRONT SECTION

CHAINCASE REAR SECTION

CHAINCASE BOTTOM SECTION

BSA's pre-unit four-piece fully enclosed chaincase alongside the standard open chainguard .

similar to the later version, which can be adapted to fit in the home workshop without recourse to specialist assistance. So, don't worry too much about the chainguard: if you can't get the right one, get the one nearest to it and with a little cutting and perhaps the odd spot of weld here and there, you'll soon have one that looks the part.

A classic example of such conversion was the BSA Gold Star fuel tank. In the early days of the classic movement, the Gold Star 4in round badge (and Shooting Star, it was/is the same tank minus the curly filler cap breather) tanks were very scarce, but it was soon noticed that the WD and various ministry versions of the 350cc B40 had exactly the same tank but without the tank badge indentations. In no time, B40 tanks by the barrowload were being bought up cheaply, stripped, indents banged into their sides, badges and filler cap details added and sold off for a whopping profit for Gold Star use. Such tanks are now available for much less from India.

NUMBER PLATES

It's not been an obligatory legal requirement to fit a front number plate since the 1970s, when it was deemed by those in the Ministry of Transport to be an item of carving knife potential if involved in an accident. However, it can still be fitted if you want to do so and will not cause any concern to the MoT tester or the local constabulary. Many have used is as a means of identifying their particular machine with make, model, capacity and year painted in place of the registration number, though that too can be lettered into place without detriment. Most machines had a basic curved plate, which fixed to, and followed the line of, the mudguard, though some had a straight plate affixed across the front of the forks. Royal Enfield made quite a design thing about their front number plates at one time, giving them a sweeping edge, which set them apart from the stock plates the others used. Triumph used a chrome-plated surround to their front plates during the early 1960s, again adding a little bit of bling to the bathtub models. These are illustrated in Chapter 4.

The rear plate, by contrast, is varied, though mostly falling into a series of patterns to suit the style of machine and the rear lamp shape. Like the mudguards, the everyday models would have had an all-enclosed lamp unit and number plate combined, whereas the sports jobs would have had a more minimalist style. Some units were used as the number plate itself, with letters and numbers either painted on, or later with stickers, whereas others had perhaps a bolt-on embossed letter, pressed aluminium plate.

The Vincent number plate was shapely but stood out as a little special with its bespoke stop light.

No front plate necessary and reflective rear plate for this mid-1970s Commando.

FAR RIGHT: Painted at the Meriden factory in 1953, this Thunderbird number plate is getting ready for a repaint.

From January 1973 vehicles had to have number plates of reflecting material, white at the front and yellow at the rear, with black characters.

If you know a good signwriter and you don't fancy an embossed alloy plate on your 1950s or 1960s classic, then get them to paint the letters on in a nice, bold script – you'll be amazed how many people will comment on how good it looks.

RUBBER GOODS

There is simply no excuse nowadays to have worn footrest rubbers or a missing kick-start or gearchange lever rubber because there are pattern replacements available for practically every machine and model. Footrest rubbers come with the name of the machine embossed on them, while the twist grip rubber and its twin on the left hand of the handlebars can be had in a host of patterns, which replicate the original.

Sometimes you'll find that getting the rubber all the way onto the footrest or handlebar may be a little difficult. It's a good idea to lightly lubricate both the footrest and the inside of the rubber, likewise the handlebar and rubber so it can be twisted into place. Don't use washing-up liquid; it might be all right for plumbers and their plastic pipes but it contains salt, which may corrode the metal. If the footrest rubber comes to dead stop, it may be an air lock in the end of the rubber and you may have to drill a very tiny hole in the end of the rubber to allow the air to be released as you press the rubber into place. It can easily be filled once the rubber is in place by simply applying a little heat to the end of the rubber and working the soft rubber into the hole.

Fuel tank knee grips are also available as patterns, perfectly replicated in shape, size and style to suit your machine, as illustrated earlier in this chapter. Some are fixed by means of simply screwing one or two screws into countersunk holes in the rubber and into the purpose-made threaded bosses on the tank. Triumph have a kind of framework, which is screwed to the tank, and the rubber has an internal face lip, which then is worked over the framework and thus held in place. It can be a bit tricky but once in place the grips are usually a good fit against the tank face.

There are companies who specialize in such rubber goods, but you can readily find what you want for your machine via your marque specialist.

RIGHT: Norton is typical in using the embossed logo on their footrests – well, at least until the company accountants decided they were too expensive and changed to plain ones.

FAR RIGHT: Rear view of Triumph's fuel tank knee grip rubber showing the area where the framework hooks under the rubber to hold it in place.

Get yourself a basic polishing kit to begin with and have a go at something fairly small before you invest in a comprehensive and expensive kit.

With patience and the right kit you can make a really good job of your alloy.

the big finish

The first thing that hits you when you cast an eye over a restored machine is the fuel tank. The rest of the job can be perfect but if the tank is anything less than 100 per cent, then the whole job is spoiled. On many tanks, there's both chromium plate and paint, so when years of oxidization have taken their toll there are questions to be asked. Has the rust eaten so far into the metal that polishing back to good metal will render it too thin to take a re-plate, or worse wear holes in the tank, or is it merely a cosmetic flaw that can be polished out? If the former, the options are either find another tank – check out the internet or pop along to one of the major autojumbles, where you'll find a few specialists who restore and sell refurbished fuel tanks, albeit at a price – or settle for a full paint job and forget originality – difficult. If the latter, then plating specialists can utilize their chemical concoctions to strip off the existing chrome before polishing the metal back to perfection and reapplying the plate. Most restorers are aware that the thickness of decorative chromium, or any other plate come to that, is measured in microns and thus does not fill; if there's a pit in your metal it becomes merely a chrome-plated pit afterwards, hence preparation is paramount to a first-class finish.

The panels to be plated are polished, whereas the areas to be painted are left unpolished to allow the paint to bond better. Wheel rims are similar but can be blasted clean to remove the old chrome and rust, then the edges can be polished – though many professional polishers shy away from this because the spoke holes can tear their mops. After re-plating, the central section remains with the blasted finish, which helps to grip the paint if a central band and coach lines are to be applied.

With regard to the alloy parts, you have a choice. Generally speaking, the crankcases and inner covers were fairly roughly cast and produced with little more than a clean cast finish, the outer covers being the only ones polished. Now, if it's your desire to try to obtain as original a finish as possible then bead blasting, or vapour blasting or any blasting with a light medium will give a similar to original finish. You will also often find that the mating faces of two alloy cases have a considerable 'step' between them. This is mechanically and practically unimportant if the mating face itself has plenty of 'meat' on it, it's just not very aesthetically pleasing and many like to have the step ground down to give a flush finish. Likewise, the heavy casting marks on crankcases, cylinder heads and rocker covers can benefit aesthetically by being ground

and polished off. As mentioned previously, the reason the factories produced their wares in this way was for economy, and had you ordered a fully polished engine, you could have had it that way, provided you paid the going rate for the labour involved. It's doubtful that anyone did, as these machines were at the time generally just means of basic transport.

If you fancied polishing up a case or two, then first it needs to be clean of muck, oil and grease, so give it a thorough going-over in the degreaser. Once it's dry, begin on the linishing wheel by grinding away those casting marks. This will rough up the alloy so then it needs to be brought down to a finer 'rough' finish. This can be done by using a mop covered in Satene, a greaseless compound that contains abrasive grit. It hardens when exposed to air, so it needs to be returned to a sealed bag to prevent it from turning into a brick. On the mop it hardens and essentially turns the mop into a soft grinding wheel, which then abrades the alloy further but in a less aggressive manner. After the Satene stage a change of mop to coarse polishing compound will take the alloy further toward a polished finish, then to an even finer finish and finally to a soft mop with finishing compound – by now the alloy should be a mirror finish.

The secret is in getting heat into the metal to make the compound work efficiently. There is only so much you can do at home with a limited power motor and a small diameter mop – the professionals use high-powered three-phase motors and huge mops, which can spin at terrific speed, generate colossal heat and cut through the metal to a fantastic finish. There are excellent home-polishing kits available from a number of specialists, all good value for money and capable of doing a good job, at least on smaller items, but like most things in the restoration game, patience is the key.

OFF WITH THE OLD

What about other parts, which are perhaps not so sensitive as the fuel tank focal point, such as the frame? Firstly, you've got to decide which finish to go for and how much you wish to do yourself. The parts have to be free of old paint, rust, grease or any other form of dirt, or the new paint will not adhere.

If you intend to undertake this kind of work then a compressor is a must, and the suppliers will be able to provide ancillary air tools such as blasting and spray guns. Blasting is another operation that requires care. Not only does it have to be done in an enclosed area but it is important to use the correct type of medium. If the medium is too aggressive, it can savage the metal to the extent that little of it remains – though usually not in the case of a heavy-tubed frame – so it is important to know what you're doing. Indeed, for what it costs – and peace of mind – it

is better to use a blasting specialist who is experienced in the field and who will use the right kind of medium, at the right pressure, for the job. For example, glass beads will not remove old paint but will return an alloy case to almost factory-like cleanliness, while iron grit – shot – will transform your rusty old frame but destroy your cases. If you've never seen a frame when it first reappears from within an industrial shot-blasting booth, you will be amazed by the results. You'll be spellbound by the bright golden brazing around the tube joins and the fact that the tubes themselves are bright grey with not an element of anything previously applied to them remaining; and the frame is also quite hot. It's fantastic but you must act quickly because within a couple of days the tubes will begin showing signs of rust, particularly where your moist hands carried the warm frame back to your car!

There are various mediums used to give different finishes. Usually strong metal like a frame tube can stand the shot, but lighter items, such as mudguards and other less strong panels, may dictate the use of sharp sand, for example – enough to cut through the paint and clean the metal without eating into it; likewise soda blasting, which is bicarbonate of soda applied at high pressure. Other gentle media include walnut shells, recycled bottle glass, polyester resin particles, corn cob, zirconia and many more.

Bead blasting, using glass beads, is a gentle means of cleaning alloy and actually peens the surface, while vapour blasting – high-pressure water

containing a mild abrasive – is a good cleaning method on alloy, though the very fact that vapour is present will cause rust to form almost immediately on steel or iron.

Chemicals can also be used to remove the paint – paint stripper and patience can be used on cycle parts – but getting into the corners is practically impossible so if you don't fancy blasting, the only alternative is to take the parts to a specialist for a dip into the cauldrons of the most evil-smelling fluids imaginable.

You may find that some of the enamel paints applied to oil tanks, toolboxes, mudguards and so on is exceptionally hard to shift, and once blasted off, the primer used beneath it can sometimes be incredibly dusty. The quality of finishing materials used in some of the factories, particularly AMC, was exceptionally high, hence the difficulty in removing it.

Powder coat is another difficult covering to remove. The average high street paint stripper will barely touch it, nor will anything but the most powerful and abrasive blasting. However, there are proprietary powder-coat removal chemicals available from automotive restoration specialists such as Frost Auto Restoration Techniques but they are quite expensive and a fair amount is needed as the item to be stripped needs to be immersed within the fluid. If you can do this, the results are amazing, in that the powder coat simply dissolves into the removal fluid, leaving behind little more than a light residue on bright, bare metal. What's more, these fluids can be reused several times.

ABOVE: Home blaster media: left are glass beads for gentle work, right iron oxide for coarse work.

LEFT: Before blasting or any stripping, get rid of all the old congealed oil, grease and muck.

Frost's powder-coat remover is specially designed for the job and works exceptionally well.

BSA Bantam alloy head before bead blasting.

BSA Bantam alloy head post bead blasting.

If you treated yourself to a home blasting cabinet, then for most items such as fork sliders, headlamp shells and toolboxes, this will be more than adequate, though larger items such as the frame itself will probably be best taken to a specialist blaster, if for no other reason than ease of blasting due to its size. Likewise, if you have a tub of gentle medium, such as glass beads, then you can clean up your alloy parts easily in preparation for polishing, painting or simply leaving them as they are.

ON WITH THE NEW

Traditional Coach Enamel Paint

Once your metal is perfectly clean you have to protect it from the air. Some specialists will give it a coat of etch primer, which at least gives you a bit of breathing space while you work out what to do next. There again, some paintwork specialists include the blasting process in house, which lessens the time the part spends unprotected.

Paint finishes have taken huge strides forward over the past few years but a number of traditional finishes can still be had, particularly for the home painter. Make sure that all paint finishes are compatible; there's nothing more heart-breaking than spending hours in preparation only to find that one coat doesn't mix with another and it all crinkles. Don't trust that old paint finish, get rid of it completely and start from bare metal, especially if you suspect it's not original. Coach enamels and domestic glosses are available and are suitable for both brush painting and to be thinned for spraying but they often need weeks to harden properly. It's an age-old traditional method of painting, which, by virtue of everything having to be done as quickly as possible these days, has fallen by the wayside, but with patience can still give a quite magnificent finish. All high-class cars, coaches, locomotives and so on were brush enamelled at one time.

There are a few basic rules to follow if considering brush enamelling, the main one being patience. With a bare metal the first step is to apply primer. Now most primer is porous, so don't leave the component to be painted hanging around too long before you apply the topcoat. If you do and the conditions are generally damp, then remove it, or at least give it a thorough sanding down and re-apply, because moisture can get into the primer and then manifest itself after the top coat has been applied as tiny blisters within the finish. If this happens you'll have to start again anyway, so avoid the situation at the primer stage.

Be patient and don't paint in direct sunlight, or in breezy conditions. Ideally paint indoors in a well-ventilated but not draughty area. Clean up as many potential dust areas as you can, and if you have a bare concrete floor damp it down with a few water splashes. Should someone open your door while your paint is still wet, a sudden change in the air could blow up dust, which will inevitably settle onto your paintwork.

In winter, try to paint in as small a space as possible and use a dry heater – never use a paraffin heater, as for every 8 pints of paraffin burned, 9 pints of water are discharged into the atmosphere – keep the temperature constant and leave it on until the paint is dry. Hence the small space. Oh yes, and be patient.

Do not be tempted to paint in a high temperature as it may cause solvent entrapment within the surface due to drying too quickly, and again you'll end up with tiny blisters, which means you'll have to start all over again. In spring and autumn don't be tempted to paint much after lunchtime, as when it rapidly cools off outside, your gloss finish can bloom due to the atmospheric changes. Keep the temperature constant – and remain patient.

It may seem obvious but make sure the paint you choose is fit for purpose – for example suitable for metal and for an appropriate temperature range – and check the colour for accuracy; you'd be surprised at the number of different shades of black! If it's satisfactory, then stick with that paint all the way through your project to stay consistent.

Use good-quality brushes. For most work, 2in and 1in wide ones should suffice but they might need 'running in', so they are past the stage where they just might jettison a bristle or two at a critical stage. A good once-over against an abrasive brick wall will usually do the trick initially, and then a few coats of primer and undercoat, cleaning the brush accordingly in between, will result in a first-class brush when it comes to applying the top coats. Be patient. A clean brush is imperative. Wash them in proper brush cleaner, then in hot soapy water, before drying them and wrapping them in something that will not leave fluff on the bristles. Another tip – don't stand brushes on their bristles because they'll deform.

If the item to be painted has deep pits, then apply a good-quality body filler and sand down flat before applying the primer. If the item to be painted is tubular, such as a fork slider or a frame tube, wrap the sanding sheet around it and pull back and forth to get an even application; if it's flat, use a sanding block. Use a primer that can easily be spotted through the chosen colour for example, with a dark colour use a light primer, and for a light colour a red primer and so on. Pour enough paint into a jar to complete the area to be covered. This will keep the paint in the tin free from any potential contamination.

Initially apply an even coverage of paint with fast brush strokes, in all directions, over a small area. Once the brush is empty immediately dip it again and repeat the process, brushing into the same area. Do this from start to finish quickly and then keep going in the same manner until the part is complete – always brush back into the area you last finished. Don't stop until it's completed.

Bear in mind that if you can see the brush marks in your primer coat, you'll

Flowliner offer a first-class, traditional brushing enamel and they also have a range of primers and cylinder paints too.

see them through your gloss coats too, so make sure you flat them out thoroughly. However, there's no need to become obsessed, because it's really only the visible faces that need this priority treatment: is there really any need to have a completely blemish-free, immaculate, show-winning finish to the never-seen back face of a toolbox or oil tank?

If you get a run or a sag when the paint is dry, be patient and don't try to rub it down because it will still be wet underneath. Slice the top off it with a sharp razor blade and leave it to dry again. Within a few days you'll be able to rub it down successfully and recoat. Likewise, despite all the space around you, any fly or bug is practically guaranteed to fly straight onto your wet paint. Don't touch it! If you attempt to pick it out it will slip and slide around and you'll end up having to start again, so leave it until the paint is dry and then sand it out. Also, should you use masking tape then don't forget to remove it immediately you're finished.

The knack of coach painting is speed. You have to keep a 'wet edge' into which you blend the next area of paint, so work quickly. Practice with the primer and undercoats – you can't apply too many! If you find the paint is drying too quickly, then work on smaller areas at a time.

Flat down the previous coat with a medium grade wet and dry, or better still at this stage use Abranet or similar sheets. These are abrasive mesh sheets, which, with a simple shake, clean themselves of the build-up of paint dust. Like wet and dry, they are available in many grades of abrasive and are common now in most body shops.

When satisfied with the sanding process, load your brush with enough paint to give a long sweep along the longest face then finish off with light strokes in one direction only, which will help even out the paint layer and minimize brush strokes.

If you can reapply undercoats on consecutive days there is no real need to sand down the previous coat; that way you can apply a deep build before

ABOVE LEFT: *The rubber sanding block grips the sanding sheet at either end and guarantees an even rubbing surface.*

ABOVE MIDDLE: *The rubber sanding block splits into two and has pins at either end and longitudinal ribs to hold the sanding sheet in place.*

ABOVE RIGHT: *Sponge sanding blocks come in various grades of abrasive and can be used finer and finer until they run out of abrasive altogether. They are also very light and easy to use.*

Abranet sheets are available in various shapes and abrasive grades but the good bit is they do not block up with the material being sanded because the pores allow it to be blown clear.

STOVE ENAMEL

Traditional stove enamelling is still a good finish and quite tough enough for most applications. The origins of the method are pretty obvious – it was a finish designed specifically to enhance the appearance, and withstand the heat of, a domestic stove or range. Stove enamelling is a wet-paint process using specially designed paints. The enamel paint is applied by spray gun and then cured in an oven at a specific temperature, for a specific period of time. The result is a high-quality, corrosion-resistant, durable, high-gloss finish, available in a variety of colours and finish effects.

Like all paint finishes, preparation is the key to a top-quality finish, so it's imperative that the operative is experienced with the spray gun and that the facilities in which stoving takes place are clean and dust-free. The items to be 'stoved' are invariably shot-blasted back to bare metal prior to application. Professional stove enamellers will usually have an automated conveyor system, which takes the items to be enamelled through the oven for just the correct amount of time.

POWDER COAT

Over the last few years powder coating has superseded stove enamelling. This is another specialist job but make sure you use a motorcycle specialist rather than going for a cheap job out of the back door of the big industrial plant downtown. There are three types of powder – epoxy, epoxy polyester and polyester – the first two of which are suitable only for indoor use such as office desk legs and fridge doors. Polyester is the only one suitable for outdoor use; the others will be turning to chalk within a year. Look at the frame on that cheap garden lounger you left out in the rain last summer if you need proof!

It's an ingenious mixture of positively charged powder, which is attracted to a negatively earthed component, which is then baked to incredible temperatures until it melts the powder and forms a gloss coat that's as good as stove enamel these days. What's more, it's getting better all the time with more and more colours and blends available. It does suffer from the usual problem of filling, or rather not filling,

rubbing down, but don't go overboard as the paint will still have to harden for several days, perhaps even weeks, and the more paint you apply, the longer it will take, so be patient. Never apply two coats on the same day.

Once sanded down, wipe the item to remove all residue, dust and particles. A tack cloth is designed especially for the job, its slightly sticky surface picking up all foreign bodies, no matter how small.

When it comes to applying the top coats, remember – be patient. Apply evenly and quickly and once your part is covered completely, run the brush lengthwise to ensure an even coat before your finishing strokes in the same direction. Finishing strokes need only light application and hopefully you'll see the brush marks disappear as the paint settles to a flat and shiny finish. Do not succumb to the temptation to over-brush, as coach enamel dries slowly but rapidly forms a surface skin. Be patient and leave it a few days then check it out again. It'll probably need a second coat, so sand off the gloss and any light brush marks with a fine sheet, wipe down with your tack cloth and apply another coat. Leave the paint to harden. Use anything from a 600 grade to a 1,000 grade abrasive for the top

coats, before finishing your final coat with a combination of 1,200 grade and household soap. It will leave the paint with a perfectly flat but matt surface, which can then be brought to a high gloss with any mild abrasive metal polish such as Brasso. The longer you leave the painted item, the harder the paint will be and it will continue to age harden for a long time after it appears finished, so be careful when handling and do not cover it with newspaper or a cloth – the former is mildly acidic and the latter can leave an imprint.

Brushless Finishes

If you have neither the patience nor the inclination to go down the coach brushing route, there are other perfectly satisfactory methods, such as stove enamelling, powder-coating, two pack and cellulose. However, always remember that it's the preparation that makes the final finish so good. If you paint, enamel or powder over a big blemish you'll end up with simply a painted, enamelled or powdered blemish. Ask your chosen specialist about filling, masking or other options – but expect him to charge accordingly.

deep pits, and regular body fillers, presently at least, cannot stand the heat of the baking process. A way round this of course is to have the base metal powder-coated and then sand it down, fill the pits with an appropriate filler and spray over the component with cellulose or two pack: perfectly satisfactory and tough albeit a little laborious.

Two Pack

Two Pack Acrylic Enamel, to use its full title, is made up of an acrylic and melamine resin mix, to which a further resin, which acts as a hardener, is added. The hardener is called Poly-isocyanate Resin and this sets off a chemical reaction between the two resins, resulting in them setting hard. It's not everywhere you can get a two pack in an aerosol and if you can, once it's mixed it cannot be kept. Heat can increase the speed of the reaction and some professional body shops have an oven capable of accommodating a complete car, which can often see the drying time reduced to little over half an hour. Incidentally, two pack only contains a minimal amount of thinners, so 'what you spray is what you get' – more paint, less waste – and thus you don't need filler primer on minor blemishes on the metal surface. This lack of added solvents also reduces the risk of adverse reactions between the two pack and any pre-existing painted layer.

Two pack cures to hard finish and resists petrol, sunlight, stones and so on reasonably well. There is a catch,

though. The isocyanate is extremely toxic if inhaled so it's an overly expensive system for the home restorer to invest in, as specialist spray booths and air-fed breathing apparatus must – or rather should – be used, so it's best left to the professionals who use it day in, day out.

Cellulose

Cellulose paint has been used for vehicle refinishing for decades, and while the green lobby is steadily managing to get rid of it altogether in professional arrangements, presently it is still available in small quantities for the amateur painter. Essentially, it's a clear resin with a pigment suspended in it to form the basic primary colours. It's then distributed to the specialist, who has 'recipes' and a special blender to measure exact quantities of whichever colour, combining them to produce the final required colour. Metallic paints follow the same principle, except the clear resin has tiny aluminium flakes suspended in it. With metallic finishes a clear lacquer also has to be applied as a final top coat to bring out the true effect. In any paint, the serious bit is the clear base resin, in this case cellulose – nitrocellulose lacquer – and it works by solvent evaporation. The coloured paint is thinned, by up to 50 per cent, by the addition of cellulose thinners, which then evaporate when the paint is applied. A slight downside to cellulose application is that because it is so thin, many

coats have to be laid down to achieve a deep, lustrous build-up of paint. Applying spray cellulose can make it a bit 'foggy' in the workshop, so use a basic face mask to prevent inhalation. It's not as nasty as two pack but you'll be blowing the colour down your nose for hours if you don't!

Be aware also that spraying a new paint over an existing painted surface can cause a solvent reaction if they are not compatible; the solvent or thinners in the new paint can react with the old paint, causing blistering or creasing. Get your part down to bare metal again if you can and start from scratch with the new paint.

Paint, like most other things, is under constant environmental scrutiny, which is why the latest paints are water-based, though some of the major paint manufacturers have already introduced non-isocyanate hardened two packs, which will eventually be ideal for the home restorer and finally seal the fate of good old cellulose.

Spray Painting

Preparation

If you're intending to spray paint the cycle parts of your restoration project yourself – that is, mudguards, oil tank, toolbox, fuel tank and so on – then you'll more than likely be using cellulose, so here are a few hints and tips.

Treat yourself to a brand new spray gun. There might not be anything wrong with a second hand one, but

Good old cellulose, the hardy annual of every home workshop's painting for decades.

then again there just might, so unless you know about the gun in question play safe. There are some perfectly adequate spray guns on the market at reasonable prices, but, like with most other things, go for the best you can afford. The spray nozzle will vary depending on the kind of paint to be applied, but in general, the one that's fitted when you buy it will normally do. If you can, try to fit a filter on the end of the pick-up tube – the tube that sits in the paint pot – because if a bit of hard paint falls into the pot from the edge of the tin or some other foreign body gets in, this will have a detrimental effect on the paint finish in some form or other. The filter can be washed and cleaned along with the gun on completion.

If you're working slightly above, say a mudguard, then angle the pick-up tube forward so it sucks up the last bit of paint in the pot as you tilt the gun forward. Likewise, should you be spraying from below, then turn the tube to face backwards – it's only a case of undoing a nut.

Apart from surface preparation, the mixing of the paint is crucial too. We all use that old screwdriver to stir up the paint but really we should use something better, like an old steel rule, to actually scrape the sludge from the bottom of the tin. Pro body shops will use a whisk specially designed for the job and then give the tin a thorough shake too. This way, you'll be guaranteed to mix the full contents and thus get the actual colour of the blend. Pour the mixed paint into a proper mixing

jug; a glass or translucent plastic one with graduations on the side, surplus to kitchen requirements, is ideal.

More often than not a ratio of 50:50 paint to thinners is perfectly fine – but make sure you use anti-bloom thinners for spraying, as opposed to general thinners for washing out. Mix in the jug or in a separate container before pouring into the spray gun pot, to avoid a potential poor mix, leaving a thicker residue at the bottom and upsetting the paint flow.

Mixing the paint in a separate container (such as a mixing cup) then pouring it into the spray gun cup (and then mixing again) will tend to result in a reasonable mix. Mixing directly in the spray gun cup could cause problems with thick, poorly mixed paint remaining at the bottom.

With the paint mixed correctly and the compressor up to pressure, the next thing to do is check the paint flow through the nozzle, so it's best to spray against something unimportant – a sheet of cardboard will do – to gauge the fan of the paint. Obviously, the desired aim is to get an even and consistent distribution of paint throughout the height of the fan. Adjust the nozzle until you're satisfied that the layer of paint at the top and the bottom of the fan is the same as the centre. If the nozzle isn't sufficiently open, there'll be a heavy build-up in the centre, which will sag, and the edges will be light, thus requiring excessive overlap, which will give a streaky finish and potentially runs. If it's open too far the paint

distribution will be heavy top and bottom and light in the centre. A fast pass over paper or cardboard will show your settings quite clearly.

Strive for the lowest air pressure that will give good application with equally good atomization (fine spray). Too high a pressure will cause overspray, get the pressure too low and you'll get the famous orange peel effect. Start at maybe 50 psi, then drop it to 45 psi, maybe even go to 40 psi – check out the overspray and droplet size because the pressure is gun and paint sensitive – and go for the lowest pressure as there's less overspray.

TECHNIQUE

Start as you mean to go on – keep it clean. Ideally you should wipe down your workpiece with a proper panel wipe that is fibre free and soaked in solvent, which cuts through greasy fingerprints and other such contaminants that could have an effect on the paint. In turn, this should then be wiped off with a rag in order not to leave a film – but then there's the problem of fibres, which can cause a real problem. The paint gathers around the fibre and forms a blob, which when dry is difficult to sand out without going back to base metal.

Enter the tack rag. These are specialist cloths with a slightly adhesive surface to which any fibres will stick, but be warned – they only need very light application or the adhesive might actually stick to the workpiece, causing even bigger problems. What's more, at this stage at least, consider those latex gloves to avoid finger marks, and the tack rag adhesive, which seems a bit partial to sticking to hands.

The first actual coats sprayed will be primer, which is much more forgiving to spray than your colour coats; if you make a few mistakes it's not a disaster because the primer will have to be sanded down a bit anyway. Having said that, use the primer stage as a practice for your technique, and if you make a mistake remember to try to avoid doing it again.

If your metal is pitted then treat yourself to some filler primer. This has a thicker consistency than ordinary primer and is wonderfully deceptive, for as you spray it over the pits, little will appear to happen and even when

Go for a new spray gun unless you know the history of a second-hand one.

RIGHT: Cobble up some form of gantry on which to suspend your parts to be sprayed, that will give you adequate access to both sides, above and below.

BELOW RIGHT: Triumph oil tank finished in primer coat.

dry the pits will be still clearly visible. However, start to sand it and the pits will miraculously begin to disappear as the rest of the primer is rubbed down. Eventually you'll have a lovely smooth, pit-free finish on which to apply your top coats. For smaller jobs it is available in handy aerosol cans. If your base metal is good, then ordinary red or grey primer will do fine as an initial first coat.

It's easier to say than do, especially at first, but keep the gun a constant 6–8in from the workpiece and at a right angle to the area you're painting to avoid heavy application at one end of the fan and overspray at the other, and move the gun in a straight line from side to side at a constant speed. Overlap should be about 50 per cent –that is, aim the centre of your second pass at the edge of the one previous.

A light squeeze of the trigger releases air but not paint. Paint feeds in as the trigger is depressed further. When you reach the edge of the workpiece release the trigger so the paint flow stops but the air flow doesn't, then open up again as you return over the piece, thus avoiding a rush of paint as the trigger is pressed.

The paint initially goes on with a slight orange peel effect before flowing and settling down within a few seconds, so resist the temptation to over-compensate. Like everything else,

practise on something unimportant first to get the hang of it.

Light is important and nothing beats natural daylight, but if you're totally indoors then maximize the light with side lights as well as overhead lights in order to see the texture of the paint on application, in case adjustments have to be made – orange peel sands out easier than a drip.

Application and finish depend on the paint used; for example, two pack paints apply thicker than cellulose paints but take longer to dry, though

orange peel tends to settle well during the drying process. Cellulose dries quicker and how it comes out of the gun is pretty much how it will finish. Essentially, it's like all skilled jobs, practice makes perfect; lose neither patience nor heart if things don't go according to your expectations straight away.

TRANSFERS – THE FINISHING TOUCH

Most machines have some form of transfer on them, even if it's only the oil

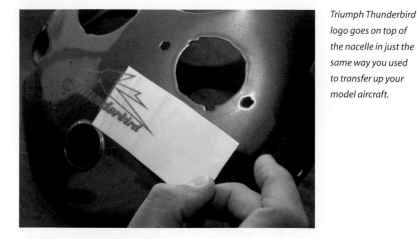

Triumph Thunderbird logo goes on top of the nacelle in just the same way you used to transfer up your model aircraft.

level on the oil tank. As seen in Chapter 11 with the fuel tanks, the Norton has a company logo transfer on the fuel tank with hand-painted coach lines around it, while the BSA has the Super Rocket transfer on the flat of the tank.

The accuracy and detail of water slide transfers, stickers and vinyl graphics today is breathtaking, such is the reprographic qualities of the computer. It's fair to say that whatever era of machine you have, from a pioneer to a 1980s rice burner, the graphics are available. With traditional water slide transfers, the principle is exactly the same as it was when you were a youngster peeling the roundels onto that model Spitfire's wings or the swastika on that Heinkel's tail plane – the difference being now that the transfer on your restored bike needs protection because otherwise it will scratch off when dry and probably slide off in the rain.

The process is the same, however. The surface to receive the transfer must be clean and free from grease or dirt. The transfer goes into a saucer of lukewarm water for half a minute until

it loosens from its backing paper; then simply slide it sideways until the transfer meets the surface then gently pull away the backing paper, position the transfer and gently absorb the excess water and any potential air bubbles from under the transfer with a small sponge, like the soft side of a kitchen scourer. Leave it to dry thoroughly, for maybe 24 hours at room temperature.

When applying a varnish to seal the transfer, protect it and hold it in place, there's always a risk that the varnish will react with either the transfer itself or the paint applied beneath it. If you've used cellulose paint for the final finish, get a small tin of modelling varnish, of the kind compatible with those traditional little tins of modelling enamel paint, and carefully apply the varnish to the transfer, covering it liberally but being a little more frugal around the edges where it meets the cellulose paint. As long as you don't go overboard, there should be no reaction and the transfer will be secured and weather-tight.

You can choose to have the whole item lacquered with cellulose lacquer.

That will give a fantastic gloss to your paintwork and seal in the transfer deeply, but it also means that all your painted parts will have to undergo the same treatment.

Coach lines are another aspect of finish where enthusiasts have divided opinions. Traditionally the coach line was applied by incredibly skilled painters with bizarre, short-handled, long and soft-bristled brushes and an awesomely steady hand and keen eye – and in certain quarters still are. The Hinckley Triumph concern has a brilliant coach line painter (or maybe more than one) who manually does all the tanks and mudguards quite perfectly in double quick time. Indeed, his father worked at Triumph Meriden and his grandfather at Triumph Coventry, both doing exactly the same thing.

However, there are excellent sticky tapes available, which are varying widths and colours and are quite fine, so that when lacquered over they are barely discernible to touch, certainly barely more so than a painted line. The only difference is that the painted line has a wonderful, very slight natural inconsistency due to being applied by the human hand – and to some that makes a big difference.

There is a long-established pinstriping tool available, which works on the same sort of principle as the white liner on a sports field. The tubular body is filled with paint, a wheel of the required width is attached, the guides fitted if required, and away you go. The wheels have tiny serrations, which pick up the paint and disperse it evenly. The adverts make it look easy, but while it does indeed make a first-class line, it's only as good as the person using it.

BSA Gold Star sports the traditional matching chronometric speedometer and tachometer.

The rigid-framed Norton just has a chronometric speedometer amidships.

13 | *clocks, dials and instruments*

THE CHRONOMETRIC SPEEDOMETER

For many years the everyday motorcycle had a speedometer positioned in a sub-housing on the top of the petrol tank or under your nose in the centre of the handlebar arrangement. It was invariably the Smiths Chronometric, some 3in in diameter. In actual fact, while generally thought of, and accepted as, 3in, they are actually a metric size – 80mm. This is because the chronometric speedometer and matching tachometer began life as a French instrument, developed by Jaeger, Paris, in the 1920s, and as such all the fittings, screw threads and so on are metric, not imperial as you would understandably think. Jaeger set up a subsidiary company in England, which, in 1927, was bought out by Smiths Motor Accessories, who duly renamed it British Jaeger. For several years, the clocks were available with either British Jaeger or the Smiths logo on the dial face, often with an accredited 'Jaeger Patent' too.

If your clocks are found to be in working order and in need of no more than a cosmetic once-over, then this is a job you can undertake on your workshop bench. The chrome plated brass bezel should simply screw off but it probably won't because the threaded area, which is still exposed, will be gummed up with years of muck and possibly paint. Strip off the paint around the body with regular paint stripper and a wire brush – wear your goggles and some light gloves because it will flick about and inevitably fly into your eyes and it burns a little on bare skin too, though nothing like as badly as it once did. If you have a small, fine wire brush, ideally on a grinding machine, get into those exposed threads as far as possible.

Now you can try to free the bezel either by applying heat, or by applying penetrating fluid and patience. If you go for heat – which is the best

This Tribsa café racer goes even more extreme than the Gold Star with the matching clocks.

ABOVE: Ariel fitted their speedometer into a perfectly formed upstanding socket cast into the top yoke.

LEFT: The Thunderbird speedometer from 1953 includes rev counter dial within it.

The daddies of them all – the Vincent 5in speedometer and rev counter.

method if the actual rubber O-ring, which seals the glass against the bezel has rotted or melted, so you have to essentially continue the melting process to soften up the joint in order to shift it – you'll have to put the body in the vice. Use the soft jaws to avoid damaging the metal body and some form of grips with a wide enough jaw to grasp around the bevel. Care must be taken here not to have the grips bite too hard into the soft brass. Some form of strap spanner would be best. Of course, if the bezel is damaged, the grips' damage will not matter, as replacement bezels are readily available off the shelf, but be careful not to squeeze the actual body out of shape or a replacement bezel will never fit. Sometimes the bezel may be so stuck, particularly if it has been struck and hence bent across the threads, that there is little alternative but to gently cut it off with a small, fine-bladed hacksaw, taking care not to damage the threads beneath. New replacements are readily available.

If you can remove the bezel without damage, then providing there are no deep scours in it, the remains of the chrome plate can be stripped and the bezel polished and re-plated by your favoured metal finisher.

The actual body needs little more than a good sanding down and a coat of primer and gloss top coat, which can be done carefully either with a brush or with everyday aerosols.

The internal workings of a chronometric speedometer and tachometer are essentially that of a mechanical timepiece and they work in exactly the same manner, with all parts integrating precisely and smoothly with their counterparts. The basis is a conventional escapement unit – a means of connecting and regulating all the moving parts from the source of motive power, in this instance the drive cable. The needle, which gives the reading on the clock face, is fixed and only moves in accordance with the spin of the drive cable. The escape-

ment is fixed on the left side of the movement. The wheel is fixed rigidly to a camshaft between it and the driving gear at the base of its shaft. This driving gear mates with the driving cable and provides the motive power to maintain the oscillations of the escapement. The ingenious part of the mechanism is that the speed of the camshaft is constant and maintained by the timing of the escapement. The clutch is designed to slip when the driving speed exceeds this figure.

Adjacent to the camshaft is the main wheel assembly. This consists of the three independently rotating wheels known as the integrator (bottom), the recorder wheel (centre) and the stabilizator (top – Smith's Instruments terminology), to which the needle is fixed via male pegs and female sockets. The integrator wheel drives the recorder wheel in one direction only, which in turn drives the stabilizator wheel and thus the needle, but in this case drive is in both directions. The integrator and recorder wheels both have toothed edges into which the ends of the springs mate, thus becoming a non-return mechanism. When the leaf springs lift, a strong hairspring causes the wheels to spring back to their original position. On the extreme right of the movement is a geared shaft, connected to the drive wheel. The tiny top bearing of this shaft fits in the outer of a rocking lever, the movement of which causes the pinion to engage with the edge of the integrator wheel. The camshaft has three cams

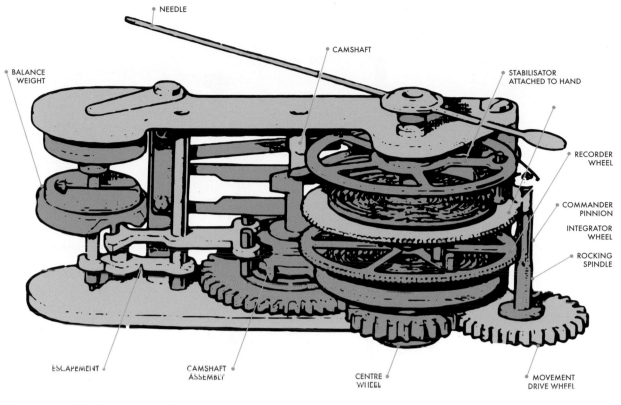

NEEDLE

CAMSHAFT

BALANCE
WEIGHT

STABILISATOR
ATTACHED TO HAND

RECORDER
WHEEL

COMMANDER
PINNION

INTEGRATOR
WHEEL

ROCKING
SPINDLE

ESCAPEMENT

CAMSHAFT
ASSEMBLY

CENTRE
WHEEL

MOVEMENT
DRIVE WHEEL

The movement of the chronometric speedometer.

controlling the rocking lever, and the two leaf springs for the integrator and recording wheels.

It sounds very complicated but it is quite simple, though magnificently precise. This is how it works.

1. The top cam on the camshaft moves the rocking lever, temporarily forcing the pinion and integrator wheel together. During this time the wheel turns through a set angle proportional to the speed of the driving cable and thus moves the recorder wheel, stabilizator wheels and of course the needle.
2. The middle cam then lifts the leaf spring controlling the recorder wheel, though no movement takes place.
3. The lower cam then raises the leaf spring controlling the integrator wheel, letting it return to its starting point, but leaves the recorder and stabilizator wheels in their new positions.
4. The sequence repeats but if the speed has dropped, then the integrator wheel will not reach its previous position. Therefore, on the second part of the sequence, when the recorder is released it

will drop to the new position of the integrator wheel, taking with it the stabilizator wheel and needle. If the speed has increased, then there will be greater deflection of the integrator wheel, which will pick up the recorder wheel and needle and move them to their new position. Each sequence takes around a half second, with the actual engagement time of the pinions around a quarter second. Hence the famous, slight twitchy movements of the chronometric.

To maintain accuracy, the integrating wheel has attached to it a tiny, spring-loaded flywheel, which prevents potential bounce during the period where the integrating wheel is returning to its zero stop. Bounce would register a false zero, which would be incorporated in the next reading and thus be an inaccurate reading.

The connection with the escape wheel and camshaft is also important as this is not a continuous operation, but actually a series of jerks. As such, in theory at least, it may be possible to hit a constant position with the pinion and integrator wheel, either fully engaged

or fully disengagement. To prevent this, two teeth are omitted from the escape wheel, thus ensuring positive engagement at all times.

The stabilizator wheel has two functions. One is to ensure an accurate zero position of the needle. A niche is cut into the edge of the wheel, into which a small V-shaped spring drops when the needle returns to zero. Its second and more important function is essentially as an averaging device. There are 135 teeth on the edge of the integrator and recorder wheels. For a given speed the final position of the recorder wheel will vary on each cycle dependent on the exact point of engagement between the pinion and integrator wheel, and between the recorder wheel and its retaining spring. By careful sizing of the hole in the stabilizator, in relation to the size of the driving pin in the recorder wheel, these variations average out.

The distance recorder mechanism consists of two ratchet wheels and two sets of counters or tumblers, the trip – where you can turn the tumblers to zero and thus record your mileage on a trip – and the total, mounted on a shaft and fitted into the alloy support frame. If you look closely at the counters, you

CHRONOMETRIC SPEEDOMETER MOVEMENT

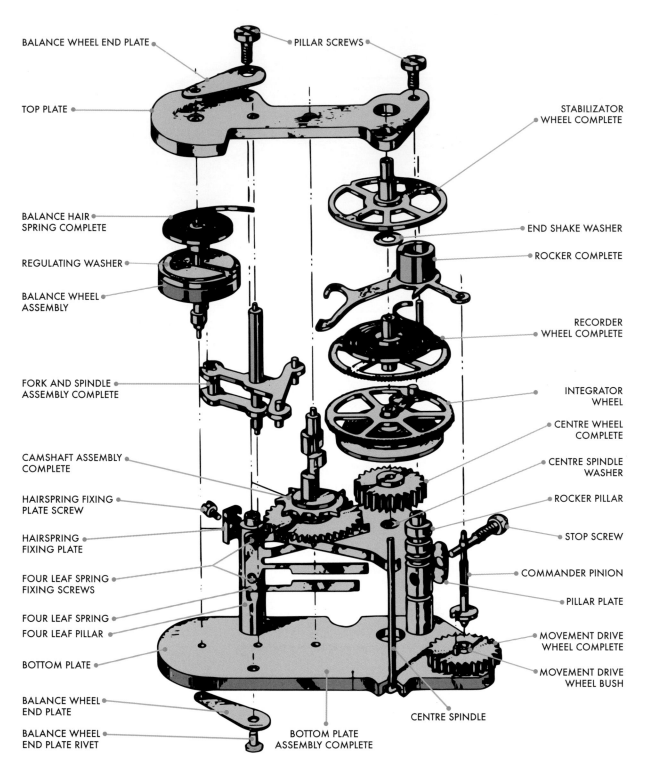

BALANCE WHEEL END PLATE

PILLAR SCREWS

TOP PLATE

STABILIZATOR
WHEEL COMPLETE

BALANCE HAIR
SPRING COMPLETE

END SHAKE WASHER

ROCKER COMPLETE

REGULATING WASHER

BALANCE WHEEL
ASSEMBLY

RECORDER
WHEEL COMPLETE

FORK AND SPINDLE
ASSEMBLY COMPLETE

INTEGRATOR
WHEEL

CENTRE WHEEL
COMPLETE

CAMSHAFT ASSEMBLY
COMPLETE

CENTRE SPINDLE
WASHER

HAIRSPRING FIXING
PLATE SCREW

ROCKER PILLAR

HAIRSPRING
FIXING PLATE

STOP SCREW

FOUR LEAF SPRING
FIXING SCREWS

COMMANDER PINION

PILLAR PLATE

FOUR LEAF SPRING
FOUR LEAF PILLAR

BOTTOM PLATE

MOVEMENT DRIVE
WHEEL COMPLETE

MOVEMENT DRIVE
WHEEL BUSH

BALANCE WHEEL
END PLATE

BALANCE WHEEL
END PLATE RIVET

BOTTOM PLATE
ASSEMBLY COMPLETE

CENTRE SPINDLE

Movement in exploded form.

will see that one face of each counter has ratchet teeth and the other has a cam-like profile. All the counters are identical, other than the tenths of a mile counter, or trip decimal counter, which is usually coloured red.

The counter drum's ratchet teeth are locked in comb springs. At every complete turn of the counter drum, a section of the comb spring is depressed by the drum's cam, allowing the next counter to turn one unit before being again locked. The distance recording counters are turned by a pawl-operated ratchet, mounted on an eccentric fitted to the worm wheel spindle, the worm wheel being driven by the mainshaft.

The wonderful and long-lasting virtue of these compact, precise instruments and their tiny component parts is their overall robustness, which has been proven for decades to be able to withstand the severe vibrations, knocks, shocks and

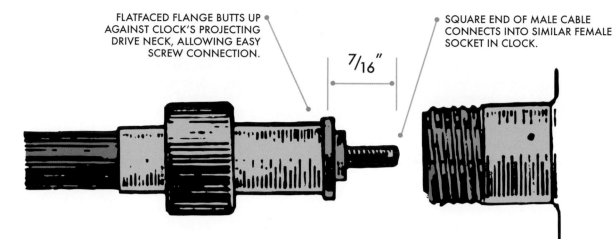

FLATFACED FLANGE BUTTS UP
AGAINST CLOCK'S PROJECTING
DRIVE NECK, ALLOWING EASY
SCREW CONNECTION.

SQUARE END OF MALE CABLE
CONNECTS INTO SIMILAR FEMALE
SOCKET IN CLOCK.

$^{7}/_{16}$"

Drive cable fixing to the speedometer head.

By the late 1960s the chronometric had been superseded by the magnetic speedometer and tachometer, which were cheaper to manufacture and equally as accurate. These are on a late 1960s Bonneville.

Matching instruments on a Norton Commando.

weather conditions handed out to them by the everyday use of a motorcycle.

As mentioned earlier, it is possible to buy newly refurbished units; or have your existing unit refurbished by a specialist; or, if you've a good eye, a steady hand and a bucket load of patience, you can buy the parts required to refurbish the unit yourself; or, if you have more than one unit, perhaps try and make one good one out of two poor ones. The bezel, clock face, needle, tripometer cable and bulb fitting are all readily available, and it's quite simple to change the specification of one clock to that of another. Likewise there are specialists who can recalibrate a clock from one machine to suit another and even convert tachometers to speedometers and vice versa. Like other things of such a precise nature, perhaps it's worth leaving it to the experts while you get on with something else on the project, because at least when it returns it will look like new, should

work like new and will have a warranty of some form with it too. It's expensive for sure, but probably worth it.

THE AMMETER AGAIN

That simple little clock in the headlamp shell measures the power going through it in amps and is the only real clue you have on how well – or otherwise – the charging system is working (other than, of course, your lights simply starting to dim to nothing when you're out at night). It makes sense, therefore, to have one that works and keeps you informed of the state of your battery and how much charge is flowing into it from the dynamo or alternator and out of it through the lights and other electrics.

As we've discussed earlier, the battery has to be kept charged otherwise in use it will go flat, like any battery. The dynamo or alternator makes the power and the regulator/rectifier governs just

how much is required and allows said amount through to the battery. The ammeter is connected into the electrical system, in series, via two connections, so the power has to flow through the ammeter at all times. So bear in mind that should your lights go out, a failed ammeter or a broken connection to it may be just as likely a culprit as anything else within the system.

The ammeter on a classic motorcycle, particularly on an original 6v system, is usually designed to measure just 8 amps either side of the central zero, to the left –8 (discharge), to the right +8 (charge). If the battery is in good condition and fully charged, then the ammeter needle will be more or less stationary on the central zero. However, put a demand on the electrical system by, let's say, switching on the lights, then there is a draw on the battery's power stock and the ammeter will show a swing to the left. When the regulator realizes this, it allows more power from the dynamo to reach the battery and so the ammeter needle then swings towards the positive as it charges. Once the battery is back to its charged state, the ammeter needle will revert to its central zero position until such time as demand further increases, or the battery power decreases slightly, and the process repeats itself. The easiest way to see the ammeter in action is to switch on the lights without the engine running. It will flick straight across to –8. Start the engine and it will immediately return to zero and above as the engine is revved, dropping down to below zero when the revs drop.

Storing a bike up without use and without the use of a monitoring battery charger will inevitably allow the battery to discharge, so when initially starting up, the ammeter should show a large charge. This means that the battery is low and a considerable amount of power is being sent to replenish the charge – a good daylight run out should soon see the battery back to full potential. However, should it not return to zero after a long time, there is a problem. The battery may be damaged, with a cell or two out of action through lack of use, in which case the dead cells will not accept a charge and a replacement is required. If the battery is good, then the problem is elsewhere, potentially within the rectifier or regulator.

Once you've got your ammeter into the system and working well, then should you ever have to remove it, there are a few simple rules to follow. Firstly, disconnect the battery, because the connection terminals on the back of the ammeter are live and the headlamp shell is earthed and with very limited space to work inside the headlamp shell, there's a good chance you'll touch the wires against something and create a short circuit, a few sparks to make you jump, a popped fuse or a melted wire or two.

Once the circuit is dead, remove the headlamp glass and reflector from shell. By this stage you will be aware that there is a screw, usually found on the very top of the headlamp shell, which, when loosened, allows an L-shaped clip to come free from the headlamp chrome surround, allowing it to be pulled forward, hinging on a tiny tag spigot that mates with a female socket slot in the rim. It can be unhooked from this socket and the bulb holder or connecting socket from a sealed beam, for example, removed.

You can then see the underside of the ammeter inside the shell. If the ammeter is in a removable mounting panel, then undo the two securing screws and lift up the panel, giving better access. Disconnect the two terminal connections as best you can as there will probably be insufficient surplus in the wires to enable it to come out fully. Mark up the two wires otherwise if you put them back the wrong way round, the ammeter will read the wrong way round, that is showing a minus when charging and vice versa. Unlike the speedometer and tachometer clocks, the little 2in ammeter does not have any form of illumination.

With the ammeter removed, a replacement unit should just slot straight into the hole in its place, though Asian-made replicas can sometimes be slightly larger than the originals and you will have to decide if you want to find another or make the hole in the shell larger to suit. A legacy of the latter action of course is that from then on, an original Lucas item will be a loose fit and a means of packing it out or support will be required.

Once the ammeter is back in place, replace the terminal wires, tighten the securing nuts and refit the headlamp arrangement.

To test the ammeter, turn on the headlight and it should flick left. The exact reading depends on if your project is still 6v or now 12v. If you divide the maximum watts of the headlamp bulb plus another five or so for the tail lamp by either six or twelve, depending on what's fitted, you'll get an approximate reading for where the needle of the ammeter should position itself. For example, if you have a 40W headlamp and 5W tail, then that adds up to 45W; 45/12 = 3.75 amps, or 45/6 = 7.5 amps, so you should see the needle either halfway across to the left, or more or less the full way across to the –8. Turn off the lights and the needle should return to zero or settle somewhere just either side. Now start up the engine and watch the needle flick right instead – how far right of course depends on the state of the battery at the time.

Out on the road is the final test, with the lights on. If all is well then the drain on the battery by the lights, when riding at normal speed, should be accommodated by the charging current from the dynamo, and the ammeter needle should be around zero or just into the positive, showing a slight trickle charge to the battery. At tickover, for example at a junction or traffic lights, then the meter will probably show a discharge as the dynamo will not be spinning fast enough to generate enough current to balance the load, but once the revs rise on getaway, all should revert to normal.

Moving-Coil Ammeters

The units used for motorcycles and cars are called moving-coil ammeters, where the movement takes place courtesy of magnetic deflection. This is where current passing through a coil causes the coil to move in a magnetic field. Usually there are two spiral springs involved to provide the returning force. The air gap between the iron core and the permanent magnet poles make the deflection of the meter linearly proportional to current. In other words, the more power that comes through the ammeter, or the more is drained, the further the needle travels in whichever direction. These meters have linear scales and because the magnetic field is polarized, the meter needle acts in opposite directions for each direction of current. That's why a DC ammeter must be connected the right way round, with the correct positive and negative terminals. The later classics gave up on the ammeter, preferring a more car-like warning light.

A belt primary drive avoids the decision as to which oil to run in the primary case.

essential fluids

Petrol and oil. It sound simple enough and quite honestly, it is. However, there has been, and indeed still is, much pontificating about what is best for particular machines, especially with regards to oil.

Before we get too deeply into the subject, it is always wise to bear the following in mind. For several years after the Second World War, the 'pool' petrol, which was forced upon the public, was pretty poor-quality stuff and of low octane. As such, all everyday machines produced were designed and built to run on this less than heady brew. In fact, it was a common wheeze to eke out the miserly fuel ration by adding a goodly percentage of paraffin into the mixture of low-revving sloggers such as the myriad ex-WD, budget-priced side-valvers that were readily available. So, unless your machine is a sports job with a high compression ratio and ignition advance, then today's basic unleaded pump fuel is more

than adequate. What's more, provided the oil is changed at regular intervals, the choice of grade and make is not of prime importance (though we will look more closely at this sweeping generalization later).

PETROL

It's not so many decades ago that dire warnings of engine self-destruction were prevalent because lead was to be added to petrol – those great old days when people were advised to eat eggs and drink milk and smoking cigarettes was a sign of sophistication in women Much has changed since then of course, perhaps not entirely for the better, as everything that was once seen as a major technological breakthrough for civilized humanity now seems to be undesirable for the environment – and that includes petrol. So, in a complete 180-degree turn-around, when everyday leaded fuel was phased out,

the doom-mongers again slipped into overdrive. All engines were going to clatter to a halt with ruined valves and valve seats, and the most credulous went out and spent a fortune in having their perfectly good cylinder heads converted to unleaded-compatible valve seats. Others didn't bother, reckoning that if valve seat recession was going to occur with the prolonged use of unleaded fuel, after years of the lead in fuel cushioning the seats against the hammering of the valve heads against them, then let it and what money was saved at the unleaded pump – compared to the inflated prices charged at specialist leaded fuel suppliers' pumps – could then be put towards having the cylinder head refurbished as and when it wore out. In the event, the issue didn't arise, and those who went for the latter option were proved the wisest. Many simply changed from leaded fuel to cheaper base unleaded in their old bikes, without recourse to any additives, and to this day have not suffered any form of mechanical malady because of it.

One particular think tank at the time reckoned that engines would wear out in as short a period as 150 miles! They were conveniently forgetting that all race and record-breaking machinery, including TT machines, in those early days ran on what was essentially unleaded before the inclusion of lead – not to mention aircraft. Tetraethyl lead was added to fuel at the dawn of the 1930s with Pratt's Petroleum running a 'drive with Ethyl' advertising campaign in 1931, using a flapper girl called Ethyl, based on the cartoon character Betty Boop. It worked.

There is a phenomenon called work-hardening. It is the process used by blacksmiths of old, who would spend hours simply belting hell out of sword blades. The more they were hammered, the harder the blade became, and the principle is exactly the same with a valve seat, which is hammered unmercifully, millions upon millions of times by the valve head. Of course, any form of competition engine using top materials should use the highest available octane of fuel, plus any available, beneficial (and allowable) additives and the best-quality, suitable oil.

When the lead was removed in 1999, individuals were given three straightforward options: a) use lead replacement fuel; b) dose the fuel with an over-the-counter lead replacement additive; c) just use unleaded and see what happens. All methods worked though a) was extremely expensive, b) saw the market flooded with additives, only a few of which were good and the bulk of which were useless, and c) proved to be perfectly fine and cheapest way. *See* more on fuel additives in Chapter 6.

It transpires that the metals used in most motorcycle valve seats are well up to the use of unleaded fuel, even in a highly strung machine like the BSA Gold Star, as well as Ariel's Square Four and all later classics, which includes most machines from the earlier 'export or die' era that have valve seats suitable for unleaded as the USA was running unleaded fuel for years before the UK introduced it.

The major oil companies all have their own lead replacement additives,

which often double as octane boosters too. These, which are readily available on the market still, are the ones that passed the tests when asked to prove the lofty claims made on the packet and as such will enhance your fuel accordingly. Having said that, it is often difficult to discern any difference when using such an additive; it will be doing more good than harm, but perhaps it's not entirely necessary to use it on every fill-up – again the choice is yours.

There are other ways of increasing octane for those with hotter or high-compression engines. Most major fuel companies sell a premium fuel on their forecourts with a higher octane rating, and claim that on these your engine will run so much further, longer and cleaner and thus not bring about worldwide environmental apocalypse. Naturally it costs a fortune in comparison to regular unleaded.

Those with access to a local, friendly airfield can buy 'avgas', a high-octane aircraft fuel, which, when mixed with pump unleaded, gives a mean octane rating equivalent to perhaps the old five-star fuel of the early 1960s. Again, though, it is very expensive and perhaps only really beneficial to race engines.

When dismantling a machine that's been standing up for a long time, the fuel system as a whole, the tank, the pipes and the carburettor will have a distinct 'old bike' smell to them. Whilst enthusiasts find this bizarrely pleasant, it does mean that the old fuel is useless and will never start your engine, so it must be emptied out and disposed of, the tank and system thoroughly cleaned out and fresh fuel added.

This is the case for old leaded fuel; old unleaded does in fact not have to be very old at all, and while it may strike up your lawnmower after having been laid up, it may not fire the sparks in your restored machine. The main tell-tale signs with unleaded are the dark colour of the fuel and it's unpleasant smell. It can however be mixed in with the new fuel and used satisfactorily in this way. Unleaded 'goes off' quicker than leaded fuel, its more volatile additives evaporating first, leaving a not very lively liquid in your tank, especially if it is in a tank that is vented, or in a container that is regularly opened.

One approach, if standing up a bike, is to keep the tank full to the brim to minimize the air space, but it's cheaper simply to drain the tank completely, which reduces the risk of any possible residues forming within the system. The carburettor can be dismantled and cleaned manually or you can choose to have it ultrasonically cleaned, while new fuel lines, taps, seals and so on should all be ethanol-resistant – but it's worth asking before you buy.

The recent introduction and increases of ethanol to pump fuel (*see sidebar*) has however caused a number of problems to classic machines. Thanks to the government's Renewable Transport Fuels Obligation announced in 2005, our petrol now contains up to 5 per cent ethyl alcohol (ethanol). Ethanol is a powerful solvent that attacks fuel system components, including the zinc in your carburettor alloy, galvanized materials, brass ferrules, copper pipes, aluminium fittings, rubber seals, hoses and pipes, cork in fuel taps, polyurethane and the epoxy resins that once acted as a liner inside your dodgy old fuel tank. Worse, though, is that it also attacks the resins within fibreglass, so classic fuel tanks such as the BSA Spitfire, which came with a fibreglass tank as standard, and any number of older café racers, have seen their fuel tanks bubble and bleb their way into a useless, sticky sludge. It's also both hygroscopic – it attracts moisture – and hydrophilic – it mixes with water, and water is not a lot of help to the combustion process.

Initially, at least, it looked like things could only get worse, as levels were then increased to 10 per cent, with suggestions that a further increase to 15 per cent is on the cards; indeed in Brazil it's 20 per cent and above as they are self-sufficient with their sugar cane. Alcohol can be brewed from any number of natural crops, but while on the one hand this is classed as a renewable energy, there is also an argument taking crops for fuel is creating a shortfall in food – but that's another story. Alcohol fuels are not new. They burn both cooler and cleaner, but an engine needs copious quantities when compared to the more familiar everyday petrol. The main benefit of alcohol fuels for the competition fraternity is their resistance to 'knock', meaning engines can

Lead and Other Additives

With the explosion of personal prosperity in the 1960s that came from finally having thrown off the shackles of post-war austerity, came an equal increase in the number of cars on the roads. This massive increase naturally meant more leaded petrol was being burned and the emissions from these vehicles in theory at least should have meant that levels of lead in our bodies increased – but this was not so, mainly because of the reduction of lead in water pipes, paints and cans. However, as the number of vehicles ever increased, so the environmentalists fought to have the fumes of the combustion process – carbon monoxide and lead – reduced, especially in built-up areas. Generally speaking, a small amount of carbon monoxide (CO), especially that from an exhaust can be readily tolerated by a healthy human and likewise, the percentage of people killed by lead is minute.

Catalytic converters clean up the CO but will not work with leaded fuel, so obviously the next step was to take the lead out of fuel.

Tetraethyl lead was introduced into motor fuel to afford higher compression ratios and greater efficiency in engines. Its elimination reduces the octane level of the fuel below the level at which modern engines would run without 'knocking'. The fuel companies' answer was to raise the octane level of the petrol by increasing the level of benzene contained in it. Benzene is a known human carcinogen, that is, it causes cancer. The obsession of governments (fortunately not in the UK, who, as ever, were years behind, though later put it down to their prudence and wisdom) with unburned hydrocarbons and carbon monoxide in petrol, led many to follow the lead of the USA and introduce methyl tertiary butyl ether (MTBE) into petrol. MTBE had been used in American fuel, albeit at a low level, since 1979, to replace lead as an octane booster, but between 1992 and 2005, MTBE was used in huge concentrations in some fuel to meet oxygenation standards of the requirements set by the 1990 Clean Air Act. Oxygen helps petrol burn more efficiently and thus reduces emissions. (Take a look at a carburettor model Hinckley Bonneville cylinder head: there is a pipe that forces compressed air into the combustion chamber just before the exhaust stroke.) The oxygen dilutes aromatics such as benzene and sulphur and also optimizes the oxidation during combustion. However, in 1996 a report was published that proved that MTBE was exceedingly carcinogenic for animals and humans and was being absorbed from the air into human tissue and was also being detected in ground water.

In 2005, another act removed the oxygenation requirements and at the same time instituted a renewable fuel standard, to which refiners made a wholesale switch, removing MTBE and blending in ethanol – a move the UK did follow, and is suffering for accordingly in the classic field.

---

run colossal compression ratios and produce more power.

However, the classic movement is nothing if it is not resourceful, and as soon as these problems began to manifest themselves, the manufacturers and retailers were right on the case, producing tank-lining mixtures that are ethanol resistant, likewise rubber pipes, seals, carburettor innards and all. It is nevertheless wise, if you are intending to stand your machine for any length of time, to drain the fuel system, as anything still within that is susceptible to ethanol attack will dissolve and form a gunge, potentially resulting in blocked carburettor jets, stuck floats and slides and all manner of other problems when you return to it. As mentioned above, just make sure the replacement parts are ethanol-resistant, otherwise you'll be dismantling your carburettor and maybe even your valve gear again before too long.

OIL

Engine oil is made up of two main components: the base stock, which is 70–95 per cent of it, and the additives. The latter are chemicals added to enhance the positive characteristics of the base stock and to withstand the purpose for which it is being used, be it in a petrol engine, diesel engine, high-performance engine or whatever. There are two forms of base stock, mineral and synthetic. Mineral, or petroleum, base stock is purified from natural crude oil and has been used since motors first needed lubricant. Its primary purpose is to prevent friction and remove heat. Synthetics, as the name implies, are additives chemically engineered for a specific lubrication purpose. Synthetics are made up of pure material and as such have no natural contaminants that need to be removed through the refining process. Synthetics first came about during the Second World War when Germany was running short of natural resources for the fuelling of their war effort.

Mineral base stock has to go through a series of refining processes in order to maximize the following lubricant qualities:

Viscosity The Viscosity Index is a measure of the oil's ability to maintain its viscosity (thickness) over a wide temperature range. The higher the number, the less change in viscosity as the working temperature increases.

Low temperature performance The better an oil will flow at cold temperatures, then obviously the better its performance within the engine at these low temperatures, certainly from a circulation point of view.

High temperature performance The way the oil holds together under hot conditions. It must not burn off or degrade, nor must it allow metal to metal contact due to a loss of viscosity (shear).

Oxidation resistance Oxidation is when oxygen reacts with the components of the oil and the chemicals formed from the combustion process and other engine deposits form a sludge. Oxidation sludge within the oil obviously makes the engine work harder to pump it around the system as its increasingly contaminated viscosity increases.

Whilst the base stock is a major factor in the lubrication quality and performance of an oil, the additives also play a massive part. The chemical additives in an oil are each designed to perform a number of specific individual tasks and the quality of the chemicals used and the way in which they are blended play a large part in just how well they do their job. As the quality of the additive chemicals increases, unfortunately so does the price of manufacture and hence the retail price to the consumer. That's why the top-quality oils cost so much

The oil companies realize the potential of the classic scene and have developed specialist oils accordingly.

more than oils with a lesser additive content – though naturally there is a premium paid for the name on the container as well as some serious mark-up for the retailers too.

The general system for engine oil classification is that established by the Society of Automotive Engineers (SAE) in the USA. The SAE system has two viscosity grades, those followed by a 'W' and those without. The 'W' grades are intended for use at lower temperatures – though the 'W' actually stands for weight and not winter as commonly believed, though it does actually fit the situation – and are based primarily on a maximum low temperature viscosity, as well as pumping temperature and a minimum viscosity at 100°C. The low temperature viscosity is measured by a test under simulated cold engine cranking conditions. Borderline pumping temperature gives the oil's ability to flow to the oil pump and provide adequate pressure during the initial stages of operation.

Oils without the 'W' are intended for use at either lower or higher temperatures, but not both, and their viscosity is measured at 100°C.

Monograde or Multigrade Oil

There has long been an argument for and against each and each has its merits.

Monogrades cover a single requirement and do not use a polymeric viscosity index improver, or VII (*see multigrade below*). There exist some eleven viscosity grades of which six are given a 'W' grade. These are for extreme cold, beginning at 0W heading up in degrees of five to 20W. The lower the viscosity grade, the lower the temperature the oil can pass. For example, if an oil passes at the specifications for 10W and 5W, but not for 0W, then it must be sold as SAE 5W. Traditionally there was a winter oil change to a lower monograde, SAE 20, to aid with hand cranking, and a higher grade in summer, SAE 50, to help maintain oil pressure. The higher the viscosity, the higher the SAE number. Remember that for any oil, if temperature is increased, viscosity will decrease – that's why the engine must be run and the oil warmed so it runs freely when it is drained. The viscosity is high at low temperatures and low at high temperatures.

However, some oils thin out less than others with increased temperature. This is the difference between a monograde and a multigrade oil.

Incidentally, the late Helmut Fath, former world sidecar champion, would never put cold oil into his engines. He would heat up the oil over a camping stove before adding it to his race outfits. 'Let the oil warm the engine, not the other way round.'

Multigrades, as opposed to monogrades that cover a single requirement, meet requirements of more than one SAE grade and are therefore suitable for use over a wider temperature range. Multigrades are made by blending a low-viscosity oil with special additives called viscosity index improvers (VII). These improve the temperature/viscosity characteristics and combine the easy starting and good friction properties of a thin oil when cold with the good lubricating and equal friction properties of a thicker oil when hot.

The VII polymers curl up into a tight ball when cold and move freely with the oil molecules but as temperature increases they open and stretch out into a long, stringy molecular mass, which restricts the normal flow of the oil. On cooling, they revert to their original shape. The result is then that when these polymer additives are blended in the correct proportion with, say, an SAE 15W oil, it flows as SAE 15W at low temperatures but like an SAE 40 when hot, hence the designation SAE 15W-40.

So, essentially, the advantages of using a multigrade are: you only need one oil all year round; easy to spin the engine over with the kick start when cold due to low drag; good high-temperature performance; and improved overall fuel economy due to shorter warm-up time and quicker circulation when cold. Multigrade oils will keep equipment operating in an optimum viscosity range, and offer consistent response and lubrication protection.

Classic monograde or classic multigrade – the choice is yours.

Monograde oils are a perfectly good and acceptable option, especially here in the UK, where oil cooling and temperature control are not serious issues.

That's the theory but in practice there is more to consider.

Many modern motor oils are naturally designed for modern car engines, with their plethora of go-faster, run-cleaner and leaner, electronic-powered devices, close tolerances, and highly filtered fluid systems. As such, these oils have high levels of detergent and dispersant added, in order to keep the engine clean and minimize sludge build-up. The oil picks up soot and other by-products from the combustion process, rather than leaving it deposited on the internal surfaces – that is one reason why fresh oil turns black so quickly after running. Likewise, contact with metal engine parts inevitably produces microscopic metallic particles from the wearing of the surfaces and these particles can circulate in the oil and act as an abrasive agent against moving parts, causing wear. Because these particles build up in and flow with the oil, it circulates through a filter,

which collects these harmful particles. The familiar car-type, round, screw-on, disposable cartridge filter is fitted to some later classics, such as Norton's Commando and Triumph Trident, but there are numerous aftermarket kits available to retro fit such a filter to most classics. Royal Enfield have had an integral filter housing built into the crankcases of their machines for many years, which simply unscrews, can be washed clean and refitted.

However, our earlier classics were designed to run on much simpler oils without the detergents of today, and therefore have little more than a gauze fitted to the oil tank outlet fitting and a similar gauze in the sump to protect the scavenge tube from the larger lumps of muck in the crankcase base. The oil passes through the centre of the crank, where the heavy muck settles into the tube, which is appropriately named the sludge trap. There will also be heavy sludge deposited in the nooks and crannies of the bottom of the oil tank and in the sump area of the crankcases too. As discussed in Chapter 6, over the years

the sludge trap tube gradually fills up with this sludge, and the oil flow becomes steadily more and more restricted until something in the engine cries enough and either breaks or seizes up.

Imagine an old engine, which has been, and seems to be still, running well. Then on the next oil change, a high-detergent oil is added, which proceeds to clean away the muck from the engine parts, out of the tank, off the flywheel, out of the sump and worst of all from the sludge trap. With no filter to catch this detritus now circulating in the oil, it will quickly ruin the engine. In this case the best choice of oil is a simple monograde, low on detergent and thin enough to make its way through the limited space it has without disturbing the years of use. Something like an SAE 30 would be ideal – though a better idea would be to clean the sludge trap. Monogrades of this type also have lower levels of dispersancy, so any solid debris collected will not remain in suspension, but fall into the bottom of the sump out of harm's way.

So, monograde or multigrade? Both are available in classic form. The older engine was designed to run on monograde oil and as such the oilways and tolerances are that much wider than in a modern engine; many parts depend on little more than the occasional splash of oil flung from an adjacent part and some get by on nothing more than oil mist. Your newly refurbished engine is clean inside and nicely run in, so for general use, a good SAE 30 is a fair compromise, SAE 40 will be good in a hot summer and SAE 50, recommended for Gold Star BSA and similar models, can also be used in the gearbox, but will need a few minutes warming up in cold weather. Maybe, then, a classic SAE 20/50 multigrade would be your choice for the engine. To be perfectly honest, with a clean engine as your starting point, the choice is yours as both multigrade or monograde will be fine. Just remember to change it regularly!

Having said that, this is a statement from Andover Norton, referring to suitable oils for the Commando:

In production times, Norton's first and foremost aim was to sell motorcycles. To do that they recommended not the oils that were technically best, but oils that could be bought at any garage. This is the *only* reason why multigrades were recommended. Friends from within the lubricant industry confirm that with the high temperatures combined with the high pressures in a roller-bearing engine, multigrade additives give up quickly and leave you with base oil within as little as 600 miles – which means your 20W-50 becomes 20 oil, which is not up to the job in a Commando engine used properly! As for the primary drive, oils have changed dramatically since the early seventies, and additives we used to put into our engine oil, like STP, are now already contained in most multigrade oils. These additives are molybdenum (graphite)-based, and will give you clutch slip very quickly.

So there's an argument in favour of monograde oil.

Running In

Now, if you have a brand-new engine – that is, freshly restored with a ground crank, clean sludge trap and new big end and main bearings, new cams and followers, good fitting, honed bore with new piston rings, clean and clear rocker and valve gear – then there is no need to worry about the aforementioned scenario. Nevertheless, there are bound to be minute elements of swarf still hiding in the engine somewhere despite your best efforts to clean it, and also there will be the inevitable microscopic particles from all the new and newly refurbished components as they meet up with each other for the first time as the engine starts. Of course you will have reassembled everything with liberal doses of assembly oil, which mixes with the engine oil as and when they come together, so friction will be minimized.

All these little pieces will be collected in the oil and circulated, so, as the engine is tight and will need careful running in for maybe 1,000 miles or so, it's wise to use purpose-made running-in oil. Most of the major manufacturers, especially those who have a bespoke classic oils division, will have their own versions of this oil. It's fairly light and is designed to clean up these newly machined areas but note the instructions on the container for how it must be used: not under heavy load and not for a long time – that is, not in place of everyday oil.

If you can get out for maybe a few steady 50-mile or so runs, when the clock reads around 200 miles, drain out the running-in oil and replenish the tank with another few jugfuls. Inspect the drain-off; hopefully it will not contain any metal particles. Repeat the exercise at around 500 miles and allow the engine to rev a little bit higher and cruise a little faster. If you have enough left in the container, drain off and use up the rest of the running-in oil at the 750-mile mark. When the clock reads around 1,000 miles, drain it out completely and then run through some special flushing oil, again available from your classic oils stockist. This is exactly what it says, it is a means of flushing off any oil and residue from

the areas through or over which the oil has passed, while still maintaining a minimum lubrication to the moving parts; as such the engine can be run slowly in the workshop but not driven under load on the road. With the engine flushed clean, it can now be refilled with an oil of your choice. Some enthusiasts essentially extend the running-in period for a further 1,000 miles or so by using a budget multigrade and changing it at regular intervals before finally settling on their preferred quality lubricant. Oil changes are then stretched out to between 1,000 and 1,500 miles. Remember, the oil is much cheaper and less time-consuming than an engine rebuild, so change that oil regularly.

What you must not do is use a synthetic or semi-synthetic oil during the running-in period because the chemical additives in synthetics are designed to prevent wear – and they do, so your new bearings, piston rings and so on will not bed in, and particularly with the latter the bore will glaze and not make a good seal with the rings, thus allowing oil to burn.

Changing the Oil

You'll be surprised at just how black your engine oil becomes in such a short time but fret not, because an oil that does not turn black is an oil that is not working. As discussed above, modern oils contain detergent-dispersant additives that keep engine internal parts clean by removing carbon deposits and maintaining them in suspension within the oil. It is better to have these deposits in the oil so they can be drained off rather than have them remain in the engine where they could do damage when they eventually decide to free off.

Don't be fooled into thinking that just because your engine doesn't burn much oil, nor does it leak a deal, then a full tank means it's fine – oil wears out like anything else. The main enemy of oil is heat. At high operating temperatures, oil oxidizes and thickens, as well as becoming laden with soot, water, acids, dust, metal particles, oxidized material and any other microscopic foreign body that your engine can ingest. Inevitably this will eventually cause problems with the oil pump, oil galleries and so on, and hence will interfere with the efficient action of the engine parts. As we've discussed above, with a multigrade, the oil contains polymers – essentially chain-like molecules – that give it the variable viscosity. Imagine the polymers on the same lines as a golf ball made up of millions of rubber bands all squashed together into a tight, solid ball. Heating up the ball and applying pressure to it will deform the ball shape as the rubber bands expand. Let it cool and it will go back to shape (more or less). Keep doing this over and over and soon the golf ball will not return to shape and eventually it will break, allowing the rubber bands to spill out, and then it is useless as a golf ball. This is, albeit a crude analogy, how oil works, once the polymers are cooked and smashed to pieces, the oil is useless and no matter how much remains in the tank, your engine will seize up somewhere. So this is another reason to change oil regularly.

Aftermarket Additives

Do not be taken in, aftermarket additives do not boost oil and engine performance. Adding these additives to your engine oil is akin to adding a spoon of sugar to your cola – you just don't need it. Premium engine oils are formulated with all the necessary additives necessary to ensure optimum engine performance for the required use. Additives cannot possibly reduce oil consumption in a worn engine or restore the protection properties of an old oil that should be changed. In fact, in a worst-case scenario, some additives may upset the oil chemistry and create problems. There are good adverts for certain additives that purport to contain PTFE and other such materials, but if these were absolutely necessary then the oils would have them included in their specification at the manufacture stage. Generally speaking these additives do no harm but it is nevertheless more sensible and economical to use approved premium classic oils.

Transmission Oil

As regards transmission oils, many manufacturers originally used grease, but as seals improved it was superseded by oil. As you can imagine, a gearbox is a pretty harsh environment for an oil, being constantly pushed and shoved between a host of spinning pinions and squashed up by male and female dogs, so it has to be tough stuff.

Down at your local car accessory emporium you will have seen plastic containers of gear oil marked up with an EP number, such as EP90. EP stands for extreme pressure and refers to the additives used to prevent metal-to-metal contact between the gearbox components. These additives are invariably based on sulphur and phosphorus and bond to the metal surfaces at points of extreme pressure and temperature, essentially forming a sacrificial chemical layer. It's the sulphur content that gives gear oils their familiar smell. It's regularly written that because many classic gearboxes contain several phosphor-bronze components, such as bushes, which contain copper, the sulphur-based EP additive attacks the copper element within them leading eventually to failure of the component. This may be the case in theory, but in practice this doesn't happen and EP90 is the recommendation of many gearbox experts in the classic movement. Indeed, one Norton Commando specialist proudly boasts of having built over 800 gearboxes, all with EP90 and not one oil-related failure. As you will see from the sample table below, even when the bikes were being built some manufacturers recommended EP90 as well as

EP90 gear oil is generally accepted as being fine for your gearbox.

heavyweight monograde mineral oil such as SAE 50.

The use of a thin oil in the primary chaincase is to ensure that the chain actually collects oil as its lower run passes through it. Some enthusiasts actually use hydraulic oil, which is very thin, and it works well but will seek out any area of leakage and so must only be used in a primary situation where the cases can be sealed perfectly. Used with, for example, Norton's hopeless pressed steel/rubber band oil bath arrangement, the fluid would quickly take up residence on your workshop floor. The primary drive chain will simply cut 'a chase' through a thick or medium-weight oil and not actually load the links with cooling lubricant. Of course, if a belt conversion is fitted then no oil is necessary and no leaks occur.

As you can see, most everyday machines ran a medium-thickness monograde oil in winter and a slightly thicker oil during the warmer months, until the multigrade was introduced and there was a choice.

Oil Recommendations from Period Manuals

Norton 1948–65, Singles and Twins

Engine and gearbox	SAE 40 summer, SAE 30 winter
Primary oil bath	SAE 20

BSA A7/10 1949–65

Engine	SAE 30 or 20W-50
Gearbox	SAE 50 or 20W-50
Primary chaincase	SAE 20 or 20W-50

Norton Commando

Engine	SAE 40 or SAE 20W-50
Gearbox	EP90
Primary chaincase	SAE 20W-50

Velocette Singles

Engine	SAE 40 winter, SAE 30 summer or 20W-50

1950-on Triumph Speed Twin and Thunderbird

Engine	SAE 20/30 winter, SAE 40/50 summer
Gearbox	EP90
Primary chaincase	SAE 20

BSA C15/B40

Engine and gearbox	SAE 30 summer, SAE 40 winter or SAE 20W-50
Side points engines gearbox	EP90.
Primary chaincase	SAE 20 or SAE W20-50

AJS/Matchless Singles and Twins

Engine	SAE 40/30 winter, SAE 50/40 summer or SAE 20W-50
Gearbox	SAE 50 or EP90
Primary chaincase	SAE 20

The selection of tax discs from over the years gives an interesting provenance to the bike.

the paperwork

THE REGISTRATION DOCUMENT

Many years ago, a friend of the author bought an ex-WD BSA 350cc B40 from a government surplus auction. It was more or less complete and a runner but it had no registration documentation, other than its now obsolete military designation, so he requested a registration from his local vehicle licensing office. The number he requested was WDB 40. Within no time he was riding his machine resplendent with its personal plate.

Alas, such easy-going times are long gone, and with the advent of the cherished number plate, the status symbol number plate and the amount of money these registrations command, not to mention criminally cloned number plates, the whole process of registration has become much more difficult and involved.

At one time there was the fold-up logbook, an official document that was completed manually and was issued with a stamp each time there was a change of ownership. If and when that booklet was full, a replacement was issued, duly marked up as such. Then, when all vehicle registration and licence issues were transferred to the central behemoth that is the Driver and Vehicle Licensing Authority, in Swansea, a computerized sheet (V5) replaced the old logbook. This was updated to the V5C a few years later, which presently remains the current document.

The V5C displays the vehicle's registration number, date of first registration, the taxation class, engine size, colour, frame and engine numbers, plus the registered keeper's name and address. Note the latter does not represent proof of ownership. The V5C has detachable slips, which must be forwarded to the DVLA on change of ownership, export or scrapping.

The registration documents, from front: current V5C, previous V5C, V5, logbook.

If your project machine comes complete with a V5C, you need do nothing other than complete the change of ownership section and send it to the DVLA. Do keep a copy of everything you send to them as it has been known for documents to go missing.

Now, way back, it was decreed by the DVLA that all vehicles with the old-style logbook must be updated to V5 status before the end of 1983. If any vehicle was not updated by that deadline then said vehicle would not be allowed to return to the road with the registration number of the old logbook; it would essentially have to be re-registered and the old number would be lost.

Of course, this decision was not important enough to make national headlines and so there were many people with vehicles tucked away in barns or garages who simply didn't know of it. Thus when it came to their vehicles being unearthed, say after they'd passed away, or simply by being persistently pressured to sell it by someone who desperately wanted to restore it, the original registration number could not be used.

The author experienced this with a Triumph. Discovered after having been stored up for years, it was purchased complete with old style logbook. The original three-letter, three-number registration could not be used and the bike was issued with an age-related plate, another three-letter, three-number plate, one of countless such registration combinations issued to vehicles in similar situations from the unused stock originally granted to thinly populated areas around the islands and highlands of Scotland. Any vehicle spotted with, for example, a plate ending in SU – such as DSU, GSU and so on – is immediately recognizable as an age-related plate.

Likewise, if the vehicle was of an era when the suffix or prefix letter was the norm, the age-related plate would have the appropriate letter, which is not so noticeable.

A few years later though, for reasons known only to the civil servants involved, this ludicrous ruling was revoked and replaced by legislation that allowed the original registration to be retained if documentary evidence was forthcoming – such as the old logbook, an appropriate tax disc, original

manufacturer's details, retailer's details and so on. The more evidence available, the better are the chances of retaining the plate. However, it was also decreed that all such reclaimed registrations were non-transferable, thus scuppering the ideas of those who fancied making a financial killing on the classic registration and then re-registering with an age-related plate – though, like everything else where potential big money is concerned, where there's a will, there's a way.

So, obtain or download form V765 – Application to register a vehicle under its original registration number – from the DVLA, get the form endorsed by the owners' club, provide a recent photo of the bike and put together the documentary evidence that links it to the original number, such as the original logbook, tax disc and so on. Send it all to the DVLA – make sure it's tracked, signed for, registered, you name it, because if these documents get lost in the post, you're doomed, especially as the DVLA often will not accept copies. In general, the original registration should be returned to you in V5C form, along with all your paperwork.

All the necessary information can be found on the DVLA website but in a nutshell, you can keep the bike's original registration number if you can prove you've used the original unmodified frame, or let's say it's beyond safe repair or restoration, a new frame of the same specification as the original. You must also have two other major components from the original bike – forks, wheels, engine or gearbox. Returning briefly to the Triumph Thunderbird saga, when the old logbook was put forward as documentary evidence, the original, but now non-transferable, registration number was returned to the bike without problem.

Sometimes of course, a 'barn find' machine may not have any documents, nor even a registration plate affixed to it. In that case, there may be someone within the owners' club but certainly at the VMCC's Burton on Trent HQ, who will have access to the manufacturers' ledgers or copies thereof, and will be able to tell you, from the frame number, exactly when that machine was built and when it left the factory. A dating certificate will be issued to you, usually for a small fee, with which

you can then apply to the DVLA for an age-related plate. Without this, a rather unattractive 'Q'-prefix registration will be issued.

Registering a Built-Up Machine

If you build a machine from parts, the process is slightly different and comes under the term 'reconstructed classic vehicle'. The application is the same but you will have to complete a Form V627/1 – Built Up Vehicle Inspection Report – and have available for inspection all official receipts for any parts used.

The DVLA will only recognize your vehicle as a reconstructed classic if it meets certain criteria. It must be built from genuine period components from more than one vehicle, all over twenty-five years old and of the same specification as the original vehicle and be a true reflection of the marque. You must include a written report from the appropriate owners' club, essentially explaining what's gone into the build and certifying that it fully meets with all their expectations as a true representation of what such a period machine should be and that it meets the reconstructed classic criteria.

The report must confirm that on inspection, it is a true reflection of the marque and is comprised of genuine parts over twenty-five years old. The DVLA will assign an age-related registration number to the vehicle based on the youngest component used. Now, it states on the DVLA website that your vehicle won't get an age-related registration number if it includes new or replica parts; it will instead be granted a 'Q'-prefix registration number and then must pass the relevant type approval test.

Before the registration is issued, the project may then still have to be fully inspected by an operative from the local DVLA office. They may come to you, but normally, you have to take the bike and all the documentation to their offices at a set time, so that means finding a means of transport to ship the bike there – as presently of course it's not legally roadworthy. When making your appointment ask them exactly what they need to see, because it's often a fair trail to said licensing office, especially as more local branches are being closed and the service centralized in some not so close town or city. If you do not have everything, they will simply turn you away and your journey is wasted.

There is a grey area surrounding the twenty-five-year-old parts ruling, as obviously it would be foolish to use tyres, brake shoes, light bulbs, or even larger parts such as wheel rims, when new replica parts are available and arguably better made from superior materials. The position taken by the VMCC, which is accepted by the DVLA, is that common sense must prevail. If the main parts of the machine are within period, such as engine, gearbox, frame, then the ancillary components can be replica. For example, a brand-new Amal carburettor, pattern mudguards, seat, handlebars, wheel rims, mirrors, levers and cables will all be visibly the same as those fitted in the period so are deemed perfectly in order. Likewise if the items are not seen, such as a solid state regulator, state-of-the-art, multi-plate clutch or brake shoes with modern material linings, even electronic ignition – these are quite acceptable.

MoT

Standing for Ministry of Transport – changed to Department of Transport in 1981 and to Department for Transport in 2002 – the annual roadworthiness test is still called the MoT test. There is a basic rule of thumb to bear in mind regarding the test – if it's not fitted it can't be tested, but if it is, then it must work, though there are statutory requirements for machines of certain age; for example, all post-1986 machines must have a front brake light switch. So a bike can be tested successfully without lights fitted, though naturally it must not be used in darkness or in weather where lights are needed. There is no such thing as a daytime MoT – that is an urban myth, which has sprung from little more than a coined phrase for a tested machine without lights. Similarly, your bike can be successfully tested without mudguards or similar accoutrements, but while it's essentially a sound machine, it does not comply with the Road Vehicle Regulations. In other words, the MoT test simply says that everything on this bike, as it was presented, was fine. For full details of what is tested during an MoT there is a downloadable booklet on the DVLA website.

A word of advice: try and find an MoT testing station that is sympathetic to classics, in other words run by someone who appreciates the limitations of a classic when compared to the test requirements of a state-of-the-art modern machine. For example, how can a BSA Bantam's simple little single leading shoe front drum brake be as efficient as a pair of massive, multi-pot calipered discs? It can't, of course, but if the brake can be shown to lock the wheel while under test, that is a 100 per cent thumbs up. Ask your local vintage/classic club members where they take their bikes – it will probably be to the same place.

A fairly recent addition to classic vehicle legislation has been the exemption from the MoT test for vehicles built prior to 1960, which is rather ironic since the late, disgraced, Transport Minister Eric Marples introduced it in that very year. It's a good idea, at least initially, to get an MoT certificate on your machine – whether or not it legally needs it – and take that along to the licensing office too with your paperwork, as every little helps. Again, you will of course have to trailer your bike to the MoT station at this stage. You could argue with the licensing office that a bike of this age is MoT exempt, but bear in mind you're trying to obtain a registration number from them, so they will have to log the frame number.

Surprisingly, when this legislation was introduced, there were many who

The moment of truth as the bike undergoes its first MoT test since restoration.

Jubilation as the tester is happy and the bike passes the test.

felt it was a bad move because it would encourage people to ride and drive vehicles in poor condition. They have a point, but the average classic owner looks after his machine very well and is unlikely to be stupid enough to ride/drive it in an unsafe condition, as this endangers both the rider/driver and others. In any case, if you so wish, you can still have your machine MoT tested in the traditional manner, irrespective of whether it legally requires it. It's up to you – if it makes you feel better, do it.

YOUR LICENCE

The legislation surrounding the motorcycle test has become increasingly difficult – indeed you could be forgiven for thinking that government has some form of hidden agenda to rid motorcycles from our roads, for while it is allowable to drive any car of any performance immediately the driving test is passed, the motorcycle test has

a host of hoops through which the rider has to jump before they have such freedom of choice. Consequently there are many youngsters who, when faced with said hoops, feel that it is easier and cheaper to go straight into four wheels than spending the traditional period on two.

Not many years ago, it was possible to simply get a bike and slap L plates on it, removing them if and when your test was passed. Then, in the 1960s, Transport Minister Barbara Castle decided motorcycles were dangerous so limited learners to 250cc or a sidecar outfit. The Japanese manufacturers responded by producing lightning-fast 250s, so the limit was further reduced to 125cc. For sixteen-year-olds the capacity limit was set at a pedal-assisted 50cc, so the manufacturers soon produced pretty nippy tiddlers with pedals, so the moped limit was then dropped to a restricted maximum speed of 28mph, which, to put

it bluntly, is a dangerously slow speed for today's UK roads.

Here are the basic rules to ride a motorcycle in the UK.

You must be at least seventeen (or sixteen for a moped) with a licence to ride Category A motorcycles. That licence can be provisional motorcycle entitlement, full car with automatic provisional motorcycle entitlement, a full motorcycle licence or a full moped licence if over seventeen. The provisional entitlement allows you to ride bikes up to 125cc with a maximum power output of 14.6bhp. Most classic 125s will generally fall well below that figure.

Learners who would rather tackle an outfit can do so as long as it has a power to weight ratio not exceeding 0.16kW/kg – which, in essence, means you can't stick L plates onto a modern superbike with a third wheel attached. Again, most classic sidecar haulers will be perfectly satisfactory.

On L plates you cannot carry a pillion passenger, unless that passenger is a full licence holder, ride on motorways, or ride without the L plates displayed.

It was once possible to ride forever on L plates, but provisional motorcycle licences were then limited to two years, before that ruling was essentially revoked on 1 February 2001, with all new provisional licences showing motorcycle entitlement valid from the issue date until the holder's seventieth birthday.

All learners must now complete Compulsory Basic Training, which is fairly expensive and has to be undertaken at an approved centre. On completion, a DL196 certificate is awarded, which must be produced before the practical test can be taken. If you do not take the test within a two-year period, then the CBT has to be retaken.

There are four types of licence available, depending on your age and the type of machine you wish to ride. This governs the type of machine on which you can undertake training and the test:

1. Age 16, max 50cc, Code AM, Moped.
2. Age 17, min 120cc/max 125cc, Code A1, Light Motorcycle.
3. Age 19, min 395cc, Code A2, Medium Motorcycle.
4. Age 24, min 595cc, Code A, Full Licence.

It's quite a complicated set-up. A1 (Lightweight) is the only option if you are between seventeen and nineteen. On passing the A1 your full licence allows you to ride on motorways and take pillion passengers, but you are limited to 125cc with a maximum of 14.6bhp. When you have held an A1 for a minimum of two years, you can upgrade to an A2 licence by retaking Modules 1 and 2. You need not take the CBT and theory test again.

If you are between nineteen and twenty-four, A2 (Standard) will be your second option. If you have not already passed the A1 test then you must first complete a CBT course and the motorcycle theory test. The test and training must be taken on a machine of minimum engine size of 395cc, producing maximum 46.6bhp. Upon passing you can ride any machine up to 46.6bhp.

If you are twenty-four or over you will be able to do Direct Access. If you've not passed the A2 test then you must complete a CBT course and the motorcycle theory test. The test and training must be on a machine min

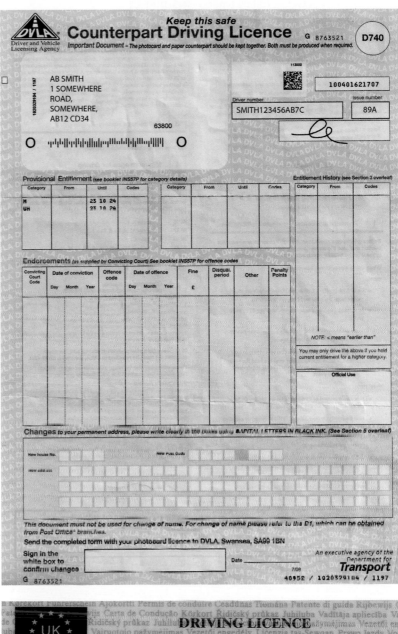

The driver's licence with the requisite allocations.

of 595cc and must produce at least 54bhp. Upon passing you can ride any size/cc of machine.

The beauty of many classics of course is that in general they are fairly low on horsepower, certainly when compared to modern machines, so a half-decent capacity machine can be ridden, but they are also endowed with loads of torque, which makes them easy, as well as great fun, to ride.

TAX

Various governments have been flip-flopping around with the historic vehicle tax situation for a few years now. Initially the Conservatives instituted a rolling twenty-five-year minimum age limit for tax-free vehicles, then Labour stopped it at 1 January 1973, then in the March 2014 budget, the Coalition government reinstated a rolling programme but for vehicles of forty years minimum. So now as soon as your project reaches its fortieth birthday, it's classified as a historic vehicle and there's no Vehicle Excise Duty (road tax) to pay. Unfortunately, until that birthday is reached, the tax bands are as per any modern machine, based on capacity.

INSURANCE

Another advantage of running a classic machine is the insurance. For many years, motorcycle insurance premiums were based on capacity limits and the experience of the rider. It soon became obvious that a seventeen-year-old with a newly passed test and a brand-new, race-bred 350cc two-stroke twin was a different risk to a thirty-year-old who had been riding and driving for over a decade and wanted to insure a twenty-five-year-old 350cc single-cylinder four-stroke plodder. So someone came up with the brilliant idea of separating them, on the grounds that the latter was a safer bet. As the classic movement gained momentum, the insurers realized that most classic owners were probably a little older and wiser than the sports bike headbanger, they cherished their machines, looked after them fastidiously, rode them carefully, secured them religiously and what's more they probably owned more than one – but could of course only ride one at once. Therefore, it was calculated that in general terms their mileage would be fairly low across their collection and as such did not constitute a high risk. Thus the premiums could be very reasonable, albeit with odd restrictions such as annual mileage limited to perhaps 1,500 or 3,000 miles.

This arrangement proved successful and nowadays whole collections can be insured very reasonably on one policy, each one covered to be on the road while the others are secure for fire and theft while in the workshop. Of course, many classic riders also have a modern machine of some form, and these can also be included into a reasonable policy premium. Most of the major insurance brokers offer some kind of classic policy, and like in any such situation, the premiums are flexible and it pays to shop around.

general maintenance

Once your newly restored machine is out on the road, there are a few things on which to keep an eye. We've spoken earlier about regular oil changes but after a few hundred miles, things start to bed in or loosen up, so after you've changed the oil, whip off the fuel tank and check that the cylinder head and rocker cover bolts are still tight; the cylinder head gasket may have settled a little, likewise the cylinder barrel nuts. Have a quick check around the mudguard nuts and bolt, the wheel nuts, fork top nuts and so on. Have a look at the fork seals and the drain outlets at the base of the sliders to make sure they haven't loosened and are weeping, and importantly peer under the sump to ensure the crankcase sump bolt is still tight and not leaking oil. On a pre-unit engine, check the gearbox adjuster is still nice and tight – an obvious sign is a drive chain like a guitar string or otherwise sagging loosely. Either way it will affect the primary chain: if the box has

pulled forward the primary will be slack and rattling against the cases, if it's pulled back you'll find the primary is so tight that the kick start will barely turn over the engine and it will be putting a colossal strain on the bearings.

Beyond that there's a basic routine to follow.

WEEKLY CHECKS

Oil level, especially with geared pump engines, as when the bike is standing, the oil tends to seep around the gears and into the sump – wet sumping. A little in the sump is no problem as the scavenge system will quickly have it returned to the oil tank, but if there's a tankful in the sump, it must be drained out as the pressure within the oil-filled cases will force oil past the piston rings on kick starting, put undue pressure on case joints and potentially break the cases. The oil can generally be returned to the tank but it is nonetheless wise to

sieve it through some form of strainer just in case. Run the engine for a few minutes and then check the oil level in the tank, replenishing as necessary.

Tyre pressures Keep the pressures as recommended, as incorrect pressure can give a dodgy riding sensation and also encourages premature tyre wear.

Battery If you have a wet cell battery, check the electrolyte level. Dry cells need no maintenance other than an occasionally boost on a charger.

Chains If the final drive chain is in good adjustment then it's safe to assume the primary will be, but most engines have an inspection eye which allows a finger or two in to feel the chain tension.

EVERY 1,000 MILES

- Carry out the standard weekly checks as above.

ABOVE: Source a good-quality tyre pressure gauge. This one is ex-RAF and saw service in the North African campaign.

RIGHT: The reading is on a spiral and 24psi is fine.

- Check pivot points on the brake mechanisms and grease accordingly.
- Adjust brake shoes if necessary now they've bedded in.
- Check the primary chain case oil level and top up as necessary.
- Check the cylinder head bolts again and torque up as required.

EVERY 2,000 MILES

- Warm up the engine and drop out the engine oil, clean/replace the filter if one is fitted and replenish with fresh oil.
- Check tightness of nuts and bolts generally.
- Check oil level in gearbox and top up as necessary.
- Remove and clean the spark plugs.
- Check rear drive chain, clean and lubricate as necessary.

YEARLY OR AS NECESSARY

- Lubricate all control cables. Disconnect them at the levers and hold them upright, forming a funnel around the top in plasticene or similar and fill the funnel with oil. Allow it to seep down around the inner cable overnight.
- Check swinging arm pivot for play.

Of course this is only a rough guide, as maintenance depends on the amount of use your machine gets and in what weather conditions.

A sad sight as the bulldozers move in on a bleak winter's morning to begin the demolition of the once mighty Meriden Triumph factory.

useful contacts

Amal Carburetters
Burlen Ltd
Spitfire House
Castle Road
Salisbury
Wiltshire SP1 3SB
Tel: 01722 412500
Fax: 01722 334221
www.amalcarb.co.uk.

Anglo Scot Abrasives
5 Bolton Road
Ashton in Makerfield
Lancashire WN4 8AA
Tel: 01942 270729
www.angloscotabrasives.co.uk

Boyer Bransden Electronics Ltd
Frindsbury House
Cox Street
Detling
Maidstone
Kent ME14 3HE
Tel: 01622 730939
Fax: 01622 730930
www.boyerbransden.com

Burlen Dry Cell Batteries
Burlen Ltd
Spitfire House
Castle Road
Salisbury
Wiltshire SP1 3SB
Tel: 01722 412500
Fax: 01722 334221
www.burlen.co.uk

Castrol Classic Oils
Wakefield House
Swavesey
Cambridge CB4 5QZ
Tel: 01954 231668
Fax: 01954 231923
www.castrol.com

Central Wheel Components
Station Road Industrial Estate
Station Road
Coleshill
Birmingham B46 1HT
Tel: 01675 462264
www.central-wheel.co.uk

Ferret's Custom Electrickery
Mobile wiring service
Tel: 07765 832420
www.motorcyclewiring.co.uk

Dave Flintoft Engineering
(BSA Gold Star B31/33)
50 Enfield Chase
Guisborough
Cleveland TS14 7LS
Tel: 01287 638677

**Frost Auto Restoration
Techniques Ltd**
Crawford Street
Rochdale
Lancashire OL16 5NU
Tel: 01706 658619
Fax: 01706 860338
www.frost.co.uk

Morris Lubricants
Castle Foregate
Shrewsbury
Shropshire SY1 2EL
Tel: 01743 232200
www.morrislubricants.co.uk

SRM Engineering
Unit 22
GlanyrAfon Enterprise Park
Aberystwyth SY23 3JQ
Tel: 01970 627771
Fax: 01970 627773
www.srm-engineering.com

VMCC Ltd
Allen House
Wetmore Road
Burton upon Trent
Staffordshire DE14 1TR
Tel: 01283 540557
Fax: 01283 510547
www.vmcc.net

C Wylde and Son Ltd
(wheelbuilding)
Aire Place Mills
143 Kirkstall Road
Leeds LS3 1JL
Tel: 0113 2468888
www.cwylde.co.uk

abbreviations and glossary

Abbreviations

4/8LS Like twin leading shoes, but with either four or eight shoes all leading. Usually found on race bikes.

AC Alternating current. A wave form that is half positive and half negative, like that delivered from an alternator, which needs to be rectified into DC.

BHP Brake horse power

CC Cubic capacity or cubic centimetres. The size of an engine, calculated by multiplying the square of the bore radius × the stroke length × 3.142 (pi) × the number of cylinders. For example, Norton ES2 with 79 × 100mm bore and stroke: 79/2 = 39.5 (bore radius); 39.5 × 39.5 = 1560.25 (bore radius squared); 1560.25 × 100 = 156025; 156025 × 3.142 = 490cc.

CVC Compensated voltage control. The mechanical cutout and regulator box used on the dynamo system.

DC Direct current. As in the power delivered from a dynamo. The faster the dynamo spins the more power is manufactured and thus needs to be regulated.

HT High tension. The lead that carries the huge voltage from the magneto to the spark plug.

OHC Overhead cam. Often preceded by an S for single or a D for double. An engine with downward-facing valves in the cylinder head opened by cams above them, driven by either a bevel shaft or, more commonly now, a chain.

OHV Overhead valve. Downward-facing valves in the cylinder head opened by rockers operated by pushrods from cams in the timing case.

QD Quickly detachable. Usually referring to the rear wheel where the wheel can be removed leaving the chain and sprocket undisturbed, or in the case of competition classics or desert sled-type machines where the lights could be quickly disconnected via a plug and socket to enable removal of the lights prior to racing.

Pre-Unit Construction Engine with separate gearbox.

SLS Single leading shoe. A brake drum of two shoes, operated by one cam; one shoe leads, the other trails.

SV Side valve. Upward-facing valves in the cylinder barrel adjacent to the piston, operated by cams in the timing case and using a shallow, flat cylinder head. Used for ease of maintenance and rugged reliability during Second World War with BSA M20/21 and Norton 16H/Big 4 and later with Triumph's twin-cylinder TRW.

TLS Twin leading shoe. A brake drum of two shoes operated by two cams making both shoes lead.

TPI Threads per inch.

WD War Department.

Glossary

Cammy An engine with an overhead cam, for example 'Cammy Norton' or 'Cammy Velo'.

Cooking As in 'a cooking model' or 'cooking version' – this odd term refers to the everyday base model within a range.

Dogs The large interconnecting male and female parts of a gearbox pinion.

Flat head A side-valve engine.

Splines Male and female castellations or fine teeth which interlock, such as a sprocket on a shaft or a QD hub arrangement.

Unit construction Engine and gearbox in the same cases

Simplex, duplex, triplex Single run chain of a single link wide, two links wide, three links wide.

Note on Spelling

Amal spell carburettor as carburetter on all their literature, so strictly when referring to Amal instruments it's carburetter; however, in this book we have used the more standard spelling of carburettor throughout to avoid confusion.

index